# BODY

## Technique & Application

### As Seen through Martial Arts

*by*

# Barry B Barker M.A., L.Ac.

Crystal Pointe Media Inc., San Diego, CA

Body: Technique and Application As Seen Through Martial Arts

Barry B Barker, M.A., L.Ac.

Copyright © 2015

2021 4th Edition - Originally Published in 2015

Published by Crystal Pointe Media Inc.
San Diego, California

ISBN-13: 978-154898517
ISBN-10: 1540898512

DISCLAIMER
The contents of this publication are intended to be educational and informative. They are not to be considered a directive to use Martial Arts on other individuals. Before embarking on Martial Arts training, you should have clearance from your personal physician or health care provider then research and find competent instruction and training.

WARNING
This book and others in this series cover mature themes regarding Martial Arts techniques, targets and methods that can do serious and irrevocable harm to another human being. Its use is only made available for Self-Defense and Sport Fighting purposes and should never be misapplied.

Cover Design by Daniel Barnier

# ACKNOWLEDGEMENTS

Thank you, G.M. Rey Leal, for reviewing my books and for writing the thoughtful Foreword that I chose to place in this book on the Body, Techniques and Applications.

Thanks to my longtime friend and classmate Tim Mullins for being in so many of the video links referenced and the pictures contained in this book.

Also, much gratitude to my Black Belt students Dr. John Hippen for reviewing several sections in this series, Daniel Barnier for his graphics work, my son Joshua Lara-Barker and Patty Alvarez for their proofreading skills in this book.

Thank you to my Poway Kenpo Black Belts, especially my son Jordan Barker, Dai Phipps, Brian Gist, and Heath Gross for covering so many of my classes so I could finish this project, and to Jennifer Nila for all your help and support.

I very much appreciate you all.

*Barry Barker, M.A., L.Ac.*

# DEDICATION

**Teachers, Classmates, Students**

A project like this is the result of many years of accumulated experience and knowledge gained and passed on to me by teachers, classmates, and students. These were absorbed sometimes immediately, other times painstakingly, or later in an epiphany of awareness. My sincere gratitude goes to all who have taught and given me perspective.

This book is dedicated to my Black Belt students, especially my senior Black Belts, who inspire me by having the same passion for martial arts as me, proved by their ongoing development. Your skill, efforts, and loyalty are always a source of pride to me.

My admiration and appreciation also go out to the memory and efforts of the late Kenpo Senior Grand Master Edmund Kealoha Parker, the founder of the American Kenpo system I have studied and taught for most of my life. He was a brilliant martial artist who literally wrote the book(s) on American Kenpo. My decision to add, revise, reformat, and re-clarify any of his works is done with the utmost respect and in the spirit of the ever-evolving martial arts system he inspired.

This book is also dedicated to the student who seeks knowledge throughout their lifetime. A desire to learn leads to learning, regardless of intellect, talent, education, or experience. A belief that we know everything about anything stops the learning process. Be humble and keep learning.

**My 1st Degree Kenpo Black Belt Test Photo from 1983**
Back L-R: Tim Mullins, Jim Mitchell, Ed Parker, Rick Hughes, Parker Linekin, Darby Darrow, Crane Ponder; Front L-R: Barry Barker, Ron Jiminez, Margaret Colfer, Derrick Jones, Reverend Mike

# PREFACE

This is one of a three book series I gave myself as an advanced Black Belt thesis project, and for the personal growth I expected would accompany the effort. Another big project of mine was attaining a Master's Degree in Chinese Medicine and subsequent Acupuncture Licensing. Rank integrity is important, so I am compelled to make a large effort towards that end. This I hope sets a good example for my children and students.

My books are intended as a reference resource for my students, along with style-related information for American Kenpo practitioners, and martial arts enthusiasts in general as several chapters are on non-style related subjects (e.g., Concepts & Principles, Pressure Points, Sport Fighting, and Martial Arts First Aid). Any athlete can also benefit from some of what is contained in this series (e.g., Breathing, Balance, Exercise & Nutrition), or even curious observers may find something of interest (e.g., Qi, Yin/Yang).

This 3-book series is formatted using one of the oldest and most accepted martial arts concepts of the 3 components, or tenets, traditionally sought for development, the *Mind, Body,* and *Spirit.* This is the book of the *Body.*

My personal biography is at the back of this book but suffice to say my formal training began in 1973, but not seriously until 1980. I opened my Kenpo Karate School in 1984 (my full-time job for over 30 years, as of the original writing of this project) and I added a Sport Fighting Gym in 1998. These experiences have given me the background to write about the subjects covered in this and my other books, Mind and Spirit.

During this time, I have also been able to put my entire system on video, so throughout my books there are names (often colorful) in parenthesis. These are techniques from my Kenpo system where whatever is being explained can be seen. Those are accessible to see at BarryBBarker.com.

The use of empty-handed martial arts can be divided into the 4 main training intentions of *Military, Law Enforcement, Civilian Self-Defense,* and *Sport Fighting,* with definite crossover value between and within these approaches. Weapon arts and movement arts are not covered, necessarily.

The *Military* objective is to attack and kill the enemy. *Law Enforcement,* including Bouncers, train to subdue the bad guy. *Civilian Self-Defense* is about not fighting yet being prepared to defend against criminal assault or interpersonal conflict. The training goal of *Sport Fighting* is to win a competition within the rules and guidelines of the sport.

The *Body* crosses into all 4 of these uses, with *Intention* the primary differentiating factor. My book series primarily addresses and comes from the *Civilian Self-Defense* and *Sport Fighting* perspectives with a large part of this volume containing my own systems curriculum information. This is a reference for my students and for those interested in Kenpo, or for martial artists who want to know more about Kenpo and/or how another system is setup.

Pictures and illustrations are contained throughout this series, and especially in this book, but the best way to visually grasp the information is by watching the video links that are listed throughout.

This book on the *Body* also contains an extensive *Pressure Point* chapter, with the *Mind* book covering important *Concepts and Principles,* and the *Spirit* book discussing some of the many intangibles including *Wisdom, Nutrition, Exercise Basics, Martial Arts First Aid* and more. Information, insight, and perspective from my Chinese medical background will be offered where useful and appropriate.

My observation is that we are all on a knowledge and wisdom continuum relative to each other. A knowledgeable reader may agree, disagree, or know more about a particular subject, but my hope is that a martial artist approaches every learning opportunity with an empty cup expecting to gain from the experience.

The contradiction with attaining knowledge and wisdom is that if we think we know everything then that is all we will know, where if we think we know nothing then knowledge is always flowing in our direction. My advice is to let others judge where you are on the continuum and keep approaching each day humble, as if you know nothing.

For myself personally and my expectation for my children and students is to always be striving for knowledge. I have noticed in myself that I have never stopped learning my entire life so there is no reason for me to think it will stop with this book series. I humbly submit this work as what I know now. After all, time may be eternal, but knowledge and wisdom are relative.

# FOREWORD
## By Grand Master Reynaldo Leal

Mind, Body, and Spirit reads like a comprehensive Encyclopedia of Martial Arts. My friend, Master Barry Barker, has not only spent years of research and dedication writing these books, but also a lifetime of learning and perfecting his art to heighten his understanding of the principles on which it is built. Reading these books took me back through my life journey to martial arts mastery, and allowed me thoughtful reflection on many of my crucial steps on that path.

Insightful and detailed information provided in these books are further augmented by a website containing videos specifically designed to illustrate the multifaceted technique concepts and principles Master Barker covers in his book series.

Whether novice trainee, teacher, or active lifestyle martial arts enthusiast, everyone will find a wealth of invaluable information by reading Master Barker's three books. They will enhance training and teaching, improve competition odds, and benefit overall physical and mental health. I highly recommend "Mind," "Body," and "Spirit."

GM. Reynaldo Leal, 9th degree
UKF American Kenpo Karate
Chen Taijiquan / Taoist Sanctuary Instructor

# BODY

## TABLE OF CONTENTS

| | | |
|---|---|---|
| **I.** | **THE BODY** | **7-8** |
| **II.** | **THE VALUE OF TECHNIQUE** | **9-12** |
| **III.** | **WEAPONS & TARGETS** | **13-16** |
| **IV.** | **ANATOMY & PHYSIOLOGY** | **17-32** |

Organs (Pg 18), Skeletal (Pg 19), Muscular (Pg 20), Nervous (Pg 22), Endocrine (Pg 24), Senses (Pg 26)
Cardiovascular (Pg 28), Lymphatic (Pg 29), Respiratory (Pg 30), Urinary (Pg 31), Digestive (Pg 32)

| | | |
|---|---|---|
| **V.** | **PRESSURE POINTS** | **33-79** |

| | |
|---|---|
| Disruption of Blood Flow | 38-42 |
| Disruption of Air Flow | 43-45 |
| Disruption of Nerve Function | 46-57 |
| Disruption of Brain Function | 58-61 |
| Disruption of Tissue & Mechanical Function | 62-65 |
| Disruption of Qi Energy | 66-75 |
| Pressure Point Summary | 76-79 |

| | | |
|---|---|---|
| **VI.** | **THE MARTIAL ARTS SYSTEM** | **80-84** |
| **VII.** | **THE BASICS OF MARTIAL ARTS** | **85-170** |

| | |
|---|---|
| Postures & Whole-Body Movements | 87-104 |

Stances (Pg 87), Foot Maneuvers (Pg 92) Body Maneuvers (Pg 99)

| | |
|---|---|
| Body Extension Movements | 105-156 |

Blocks, Parries, Checks (Pg 105), Punches & Strikes (Pg 117), Kicks & Balance Disruptions (Pg 136)

| | |
|---|---|
| Contraction Movements | 157-170 |

Grabs (Pg 157), Locks ((Pg 159), Holds (Pg 167), Chokes (Pg 169)

| | | |
|---|---|---|
| **VIII.** | **MOVEMENT ROUTINES** | **171-197** |

| | |
|---|---|
| Sets (Stances, Blocking, Kicking, Striking, Partner) | 174-183 |
| Forms (Short 1-2-3, Long 1-2-3-4-5-6, Mass Attacks) | 184-197 |

| | | |
|---|---|---|
| **IX.** | **SPORT FIGHTING** | **198-233** |

| | |
|---|---|
| What Smart Fighters Know | 200-202 |
| G.R.E.A.T. / Tips for Sport Fighters / Elements of a Champion | 203-210 |
| Fighter's Preparation & Training Guide | 211-213 |
| Sport System for the Street Stylist | 214-233 |

Concepts, Point Fighting, Kickboxing, Boxing, Ground Grappling, Takedowns, MMA

| | | |
|---|---|---|
| **X.** | **SELF-DEFENSE SYSTEM** | **234-308** |

| | |
|---|---|
| Kenpo S-D Technique Cross Reference Name Chart | 241-244 |
| Hand, Wrist & Arm Grab Attacks | 245-252 |
| Body, Neck & Head Grab Attacks | 253-259 |
| Pushing Attacks | 260-263 |
| Punch & Strike Attacks | 264-276 |
| Club / Knife / Gun Weapon Attacks | 277-286 |
| Kick & Kick/Punch Combination Attacks | 287-293 |
| Tackle & Takedown Attacks | 294-296 |
| Hugs/Holds & Locks | 297-304 |
| Multiple Attackers | 305-308 |

| | |
|---|---|
| **BIBLIOGRAPHY & ABOUT THE AUTHOR** | **309-311** |

**Person's Body**

# THE BODY
## Chapter 1

**Physical Body**

The Idea or Concept of Mind-Body-Spirit as an integrated whole is a common thread that transcends martial arts styles and practitioners. It is used and referenced on a regular basis in its teaching and practice. This concept not only applies to martial arts because every field contains mental, physical, and intangible motivational and developmental aspects.

Although appearing straightforward Mind-Body-Spirit can be interpreted by the human mind differently. A martial arts teacher or organization may prefer a different order of importance, place more emphasis, or have another interpretation on one aspect or the other. The reality of course is that although these can be analyzed separately, as in this book series, they are developed simultaneously.

In teaching martial arts to adults, I would list Body after Mind since the intellectual understanding should be engaged first, then the Body can be directed until a Mind/Body connection begins to develop. With children, I would list the Body first, adding the Mind slowly as information can be absorbed (see "Spirit" chapter on "How to Teach Martial Arts").

Some call it muscle-memory, but it goes deeper as the Body at some level appears to direct the Mind, or perhaps it is the subconscious mind directing the body. This is when the Mind sees, the brain generates an impulse, and the Body reacts instantly with no interference from conscious thought. This is one reason for repetition and training.

Another important "Body" consideration is physical health as we should enjoy life, have a good attitude, be positive, rest, drink quality liquids, eat well and stay fit through exercise. These along with the ability to protect our self increases the chance of living a long healthy life.

Leading a balanced life where Mind, Body, and Spirit are in harmony can be difficult. It takes discipline and a positive self-vision throughout life, hopefully from youth into old age. We all have times, or perhaps years, of inconsistency, but having a positive vision of our future self into old age can become our conscience when making long term or spontaneous health and lifestyle related decisions.

My martial arts self-vision is of the old Kung Fu master I saw in the Kung Fu movies I watched in the 1970's. Whilee others were admiring the great fighters depicted in those movies I was fascinated by their teachers, or masters. Those gray-haired, long eye-browed icons, at least a hundred years old, epitomized by the Pai Mei character in the movie "Kill Bill 2," often ornery and belligerent as they can no longer suffer the fools.

Whether ornery or sublimely humble they are admired by their students for their wisdom and are of course still phenomenal at martial arts. They positively affect those around them seeming to know everything about everything and are always teaching life lessons to those who will listen. My path is in striving to be that guy, but the nicer version of course and without the long eyebrows.

This book's primary focus is in describing the martial arts as a *System* that can be taught to anyone motivated to learn. My base style is Kenpo, so I have taken the opportunity of this book to index my Kenpo System for my students and lineage.

Even if the names of basics, patterns and specific techniques are or are not familiar, or perhaps different, to readers from other backgrounds it is recommended that one see new information with an empty cup so to recognize something different. Since we're all the same species with the Concepts and Principles of motion universal this is the best way to approach any learning opportunity.

The *Anatomy & Physiology* and *Pressure Point* chapters should be of interest to every martial artist with much of the *Basics* chapter also able to cross styles. The *Sets & Forms* chapter is mostly style specific with most of the *Sport Fighting* chapter useful to anyone training or competing in a fighting sport, and the opening discussion in the *Self-Defense System* chapter and the attack category description also useful information that transcends style.

How the body can be used for martial arts is a fascinating and varied adventure that many people spend their entire lives pursuing so this book is also for those nerdy martial arts junkies who can spend hours discussing the difference between a hook and a roundhouse punch. I hope you enjoy my efforts.

# THE VALUE OF TECHNIQUE
## Chapter II

Techniques are developed, refined, and practiced procedures executed with intention by people to conduct a task. They are efficient and effective methods for carrying out an artistic work or a physical procedure with the techniques and precision used considered as someone's skill level in that field or endeavor.

Actor Nick Nolte delivers one of my favorite movie lines from *Way of the Peaceful Warrior*, adapted from the book of the same name by Dan Millman. I highly recommend the book and the movie, but the line Nolte delivers takes place in a small dining area where he has taken a cocky but talented gymnast as a Zen student and invited him over to eat sushi.

As the scene begins the student plops himself at the table and begins sloppily and aggressively grabbing food with his fingers and shoving it into his mouth, elbows on the table, talking and chewing with his mouth open, displaying absolutely no manners or dining etiquette. Nolte on the other hand is very proper and controlled while eating his meal.

In the ensuing conversation, the student rebels against the indication that he needs table manners to which Nolte says, "that is the difference between you and me, you practice gymnastics and I practice everything."

Martial arts technique is what's discussed here but we should be aware of technique in everything we do. The mind should strive and search for the best technique to accomplish successfully and efficiently simple to complicated tasks. From making our bed and tying our shoes, to learning a martial art, playing a musical instrument, doing brain surgery, etc.

Technique is in everything and it is also in nothing at the same time. It's easy for a martial artist to become filled with confidence knowing technique(s) or imagining their ability to apply damaging and deadly moves they learned on a deserving opponent. Before becoming too full of ourselves it is important to not only know the value but also the limitations of technique.

Anyone considered good at anything has and uses technique, from the framer building a house to the espresso clerk making a latte to the pro athlete playing a position or someone performing in any context. Technique is everywhere but it must be learned and/or discovered, and then practiced, which all help improve and and develop someone so they can attain their highest level and reach their potential in each field.

So, there is value in technique but there is also nothingness contained in that same technique. When it comes to martial arts the nothingness of technique can be expressed a few ways. An old adage says, "conditioning and determination are great equalizers" or the Ed Parker quote that "guts and conditioning take over where skill and knowledge leave off."

My son Jordan gave me a wrestling axiom that says the first period gocs to the most technical wrestler (Mind), the second to the wrestler with the best conditioning (Body), and the third to the wrestler with the most heart (Spirit).

The point is physical technique is as useful as the level of conditioning, athleticism, strength, and timing to apply it; and with the courage, determination, effort, and heart to use it under difficult circumstances.

An aggressive determined street thug with no training can defeat a skilled martial arts master who does not have the other qualities that help him or her hurt a mean, tough, and probably durable opponent. The top fighters and competitors in any sport are a combination of the best athletes with the best training, technique, and preparation, but who also have the most heart, drive, and determination to win.

In the fighting disciplines, many martial art teachers refer to this breed of student as the "tough guys." These fight athletes go where they have opportunities to be challenged. Some gain personal acknowledgement or even financial reward, but all want to prove themselves and be tested.

"Tough guys" is relative as men especially seem genetically programmed through the ego to believe this about themselves. Helping men control this powerful driving force of ego is one reason for the evolution of etiquette and discipline in martial arts and in the military, and why there are rules in sport. That subject is discussed more extensively in my "Spirit" book.

The discussion here centers on the different techniques, i.e., styles of martial arts that have benefited from the tough guy search to find a fight challenge where they can prove and improve themselves. This happens based upon where the tough guys of a culture perceive as the best place to test themself.

People around martial arts long enough have seen this with the changing popularity of martial arts styles. Karate, Kung Fu, Muay Thai, Boxing, Wrestling, Brazilian Jiu Jitsu, MMA, have all had more or less of the tough guy following at various times. Contact sports, the military, and law enforcement are other areas where this breed of person gets involved.

The history of fighting and warfare has proven that this changes over time because people adapt and adjust to adversaries. What is perceived as the best style, weapon, army, or strategy in one time and place can become less effective, minimized, or even neutralized by another style, weapon, army, or strategy in another time, and so it goes.

Another reason is as a style becomes popular teachers accept more diverse students. This can lead to training becoming less strenuous and perhaps even watered-down. The training becomes more for the masses, probably those who need it most as opposed to already tough guys, who most likely were not and are not getting picked on or intimidated in real life.

Overall, technique can make us better, smarter, and more efficient but, regardless of style, other factors are important so this knowledge should not be the only source of faith we have in our abilities. An expert, or "Black Belt" level martial artist, should strive to attain and maintain the physical capability and practiced knowledge associated with their rank.

This requires a lifetime of fitness, training, and practicing the techniques of our chosen style(s). As we become older training needs to be progressively modified, but by then you know how to make that adjustment. Healthy life habits help us stay at a level of fitness to retain the ability to apply an appropriate martial art technique should some street thug want to test our skills.

The psychological components of determination, drive, competitiveness, pride, or whatever burns inside that will not allow quitting or failure are equally, or perhaps even more important. It's good to be a nice person but even nice people need to be able to dig deep to find the will to fight ferociously to the death against anyone trying to harm them or their families.

I tell women's self-defense attendees that technique practice and training are important but then provide an analogy that a pit bull does not have training and uses only instinctive technique, yet nobody wants to fight a pit bull. One-hundred pounds may sound small in a person but the biggest toughest meanest criminal or street punk does not want to fight a pit bull, let alone a 100 pound one. We can then delve into the vastness of martial arts technique.

I hope this next statement is not too shocking or controversial but in the information age with its shared knowledge there are no martial arts secrets. What had been secret knowledge in another time is now available for all to see or read about (see my book on the *Spirit,* Chapter III).

Some organizations, like the military, still try and keep technological, strategic, and tactical secrets. They are successful to different degrees, but the techniques and information of non-technology based empty-handed fighting is out there somewhere for anyone to see.

Of course, that only means it can be seen or read about so, rare exception aside, without instruction, training, and insight most are wasting their time, and perhaps even endangering themselves and others to try and learn by this method. Without proper and informed guidance, it is exceedingly difficult to gain the insight to achieve the highest level of skill that a styles technique can offer.

The fact is the untrained eye and mind cannot fully process or understand what it does not know, and we cannot objectively see ourselves. This makes self-training or reinventing the wheel often a fool's journey, especially when so much knowledge and many talented teachers are available for the willing student.

The human mind and ego seem capable of believing anything as many have convinced themselves they know more than they do and are better at things than they really are. This "legend in their own mind" mentality limits what someone will ever know as this ego will not allow for the instruction and training to be attained for someone to reach full potential. Why humble them self to learn when they already know everything and are invincible?

Everyone else needs to find good teachers and resources to help guide, develop, and become competent in the style(s) of interest to them. The opportunity then exists to learn and discover technique within technique and to never stop learning or seeking knowledge, nuance, insight, perspective, and personal growth challenges throughout our lifetime.

Since technique is the collective accumulative knowledge discovered and developed over many years and generations not one person figured it all out in their lifetime. As martial artist's we should try to learn and at some point, contribute to this information nexus and pass it forward so others can do the same.

With all that said it is better to have technique than not. It is not only useful, but it can be interesting, challenging, and even a fun never ending journey of learning and discovery. My hope is you are always curious to know more than you know now.

# WEAPONS & TARGETS
## Chapter III

Before discussing weapons and targets, the mental intention and possible results of that intention are of crucial importance. The degree of force used is influenced by our weapons projection onto or into a target(s).

Additionally, the wide range of variables in the vast human genetic spectrum could make a punch to the chest barely felt by one person yet cause another person's heart to stop. Even with that possibility, the purpose or *intention* behind applying weapons to targets would fall within one of the 7 Levels of Force listed here and in my book on the *Mind*.

**Level #1: Distraction / Attention Getter** – Any technique or application that gets another person to focus or refocus their mind and/or eyes.

**Level #2: Control & Discomfort** – Any technique or application that neutralizes an opponent's efforts by holding in place, forcing compliance, or causing discomfort in a way that cancels attempts to cause harm.

**Level #3: Strain & Sprain** – Any technique or application that temporarily damages any part of an opponent's anatomy (internal or external) causing a level of pain and dysfunction that ends their attempts to cause harm at that moment.

**Level #4: Break & Dislocate** – Any technique or application that stops someone's ability to cause harm due to pain and/or anatomical dysfunction by the breaking of bones or dislocation of joints.

**Level #5: Unconsciousness or Knockout** – Any technique or application that causes an opponent to lose his mental awareness and function for a limited time, ranging from temporary dizziness, to relaxed sleep, to a rigid tonic seizure. These are generally recoverable long term but a fight ender short term.

**Level #6: Disable** – Any technique or application that damages an opponent in a way from which they will never fully recover. This can range from joint disfigurement, an injury affecting the spine, an internal organ, sight, or the effectiveness of the mind as in brain damage. Although permanent long term it may not be a fight ender short term.

**Level #7: Death or Kill** – Any technique or application that causes the death of another person. This should be avoided if humanly possible.

Since the mind is the most powerful weapon, directing everything else, the intention applied is a key in determining the result. Once this is established then the physical weapons and targets gain a more profound purpose. This makes analyzing and formatting them more meaningful.

The formulation described here to apply Weapons to Targets is related using the ancient Yin/Yang concept of complimentary opposites (See *Mental Concepts* in my book on the *Mind*). In this model the Yin (soft) weapons attack the Yang (hard) targets and the Yang weapons (hard) attack the Yin (soft) targets.

 Within the Yin-Yang symbol however there is flexibility as some Yin exists within Yang (black dot inside the white) and some Yang within Yin (white dot inside the black). This concept therefore does not become a universal principle at every point of contact. It does however provide a weapon to target reference that we can wrap our minds around.

**Weapons** in this context are more precisely called *Natural Weapons* and refer to those parts of our body that can be used against selected targets on an opponent's body. It does not include anything that is not a naturally attached part of the human physical anatomy.

Natural weapons are primarily the hands, arms, legs, and feet, but would also include any part of the body that can be used individually or in combination as a weapon.

If used without sport fighting protection the natural body weapon surfaces are either hard (Yang) and bony like the knuckles, elbows, knees, and shins; or soft (Yin) and padded like the palm, handsword, hammerfist, and ball of the foot.

Generally, the hard-surface (Yang) natural weapons have less chance of injury against softer or less reinforced surface targets (Crossing Fist) with soft-surface (Yin) and more absorbing natural weapons used against hard less reinforced soft surface targets (Thrusting Palm).

Natural weapons can be enhanced and protected with accessories such as sparring equipment, joint or muscle support braces, body armor, brass knuckles, a roll of quarters, etc. Reinforcing weapon surface(s) and structures does not take away from them being natural weapons.

Individual natural weapons are covered in the *Basics* chapter where each is categorized and explained in the context of their use. Mr. Parker also did a thorough job of covering this subject in his *Infinite Insights into Kenpo Books 3 & 4*, so those are also a recommended resource.

The 3 "Point of Contact Variables" (See *Motion & Movement* in my book on the *Mind*) for applying natural weapons are *Impact* (punch, strike, kick, hit, bump, push, crash, tackle, etc.); *Connect* (press, slide, check, pin, rub, scrape, etc.); *Attach* (grasp, grab, grapple, lock, hold, twist, stretch, pinch, squeeze, etc.).

*Impact* movements (i.e., striking) accelerate quickly with the intention to penetrate a target, then either retract or slide through. *Connect* movements (i.e., touching) are done on the body surface area to control movement and possibly damage tissue. *Attach* movements (i.e., grabbing) hook onto or wrap around a surface area to affect it or a nearby area directly, or a person's posture and balance.

Several related factors make the application of natural weapons effective while not getting damaged. These include posture, structural alignment and reinforcement, target availability, path of motion, weapon formation, weapon development, target contouring, angle of contact, vector of penetration, timing, precision, acceleration, etc.

The environment we find ourselves can also assist the application of natural weapons. The ground, a wall, cage, boxing ring can provide an additional bracing, rebounding, or contact surface. Once a best method is chosen the weapon would be applied directionally contacting at a vector to best influence the target, based upon our intention.

This would hopefully result in the "Level of Force" we intended by penetrating, smashing, breaking, controlling, manipulating, tearing, pushing, pulling, squeezing, collapsing, etc.

**Targets** can also be looked at as soft tissue and hard-surface targets. Pressure points, internal organs, nerve centers, and circulation paths lie under many or perhaps most target locations. These can be disturbed, interrupted, shocked, and damaged with the right type and angle of impact or pressure, then compounded with follow up attacks.

Some targets are used more for manipulation where others distract or can devastate an opponent. The natural weapon and technique used to attack a target should have the capability to defeat that target without injury to the weapon. Training and knowledge make this more likely.

For example, a hard-bare-knuckle punch to the frontal lobe of the skull could result in a broken knuckle as the target is a larger stronger bone surface than the weapon. This is one reason why the first thing a boxer does before punching anyone is wrap and protect their hands, a luxury not available in a street altercation.

Another choice for striking this target would be the padded palm or hammerfist. Punching the head can still be done, but with precision to more vulnerable targets like the less reinforced temple, mastoid, jaw, or nose where the punch can win at the point of contact. Numerous weapon-to-target options can vary based upon changing circumstances or personal preference.

**Soft Tissue *(Yin)* Target Areas** consist of those places on the human body without a bone directly under the skin. These would include the side of the neck, solar plexus, abdomen, and groin that can be penetrated with various weapons from different directions, angles, and entry vectors (Raking Fist).

The deeper this attacking energy goes into the body the more internal damage is possible causing a type of pain that is difficult to ignore. Striking or pressing a soft tissue target with a sharp natural or perhaps heavy weapon increases the chance of affecting the deeper layers, if that is the intention.

A basic punch (Yang surface weapon) to the solar plexus (Yin surface target) can be enhanced by extending the middle knuckle to gain extra penetration into the tissue. A heavy knee to the solar plexus can hit with more surface area and a heavier mass to affect deeper layers.

Soft padded (Yin) weapons can also be used effectively onto these soft padded (Yin) targets, such as a handsword strike to the side of the neck or a hammerfist strike to the groin.

**Hard-Surface *(Yang)* Target Areas** are body parts where the bone(s) lie directly under the surface of the skin. Attacking the skull, chin, sternum, and spine can affect organs and consiousness, along with all the joints and bones where nerves and blood vessels can be compressed into bone, and all where skin can be easily torn.

Striking attacks to these targets are most often done with a padded weapon such as a hammerfist, handsword, palm strike, ball of the foot, bottom of the heel, etc.

Exceptions exist when mismatches occur in opposing structures. This can justify hard weapons to hard targets, like a knee to the spine, or a well-conditioned punch into a bony sternum to affect the Qi (CV17) or hitting the chin to affect consciousness.

Pressing and rubbing a nerve into a bone is another way a hard Yang surface can attack a hard Yang target successfully. A bone on bone joint-lock (Yang on Yang), using the ulna bone pressing the elbow joint for manipulation, pain compliance, or to cause injury (Obstructing the Club) is an example of this.

Whatever the formula for attacking soft or hard targets it is useful to have well-conditioned natural weapons while using the best method (Impact, Connect, Attach) at the most precise angle (Contouring) allowing the most effective vector to be applied into a vulnerable area or pressure point. This, when done with mental intention, maximizes the potential of a technique being successful while minimizing the possibility of the natural weapon becoming damaged.

# ANATOMY & PHYSIOLOGY
## Chapter IV

In my view, a martial artist should have a basic understanding of human anatomy (the parts) and some physiology (the functions). Without this knowledge a techniques intention is missing a major component of its effectiveness.

The choice to use martial arts technique to harm or not to harm another person requires we have this basic understanding of where things are located and what they do. This allows our intention to be more precise.

Additionally, at the root of martial arts is our own health. This human survival motivation includes being safe in our environment with a healthy body, mind, and spirit. Enemies exist not only on the outside but can enter to the inside by force, be allowed to enter, or brought in through the environment, our lifestyle, and our diet.

The skeletal and muscular systems are only the surface (pun intended) of what a martial artist should know. Some systems, like the endocrine, are not critical to making a punch more effective, but it does give insight into human development. This bigger view can be beneficial from not only a fighting standpoint but for our own overall health.

The *Anatomy Systems* presented here can be studied for martial art applications and for general knowledge. A martial artist should, in my opinion, eventually know how to heal the body to some degree as this allows for longer and more consistent training by our self and those around us, and it is much more difficult than causing damage. It can also be rewarding on many levels to become a healer with an expertise in a health and wellness discipline.

A working knowledge of basic human anatomy and physiology should be considered a pillar of martial arts, in my opinion, as our claimed expertise is in how to damage another human being. Ignorance of the human body is unacceptable for someone with those professed skills.

There is also a moral obligation that trained practitioners have, as they should try to accomplish a task with the least amount of permanent damage to an opponent or opponents.

Mostly common terms are used here, with some medical or professional terms where they are more precise. This is by no means a complete medical text, so the reader should do whatever additional research they require to attain more knowledge and information as they require it. Use this chapter and the next as reference reminders, and for clarification when studying and practicing martial arts applications.

# Human Organ Systems

Anatomy and physiology knowledge for martial arts starts with an overview of the 10 Human Organ Systems shown below. Note: The male and female Reproductive Systems are not included here since the groin as a target is covered under the Urinary System.

The first 5 systems are the *Skeletal* and *Muscular* for Support & Movement, the *Nervous* and *Endocrine* for Coordination & Integration, and the *Integumentary* system that covers the body is listed but not covered indepthly here.

The next 5 are Processing and Transporting Systems. Those are *Cardiovascular* for blood, *Lymphatic* for lymph, *Respiratory* for air, *Urinary* for liquid, and *Digestive* for solids.

All these systems have martial art targets with some mentioned in the system descriptions but covered more thoroughly in the Pressure Point chapter.

Also discussed in this chapter are the 5 Senses of *Sight, Hearing, Taste, Smell* and *Touch* along with the 4 Sensation Senses of *Balance, Pressure & Temperature, Pain,* and *Position & Coordination.*

10 Human Organ Systems illustrated and discussed in this chapter are:

| **Skeletal** | **Muscular** | **Nervous** | **Endocrine** | **Integumentary** |
|:---:|:---:|:---:|:---:|:---:|
| *206 Bones* | *Cardiac / Skeletal* | *Central (CNS)* | *Glands* | *Skin/Hair* |
| | *Smooth* | *Peripheral (PNS)* | *Hormones* | *Nails* |
| ***Support & Movement*** | | ***Coordination & Integration*** | | ***Body Covering*** |

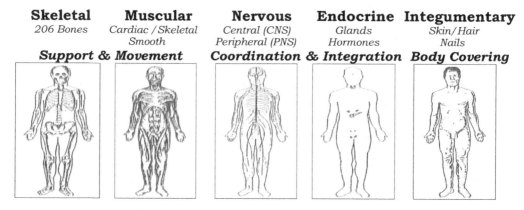

### Processing & Transporting Systems

| **Cardiovascular** | **Lymphatic** | **Respiratory** | **Urinary** | **Digestive** |
|:---:|:---:|:---:|:---:|:---:|
| ***Blood*** | ***Waste*** | ***Air*** | ***Liquid*** | ***Food*** |

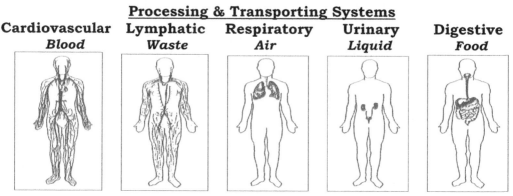

# Human Skeletal System

The human Skeletal System consists of 206 bones that connect at 6 distinct types of joints, many of which can be effectively manipulated in the application of martial art techniques.

This is the framework the Muscular System (muscles, ligaments, & tendons) is built upon, that then holds the skeletal system together.

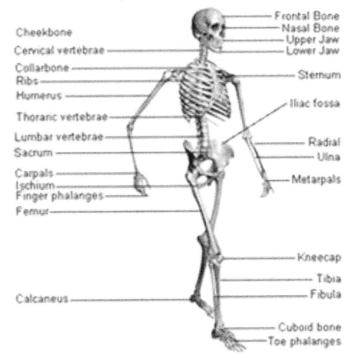

Bones are living tissue but still extremely hard. Ligaments hold bones together, and tendons connect muscles to bones. Attacking the areas where bones connect or articulate (joints) is used often in martial arts.

The nerves and blook that flow along these surfaces under the skin can also be attacked, often using our own bones to apply force for disrupting blood flow, or to generate a nerve response.

A bone that becomes broken not only affects function. Besides painful from the physical break it could also potentially damage muscles, tendons, ligaments, nerves, blood vessels, and nearby skin.

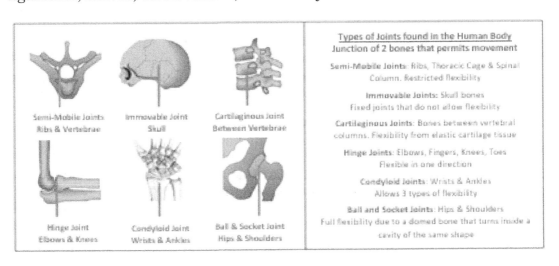

# Human Muscular System

The Muscular System includes muscles, tendons, ligaments, and the encompassing fascia structure. These vital components allow us to put our bodies in motion and apply force.

Knowing how muscles work together is useful for developing and maintaining a balanced muscular framework in our body. It is also beneficial to understanding where and how an opponent is or can be weak at a given moment.

Awareness of posture, knowledge of muscular alignment, and how muscles function is important. Muscles work in pairs so when one direction contracts (is engaged) the opposite complimentary muscle relaxes but is ready to engage.

**FRONT (ANTERIOR VIEW)**

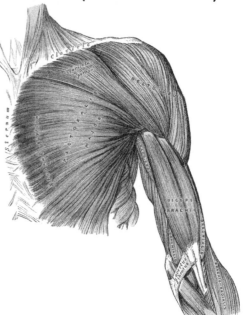

**REAR (POSTERIOR VIEW)**

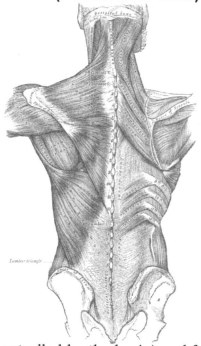

An opponent with hands up to punch is preparing (pre-loading) his arms extensor muscles (triceps) for action (pushing). This means his (pulling) flexor muscles (biceps) may not be as prepared for resistance. This could make it easier to pull his hand down, and if he resists, his muscle focus has changed so then is easier to push his hands.

In either case his internal and external shoulder rotators are not engaged so his arm can be moved or checked inside or out at different angles at his hand or elbow.

**Muscular System facts:**
There are over 630 muscles in the Human Body made up of 3 types:
**1) Cardiac muscles** are involuntary (not controlled by the brain) and found only in the heart.
**2) Smooth muscles** are also involuntary and make up all the muscles in the internal organs, except the heart.

**3) Skeletal muscles** are the only voluntary muscles in the body. They work in pairs to move bones so when one-muscle contracts its complimentary partner muscle relaxes.

*Skeletal Muscles work together in different ways*:
1) *Flexors* bend (flex) at the joint to make its muscle shorter. *Extensors* un-bend (extend) at the joint making its muscle longer.
2) *Agonist* refers to a prime moving or contracting muscle (Flexor flexing or Extensor extending) as its complimentary *Antagonist* muscle opposes while relaxing (Flexor extending or Extensor flexing).
3) A *Concentric* contraction is when a muscle shortens as it contracts. An *Eccentric* contraction is when the muscle lengthens as it contracts. An *Isometric* contraction is where the muscle does not change length.
4) <u>*Abductors*</u> move away from the body. <u>*Adductors*</u> move towards it.
5) The limbs are turned using *Internal* and *External* rotator muscles.

*Other Terms to Know About Muscles:*
Actions (What a muscle does)
Origins (Where a muscle starts)
Insertions (Where a muscle goes)

**Note:** Muscles only contract as the *Insertion* moves closer to the *Origin*, so knowing Origin and Insertion tells what moves what.

*Tendons and Ligaments:*
**Tendons** connect muscles to bone. Contracting limb muscles pull the tendon, attached over a joint to another bone, making for skeletal movement.

**Ligaments** hold bones together by connecting at the ends of two bones.

*Reflexes:*
**Golgi Tendon Organ (GTO) Reflex** – The neurological protection mechanism located in a muscles tendon that protects the muscle from too much tension. Too much weight or a rubbing stimulation to a GTO disengages a muscles contraction, causing it to relax.

**Muscle Spindle Cell (MSC) Reflex** – The neurological mechanism within the muscle belly protecting it from being overstretched. Too much stretch or hard impact to a MSC causes the muscle to contract.

*Fascia:*
This fibrous flexible connective tissue covers the entire body and binds all its structural components together like a web. The superficial layer connects with the skin and surface level muscles while deep layers surround and connect with deeper muscles, bones, nerves, and blood vessels. At a visceral level the internal organs are suspended in their cavities by being wrapped in this fascia structure.

# Human Nervous System

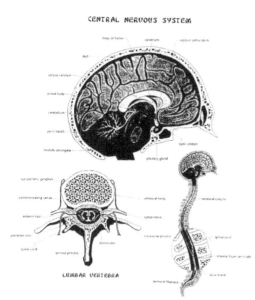

CENTRAL NERVOUS SYSTEM

LUMBAR VERTEBRA

The Nervous System coordinates all bodily functions and is divided into the Central Nervous System (CNS) and Peripheral Nervous System (PNS). The CNS consists of the brain and spinal cord. The PNS consists of the nerves that branch out from that central system. The nervous system covers the entire body, so some part is always available for attack. Nerves are effective targets that can even be lethal.

The PNS is divided into somatic and autonomic systems. The somatic system consists of nerves connecting to skin and skeletal muscles (voluntary nerve control). The autonomic system consists of nerves connecting to organs and glands (involuntary nerve control).

Cranial Nerves (CN) are important Nervous System components emerging directly from the brain, unlike spinal nerves, from the spinal cord. Function is covered here with Targets covered in the Pressure Point chapter.

There are 12 pairs of cranial nerves. CNI and CNII emerge from the cerebrum at the front of the brain. The other 10 Cranial Nerves emerge from the brainstem located at the back of the brain. The brainstem provides the motor and sensory system innervations to the face and neck through these cranial nerves.

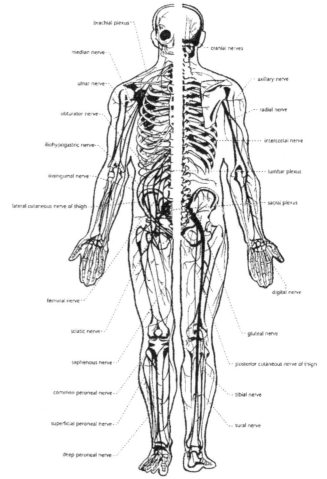

PERIPHERAL NERVOUS SYSTEM

brachial plexus
median nerve
ulnar nerve
obturator nerve
iliohypogastric nerve
ilioinguinal nerve
lateral cutaneous nerve of thigh
femoral nerve
sciatic nerve
saphenous nerve
common peroneal nerve
superficial peroneal nerve
deep peroneal nerve

cranial nerves
axillary nerve
radial nerve
intercostal nerve
lumbar plexus
sacral plexus
digital nerve
gluteal nerve
posterior cutaneous nerve of thigh
tibial nerve
sural nerve

All 12 Cranial Nerves are listed for reference. CNV (Trigeminal), VII (Facial), X (Vagus), and XI (Accessory) are the ones primarily attacked in martial arts.

I.    Olfactory Nerve –Smell

II.   Optic Nerve – Vision

III.  Oculomotor Nerve – Eyelid & eyeball movement

IV.   Trochlear Nerve – Turns eyes downward and sideways

V.    Trigeminal Nerve – Chewing plus sensation to the face and mouth. The 3 branches are: Ophthalmic, Maxillary, and Mandibular with the first two only sensory and the mandibular sensory and motor, where a nerve disruption could lock the jaw.

VI.   Abducens Nerve – Turns eyes sideways

VII.  Facial Nerve – Controls most facial expressions, the front two-thirds of the tongue along with secretion of tears and saliva

VIII. Vestibulocochlear Nerve – Controls hearing & equilibrium sensation

IX.   Glossopharyngeal Nerve – Taste & senses carotid blood pressure

X.    Vagus Nerve – Senses aortic blood pressure, slows heart rate, stimulates digestion, and controls some taste

XI.   Accessory Nerve – Controls trapezius, SCM muscles, and swallowing

XII.  Hypoglossal Nerve – Controls tongue movement

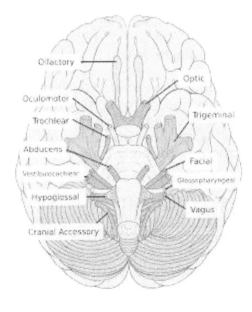

# Human Endocrine System

The Endocrine System describes a system of glands that secrete *Hormones* into our bodies throughout our lifetimes to regulate growth and development, tissue and bodily function, metabolism, and mood. Many glands work in a sequence such as the hypothalamus releasing a hormone into the pituitary that releases one into the adrenal medulla that releases one into the bloodstream.

Chinese Medicine describes these human development and aging functions differently, but usefully, with females evolving over 7-year *Life Cycles* and males evolving over 8-year *Life Cycles*. Although this is a general overview of growth and aging it can provide insight into human development and the complicated human health matrix viewed over a lifetime.

## Female Life Cycle (7x7)
7 years   – Abundant kidney Qi with permanent teeth and body hair
14 years – Starts to menstruate and can then conceive
21 years – Kidney Qi peaks, body development stops, wisdom teeth grow
28 years – Peak physicality with strong muscles & bones, & hair thickest
35 years – Body starts decline, initial aging signs (sallow face, wrinkles)
42 years – Yang meridians begin decline; facial sagging & hair whitening
49 years – Body deteriorates & ability to menstruate & give birth ceases

## Male Life Cycle (8x8)
8 years   – Kidney Qi consolidates, grows permanent teeth and body hair
16 years – Kidney Qi abundant; kidney essence can transform to sperm
24 years – Kidney Qi peaks, wisdom teeth grow & limbs are strong
32 years – Body reaches peak, with sturdy powerful bones & tendons
40 years – Kidney starts to decline, leading to hair loss or loose teeth
48 years – Yang-Qi starts depleting, face can sag & hair start graying
56 years – Liver & kidney Qi weakens; joint issues; less essence & vitality; body ages
64 years – Hair and teeth may be lost

Although the human hormonal system described does not necessarily contain martial arts targets in the normal sense, they can be affected with severe trauma to areas where glands are located. They are listed here as an informational reference since they are intricately connected to all functions and processes within the human body.

## Gland: Hypothalamus
Thyrotropin-Releasing Hormone (TRH) - Stimulates TSH & Prolactin
Corticotropin-Releasing Hormone (CRH) - Triggers ACTH release
Growth Hormone-Releasing Hormone (GHRH) - Triggers GH release
GH-Inhibitory Hormone (GHIH) (somatostatin) - Inhibits GH secretion
Gonadotropin-Releasing Hormone (GnRH) - Triggers LH & FSH release
Dopamine/Prolactin-Inhibiting Factor (PIF) - Controls release of Prolactin

**Gland: Anterior Pituitary Gland**
Adrenocorticotropic Hormone (ACTH)
Stimulates synthesis & secretion of Cortisol, Androgens and Aldosterone
Follicle-Stimulating Hormone (FSH)
Stimulates the growth of the ovarian follicle in women
Stimulates the maturation of sperm in the testes of men
Growth Hormone (GH)
Stimulates synthesis of proteins for the growth of cells & tissues
Luteinizing Hormone (LH)
Stimulates ovulation & production of estrogen & progesterone in women
Stimulates the testes to produce testosterone in men
Prolactin
Promotes development of breasts and milk production in women
Thyroid-Stimulating Hormone (TSH)
Stimulates the synthesis and secretion of thyroid hormones

**Gland: Posterior Pituitary Gland**
Antidiuretic Hormone (ADH) / Vasopressin
Stimulates re-absorption of water from urine in the kidneys
Triggers vasoconstriction (Both can increase blood pressure)
Oxytocin - Stimulates breast milk, enhances uterine contractions

**Gland: Thyroid**
Thyroxine (T4) & Triiodothyronine (T3)
Controls metabolic process rates in blood
Calcitonin - Promotes calcium in bones -
Reduces calcium in blood & tissue fluid

**Gland: Parathyroid**
Parathyroid Hormone (PTH)
Triggers calcium release from bones &
increases calcium gastrointestinal tract
absorption - Together increases calcium
concentration in blood

**Gland: Adrenal Cortex**
Cortisol - Glucocorticoid with wide range of
metabolic & anti-inflammatory effects
Aldosterone - Mineralocorticoid regulates
concentration of essential electrolytes

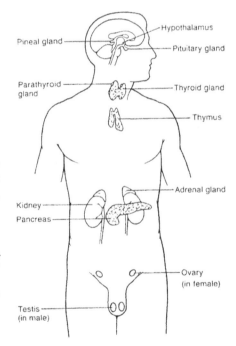

**Gland: Adrenal Medulla**
Norepinephrine & Epinephrine - Stimulates Sympathetic Nervous System
Insulin - Acts on cells to increase glucose (sugar) uptake from the blood
Glucagon - Promotes the release of stored glucose from the liver

# The Human Senses

Each of the 5 generally described senses consists of organs with specialized cells that have receptors for specific stimuli. These cells have links to the nervous system, and thus to the brain. Sensing is done in the cells and integrated into sensations in the nervous system.

In addition to sight, hearing, taste, smell, and touch, humans also have a sense of Balance (Equilibrioception), Pressure & Temperature (Thermoception), Pain (Nociception), and Kinesthetic (Proprioception) or position in space, all or some of which involve the coordinated use of multiple sensory organs.

Proprioception, for example, enables us to touch the tip of our nose with our eyes closed or know which part to scratch when we itch. Closely related to Proprioception is Kinesthesia, the sensory awareness of muscle and joint movement that allows us to coordinate our muscles when we walk, talk, and use our hands.

This can be an extensive topic where distraction and intimidation can be used to affect these different processes. This relates to the effect a ferocious "war face" or a thundering war/battle cry or powerful kiai can have on the human psyche.

Deception is also used to fool these senses. As Mr. Parker put it "to hear is to doubt, to see is to be deceived, but to feel is to believe." Expand that to add: We see and we are seen, we hear and we are heard, we touch and we are touched.

**Sight:** Although the eye is the primary organ of sight, its functions are assisted by the eyelids, eyelashes, and eye muscles, all of which help to protect it. The eye muscles are the smallest muscles found in the body. The eye itself is hollow. It has three layers: outer, middle, and inner. The spaces within the eye are filled with fluids that provide support for its wall and internal parts, and to help maintain its shape.

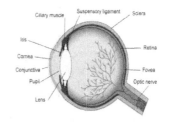

**Hearing:** The organ of hearing is the ear. It has external, middle, and internal parts. In addition to making hearing possible, the ear functions in the sense of equilibrium.

The tube leading into the ear is guarded by small hairs and lined with skin containing numerous modified sweat glands that secrete wax. The hair and wax together help to keep relatively large foreign objects like insects from entering the ear. Vibrations (sounds) are transmitted through the auditory ossicles from the eardrum to the inner ear.

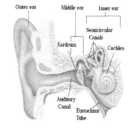

The sense of balance is maintained by the inner ear vestibular system along with a complex interaction of visual inputs and proprioceptive sensors (affected by gravity and stretch sensors found in muscles, skin, and joints), and the central nervous system. Disturbances occurring in any part of the balance system, or even within the brains integration of inputs, can cause a feeling of dizziness or unsteadiness.

**Taste:** The tongue, teeth, and mouth cavity work together with saliva to break food down into a size that can be swallowed. The taste buds are the organs of taste and mostly located on the tongue.

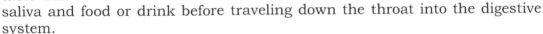

The four primary taste sensations are: Sweet, Sour, Salty, and Bitter (with TCM adding Spicy). Before the taste can be detected however it must be mixed with saliva and food or drink before traveling down the throat into the digestive system.

Generally, the taste buds closer to the tip of the tongue are sensitive to sweet tastes with those at the back of the tongue more sensitive to bitter tastes. The taste buds on the top and sides of the tongue are sensitive to salty and sour tastes.

**Smell:** The smell, or olfactory receptors, are like those of taste as they sense close together and aid in food selection. This explains why food tastes differently with a stuffed-up nose.

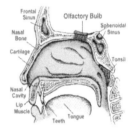

The seven major groups of odors are camphoraceous (medicine smell), musk, floral, peppermint, ether (cleaning solutions), pungent (spices), and putrid (rotten).

**Touch:** The sense of touch is considered a somatic sense. It involves receptors associated with the skin, muscles, and joints, with some areas more sensitive than others. The four sensations are cold, heat, contact, and pain.

The epidermis is the outer most layer of skin. Pressure factors for determining pain, pleasure, or incidental contact include the contact surface shape, size, and speed of the applied pressure. Temperature is another way to stimulate the sense of touch.

# Human Cardiovascular System

The heart is the primary organ of the Cardiovascular System, sometimes known as the Circulatory System. It is partially located behind the sternum and mostly on the upper left part of the chest cavity where it shares space with the left lung lobe. From top to bottom the heart organ occupies space from about the 2nd rib space (under the left collar bone) down to about the 6th rib space (two rib spaces under the left nipple).

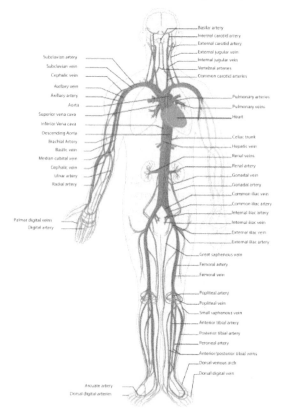

Arteries carry pressurized blood away from the heart to the entire body delivering oxygen and substance. Veins return de-oxygenated blood back to the heart.

It is said in Chinese medicine that "Blood is the Mother of Qi & Qi is the Commander of Blood." This symbiotic relationship between Blood (substance) and Qi (energy/life force) helps explain the dynamic quality of our blood.

Arteries are frequently attacked in martial arts, and even the heart organ behind the hard chest cavity that protects it is vulnerable.

The liver (Multi-System Organ), spleen (Lymphatic System) and kidneys (Urinary System) are all blood-filled so their locations and general dimensions should be known.

The large liver organ, on the human torso right side, accounts for about 25% of the circulating blood at any given time. It can be attacked from the front, side, or rear with trauma that can make the body and legs weak, or even cause shock, all of which can make a person collapse in pain.

The spleen, on the left side opposite the liver, can be ruptured creating lots of internal bleeding and pain. For liver or spleen, attacking the lowest unattached rib (floating rib), generally with strikes, is a good marker.

The kidneys are two bean-shaped organs on either side of the spine in the lower back, just above the hipbones. Striking into or grasping the surface area near them can have an instant and dramatic effect on someone's Qi.

# Human Lymphatic System

This part of the Circulatory System is an important part of our Immune System. When substances are exchanged between the blood and tissue more fluid leaves the blood capillaries than returns to them.

If the fluid remaining accumulated, the pressure inside this tissue would increase. The Lymphatic System helps to prevent such an imbalance by providing pathways through which tissue fluid can be transported as lymph from these spaces, filtered, then deposited into the veins where it becomes part of the returning blood.

This filtering by the Lymphatic System helps defend the body tissues against infections by removing toxic particles from the lymph and by supporting the activities of the lymphocytes that furnish immunity against disease. Although not necessarily used as martial arts targets this is a critical system in the human health matrix.

The Lymphatic Pathway: Excess fluids between the blood and tissue become *Lymph* then enter *Lymphatic Capillaries*. These merge to form *Afferent Lymphatic Vessels* that empty into *Lymph Nodes* where the *Lymph* is filtered. The *Lymph* then leaves through *Efferent Lymphatic Vessels* to *Lymphatic Trunks* that merge into *Collecting Ducts* emptying into the *Subclavian Vein* where the lymph is added to the blood.

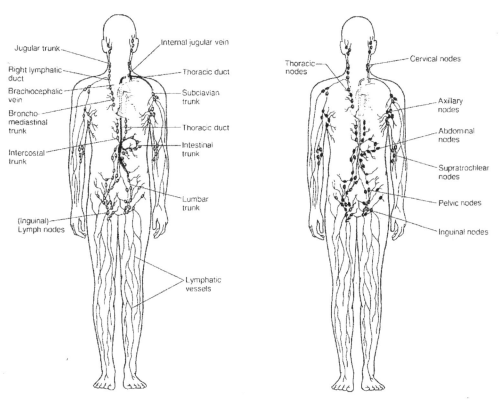

# Human Respiratory System

The Respiratory System processes environmental gases into and out of the body. It consists of a group of passages that filter incoming air (oxygen) as it is pulled into the lungs by a diaphragm muscle contraction. The outgoing air (carbon dioxide) is then expelled by the Lungs contracting. This exchange of gases makes human life possible.

The nose and mouth are where air/oxygen is brought into the body and where carbon dioxide is expelled. There are different breathing techniques depending on what we are using the air for, and many visuals that can help improve the quality of our breath, as the quality of air we breathe is only equaled by the technique we use to bring that air into our bodies. See *Breath* in the *Mind* for details.

Fighting techniques that attack the lungs include interrupting or stopping the airflow, attacking the breath muscle (diaphragm), or damaging the lung organ directly. This is covered more thoroughly in the *Pressure Point* chapter.

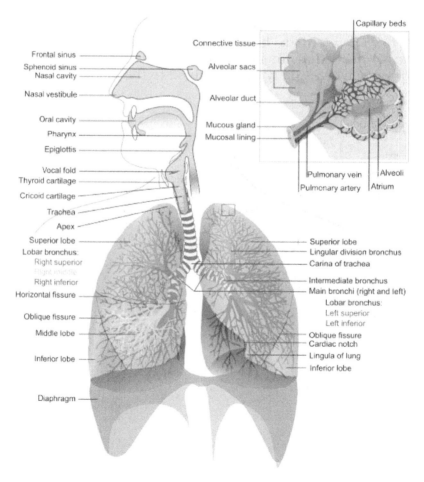

# Human Urinary System

The Urinary System processes liquid waste from the body. It consists of a pair of kidneys that remove substances from the blood, form urine, and transport it through ureters into the urinary bladder. The urine is then stored until the urethra releases it outside the body at the groin.

In addition, the adrenal glands are attached to the kidneys making for more vulnerability in this area. Low blood pressure and anemia may occur if a significant amount of blood is lost internally or externally (shock).

The primary places to attack this system would be at the kidneys, urinary bladder, and the groin in front or underneath. Symptoms caused by trauma to the kidneys may include pain in the upper abdomen or flank (between ribs and hip), bruising of the flank, blood in the urine, or pain resulting from lower rib fractures.

The kidneys can be struck, or the surface grasped, squeezed, and twisted in any number of ways depending on available angles. Located on the backside of the body these can be difficult to access, but position and technique can often be adjusted to fit this target area.

The urinary bladder on the front lower abdominal area (dantien), just below the navel/belly button, is a weaker abdominal area to attack.

The groin area is at and just below the urinary bladder. This is a popular target in self-defense arts, but generally illegal in sport fighting arts due to the powerful effect of trauma to this area.

The groin can be attacked from the front to affect the bladder, pelvic girdle, or hips and hip flexors causing pain and affecting posture. It can also be attacked underneath between the legs to crush a man's testicles against his pubic bone causing severe pain and inability to function.

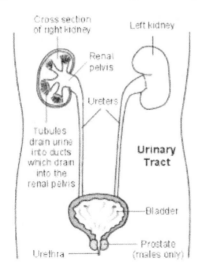

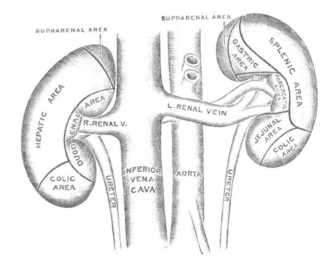

# Human Digestive System

The Digestive System processes the solid foods we eat. The alimentary canal extends from the mouth to the anus. Food is taken into our mouths, then chewed and mixed with saliva, then swallowed into the stomach where further digestion occurs before it moves through the intestines by mixing and propelling motions.

Accessory organs along the way release secretions at various stages that change food substances into forms that can be absorbed by cell membranes. The solid leftover waste is then excreted from the body at the end of the canal.

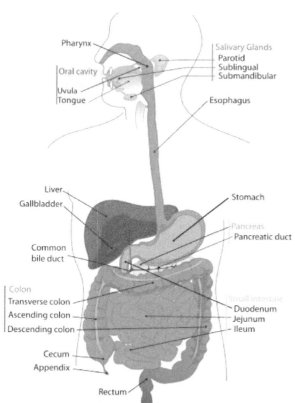

From a health standpoint one of the critical junctures in this process is the ability of the stomach to break down the food we eat with acids and enzymes, and our ability to absorb the nutrients from that food in our Small Intestines.

The small intestine is where about 90% of nutrients are absorbed. Bile from the liver mixes with food product and is slowed by small hair-like villi in the 28' long small intestine organ.

Poor diet, diminished stomach Qi, and aging affects the production of stomach acids, enzymes, bile, and the villi, all making nutrient absorption less productive or even difficult. This body metabolism interaction affects our energy and health.

Without cleansing, supplements, and diet modifications to protect and reinvigorate this process, especially as we age, then fatigue, digestive problems, and disease can develop (See *Nutrition* in the *Spirit*). After absorption, waste products continue into and through the large intestine for processing and elimination.

From a martial arts standpoint, this system is attacked primarily from the front and possibly sides of the body. Several internal organs contained in this system, or near it, are useful targets. The stomach, appendix (lower right side), liver, and spleen are all organs associated with this system that are reactive to trauma.

# PRESSURE POINTS
## Chapter V

The anatomy and physiology information from the previous chapter can be used as a reference when practicing and understanding what is contained in this chapter. Care should always be used when practicing this subject, and sound judgment as to when it may ever be appropriate to attack many of the targets in the ways described.

Additional research can help to gain a more complete picture and clear understanding of how the human body functions. This can stimulate other ideas as how to affect the different body systems and may have the additional bonus of leading you down a path towards better health, and possibly even empower you as a healer.

The human body is a complex but understandable matrix with information here gleaned from Western and Eastern health paradigms. Both contain valuable knowledge, but both can also be lacking in perspective which can lead to inconsistent results.

Ancient systems can seem complicated away from where and when created and are often supported by anecdotal evidence and unproven exaggerations. Western science-based systems can be lacking in acknowledging the wide range of human variables and holistic relationships taking place in the body.

Regardless of the paradigm, every part of the human body is a pressure point to one degree or another. The human body is constructed in layers making for compounding as deeper layers of the body are accessed. In the spectrum of mapped points there are hurting ones and healing ones, and those that can do both as determined by intention and technique. This chapter will try to narrow down the points for martial arts use.

In Traditional Chinese Medicine (TCM) there are about 360 standard acupuncture points, plus many *Extra Points (EP)* and the longstanding tradition of the *Ahshi (Ah-sure) Point*, which is any unnamed point or spot on the body that has an effect. Many of the micro-system points also exist on the Scalp, Ears, Face, Hands, and Feet, but are not covered here.

Individual points are listed by one of 12 bilateral organ system channels plus front and back centerline channels. Internal pathways that connect these channels are not covered. Points on the channels discussed will have the organ abbreviation and assigned Western number. Also included is the Chinese Pinyin with its English translation as these can be interesting and provide point insight.

## Acupuncture Meridian Abbreviations:

| | | | |
|---|---|---|---|
| Lu = | Lung Meridian | LI = | Large Intestine Meridian |
| St = | Stomach Meridian | Sp = | Spleen Meridian (Pancreas) |
| Ht = | Heart Meridian | SI = | Small Intestine Meridian |
| Ki = | Kidney Meridian | UB= | Urinary Bladder Meridian |
| P = | Pericardium (Heart Cover) | TW = | Triple Warmer (3 Sections) |
| Lv = | Liver Meridian | GB= | Gall Bladder Meridian |
| CV = | Conception Vessel (Front Centerline) | GV = | Governing Vessel (Back Centerline) |
| EP = | Extra Point | Ahshi Point = Felt Unnamed Point | |

Many standard acupuncture points are not necessarily for martial arts use so are not covered. The points listed here, if stimulated, will have some effect. The degree of which is determined by the interactive variables within the vast human genetic spectrum, along with applied intention and technique. Some reactions are consistent such as nerve stimulation tending to cause a reflex action away from the stimulation and internal organ or groin damage tending to cause the body to contract around the stimulation.

Individual people are different with regards to relative body size, dimensions, tissue density, pain tolerance, functional recovery time, reflexes, instincts, determination, target depth, and even target location. These very real human dynamics make many targets and techniques not as effective for some people to use on certain other people. The fact is that different people can take, absorb, mentally block, or deal with system disruptions and there affects to different degrees.

This makes good technique and setting up targets important, while matching or exceeding an opponent's motivation and determination to win and survive for this higher intellectual knowledge to assure victory, so keep fighting! Never assume everyone will respond equally to any of the points covered. The ability to generate enough force with accuracy to affect a small target with an appropriate weapon on an unpredictably moving location at the most effective angle, vector, and depth in a dynamic environment is not guaranteed. Translation: You might miss!

With that said, *Points* covered here are divided into 6 categories that I call "Areas of Disruption." Those are *Disruption of Blood Flow, Disruption of Air Flow, Disruption of Nerve Function, Disruption of Brain Function, Disruption of Tissue & Mechanical Function,* and *Disruption of Qi Energy.* The first 5 use mostly Modern Western Medicine (MWM) system references with the last one anchored in Traditional Chinese Medicine (TCM) theory.

Overlap exists among these categories, due to the body's holistic nature, and many points are near areas or points in more than one *Area of Disruption.* A broken bone for example disrupts mechanical function but can also cause collateral damage to nearby blood vessels and nerves, increase respiration, and affect brain function, all of which disrupts Qi.

*BarryBBarker.com for the SELF-DEFENSE Technique video references*

The body is constructed in layers, so deeper layers of damage affect every layer on the way in. A punch to the solar plexus could cause a change in posture, or deeper affect the diaphragm muscle to take someone's air, or deeper to impact the heart organ causing a life-threatening fibrillation.

Torso and musculoskeletal points, except for the body centerline, are bilateral with two points, one on each side of the body's sagittal plane. The body is also 3-dimensional, so large organs can be attacked at various positions around the body.

**Anatomical Body Reference Terms:**
Body references, relative position, location, and direction as used in the Western medical field.

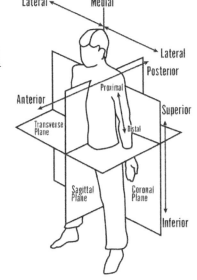

Transverse Plane – Top/Bottom halves
Sagittal Plane – Left/Right sides
Coronal Plane – Front/Back halves
Anterior – Front
Posterior – Rear
Superior – Above
Inferior – Below
Lateral – Towards the outside
Medial – Towards the middle
Proximal – Nearer the body
Distal – Further from the body

Points can be attacked individually, simultaneously, or sequentially along acupuncture meridians, nerve pathways, energetically connected channel & organ correspondences, and body quadrants.

Multiple point attack sequences include *limb to body* (Six Hands), along the *centerline* (Hidden Elbow), on *one side* (Reversing Fist), *horizontally* along the *upper* (Hidden Hand) or *lower* body (Scraping Stomp), *diagonally* (Conquering Arm), and *front/back* (Blinding Vice). They can also be applied simultaneously *(Twins of Destruction).*

Combining and overlapping these lines only enhances them. They all can affect the physical body from simple posture and position changes to creating energetic, functional, internal, and/or mental dysfunction.

As anyone familiar with contact sports knows, it hurts more if you don't see it coming. This is how a boxing combination can be so devastating and is how Kenpo techniques are devised.

This chapter however is not a particular style of fighting, but a list of effective points and areas categorized using Western and Eastern anatomy and physiology paradigms. Kenpo techniques and basics are referenced for those interested but what is covered can be used and adapted to any martial art style or system.

Pressure Point systems often use acupuncture theory to emphasize attacking points within a channel / organ correspondence, a 5-element sequence, or even at a specific time of day, or season of the year.

This often complicated and seemingly mystical analysis may or may not be a noticeable refinement of their use, but the points covered here stand on their own merit. Western and/or Eastern health models can both explain them, with Disruption of Qi Energy an exception to the Western paradigm, yet still a real phenomenon.

All points and body areas are attacked best at precise angles, vectors, and depths using various weapons and methods. Body contours are also important in determining the best entry angle and attack method with body density a factor in determining attack depth. The vector is applied after arriving at the point and may not be the same as the angle of entry.

Some targets have a solid structure behind them, like a backstop (e.g., nerve pushed against a bone), others are areas with targets under a solid structure (e.g., brain under skull), or soft targets with no solid support structure nearby (e.g., solar plexus into diaphragm muscle). At the point of attack, the directional options depend on the point structure and type of weapon.

*Point of Contact Variables* (see *Motion & Movement* in the *Mind*) are *Impact* (strike, hit, punch, slap, bump, tackle, push, etc.), *Connect* (slide, press, check, pin, rub, scrape, gouge, stick, track, etc.), and *Attach* (grab, grapple, lock, stretch, twist, hold, pinch, squeeze, pull, etc.). These can be used individually as in only striking (Six Hands) or combined to connect multiple methods (Piercing Blade).

What works is to use the best weapon and method to fit and affect that target. The radial arm nerve is affected best when pressed and rubbed back and forth with a sharp tool, the arms bicep muscle struck with blunt force then raked, the carotid arteries surrounded and squeezed shut.

Since formulations are seemingly endless this chapter will cover individual points with a few combinations, notations, and Kenpo technique references. This should help the reader form a visual to help gain an understanding and knowledge baseline for creative practice.

It's better to have this knowledge than not but Ed Parker's quote that "Guts and conditioning take over where skill and knowledge leave off" or the Russian General's quote "Quantity has a Quality all its own" are good advice when using this sophisticated target knowledge in a fight.

To that end there are many effective points on the human body that can affect someone's ability, capability, or motivation to fight. Following are ways to attack the human structure with a focused educated intention that can increase your chances of success and victory.

## Recovery and Revival Techniques:

Potentially damaging techniques must always be done with control and awareness of everyone's safety. Attacking points on the body focuses energy into those points so recovery methods for structurally undamaged surface level tissue generally involves rubbing, stimulating, and moving.

This helps to return Qi flow and is the normal human instinct to surface level trauma (i.e., "rub some dirt on it", "walk it off"). Note: First aid and possibly professional medical attention would be required for a damaged tissue injury (torn skin, broken bone, or severe pain).

Revival techniques for blood flow disruption to the brain involve getting blood back into the head so stimulating the muscles in the chest and neck help to accelerate that flow.

Brain Function revival is done at GV26 (Du26 -philtrum upper-third under the nose) by gently tapping with a finger pad. Sit them up when able with legs crossed, bracing them, and rubbing the back of their neck on the opposite side of trauma. Place a finger pad on their GV20 (Du20 - highest point on head) until you feel a pulse. This also brings Qi and focus back up into the brain.

Note: Trained medical personnel should be called (911) or take them to a nearby hospital emergency room if they don't revive so they can be evaluated for potential concussion trauma, long-term unconsciousness, or any neck injury (don't move them until seen).

Depending on recovery time after using any revival techniques, stimulating other areas of the body can help bring Qi back to normal faster. Rub a palm side to side across the lower and upper back. Slide the palm and finger pads up the spine, and the nearby parallel back muscles (erector spinitus) from low to high. Gently rub each finger digit and pinch off the fingertips with a snap or pop.

In any case the injured person is probably done training for at least that day and should be followed up on within a day to assure any injury or condition is not getting worse. See *Martial Arts First Aid* in my book on the *Spirit*.

## Disruption of Blood Flow

The blood flowing through the body is analogous to how water flows in the world through seas, rivers, lakes, streams, and ponds. The heart is the primary pumping organ of blood flow, with Qi as the current. A disruption is caused by attacking the heart organ directly or the blood flow through an artery where pressurized oxygenated blood moves through the body.

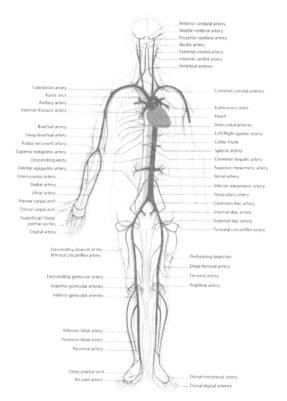

This Circulatory System is closed so affecting an artery also affects the heart organ to some degree. Veins return deoxygenated blood back towards the heart, with the jugular vein in the neck returning blood from the brain and face, but otherwise there's minimal short-term benefit to attacking the venous system.

The heart organ can be traumatized temporarily or permanently by interrupting the heart rhythm, and/or collapsing a valve within the physical structure. Heavy trauma to any area around the heart organ can result in a fibrillation (abnormal heart rhythm or skip) or physical damage.

Note: A Western medical procedure called a "Precordial Thump" was formerly part of standard CPR training but was removed as it resulted in too many injuries. Now it can only be done legally by a trained medical professional under special conditions.

That technique uses a hammerfist to strike the sternum of someone whose heart has stopped beating, trying to restart it. This striking can also traumatize the Heart and can be applied to the back as well.

Precise accuracy is not required if the trauma were great enough, and near enough, to affect the heart rhythm. A sharp weapon can also be precisely applied by striking or pressing a finger knuckle (Parting Arms) or elbow tip (Hidden Hand) between the intercostal rib spaces. Impacting or pressing after connecting are methods used to attack the heart organ directly. Grabbing the heart however is impractical, except in a Kung Fu movie.

The heart and blood flow can also be affected at various places in the body to cause fainting, chest pain, shortness of breath, or even heart failure.

## Heart Organ Points

The hard breastbone protects the heart, with the softer angle to the heart organ up through the diaphragm muscle at the solar plexus, CV14 (Disruption of Air Flow). This is the access point spawning the martial arts legend of ripping the beating heart out of someone's chest.

The Heart organ has 4 main valves, with damage to any prohibiting blood from flowing to the next processing stage. This would be fatal without

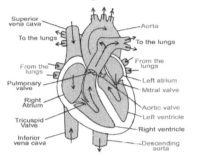

immediate medical attention, although it would take some time for an effect to be noticed as blood is still contained within the system, so keep fighting.

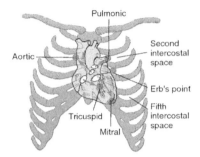

**Ki25 / Shen Cang / Spirit Storehouse** is between the 2nd intercostal rib spaces on either side of the sternum. The left side point is over the Pulmonary Valve. This gate is where deoxygenated blood in the right ventricle is carried into the pulmonary artery before going into the lungs to be oxygenated.

The Aortic Valve is also on this point but on its right point side, although it could be under the sternum or partially sharing the left point side. It is the gate that carries newly oxygenated blood from the left ventricle into the aorta for distribution into the Arterial System.

**St17 / Ru Zhong / Chest Center** is in the 4th rib spaces over the nipple, with the left side point over the Triscupid Valve. This gate is where deoxygenated blood from the right atrium moves into the right ventricle until pumped through the pulmonary valve into the lungs to be oxygenated.

**St18 / Ru Gen / Root of the Breast** is in the 5th rib spaces, just under the nipples with the left side point over the Mitral Valve. This gate carries newly oxygenated blood stored in the left atrium into the left ventricle where it is pumped through the aortic valve into the aorta.

Body landmarks are the best way to locate vital points like these but can prove difficult to find in a fight. Other factors include tissue density and location, as they are not universal. Valves can be higher or lower in the chest, with the heart organ even on the body's right side in rare occurrences.

Presuming targets are in their standard location these vital spaces can be attacked by striking or pressing after connecting. A support structure, like the ground or a wall, can help to penetrate these points more easily.

Pressing with steady heavy pressure may be more successful, or a press/strike method with pressure applied like a strike but with little or no separation. Points could also be rubbed. In any case it requires target sensitivity and timing as an opponent would feel and react to any pressure, probably by changing body position. Striking small targets on a moving, and probably clothed person, requires great skill and probably some luck.

## Arterial System Points

Arteries carry oxygenated blood to body parts that all need this oxygen to function. Attacking arteries is common in martial arts. Away from the physical heart organ, the Aorta runs vertically along the body centerline from above the heart down to the lower abdomen.

The upper body arterial blood flow travels from the Aortic Arch up through the Carotid Arteries into the brain and into the Subclavian and Axillary Arteries that nourish the chest, armpits, and shoulders. These become the Brachial Arteries into the arms and hands.

The lower body arterial supply starts and then travels from the Abdominal Aorta, where it splits (just below the navel) into the Common Iliac Arteries (left & right) then becomes the Femoral Arteries into the legs, where they then split further.

The 3 ways to disrupt upper body blood flow are to temporarily close an artery making the tissue it feeds momentarily weak, stop the blood flow by longterm compression causing unconsciousness, or by damaging the vessel so blood flows out causing from a bruise to internal or external bleeding. Note: The unsanitary and messy nature of causing external bleeding should be avoided except in a life or death situation (e.g., biting carotid artery).

Temporarily affecting arterial blood flow is best used with follow-ups to take advantage of this momentary effect. Stopping blood flow is more easily regulated and consistently applied using grappling methods.

Note: A *Karate Chop* to the side of the neck is commonly thought to affect blood flow, and it does to some degree. The knockout effect however is elicited by a blood pressure and/or nervous system response.

The blood pressure response occurs by stimulating the Carotid Sinus, convincing the brain that blood pressure has elevated so the body responds by slowing the heart rate to lower BP. This tricking the body system results in lightheadedness, disorientation, and unconsciousness.

The nervous system is affected in the neck at the Vagus Nerve (CNX) that runs parallel with the Carotid Artery. Both are most easily attacked at the side of the neck at St9 to affect not only blood pressure, but also brain and organ function so is covered again under *Disruption of Brain Function.*

### Upper Body Blood Flow Points - Carotid Artery:

**SI17 / Tian Rong / Heavenly Appearance** between the angle of the mandible and SCM muscle anterior border and **St9 / Ren Ying / Mans Welcome** on the carotid artery level with the throats Adams Apple.

The powerful *Carotid Sinus* is just under SI17 and above St9 level with the top of the thyroid cartilage. This bulb shaped tissue is where the artery splits into internal and external carotids and contains sensitive baroreceptors that if stimulated cause a decrease in blood pressure.

The SI17 contact angle to affect the carotid sinus is perpendicular into the soft tissue, as the same point struck against the bone can affect the jaw hinge so is also listed under *Disruption of Mechanical Function.*

The carotid artery pulse can be felt at St9 on both sides of the thyroid cartilage (finger pads slide off until felt). This supplies blood to the brain and is disrupted by compressing both sides simultaneously. The Sleeper Choke, or Carotid Restraint, is often how this is attacked (Turn of Fate) but the hands, legs, or clothing can also be used to interrupt blood flow.

Note: Once the arterial blood (and oxygen) to the brain stops flowing, and after a couple panicked seconds, a person's brain shuts down and they will be asleep. These holds then need to be released to avoid permanent brain damage from lack of oxygen. The ability to subdue a person without permanent injury makes this a very humane technique when applied with that intention.

**TW17 / Yi Feng / Wind Screen** is located at the Temporomandibular Joint (TMJ) behind the ear lobe. Much of the blood flow into the brain flows through this area. This powerful point is also covered under *Disruption of Brain Function* and *Disruption of Mechanical Function.*

## Subclavian & Axillary Artery:

The Subclavian artery travels under each collarbone to supply the chest with blood, then into the armpits where it becomes the Axillary artery. St12 and St13, in the middle of the collarbones, are covered under *Disruption of Nerve Function* as it would take a complete fracture to affect blood flow through this artery.

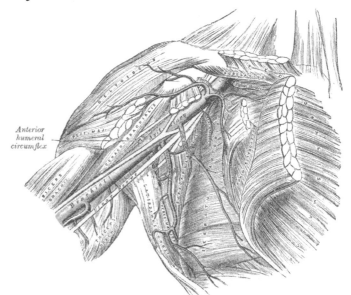

Anterior humeral circumflex

**Ht1 / Ji Quan / Summit Spring** is where the axillary pulse can be felt on the underside of each armpit. A strike collapsing the axillary artery (Protective Circles) could cause major upstream damage as blood backs up into the heart. Defensively, this vital area must be checked whenever our elbow is away from our body (Deflecting Pendulum).

The Brachial arteries continue from here with the pulse felt at Ht2 and Ht3 as the blood and Qi move down the arm, with points most effectively attacked against normal bloodflow. These powerful points however are listed under *Disruption of Nerve Function.*

It splits distal to the elbow forming the Ulnar and Radial arteries, supplying blood to the forearms and hands. The more palpable radial artery wrist pulse can be grasped to affect blood flow at the medial wrist crease at **Lu9 / Tai Yuan / Supreme Abyss** or an inch proximal at **Lu8 / Jing Qu / Channel Gutter**. Lu8 is also a radial arm nerve rub point along with Lu6. Anywhere along this blood flow line can be grasped or pressed to delay, stop, or damage the blood flow downstream.

### Lower Body Blood Flow Points - Abdominal Aorta
This large artery runs parallel and in front of the spinal column from just under the diaphragm muscle down to about the 4th lumbar vertebrae. Any centerline attacks powerful enough to overwhelm the abdominal muscles, or if relaxed, could affect this vital blood supply to the lower body and push arterial blood back towards the heart organ.

**CV6 / Qi Hai / Sea of Qi** is just below the navel where the abdominal aorta splits to become the Common Iliac Arteries. Due to its powerful systemic effect this target area is also covered under *Disruption of Qi.*

### Common Iliac Arteries
**Sp12 / Chong Men / Rushing Gate** is where the pulse can be felt at the groin crease. A front kick can cause a brief disruption in blood flow causing an exploitable weakness (Hand of Destruction).

### Femoral / Popliteal / Tibial Arteries
Blood flow in the legs is less commonly attacked due to arterial depth and leg musculature but is still possible. The Femoral arteries supply the upper legs then split to pass through the back and front of the knee and lower leg. The pulse can be felt at the posterior knee crease point UB40 (*Disruption of Nerve Function*).

The pulse can also be felt at the feet between the 2nd and 3rd bones (metatarsals) at **St42 / Chong Yang / Rushing Yang** (Dorsal Artery); the inner ankle between the Achilles Tendon and medial ankle bone (medial malleolus) at **Ki3 / Tai Xi / Supreme Stream** (Posterior Tibial Artery); and between the 1st and 2nd metatarsals at **Lv3 / Tai Chong / Great Rushing** (Dorsal Artery). Attacking foot targets, usually with stomps, is mostly used to distract and set up other targets.

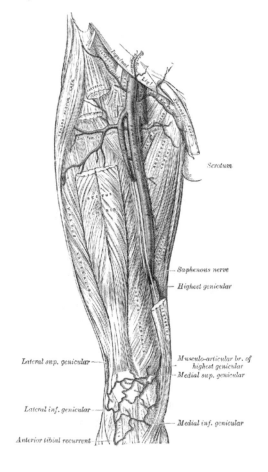

Scrotum

Saphenous nerve

Highest genicular

Lateral sup. genicular

Musculo-articular br. of highest genicular

Medial sup. genicular

Lateral inf. genicular

Medial inf. genicular

Anterior tibial recurrent

# Disruption of Air Flow

The Lungs are the organ of airflow, occupying most of the chest cavity from the collarbone down to about the 6th rib space and from left to right across the chest. They pull oxygen into the body through inhalation then push carbon dioxide out through exhalation.

An old survival saying about the value of air say's "a man can go 3 weeks without food, 3 days without water, but only 3 minutes without air." Disrupting this airflow can be accomplished by attacking the lung organ directly or along an air pathway.

## Lung Organ

The lung organ can be affected at the diaphragm muscle, or by causing a pneumothorax where the lung becomes punctured, perhaps by a broken rib. This would disrupt the compression needed to exhale and would limit inhalation capacity while causing chest pain and probably mental panic.

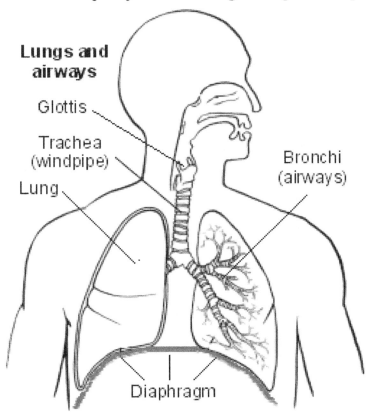

**Lungs and airways**

Glottis

Trachea (windpipe)

Lung

Bronchi (airways)

Diaphragm

The diaphragm muscle is responsible for the inhalation part of the breath cycle, as the lung organ does not have inhalation muscles and can only contract to exhale.

This diaphragm muscle is an umbrella shaped muscle just under the lungs but above the stomach. It separates the upper torso where the heart and lungs are located (clean area) from the liver, stomach, and intestines in the lower torso (dirty area).

Many have experienced and/or observed having the wind "knocked out." This can be caused by the ground after falling or by a heavy striking trauma often directed at the "A" shaped angle of the solar plexus in the center of the torso, where the ribs meet at the bottom of the sternum. The *xiphoid process* (boney prominence under this angle) has 3 points close together on a vertical centerline that if impacted can affect the diaphragm muscle.

**CV16 / Zhong Ting / Central Courtyard** (top), **CV15 / Jiu Wei / Turtledove Tail** (middle), and **CV14 / Ju Que / Great Gateway** (bottom). Depending on weapon and angle a strike would probably hit all 3 points simultaneously due to their close proximity to each other.

Note: To find the solar plexus on a clothed opponent draw two lines in your mind on them from each shoulder to opposite hip, or hip to opposite shoulder forming an X. Where the two lines intersect is the solar plexus.

Trauma applied up into this tissue (Defending Cross) can literally knock someone's wind out, leaving them gasping for air. Since the body is 3-dimensional the lung organ it can be attacked from the front, side, rear and top using striking or pressing.

Heavy blunt force weapons applied at or near the lung organ at different body angles and locations can also do this. A punch (Crossing Fist), hammerfist (Buckling the Leg), kick (Hammerlock), stomp (Brushing the Club), or a sharper weapon like an elbow point can attack with even more precision and penetration (Twisted Wrist).

Nearby organs can also be affected as the heart shares the left lung lobe space with the liver and spleen also susceptible to puncture from a broken rib (Parrying Grab).

Note: In ancient times, martial artists would train their hands to penetrate hard/dense body surfaces. The goal to make "every finger a dagger, every hand a sword, every arm a spear" is less common in modern times as the time-to-benefit ratio, and body part disfiguration, make soft target, combination striking, pressure point applications, and more natural weapon/target mismatches more popular.

## Air Pathway

Collapsing or smothering of an air pathway also has a dramatic effect. The 3 places away from the physical lung organ where this flow of air can be interrupted are the trachea (throat), mouth, and nose.

**Ahshi Point - Thyroid Cartilage** is the hard cartilage lying vertically at the front of the throat where it surrounds the trachea (windpipe). Some have a visible bony prominence commonly called the *Adams Apple*. This is not a specific acupuncture point, but it is a very real martial arts target.

Unlike arteries, cartilage is not flexible so if collapsed it would not rebound open. Crushing someone's windpipe closes the air pathway and would result in death unless a tracheotomy was performed very quickly.

Note: A tracheotomy is one of the oldest known surgical procedures. It is where an external cut is made at the base of the throat to open the trachea to the outside, so air can get in and out of the lungs.

A common strike in self-defense arts is the handsword strike (karate chop) that can be used effectively against this target (Hidden Hand). This lethal strike should only be used under extremely serious circumstances.

The half-fist or "panther punch" also fits into this throat target (Pursuing Panther) along with the thumb/index web hand strike (Tripping Leg). The length of someone's neck would determine whether an elbow, shin, or closed hand strike could fit into this neck pocket.

Grasping with the hands can also be effectively used to attack the trachea and possibly crush the windpipe. The *Eagles Claw* is a martial art basic that can grasp around a windpipe to surround and close the airflow (Raining Blade). Ripping the tissue is even possible by some and made famous by Patrick Swayze in the movie "Roadhouse."

Pressing is another method, often done with the forearm bones. The radius bone can be pulled against the trachea as in a Guillotine choke (Dangerous Tackle B); or the ulna bone can be pushed into this cartilage and is best done with a support structure behind (Taming the Fist).

**CV22 / Tian Tu / Heavenly Prominence** is at the base of the throat at the top of the sternum in the suprasternal notch. This quarter-sized hollow, or *esophageal dent,* can be affected with a sharp weapon such as a finger strike or press (Returning the Gift).

Against a standing opponent, pushing into this point will back them up and elicit a slight gag reflex. This creates space, changes posture, and causes a mental distraction that could open other targets. With the ground or a wall for support then deeper pressure could be applied causing trauma, swelling, or more severe tissue damage.

The nose and mouth work together, so if the nose were pinched shut, broken, or the sinuses damaged then a person could still breathe through their mouth, and if the mouth were covered, they could still breathe through their nose. Both nose and mouth would need to be blocked or interfered with to completely stop air flow in and out of the lungs.

Note: Sport fighters when given an opportunity often try to disrupt an opponent's breathing by covering (smothering) the nose and mouth with their hand(s) and/or body.

**GV25 / Su Liao / White Crevice** at the nose tip is generally hit straight (Twins of Destruction). Bilaterally, sinus points **LI20 / Yang Xiang / Welcome Fragrance** at nose base, **EP / Bi Tong / Penetrating the Nose** just above it, and **UB2 / Zan Zhu / Gathered Bamboo** at the medial corner of each eyebrow are often hit diagonally (Raking Fist).

# Disruption of Nerve Function

Nerve Function looks at the Peripheral Nervous System, the physical spine of the Central Nervous System (CNS), and Cranial Nerve XI (Accessory). The Brain of the CNS is covered under *Disruption of Brain Function,* along with a few other useful Cranial Nerves.

Cranial Nerve XI is covered here because its function begins outside the skull, unlike the others that begin inside the brain. The Accessory Nerve controls the SCM and trapezius muscles needed for shoulder and neck movement. It runs through the neck parallel with the Vagus Nerve and is part of the Carotid Sheath of vital components.

The peripheral nerves carry impulses for voluntary and involuntary muscle contractions and relaxation. These *motor nerves* carry those impulses from the brain and spinal cord to the muscles (efferent), which also communicate back to the brain and spinal cord (afferent).

*Voluntary* movement is driven by the purposeful mental intention to move. *Involuntary* movements are the nervous systems hard-wired reflexes. Martial arts technique can be used to affect voluntary muscle capability or take advantage of these involuntary reflexes.

Note: Through repetitive training voluntary movement appears to bypass conscious thought. See the *Spirit* book for a full treatise.

**Voluntary** movement can be affected directly at the structures of the musculoskeletal system, or at a spinal segment causing difficulty downstream at its related voluntary muscle, and internal organ.

The 4 major spinal sections from top to bottom are the Cervical, Thoracic, Lumbar and Sacral/Coccygeal. This will be the starting point used here to follow the peripheral system nerve flow as it branches out and innervates the rest of the body.

Striking the spine with the hands (Crossed Arms), elbows (Sweeping the Leg), knees (Broken Kneel), and feet (Jumping Crane) can cause trauma and affect posture. Pressing and rubbing can also be used (Meeting the Tackle) with grasping the spine not practical, except at the back of the neck (Scraping Stomp).

Once nerves leave the spinal column many pressure points open at different places on the neck, torso, arms, and legs. Since the flow of energy in these nerve channels goes in both directions attacking a point can affect and be compounded up or down the nerve pathway.

Striking points on the larger torso are often easier to find than the smaller limbs, especially when in close contact, or if the limbs are moving. The limbs however are often the first contact, especially if defending. The torso and spine could then be attacked as part of a progression.

Attacking points on moving limbs can be inconsistent due to point entry vectors so would work best if held in place or with a supporting structure (Clipping the Blade). Moving a limb off its intended path however may be more important initially, with nerve strikes a bonus (Thrusting Blade).

Grasping points can be used for pain compliance or to affect a release. Pressing needs a backstop support to be effective (Cross of Destruction), or the point held open (Unexpected Blade). Once connected, rubbing can greatly increase the electric sensation felt at nerve points.

**Involuntary** nerve reactions or "reflexes" occur along a nerve pathway. These affect an area directly, another area indirectly, or are even at the skin surface. Understanding them can be useful as every muscle function comes from a nerve impulse with reflexive defense mechanisms built in.

A strategy against the muscle structure is to override its voluntary mechanism causing an involuntary muscle contraction or relaxation. Two complimentary mechanisms within every muscle that do this are the Golgi Tendon Organ (GTO) and the Muscle Spindle Cell (MSC).

The **GOLGI TENDON ORGAN (GTO)** is a neurological mechanism located in a muscle's tendon at the end of a muscle where it connects one bone with another bone via the muscle structure to allow for skeletal movement.

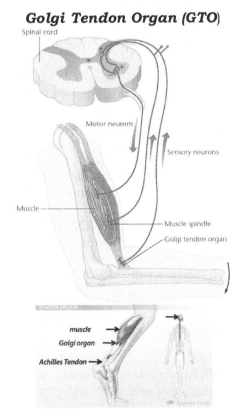

*Golgi Tendon Organ (GTO)*

This GTO is a protective reflex against too much muscle tension that if stimulated causes that muscle to relax. This *involuntary* mechanism protects the muscle attachment from tearing because of bearing too much weight. It is used in martial arts to cause a joint hyperextension, affect a grip release, or manipulate a body.

It can be tricked into relaxing with a quick short rubbing motion (Obstructing the Club), by stretching the tendon as when a limb is twisted (Piercing Blade), or by striking a tendons GTO (Snapping Arm).

Common GTO targets are the posterior elbow joint at the base of the tricep tendon (TW10-11), the forearms brachioradialis tendon (between Lu6-Lu8), and the quadriceps tendon just above the knee (EP-Heding), or the Patellar Tendon below the knee (Ahshi).

The **MUSCLE SPINDLE CELL (MSC),** or motor point, is a neurological mechanism within the belly of a muscle, and the complimentary opposite of the GTO. The MSC is where nerves accumulate or bundle within each muscle before branching out to nourish individual fibers.

Stimulating a motor point causes an involuntary muscle contraction, immediately followed by relaxation. Also known as the "stretch reflex" it protects the muscle from being overstretched, and possibly tearing from too much extension.

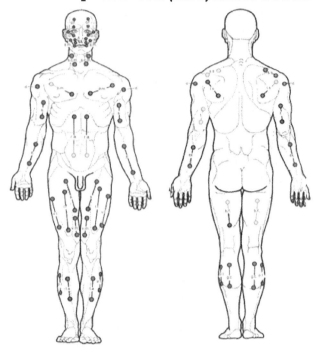

*Muscle Spindle Cell (MSC) Motor Points*

Note: Most of these are <u>not</u> located at standard Acupuncture points so location descriptions are often Western anatomy based. The illustration above contains many but not all of these motor points.

This mechanism can be tricked into contracting with a strong impact (Six Hands), or sudden heavy pressure (Straddling the Leg). Since this mechanism reacts to being over stretched, adding a slight drag in the direction of the fibers upon contact increases the reaction.

Popular MSC targets are the bicep muscle, the anterior shoulder (EP-Jian Qian), and anterior quadriceps. See illustration and technique examples in the previous paragraph.

The **CROSSED EXTENSOR REFLEX** compliments and follows the withdrawal or *touch reflex*. As one limb retracts from harm the opposite limb reflexively extends and engages. One side of the body is affected directly while the other side is affected indirectly. The common example used is stepping on a nail where the damaged foot retracts as the opposite foot plants. In martial arts, if the right arm is damaged it will reflexively retract as the left arm reaches forward or towards it.

This knowledge can be used defensively for checking (Hooking Arms), or offensively to shift body weight (Sweeping the Leg), or as a setup whereby attacking one limb will draw the other limb to position (Parrying Grab).

**SKIN RECEPTORS** are where the nervous system reaches out to the body surface for sensory input. They are located everywhere on the body, so are not at a specific point site. Some areas have a higher concentration of these receptors, or are located at more sensitive body areas, or are anatomically easier to grasp.

Note: Pinching is the primary method used to grab this tissue. Methods include four-fingers folded into the palm or "horsebite pinch" (Pinch from Death), thumb/2nd index joint pinch (Arms of Silk), thumb/index/middle fingertip "crab pinch" (Raining Blade), or the ground (Dance of Death).

Tender areas to grab include the upper pectoralis muscles (Fatal Variation), the kidney area (Crossed Arms), sides of the abdomen (Locked Arm), and the upper inner thigh (Pinch from Death).

**The Spine** consists of four major sections. Regardless of the exact, location any powerful unimpeded strike to any part of the spine could be devastating. Damage ranges from local pain and discomfort to permanent disability, or from recoverable knockout to a fatality.

The *Cervical* (C) spine consists of 7 vertebrae at the back of the neck that provide nerve function to the shoulders, arms, and hands.

The *Thoracic* (T) spine consists of 12 vertebrae in the upper and middle back that provide nerve function to the chest, abdomen, and internal organs.

| | | |
|---|---|---|
| **CERVICAL SPINE** | C1 | Atlas (skull mobility) |
| | C2 | Axis (skull mobility) |
| | C3 | Diaphragm (breathing) |
| | C4 | Diaphragm (breathing), shoulder shrug |
| | C5 | Deltoid (lifts arms), Biceps (bends elbows) |
| | C6 | Wrist extensors (lifts wrists back) |
| | C7 | Triceps (straightens elbow) |
| | C8 | Hands & fingers |
| **THORACIC SPINE** | T1 | Hands & fingers |
| | T2 | Chest muscles |
| | T3 | Chest muscles |
| | T4 | Chest muscles |
| | T5 | Chest muscles |
| | T6 | Chest & abdominal muscles |
| | T7 | Chest & abdominal muscles |
| | T8 | Chest & abdominal muscles |
| | T9 | Abdominal muscles |
| | T10 | Abdominal muscles |
| | T11 | Abdominal muscles |
| | T12 | Abdominal muscles |
| **LUMBAR SPINE** | L1 | Hip muscles (bends hips) |
| | L2 | Hip muscles |
| | L3 | Knee muscles (straightens knee) |
| | L4 | Knee & ankle muscles |
| | L5 | Ankle & toe muscles (lifts big toe & foot) |
| **SACRUM COCCYX** | S1 | Leg & toe muscles (points foot) |
| | S2 | Toes, anal & bladder sphincters |
| | S3 | Anal & bladder sphincters |
| | S4 | Anal & bladder sphincters |
| | S5 | Anal & bladder sphincters |

The *Lumbar* (L) spine consists of 5 vertebrae in the lower back with the *Sacrum* (S) attached just underneath as one triangular shaped vertebra with the *Coccyx* (tailbone) attached underneath. These lower spinal sections provide nerve function to the hips, legs and feet.

## NERVE FLOW STARTING AT THE SPINE:

The **CERVICAL VERTEBRAE** (C1-C7) from the skull base to the tops of the shoulders innervate the shoulders, arms, and hands. This area also influences the throat, sinuses, nose, thyroid gland, lymph nodes, and diaphragm muscle.

Note: When training, especially in a street style, the back of the neck must be guarded always. Partners must always use control, but accidents can happen so for safety and to develop a good habit, lift your shoulders against these attacks so the trapezius muscles can provide some protection.

### Accessory, Phrenic, & Brachial Plexus Nerve Points:

The Nervous System branches from the cervical spine to the sides and front of the neck. The *accessory nerve* (CNXI) from C1-C5 lifts the shoulders (trapezius muscles), the *phrenic nerve* from C3-C5 is for breathing (diaphragm muscle), and *brachial plexus nerve bundle* from C5-C8 & T1 innervates most shoulder and arm muscles.

Note: Due to the proximity of vital nerve, blood, and air components attacking the neck can affect multiple systems simultaneously. A focused strike can cause injury, loss of consciousness, or even death. The neck can also be grabbed and squeezed with the fingers (Securing the Club) or pressed and rubbed (Ducking Dragon).

The *Brachial Plexus* path starts on the front of the body under the collarbones, parallel with the *subclavian artery,* on its way to the armpits. From there it travels down the arms to the hands.

The *axillary* and *suprascapular* nerves branch off the brachial plexus. They innervate the deltoids (shoulder muscles), teres minor, infraspinatus, and supraspinatus (3 of 4 rotator cuff muscles), then branch to become the radial nerve.

**SI16 / Yian Chuang / Heavenly Window** is level with the Adams Apple on both sides of the neck at the posterior edge of the SCM muscle. **LI18 / Fu Tu / Support the Prominence** is level with the Adams Apple on both sides of the neck between the two SCM muscles, near SI16 and St9.

Note: Level with the Adams Apple in a straight line across the SCM are the 3 points SI16 (posterior), LI18 (middle) and St9 (anterior). Layers can be affected at the SCM, into the Scalene Muscles, Brachial Plexus, Vagus Nerve, and deeper. Points are attacked with a strike (Delayed Hand), push (Tripping Leg), rub (Blinding Vice), hold (Securing the Club), etc.

**GB21 / Jian Jing / Shoulder Well** at the high point of the trapezius muscle on both sides, halfway between the neck and shoulder. It is innervated by the accessory nerve and part of the supraclavicular nerve. Striking (Blinding Vice) or grasping (Compulsive Kneel) is used.

Note: This is the Mr. Spock "Vulcan death grip" location of Star Trek fame but depending on the muscle mass to grip strength ratio the necks ultra nervy scalene muscles (SI16, LI18, St9) would be more likely to simulate that paralyzing effect.

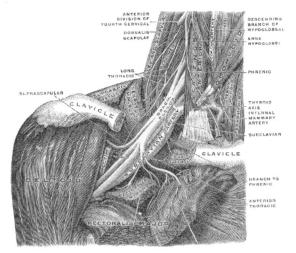

**St12 / Que Pen / Empty Basin)** above the center of the collarbone is innervated by the Brachial Plexus, and **St13 (Qi Hu / Qi Door)** below it is innervated by the anterior thoracic nerve, both using the supraclavicular nerve. Striking the collarbone (Entwined Fists) or pressing with a firm weapon like an elbow tip (Twisted Gun) is effective.

**Lu1 / Zhong Fu / Middle Palace** under the outside collarbone edge, lateral to the pec muscle, and **Lu2 / Yun Men / Cloud Gate** about an inch below are innervated by the supraclavicular and anterior thoracic nerves. Trauma can affect lung respiration, but this target is primarily used to manipulate posture at the shoulder line with striking (Fist of Aggression) or pressure (Falling Eagle).

**EP / Jian Qian / Front of the Shoulder** is an MSC point in the center of the anterior deltoid innervated by the axillary nerve. Striking (Hidden Hand) or pressing are used with grasping possible at certain angles. The pressure from a "Kimura" lock is commonly felt at this point (Dangerous Tackle).

**Ahshi Point / Between the Bicep Muscles** in the middle of the upper arm and innervated by the musculocutaneous nerve. Any method can be used against a relaxed or overpowered muscle (Defying the Club).

### Axillary & Suprascapular Nerve Points:
**LI16 / Ju Gu / Great Bone** in the groove where the collarbone attaches to the scapula (acromio-clavicular or AC Joint) is innervated by the axillary and supraclavicular nerves. This point gives access to the supraspinatus muscle (one of 4 rotator cuff muscles).

Two other sensitive upper back points at the top scapula edge, at the Supraspinatus muscle, are **SI12 / Bing Feng / Grasping the Wind** in the center and **SI13 / Qu Yuan / Crooked Wall** at the medial edge. Both can be struck (Piercing Blade), and SI13 also a brace point for the neck (Crashing Elbows).

**SI9 / Jian Zhen / True Shoulder** is at the back of the armpit crease where the long tricep head attaches the arm to the scapula. Striking (Arms of Silk) or manipulating this point (Spiraling Wrist) is mostly used to affect posture, but if damaged would affect shoulder and arm function.

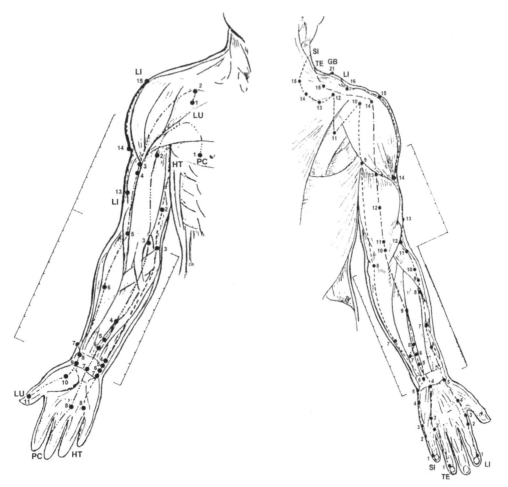

Anterior (Front) View                                    Posterior (Rear) View

The *Brachial Plexus* continues branching into the *radial, median* and *ulnar* nerves, all of which innervate the arms and hands. They can be attacked in many ways, depending on the point.

The **Radial Arm Nerve** has two branches, one deep and one superficial. It travels across and around the upper arm to innervate most of the tricep muscle (arm extension) and others. Points on this nerve pathway include:

**LI14 / Bi Nao / Upper Arm** at the lateral deltoid, **LI13 / Shou Wu Li / Arm Five Miles** about 1/3 proximal from elbow to shoulder, both often shin kicked in Muay Thai to cause arm fatigue. **TW10 / Tian Jing / Celestial Well** at the arms tricep muscle base near the elbow joint, and about 1" above **TW11 / Qing Leng Yuan / Clear Cold Abyss.** Both are GTO reflex points susceptible to striking (Snapping Arm), pressing (Obstructing the Club), or twisting (Hammerlock).

**LI11 / Qu Chi / Pool at the Crook** at the outside elbow crease over the brachioradialis muscle. Manipulation causes weight and posture to shift (Triggered Palm).

**Lu5 / Chi Ze / Cubit Marsh** is medial to LI11 in the middle of the elbow crease between the tendons. Manipulation affects posture and causes a weight shift down and forward onto the toes (Raking Fist) and is also the access point for the biceps GTO (Flashing Fist).

**LI10 / Shou San Li / Arm Three Miles** is about 2" distal to LI11 on the forearm at the high point of the extensor carpi radialis muscle. This muscle affects the grip and is above the deeper supinator muscle (external rotation). It can be held and squeezed (Destructive Parries) or hit (Alternating Fist) to affect wrist integrity and grip strength.

Note: Rotating the hand, as often done when punching, can cause the 2 wrist bones to cross, unless the elbow is also rotated, weakening wrist stability. For this reason, some profess the vertical punch as the more powerful hand position for punching, especially without wrist support as used in sport fighting.

**Lu6 / Kong Zui / Maximum Opening** is an MSC point on the brachioradialis muscle, proximal to the forearms halfway point, at the medial angle of the radius bone.

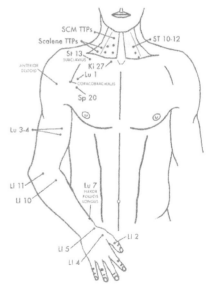

**Lu7 / Lie Que / Broken Sequence** proximal to the styloid process on the lateral wrist, and **Lu8 / Jing Qu / Channel Gutter** about an inch proximal to the wrist crease on the thumb side, both radial arm nerve points that affect thumb and index finger grip.

Striking between Lu6 and Lu8 makes the hand contract causing a grip release (Thrusting Blade).

**Lu10 / Yuji Lu / Fish Border** is in the meaty area of the thumb base, on the palm side, and is influenced by radial and some median nerve function. Damage at this point affects the thumb and thereby the grip.

The **Median Arm Nerve** travels down the medial forearm in the middle of the wrist joint on the palm side of the hand. It is the only nerve that passes through the carpal tunnel.

This innervates the ring, middle, and index fingers plus some of the thenar eminence (thumb base). It passes through **P7 / Da Ling / Great Mound** on the medial wrist crease, **TW4 / Yang Chi / Yang Pool**, with **EP / Zhong Quan / Posterior Spring** on the lateral wrist crease.

Note: Carpal Tunnel Syndrome is an overuse injury where the median nerve gets pinched inside a small wrist tunnel pathway, usually from swelling. It causes numbing that affects grip and hand strength.

A sharp knuckle can affect the opposable grip at this juncture (Clipping the Blade 2) or be tightly held to cause a grip release (Entwined Blade), twisted (Crossing Grab), or have pressure applied against a bent wrist joint (Entangled Arm).

The **Ulnar Arm Nerve** travels along the medial upper arm, along the inner elbow and down the ulnar bone. It controls the little finger and part of the ring finger.

**Ht2 / Qing Ling / Green Spirit** at the inner bicep muscle is about two-thirds down the Humerus bone and is vulnerable to grasping (Flashing Fist).

**SI8 / Xiao Hai / Small Sea** (one of 3 "funny bone" points, with TW10 and medial elbow ahshi) is at the inside corner of the medial elbow bone between the ulnar and median nerves. Striking or rubbing causes an intense nerve reaction causing pain and the hand to open (Cradling the Baby).

**Ahshi Point / Medial Epicondyle of Humerus** is a sensitive elbow point next to SI8. Stimulation into the bone at the medial supracondylar ridge causes an intense electrical sensation (Entwined Blade).

**Ht3 / Shao Hai / Lesser Sea** about an inch lateral to SI8 at the medial elbow crease can be used as a lever to move the elbow to escape a hold (clinch counter) or be used to apply a lock (Evading the Club).

The 12 **THORACIC VERTEBRAE** (T1-T12) start below the cervical vertebrae at the base of the neck down to the lowest rib attachment. Each has a rib connected on each side that makes up the cage that wraps around our upper and middle torso.

These vertebrae innervate the back and abdominal muscles but also have a close relationship with the internal organs. Damage to any of them can interrupt nerve flow to the erector spinatus muscles parallel with the spine, intercostal rib spaces, the upper, middle, and oblique abdominal muscles, along with nearby internal organs. The scapula (upper back "wing" bones) provides some structural support and protection on each side of this spinal section.

**UB41 / Fu Fen / Attached Branch, UB42 / Po Hu / Po Door, UB43 / Gao Huang Shu / Gao Huang Shu,** and **UB44 / Shen Tang / Shen Hall** are all on a vertical line along the scapula's medial border from T2 to T5, respectively. Each land on rhomboid or trapezius muscle motor points.

Individually or together, these are susceptible to impact (Desperate Fists), pressure (Evading the Club), or as a bracing structure (Turning the Cross).

**GV9 / Ahi Yang / Reaching Yang** below the T7 spinous process at the Scapula's bottom edge is perhaps the weakest structural thoracic section. Striking with an elbow (Crossed Arms), punch (Reversing Fist), knee (Backbreaker), kick (Sweeping the Leg), or stomp (Straddling the Leg) can cause serious problems, regardless of exact location. These same methods can also be used in reverse against the organs at the torso location to affect the spine.

The 5 **LUMBAR VERTEBRAE** (L1-L5) are below the thoracic vertebrae down to just below the hipbones. These are the largest moveable structures in the spine and bear the most weight. The lumbar plexus innervates the lower torso, hips, and legs. A punch (Kick into Darkness), knee (Hidden Hand), or kick (Jumping Crane) can dramatically affect someone's posture while causing pain and possibly severe injury.

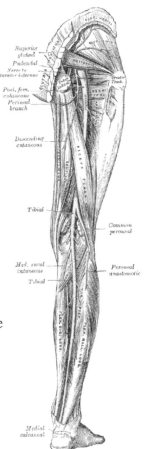

Just below the lumbar vertebrae are the **Sacral/Coccygeal** sections of the spine. The triangular shaped **Sacrum** (S1-S4) is wedged between the two hipbones, where it primarily innervates the lower legs and feet. The **Coccyx** (tailbone) is the lowest solid surface of the spine.

Branching from the lumbar and sacral vertebrae down the legs are the **Sciatic Nerve** in the back and the **Femoral Nerve** in the front.

The **Sciatic Nerve** at the back of the leg is the largest and longest nerve in the body. It is actually two parallel nerves combined stemming from L4-S3 separating and branching just above the knee.

The **Tibial Nerve** branch runs down the middle posterior lower leg through the popliteal fossa at **UB40 / Wei Zhong / Middle of the Crook**. The common peroneal nerve branch runs in the posterior lateral knee pocket at **UB39 / Wei Yang / Bend Yang.**

The knee crease is a weak line in the leg structure as nerve and blood flow are close to the surface. Trauma can cause the knee to reflexively buckle (Evading the Club) to affect posture and position while possibly disrupting knee function.

The **Tibial** and **Common Peroneal Nerves** provide function to the back and outside lower leg and feet. The tibial nerve travels down the back and medial calf, the peroneal nerve around the lateral calf.

Lower leg attacks are generally used to disrupt balance, break concentration, affect mechanical function, or stimulate an energetic pathway. Targets below the knee are generally attacked after pre-positioning, so driving a knee to the ground leaves their lower leg exposed to a stomp (Jumping Crane) or knee drop (Evading the Club).

The **Femoral Nerve** at the inner leg branches from the lumbar plexus and is made of nerves mostly from L1-L4. It passes in front of the hip joint along the groin crease (inguinal groove) running parallel with the femoral artery *(Disruption of Blood Flow)*. A front kick on either side of the groin into this crease can affect nerve function and/or temporarily affect blood flow and leg strength while disrupting posture and balance.

**Lv11 / Yin Lian / Yin Corner** is at the upper inner corner of the thigh on the adductor longus muscle moves the leg forward and inward. It is just below Sp12 *(Disruption of Blood Flow)*.

The femoral nerve travels down the leg where it splits into the anterior and posterior divisions. These innervate the anterior and inner thighs and knees at the saphenous and anterior cutaneous (surface) nerves.

**Sp11 / Ji Men / Winnowing Gate** at the middle of the inner thigh on the Saphenous nerve line midway up on the inner thigh, just posterior to the sartorius muscle. The pulse can be felt here and is an area sensitive to pinching (Pinch from Death) and kicks to affect posture and balance (Cradling the Baby).

**Sp10 / Xue Hai / Sea of Blood** above the kneecap on the inside part of the leg at the base of the medial quad muscle (Vastus Medialis) is innervated by the anterior cutaneous nerve and a muscular branch of the femoral nerve. It is susceptible to kicks (Unrolling Crane) and knees (Triggered Palm) to mostly affect posture and position.

**Sp9 / Yin Ling Quan / Yin Mound Spring** just below the medial kneecap at the top of the calf muscle is innervated by a cutaneous branch of the saphenous and tibial nerves. This tender area is susceptible to impact causing the knee to bend outwards (Scraping Stomp).

**Lv8 / Qu Quan / Spring at the Crook** and **Ki10 / Yin Gu / Yin Valley** are points close together further around the inside of the knee between the semitendinosus and semimembranosus tendons at the inner knee crease and innervated by the tibial nerve.

**Ahshi Point / Medial Knee** between Sp10 and Ki10 on the sartorius muscle near its knee attachment where the saphenous nerve passes underneath. It is susceptible to outward buckling (Locked Horns).

Sp9, Lv8, Ki10, and Ahshi Medial Knee point are all near each other where the knee can be manipulated outward to affect posture, balance, and expose the groin (Circling the Arm). It can be buckled (Snapping Arm), punched (Entangled Arm B), pressed (Scraping Stomp), or pushed with a sharp elbow (can be used to open the guard in grappling).

**EP / Heading / Top Crane** is a GTO reflex point just superior to the anterior knee at the vastus medialis quad muscle tendon. Impacting can cause the knee to hyperextend (Twins of Aggression).

**Ahshi Point / Lateral Knee** is a GTO reflex point just superior to the lateral patellar at the vastus lateralis quad muscle tendon. Impacting can cause severe knee damage (Hand and Shield).

**GB34 / Yang Ling Quan / Yang Mound Spring** is just below the knee where the fibula bone (smaller lateral shin bone) attaches to the tibia (large shin bone). It is susceptible to impact (Hand and Shield) that could cause the knee to buckle inwards (MCL strain or separation).

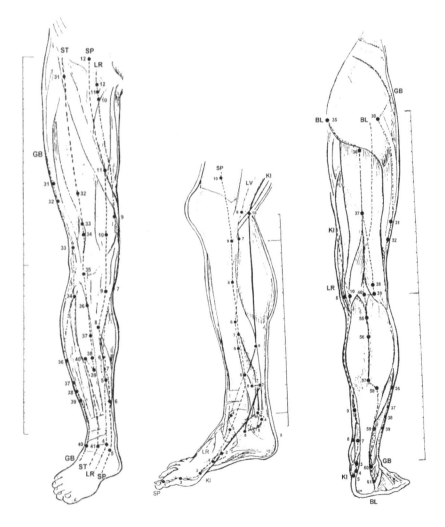

# Disruption of Brain Function

This section discusses the skull, the enclosed physical brain, plus the Trigeminal (CNV) and Facial (CNVII) Cranial Nerves of the Central Nervous System (CNS). Attacking the brain, via the skull and specific points on the face, can affect consciousness, mental thought, or focus as observed through the eyes. Disrupting these functions can occur from blunt force trauma, a sudden violent head movement, precise point stimulation, or a more benign mental distraction.

A violent impact anywhere to the head from a martial art strike, the ground, a wall, a car bumper, baseball bat, etc. could fracture the skull bones and force the brain against the inside of its encasing skull structure.

This impact can bruise or damage brain and blood tissue causing bleeding and pressure to build from swelling in and around the brain. At a minimum this is a concussion, made worse by any accumulation of swelling inside the brain. Symptoms range from head pain, dizziness, and lightheadedness, to unconsciousness, or even death.

The effect depends on the force of the trauma and the time until medical attention is available. A sport fight is stopped if a fighter can no longer consciously defend himself where a street encounter can be less forgiving.

Unconscious knockouts range from the stiff body tonic version to the limp body knockout. The more serious stiff body knockout indicates swelling or herniation inside the brain, or from brainstem damage. The limp body knockout results from a disruption of arterial blood flow to the brain and/or interruption of nerve function at the reticular formation of the brainstem.

Note: Besides mental unconsciousness another type of sport knockout is when a fighter cannot physically continue after taking a powerful body shot. The liver punch (*Disruption of Qi*) does this and is often seen in Boxing (see Hopkins vs. De La Hoya 2004).

Sudden violent head movement can affect the neck, and with-it brain function, resulting in dizziness or unconsciousness. Major head motions are *flexion/extension* (nodding head "yes"), *lateral rotation* (shaking head "no"), and *lateral flexion/extension* (ear to shoulder).

The chin is the primary pivot point to move and lever the head with four major contact vectors. The chin can be forced down or back at the tip (Ascending from Death), or up, left or right at underneath (Hooking Arms) or side of chin points (Darting Fist). Attacking the sides of the head can force an ear towards a shoulder (Tripping Leg), with grappling methods that use the chin as a lever to manipulate (Flashing Hands) or crank the neck (Sweeping the Leg).

Falls can also force the head to move uncontrollably causing a neck injury and possible skull trauma from the ground. Pain, mental confusion, unconsciousness, or death are among the layers of injury possible, and a good reason to learn proper falling and rolling techniques.

Knowing skull anatomy, and vulnerable nerve points that ride the skull surface, is useful not only for maximizing technique but also for protecting our own head. This includes defensive posturing, aligning to take an unavoidable impact, and proper alignment to use the head as a weapon.

**The Skull** that surrounds and protects the brain is made up of 28 bones, most connected at sutures, with the physical brain housed inside the 8 cranial bones. The mandible (jawbone) connects at hinges so the mouth can open and close with 14 bones associated with the face, 6 with hearing, the hyoid (only free-floating bone), and larynx in the throat. This skull structure also contains nerves, blood vessels, sinus cavities, and numerous holes.

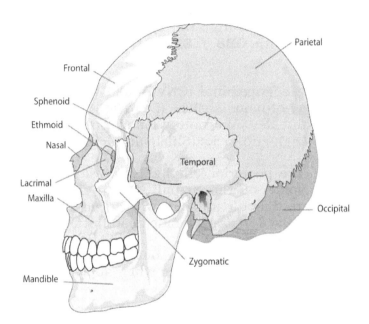

The **Frontal Bone** is from the eyebrows up the forehead past the hairline about a third of the way back along the top of the head. The hardest and best structurally aligned angle of this bone is above the forehead, just inside the natural hairline. This is the front head butt weapon, and where a boxer would try to take an unavoidable face punch. This area houses the brains emotional control center and where personality is located.

The forehead, below the hairline, and frontal sinuses at the eyebrows are most vulnerable at each eyebrow center, **EP / Yin Tang / Hall of Impression** between the eyebrows, **EP / Yu Yao / Fish Waist** at each middle eyebrow, and **Ahshi Point / Middle forehead**, between Yin Tang and the hairline as a useful neck lever point.

Striking can cause disorientation, whiplash (Hidden Hand), or a hangman's fracture (Wraparound) using a palm strike (Thrusting Palm), knee (Entangled Arm B), or elbow (Hand and Shield) all able to cause layers of damage.

The **Temporal, Sphenoid,** and **Zygomatic Bones** are on the sides of the head from the lateral eye sockets to just past the ears. These bi-lateral smaller bones are vulnerable to impact, housing some visual control functions and hearing components that make the ear holes a valuable target *(Disruption of Tissue & Mechanical Function)*.

**TW23 / Si Zhu Kong / Silken Bamboo Hollow** at each eyebrow lateral end, **GB1 / Tong Zi Liao / Pupil Crevice** at the lateral corner of each eye, and **EP / Tai Yang / Supreme Yang** about an inch posterior the other two making a powerful triangle of temple Cranial Nerve points (Blinding Vice).

**GB4 / Han Yan / Jaw Serenity, GB5 Xuan Lu / Suspended Skull, GB6 Xuan Li / Suspended Hair,** and **GB7 Qu Bin / Crook of the Temple** are a vertical line of sensitive points from the upper corner of the face down to in front of the ear, along with **GB8 / Shuai Gu / Leading Valley** about an inch above the ear apex.

These areas overlap the Trigeminal (CNV) and Facial Nerves (CNVII). They are vulnerable to heel-of-palm strikes (Destructive Circles), palm strikes (Tripping Leg), backknuckles (Alternating Fists), punches (Circling the Arm), knees (Sweeping the Leg), and kicks (Shield and Punch).

The **Parietal Bones** are posterior on the upper sides of the head. These large bones house some of the visual system and perception control functions, but they are difficult to affect with basic striking as this is also the skull bone weapon used to apply a side head butt.

The **Occipital Bone**, at the back of the head, is where the primary visual center is located. This is the weapon used when applying a rear head butt.

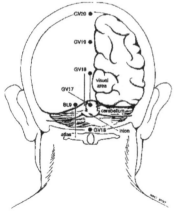

**GV17 / Nao Hu / Brains Door** and **UB9 / Yu Zhen / Jade Pillow** are at the back of the head that, if struck (Destructive Circles), could affect the visual field. Hitting this area against a hard ground surface increases any effect (Crossed Arms).

The more vulnerable *Cerebellum* is just below the occipital bone and accesses the motor control part of the brain, affecting balance and athleticism, so any heavy trauma can affect equilibrium and mental focus.

**GV16 / Feng Fu / Palace of Wind, UB10 / Tian Zhu / Celestial Pillar** and the powerful **GB20 / Feng Chi / Wind Pool** (a great headache relief point) are across the base of the rear skull. Stimulation can affect posture, equilibrium, mental focus, or consciousness. Palm strikes (Destructive Circles), punch (Pinch from Death), grasp (Scraping Stomp) or press/rub (Jamming the Tackle) technique can be effective.

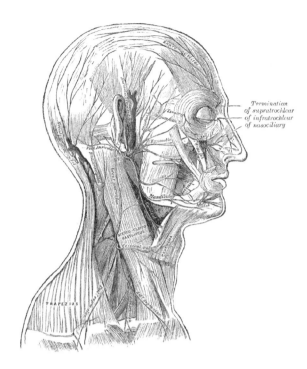

**Cranial Nerves** accessible on the face are the Trigeminal (CNV) and Facial (CNVII) nerves. Since these emerge directly from the brain any aggressive stimulation is not only felt at sensitive points but can reverberate to interrupt brain function.

The **Trigeminal Nerve (CNV)** is the largest cranial nerve. It emerges at the temple with three major sections that control much of face sensation and motor function. The *Ophthalmic* (upper) innervates around the eyes up to the forehead. The *Maxillary* (middle) innervates the cheeks and upper teeth. The *Mandibular* (lower) innervates the jaw and lower teeth.

The **Facial Nerve (CNVII)** emerges behind the ear lobe at the Stylomastoid Foramen and TW17 (*Disruption of Blood Flow*). It has 5 major branches that primarily control the muscles of facial expression. The *Temporal* branch controls the forehead. The *Zygomatic* branch is how the eyes are closed and opened. The *Buccal* branch controls facial expression. The *Mandibular* branch controls the lower lip and chin. The *Cervical* branch controls the platysma neck muscle and connects with the cervical cutaneous nerve.

Facial bones like the **Ethmoid, Lacrimal, Maxilla,** and **Nasal** make up the eye socket and nasal structure. LI20 and Bitong (*Disruption of Air Flow*) along with **St3 / Juliao / Great Crevice** under eyeball center below the cheekbone are 3 points on the side of the nose that can affect CNV, CNVII, and the maxillary sinus (Fist of Aggression).

**St5 / Da Ying / Great Welcome** at the front side of the masseter muscle (visible when teeth clenched) and **St6 / Jia Che / Jawbone** in the middle of that muscle are all effective CNVII points. St5 can be hit or rubbed, compressing it into the mandible bone and muscle, and St6 activates the MSC reflex causing the jaw to clench.

Note: Combining points simultaneously or sequentially can compound their affect. The triangle of points TW23/GB1/Tai Yang (Circling the Arm), or GB20 with Tai Yang are more powerful when used together, or on opposite sides (Twirling Fist).

The **Vagus Nerve (CNX)** is a powerful Cranial Nerve that can generate a vasovagal response (fainting) with neck access at LI18 between SCM muscles or St9 where the neck pulse is felt (*Disruption of Blood Flow*).

# Disruption of Tissue & Mechanical Function

This refers to damaged body parts that results in temporary to permanent non-use of that part. *Tissue* are the soft targets like eyes, ears, and some muscles, with *Mechanical Function* the hard targets like bones and joints.

These are affected in such a way so even if pain is blocked from drugs, alcohol, mental illness, or mental toughness, the disability caused makes someone physically unable to utilize that piece of their anatomy.

## Tissue Function

**Eyes:** Attacking the eyes is a serious escalation only justified under the worst of circumstances. If needed and successfully damaged, then temporary, or permanent inability to see out of one or both eyes results.

A sport fighting tactic to affect the eyes is to cause a cut above one or both eyes so blood drip's down, making unobstructed vision problematic. A sport fight is stopped if one of the fighters cannot see.

The *blink reflex* can also be stimulated by making a motion towards the eye(s), causing them to flinch closed briefly (blink), at which time other attack options can be used. A street tactic may be to throw dirt, liquid, a hard object, or even spit in someone's eyes.

Since the eyes are small surface targets it takes a small weapon to fit into the socket holes making fingers, thumbs, and knuckles the most common choice. Larger and powerful blunt force weapons could however penetrate the eye socket by breaking the orbital bone around the eye.

Four methods using the fingertips and thumbs are to *Poke* (Blinding Vice), *Whip* (Protective Parries), *Slice* (Turning Windmills), or *Claw* (Hooking Arms). Extending an index or middle knuckle when punching is also effective (Flashing Fist). See Basics.

Note: Eye attacks are used in street systems as equalizers but must be practiced with control always. Any contact in practice is done near the eye with a less damaging part of the fingers, like a finger pad tapping the forehead or sliding across the temple. Developing these weapons is done only on inanimate objects or isometrically (Kenpo "Finger Sets").

**Ears:** Attacking the ears are done by striking or slapping one or both with a slightly cupped hand. Using two hands to slap (box, clap) together around the ear holes can rupture the tympanic membrane (eardrum) to dramatically affect equilibrium, balance, and mental focus (Tripping Leg).

**Nose:** The nose can be attacked at the physical structure and the nearby sinuses. The most protruding part of the nose is flexible cartilage with the nasal bone underneath connected to the skull. Noses vary in length and thickness based upon ethnicity and genetics.

Damage at GV25, LI20, and Bitong (*Disruption of Air Flow*) can affect the nose structure and sinuses on the sides and above the nose. This can be accompanied by blood flow, watery eyes, and intense headache that can make it difficult to concentrate, see, and may even contribute to some panic.

Note: A palm strike driving the nasal bone up into the frontal bone into the brain killing someone is a martial myth. This is anatomically and therefore physically impossible since the nasal bone is not long enough, sturdy enough, or lined up with an accessible entry vector to cause this to occur.

**Throat & Neck:** Perhaps the most vital area of the human body where blood, nerve, and air pathways all traverse this trunk crucial for life between the head and body. This vulnerable area can be attacked 360° around, from bottom to top, and is susceptible to manipulation.

Depths and layers of damage range from a choking sensation to a collapsed windpipe, from unconsciousness to paralysis or death. Application practice must always be done with control, while also learning how to check and protect our own throat and neck.

St9 (Delayed Hand), Ren22 (Returning the Gift), SI17 (Fatal Variation), and the trachea (Hidden Hand) are throat points covered in other categories. SI16 and LI18 are side of neck points on the SCM (Sleeper), with any vertebrae on the cervical spine a vital target (Six Hands).

### Mechanical Function
**Jaw Hinge:** Where the lower jaw attaches to the temporal bone and is most vulnerable when the teeth are not clenched. Dislocation is painful and makes opening and closing the mouth difficult (a good reason to wear a mouthpiece).

Points already covered at this hinge are TW17 and SI17 (*Blood Flow*), with blunt force anywhere at this joint able to separate these bones (Flashing Hands). TW21, SI19, and GB2 (*Brain Function*) are another group of points in front of the ear that can affect this structure (Fist of Aggression).

**Collarbone:** This *Clavicle* bone connects the arms at the shoulder (AC joint) with the sternum in the middle chest. Dislocating the joint at either end or breaking the bone along its shaft makes the arm it is connected to structurally unusable (Blinding Vice).

**Ki27 / Shu Fu / Shu Mansion** at the lower border of the medial clavicle or nearby St12, St13, Lu2 and LI16, are all vulnerable targets. A hammerfist (Entwined Fists), elbow (Pursuing Panther), or backknuckle (Rear Belt Grab) can cause a structural disconnection immobilizing that arm.

**Shoulder:** The shoulder is attacked against its natural ranges of motion by twisting the arm (Hammerlock) or bent elbow pressure applied using the hand above, "Americana" (Dangerous Tackle), or below, "Kimura" (Returning Club) that shoulder for compliance, submission, or dislocation. There are many creative ways to apply these locks using the arms or legs.

EP Jian Qian is a shoulder strike point on the anterior muscle (Alternating Fist) and SI9 on the posterior crease a manipulation push point (Arms of Silk), both covered under *Disruption of Nerve Function*.

**Elbow Joint:** This joint has 360° of surface area but generally is attacked on two primary sides to bend or hyper-extend. Bending is done at the LI11, Lu5, Ht3 (*Disruption of Nerve Function*) joint crease angles or by striking the bicep MSC (Muscle Spindle Cell) causing a bicep reflex contraction.

The back of a straightened elbow joint is attacked to cause hyperextension at TW10/TW11 to affect the GTO (Golgi Tendon Organ) causing the joint to lock straight. Force is applied with striking (Snapping Arm), grasping (Returning the Club), and pressing (Reversing Circles), with grappling methods also used to attack at this vector (Pinch from Death C).

Note: Numbing the arm/hand can be done at one of the elbows three "funny bone" points *(Disruption of Nerve Function)*, SI8 (Jumping Crane), TW10 (Hammerlock), and the medial epicondyle Ahshi point (Unexpected Blade). The elbow is also vulnerable to dislocation from the joint side near LI11 (Conquering Arm).

**Arm Bones:** The humerus bone in the upper arm, plus the radius and ulnar bones in the forearm is the framework for arm muscles, nerves, and blood flow. Damaging any of these bones makes them difficult to use and can compound into a more serious medical issue

**Wrist:** Where the radius bone meets and articulates with 3 of the hand's carpal bones. The ulna bone articulates with the radius bone but not with any of the hand bones.

Along with nerve and blood flow, many small tendon and ligament structures exist that, if damaged, can affect the use of that hand. These flexible joints move in 6 directions, 2 each that bend, twist, and flex, or combined to rotate the hand internally or externally. The wrist is often locked in body manipulation, to cause damage, or for submission.

**TW2 / Yemen / Humor Gate** on the back of the hand between the little and ring finger knuckle can be pushed while Lu9 at the medial thumb side crease is pulled to twist the wrist outward (Piercing Blade). **SI3 / Wan Gu / Wrist Bone**, on the hands ulnar side between the little finger and hamate bone with LI4 can be ulnar flexed to manipulate (Desperate Fists), submit, or break (Thrusting Blade).

**Hands & Fingers:** The hand has 8 carpal bones, 5 metacarpals, and 14 phalanges. All connect with ligaments, tendons, supplied with blood, and innervated by nerves. Damage makes it difficult to use the grip or digit(s). Striking (Clipping the Blade 2), pressing (Spiraling Wrist), or grasping individual digits (Gripping Wrist) are ways to attack this area.

**Hips & Thighs:** The hip joint and thigh muscles (quads, hamstrings) make up this most powerful area of the body. **St31 / Bi Guan / Thigh Gate** where the lateral superior leg connects at the hip. **GB31 / Feng Shi / Wind Market** on the middle lateral thigh where the middle finger touches when the arms hang by the side.

This *Iliotibial Band* is the vertical indention at the sides of the thighs between the front quad and rear hamstring muscles. This "Charley Horse" area is often attacked with roundhouse (Six Hands) or knee kicks (Sleeper).

**Ahshi Point / Middle Anterior Quad**, or any quad motor point (MSC), when stimulated causes the muscle to fire, flexing the knee. This can be done with striking (Destructive Gift) or pressing (Straddling the Leg).

**Ahshi Point / Hamstring Muscle Group** at the back of the thighs can be affected with trauma to the middle causing leg weakness to affect posture and balance (Evading the Club).

**Knee Joint:** The knee joint can be attacked at 4 major angles with the medial and rear knee crease used mostly to bend, while the lateral and front angles are used to cause a hyperextension or dislocation. The knee can be forced to bend inside out at Spleen 9/10 (Scraping Stomp), the medial knee Ahshi point (Triggered Palm), or back of the knee at UB40 (Reversing Fist), all covered under *Disruption of Nerve Function.*

Attacking the front knee can cause a hyperextension, ACL tear, or dislocation with kicks (Twins of Aggression), pressure (Nutcracker), or even rolled into (see Lawrence Taylor tackle of Joe Theisman 1985). Damage can also be caused at the lateral knee with kicks possibly causing an MCL strain or tear (Evading the Club).

**Calf Muscle & Achilles Tendon:** Damage along these connected lower leg targets causes pain and affects the ability to put weight on the foot. Force is applied for pain compliance, submission, to traumatize the tissue or at the Achilles tendon to cause disability. These targets are exposed to compression with the arms (Dance of Death) or legs as in a knee drop (Broken Kneel).

Note: With the knee on the ground observe whether the top of their foot is flat or if the heel is up with the ball of the foot on the ground. The flat foot relaxes the calf muscle making it the vulnerable target where the heel up flexes the calf making the Achilles tendon the more vulnerable target.

**Feet & Ankles** – The feet have 7 bones (metatarsals), with the talus connecting with the tibia and fibula to form the ankle joint. All are connected by ligaments, tendons, and cartilage, are supplied with blood, and innervated by nerves. Damage can severely limit someone's mobility and ability to function on their feet. Stomps on top (Captured Arms) or across the arch of a turned foot (Scraping Stomp) or grabbing to manipulate (Straddling the Leg) are all ways to attack this structure.

# Disruption of Qi Energy

The topic of Qi (Chi/Chee/Ki) can seem illusive or controversial for some to grasp (see the *Mind*). Gravity is a comparable concept where it is not imperative to have an understanding for it to be present. In fact, gravity was just an accepted and utilized truth until Sir Isaac Newton "discovered it" and defined the terms surrounding the phenomenon. Qi also defines something real and even if defined differently is a valuable concept worthy of evaluation and thought.

The previous Pressure Point categories have all affected someone's Qi. This section covers points and areas that fall between those Western defined categories. Some affect internal organs, glands, physical structures, the nervous system, but all affect a person's Qi at the essence of their internal energy and life force.

In ancient times this was secret knowledge handed down only to the advanced and hopefully responsible practitioners. In modern times where anyone can see and research this, my hope is to demystify it while encouraging safe knowledgeable practice, and situation appropriate use.

With that said a person's Qi can be dynamic and not noticeably vulnerable to some pressure point attacks. People can block pain (shift their Qi) and its affect long enough to survive a situation. Stories of people demonstrating incredible strength and determination in dangerous and life-threatening situations abound in all cultures.

Previously, TCM names and references were defined mostly using the MWM model. Points in this section are defined emphasizing the Eastern energetics and TCM model.

The 12 bilateral Yin/Yang channels (Lu, LI, St, etc.) stem from their named internal organ, with the front centerline Conception Vessel (CV) and rear Governing Vessel (GV) nourishing those organs.

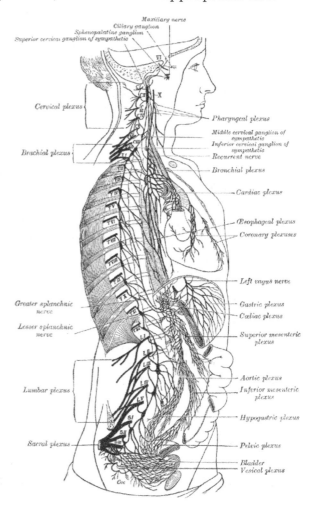

Each TCM organ system has an *Alarm Point* on the anterior torso, with 6 centerline and 6 bi-lateral points that connect directly too and affect that organ. A few of these were listed in other sections but all are listed and shown here in this context.

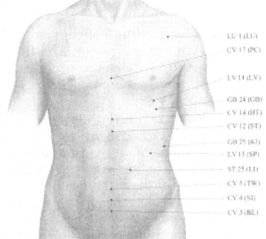

Impacting any of these points can disrupt someone's Qi. The Alarm Point for the Lungs is Lu1 (*Disruption of Nerve Function*), the Heart is CV14 (*Disruption of Air Flow*). Other points are St25 for Large Intestine, CV12 for Stomach, Lv13 for Spleen, CV4 for Small Intestine, CV3 for Urinary Bladder, GB25 for Kidney, CV17 for Pericardium, CV5 for Triple Warmer, GB24 for Gall Bladder and Lv14 for Liver.

The Qi-flow along the limbs is where many people start questioning the credibility of applying this in a fighting environment, so here's the basic concept. Starting inside the body, at the Organs, the Qi flows out to the limbs where it eventually reaches and connects to a finger or toe tip.

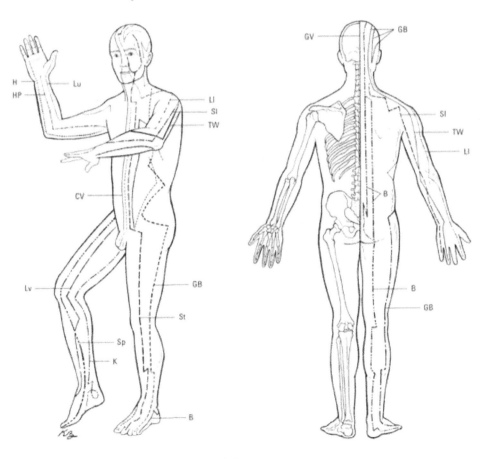

Think of a tree growing from the trunk to larger (arms & legs) then smaller branches (fingers & toes). A "System of Correspondences" therefore exists between the organ systems and these branches along "channels" or "meridians" where Qi flows in a predictable direction and known cycle.

Note: An interesting concept in TCM is called the "organ flower" at the end of each Yin organ system. The flower of the lung is body hair, the spleen is the lips, the heart is the tongue, the kidney is head hair, and the liver are the finger and toenails.

Each Organ and related Organ System is also known to be on a natural timer of activation and rest commonly known as a Circadian Clock or Rhythm. This observation points out that there is a 2-hour period in each 24-hour cycle where the organ is most active and vibrant, meaning on the opposite end of that 2-hour cycle an organ system is at it's weakest. Therefore, the Lungs are strongest from 3-5am and weakest from 3-5pm, etc. In martial arts this has been used to understand the best time of day to attack an organ system, or what particular time of day an organ system is best attacked.

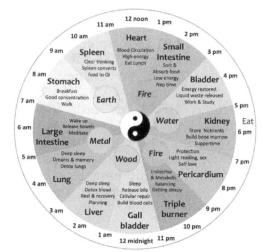

The Qi of the 6 *Yin* organ systems (Lu, Sp, Ht, Ki, P, Lv) and CV flow along the anterior and medial sides of the body. The normal *Yin Qi* in the arms flows distally from the torso along the medial arms to the fingers, in the medial legs proximally from toes to torso. The CV Qi travels upward anteriorly from perineum to chin.

The complimentary Qi of the 6 *Yang* organ systems (LI, St, SI, UB, TW, GB) and GV flow along the posterior and lateral sides of the body. The normal *Yang Qi* in the arms flows proximally along the lateral arms from fingers to face, and in the lateral legs distally from face to toes. The GV Qi travels upward from coccyx to top of the head.

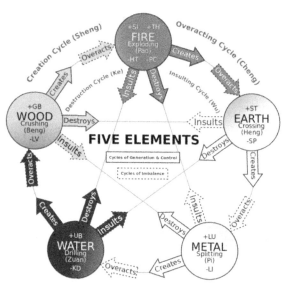

68

Ancient, Chinese influenced, pressure point fighting systems use a "5-Element Theory" to conceptually define how these channels interact and how vital points along them can
be affected. The 5 elements are Fire, Earth, Metal, Water, Wood, with each attached to human organ systems and bilateral channel correspondences.

They are also associated with sensory organs, emotions, odors, tastes, colors, emotions, sounds, seasons, body tissue, movement qualities, etc.

Wood creates Fire, is created by Water, controls Earth, is controlled by Metal. Wood (Lv/ GB) is represented by the tendon and ligament connecting tissue; it is strong yet flexible. Its martial quality is twisting, bouncing, torqueing, gripping, with its energy to grow and expand.

Fire creates Earth, is created by Wood, controls Metal, and is controlled by Water. Fire (Ht/SI/P/TW) is represented by the blood vessels; it is dynamic and relentless. Its martial quality is leaping, lunging, and fast striking combinations, with its energy up and out.

Earth creates Metal, is created by Fire, controls Water, and is controlled by Wood. Earth (Sp/St) is represented by the muscle structure; it is heavy, settled, using gravity to pull down. Its martial quality is grabbing, grappling, and takedowns, with its energy centered and inward.

Metal creates Water, is created by Earth, controls Wood, and is controlled by Fire. Metal (Lu/LI) is represented by the skin and hair; it is strong and determined. Its martial quality is accuracy, focus, pointed, sharp, and penetrating, with its energy inward and contracting.

Water creates Wood, is created by Metal, controls Fire, and is controlled by Earth. Water (Ki/UB) is represented by the bones; it is fluid and circular. Its martial quality applies force from one movement to the next while absorbing and redirecting an opponent's energy, with its energy down and out.

This is an ancient tool that provides a framework for recognizing and evaluating the interactive nature of different correspondences. Although not always applicable, it does give a theoretical baseline for understanding the interaction among these various components.

In 5-element theory, each element influences and is influenced by other elements in *Creating, Controlling* and *Destructive Cycles*. In TCM, and the lifestyle art of Feng Shui, balance and harmony are the goal, but in martial arts the intention is disrupt that harmony by attacking meridians and points against, or excessively with the normal *Cycles ("Insults" and "Destroys" in illustration).*

Using this theory as a martial arts concept in modern times can seem metaphorical, but any interaction can be plugged into the model, or the model can be used to evaluate the interaction. It's a theory so the efficacy can be debated.

Using organ systems, a hard punch to the sternum (Lung-Metal) can deflate the chest and quiet an aggressive spirit (Heart-Fire), i.e., Metal "Insults" Fire. A hard punch to the ribs (Liver-Wood) can weaken the muscles (Spleen-Earth), i.e., Wood "Destroys" Earth.

Plugging all 5-elements into the theory using the *"Destroys Cycle"*, then flexible expanding Wood can overwhelm (contain) deliberate grabbing Earth, that can overwhelm (absorb) fluid illusive Water, which can overwhelm (extinguish/absorb) fast hitting Fire, which can overwhelm (melt) hard penetrating Metal, which can overwhelm (destroy) flexible expanding Wood.

Following the *"Insults Cycle"* large expanding Wood is drained (swallowed) by deliberate grabbing Earth, which is drained (muddied) by fluid illusiveness Water, which is drained (dissipated) by fast hitting Fire, which is drained (put out) by linear penetrating Metal, which is drained (contained) by large expanding Wood.

This can be a way to conceptually evaluate an opponent for sport or street by style, temperament, body type, etc. Since sport and non-sport styles contain movement attitudes from all 5 elements, adjustments can counter an opponent's strength while attacking weaknesses.

Points can also be used so a vertical punch blocked at P6 and Ht3 (wrist and elbow Yin Channel Fire points) would weaken LI18 (neck Yang Channel Metal point) for a follow up handsword, or *"Fire Destroys Metal."* Blocking a horizontal punch at Lu7 and LI11 (wrist and elbow Yin channel metal points) would weaken SI17 (neck Yang Channel Fire point) for a follow up handsword, or *"Metal Insults Fire"* (Six Hands).

In both cases using a MWM model, the radial or median arm nerves are stimulated causing a weakness upstream along the brachial plexus into the neck making the handsword strike more potent at the Vagus Nerve or Carotid Sinus (Six Hands).

The ancient style of Dim Mak is a well heard of pressure point fighting system with many points common to my list here, but with its combinations mostly left out as they are style specific, often not flexible, and have questionable consistency to many in the modern martial art community.

Another issue is many points and combinations used in ancient times have become obsolete. One of the primary reasons is that to damage or disrupt the Qi at many ancient Dim Mak points, highly developed natural weapons are needed. Ancient practitioners would develop these based upon personal preference, talent, a genetic gift, or a training opportunity.

This is less common among modern day martial artists who generally do not train hours every day to develop their hands into a "quivering" or "iron palm," or have the goal to "make every hand a sword and every finger a dagger."

Modern technology and training methods do not encourage what for many generations of martial artists became disfigurement of their hands and other body parts for purposes of durability in empty handed fighting.

With gun powder weaponry readily available and used predominantly by those whose professions involve regular violent interactions, like military and law enforcement, this type of natural weapon development training has become impractical for most due to a time to benefit ratio, and other factors.

Additionally, modern people are bigger, less frail, have more muscle mass and stronger immune systems than the ancient Chinese where these systems evolved. Most generally wear shoes making most foot points inaccessible, and modern medicine can treat what might have become a more serious problem after a fight in ancient times.

The subject is still interesting, but to transfer an ancient system like Dim Mak into modern times is not always practical and may not even be interesting to many modern-day martial artists. A simplification allows more to benefit from the information on how to affect someone's Qi.

*Disruption of Qi Function* in this book therefore is less complicated as points covered are dynamic effective points not covered in other sections. These points can change someone's physical posture, mental focus, and the ability or desire/spirit to fight. Starting at the head they are:

## Head & Neck Points
**GV20 / Bai Hui / Hundred Meetings** is the highest point on the head where the parietal and occipital lobes connect (baby's soft spot area). It is a vulnerable human structure where a knee driven into the top of the head of a bent opponent could cause a cervical spinal compression and/or head trauma that could be fatal (Deflecting the Kick). It is used in Acupuncture primarily to lift blood and Qi into the head.

**GV26 / Ren Zhong / Mans Middle** is located just under the tip of the nose in the area at the top of the philtrum (vertical indention between upper lip and nose). In TCM this is a revival point that is gently tapped to revive consciousness, where impacting this Qi point can cause unconsciousness or death (Flashing Hands).

**CV24 / Cheng Jiang / Sauce Receptacle** is on the anterior face in the mentolabial groove between the lower lip and the tip of the chin. This sensitive press and rub point are felt in the teeth and tongue (Twins of Destruction).

**Ahshi Point / Tip of the Chin** just under CV24 at the center of the most prominent forward part of the chin and susceptible to striking. Hitting this target in boxing is colloquially called "on the button" where straight contact drives the chin down towards the chest stretching the cervical spine affecting consciousness (Calming the Club), although the chin can be hit on several vectors to affect consciousness.

**EP / Shang Lian Quan / Upper Spring of Integrity** under the mandible between the chin and top of the throat, and **CV23 / Lian Quan / Corner Spring** under the chin at the top of the throat over the hyoid bone, both tender areas under the tongue root. Boxer's can use it as an uppercut target, but an empty-handed sharp weapon can strike or press causing serious disruption to someone's physical and mental Qi (Captured Arms).

**Ahshi Points / Under Lateral Jaw (Mumps Area)** are points under the sides of the jaw innervated by the inferior alveolar nerve, where the parotid glands are located and innervated by CNVII. Pressure here is painful and drastically affects the entire area, along with mental focus (Entwined Fists).

**Ahshi Points / Scalene Muscles** in the neck, especially anterior and middle, are best accessed between the trachea and SCM muscles, which they are behind. Grasping or pressing these tender muscles above the brachial plexus has an extremely dramatic effect (Securing the Club).

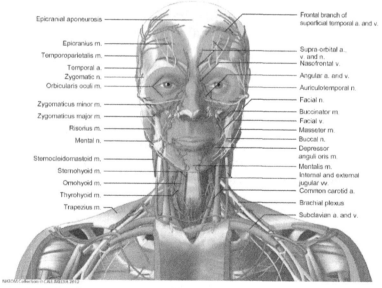

### Arm, Upper & Middle Torso Points:

**P6 / Nei Guan / Inner Pass** a couple inches proximal to each medial wrist crease between the palmaris longus and flexor radialis tendons on the median arm nerve line. This point affects the nervous system up the channel into the head, diaphragm, and Heart organ. It is often the point blocked to defend a punch, depending on hand rotation, that in combination with Ht3 at the elbow can be a devastating set up (Six Hands).

**SI11 / Tian Zong / Heavenly Gathering** is one-third down each scapula in the middle. The teres minor, teres major and infraspinatus muscles all originate here. A reflexive nerve response is generated by striking (Broken Tackle), and/or pressing, that is enhanced by rubbing, (Crossed Arms). It is also a brace point for the knee to dislocate the shoulder (Returning the Club).

**CV17 / Shan Zhong / Chest Center** is the *Pericardium Alarm Point* on the sternum between the two nipples, known as the "Sea of Qi" in TCM circles. Impacting this tender Qi filled area can drastically and immediately affect someone's attitude, enthusiasm, and spirit to fight.

Striking/pressing a sharp knuckle (Parting Arms) or elbow point (Entangled Arm) would be a common attack method.

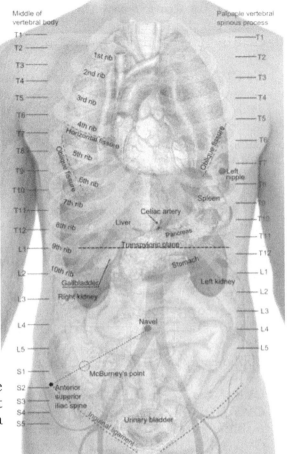

Note: An observation can be made of people's chest (especially men) swelling up when angry or motivated to action. Men often hit their own chest and let out noises as their lungs fill with air and their Qi rises. Attacking CV17 is a way to deflate the chest and disrupt this rising Qi.

**St15 / Wu Yi / Roof** is in the 2nd rib spaces, 2 ribs above the nipple between the pec muscles. This juncture is vulnerable to a hard push, strike, or pinch to affect lung Qi (Bear and the Ram).

**GB22 / Yuan Ye / Armpit Abyss** and **GB23 / Zhe Jin / Flank Sinews** are points about an inch apart in the 5th rib spaces under each armpit. These intercostal spaces are innervated by the spine where a punch or sharp weapon can disrupt Qi, breath, and mental focus (Grabbing Hair).

**Lv14 / Qi Men / Cycle Gate** is the *Liver Alarm Point* located in the 6th rib space directly under each nipple. A sharp knuckle can penetrate this tender area causing severe pain, trauma, and potentially cause future health issues (Turning the Cross).

**GB24 / Ri Yue / Sun and Moon** is the tender *Gall Bladder Alarm Point* directly below Liver 14 in the 7th rib spaces (Glancing Poke).

**St19 / Bu Rong / Not Contained** at the medial border of each 7th rib, on a line with the tip of the xiphoid process. This tender rib edge is an opening to nearby internal organs (Arms of Silk).

**Lv13 / Zhang Men / Completion Gate** is the *Spleen Alarm Point* at the end of the 11th rib, and **GB25 / Jing Men / Capital Gate** the *Kidney Alarm Point* at the end of the 12th rib. These "floating ribs" (not attached at the sternum) are more easily damaged due to the lack of structural support on the unattached side. Breaking off a rib end would be painful and could puncture a nearby internal organ (Crushing Palm).

Note: Even if not punctured heavy trauma near Lv14, Lv13, GB25, GB24, St19, or any angle around the blood-filled Liver or Spleen organs can take someone's Qi away leaving them weak and unable to fight.

**CV12 / Zhong Wan / Central Venter** is the *Stomach Alarm Point*, midway between the navel and sternum base (Checking the Club).

**Lower Torso Points:**
**CV8 / Shen Que / Spirit Gate** (the navel), and **St25 / Tian Shu / Celestial Pivot** about 2" on either side of the navel is a weaker lower abdominal area (Hidden Hand)

**CV4 / Guan Yuan / Gate of Origin** the *Small Intestine Alarm Point*, and **CV6 / Qi Hai / Sea of Qi** are lower abdomen points between the navel and pubic bone. There are over 20 points, including the CV3 *UB Alarm Point* and CV5 *TW Alarm Point* in this extremely Qi-filled area of the body. Only CV4 and CV6 are listed but the Qi of this entire area is very dynamic. This is a blunt force area as the opportunity to strike specific points in a fight is unlikely.

This lower abdominal, or "core" in Western exercise physiology, is where Qi and breath come up from, and where power and balance are rooted. This 3-dimensional area fills the lower abdomin below the navel (dantien area). A front kick (Delayed Hand), knee (Rear Belt Grab), punch (Ducking Dragon), or other strike (Thrusting Thumbs) can severely damage one's Qi energy, and possibly have a negative effect on short or long-term health.

**CV1 / Hui Yin / Meeting of Yin** is located at the Perineum at the bottom of the body between the anus and scrotum in men, and posterior labia in women. Striking this vital lower body point can cause unconsciousness and death (Crushing Palm).

**GV1 / Chang Qiang / Long Strong** is located near CV1, except is between the anus and the coccyx. Attacking this point can dramatically affect someone's posture and Qi (Hidden Hand).

## Limb Points:

**LI4 / He Gu / Joining Valley** is a strongly felt point between the thumb and index finger knuckles in the middle of the first interosseus muscle (bulges when thumb pressed to index finger). Damage affects the opposable grip at the thumb and can disrupt the body's surface Qi (body force field) compromising the immune system, allowing illness to invade.

It can be struck (Clipping the Blade) or pressed as in a handshake attack or counter where the thumb pad shifts to press this point before or while other moves are done (Returning the Gift).

**EP Yao Tong Xue / Lumbar Pain Point** consists of two dynamic points on the back of the hand located between the 2nd/3rd & 4th/5th metacarpal bones in depressions proximal to the punching knuckles. These are powerful low back pain relief points that if struck can weaken the grip (Crashing Elbows).

**St36 / Zu San Li / Leg 3-mile** is about one hand width below the patella and one finger width outside the shinbone over the anterior tibial artery, that stems from the femoral artery, that stems from the iliac artery, that stems from the abdominal aorta, that stems from the heart.

In 5-element theory this is an Earth Point on the Earth Channel (St) so damaging it damages the earth element crucial for energy and health. If the ankle is flexed the anterior tibialis muscle surrounds the point so becomes difficult to access, but not impossible (Prancing Tiger).

Note: For health, this longevity point can be stimulated gently or warmed with moxa (see the *Mind, Qi*) to increase energy and boost the immune system.

**Sp6 / San Yin Jiao / Three Yin Intersection** is about a hands width above the medial maleolus (anklebone) innervated by a cutaneous branch of the saphenous and tibial nerves. This energetically charged point is where 3 yin organ channels intersect (Lv, Sp, Ki). A strike can take the energy out of the legs, and it is an excellent inner ankle sweep point (Glancing Poke).

# Pressure Point System Summary
## Disruption of Blood Flow Review
**Heart Organ Points**

*Ki25 / Shen Cang / Spirit Storehouse:* 2nd rib space next to the sternum, where the pulmonary valve is located on the left side

*St17 / Ru Zhong / Chest Center:* 4th rib spaces on the nipple line

*St18 / Ru Gen / Root of the Breast:* 5th rib space just below the nipple, and where the mitral valve of the heart is located on the left side

**Arterial System Points**

*SI17 / Tian Rong / Heavenly Appearance:* between angle of mandible and anterior border of SCM muscle

*St9 / Ren Ying / Mans Welcome:* carotid pulse felt on either side of trachea

*TW17 / Yi Feng / Wind Screen:* Temporomandibular joint (TMJ) behind ear

*Ht1 / Jing Qu / Summit Spring:* under armpits where axillary artery pulse felt

*Lu9 / Tai Yuan / Supreme Abyss:* medial wrist crease where pulse felt

*Lu8 / Tai Yuan / Channel Gutter:* medial wrist crease about 1" proximal to Lu9

*CV6 / Qi Hai / Sea of Qi:* inch below navel on body centerline

*Sp12 / Chong Men / Rushing Gate:* groin creases on either side where femoral artery pulse felt

*St42 / Chong Yang / Rushing Yang:* foot top between 2nd &3rd metatarsal bones

*Ki3 / Tai Xi / Supreme Stream:* inner ankle between Achilles tendon and inner ankle bone (medial malleolus)

*Lv3 / Tai Chong / Great Rushing:* top of foot (metatarsals) between 1st and 2nd bones, between big and second toe

## Disruption of Air Flow Review
**Lung Organ Points**

*CV16 / Zhong Ting / Central Courtyard:* bottom of sternal angle

*CV15 / Jiu Wei / Turtledove Tail:* middle of xyphoid process

*CV14 / Ju Que / Great Gateway:* bottom tip of xyphoid process

**Air Pathway Points**

*Ahshi Point / Thyroid Cartilage:* middle anterior throat or "Adams Apple"

*CV22 / Tian Tu / Heavenly Prominence:* suprasternal notch indentation at top of sternum and base of throat

*GV25 / Su Liao / White Crevice:* nose tip

*LI20 / Yang Xiang / Welcome Fragrance:* nose base

*EP Bi Tong:* just outside LI20

*UB2 / Zan Zhu / Gathered Bamboo:* medial corner of each eyebrow

## Disruption of Nerve Function Review
**Points Branching from the Cervical Spine**

*SI16 / Yian Chuang / Heavenly Window:* posterior edge of SCM muscles, level with Adams Apple

*LI18 / Fu Tu / Support the Prominence:* between SCM muscles, level with Adams Apple

*GB21 / Jian Jing / Shoulder Well:* top of trapezius muscles halfway between neck and shoulder

*St12 / Que Pen / Empty Basin:* above center of collarbone

*St13 / Qi Hu / Qi Door:* below center of collarbone

*Lu1 / Zhong Fu / Middle Palace:* under outside edge of collarbone

*Lu2 / Yun Men / Cloud Gate:* under Lu1 at outside edge of collarbone

*EP / Jian Qian / Front of the Shoulder:* middle anterior shoulder

*Ahshi Point / Between the Bicep Muscles:* high point between bicep muscles, innervated by the musculocutaneous nerve

*LI16 / Ju Gu / Great Bone:* AC Joint where collarbone & scapula attach

*SI12 / Bing Feng / Grasping the Wind:* top center of scapula

*SI13 / Qu Yuan / Crooked Wall:* superior medial scapula edge

*SI9 / Jian Zhen / True Shoulder:* back of armpit crease where long tricep head attaches arm to scapula

*LI14 / Bi Nao / Upper Arm:* lateral deltoid (shoulder) muscle

*LI13 / Shou Wu Li / Arm Five Miles:* about one-third the distance proximal from the elbow to the shoulder

*TW10 / Tian Jing / Celestial Well:* tricep muscle near elbow

*TW11 / Qing Leng Yuan / Clear Cold Abyss:* about 1" proximal to TW10

*LI11 / Qu Chi / Pool at the Crook:* outside edge of elbow crease over brachioradialis muscle

*Lu5 / Chi Ze / Cubit Marsh:* medial to LI11 at elbow crease between tendons

*LI10 / Shou San Li / Arm Three Miles:* about 2" distal to LI11 on forearm at high point of extensor carpi radialis muscle

*Lu6 / Kong Zui / Maximum Opening:* on brachioradialis muscle proximal to forearms halfway point at radius bones medial angle

*Lu7 / Lie Que / Broken Sequence:* proximal to radius styloid process

*Lu8 / Jing Qu / Channel Gutter:* an inch proximal to thumb side wrist crease

*Lu10 / Yuji Lu / Fish Border:* meaty thumb base area on palm side (Thenar Eminence)

*P7 / Da Ling / Great Mound:* medial wrist 3 finger widths from crease

*TW4 / Yang Chi / Yang Pool:* posterior wrist crease on little finger side of extensor digitorum tendon

*EP / Zhong Quan / Posterior Spring:* posterior wrist crease on index finger side of extensor digitorum tendon

*Ht2 / Qing Ling / Green Spirit:* inner bicep muscle about two-thirds down humerus bone

*SI8 / Xiao Hai / Small Sea:* inside corner of medial elbow bone between ulnar and median nerves

*Ahshi Point / Medial Epicondyle of Humerus:* distal medial supracondylar ridge

*Ht3 / Shao Hai / Lesser Sea:* lateral to SI8 at medial elbow crease

**Points Branching from the Thoracic Spine**

*UB41 / Fu Fen / Attached Branch:* medial scapula level with T2

*UB42 / Po Hu / Po Door:* medial edge of scapula level with T3

*UB43 / Gao Huang Shu / Gao Huang Shu:* medial edge of scapula level with T4

*UB44 / Shen Tang / Shen Hall:* medial edge of scapula level with T5

*GV9 / Zhi Yang / Reaching Yang:* below T7 spinous process level with lower border of scapula

**Points Branching from the Lumbar & Sacral Spines**

*UB40 / Wei Zhong / Middle of the Crook:* back of knee between tendons where pulse can be felt

*UB39 / Wei Yang / Bend Yang:* lateral knee crease

*Lv11 / Yin Lian / Yin Corner:* upper inner corner of thigh on adductor longus muscle, just below Sp11

*Sp11 / Ji Men / Winnowing Gate:* middle inner thigh on saphenous nerve line midway up and behind sartorius muscle

*Sp10 / Xue Hai / Sea of Blood:* above kneecap on meaty base of medial quad muscle

*Sp9 / Yin Ling Quan / Yin Mound Spring:* below kneecap on inner leg at top of calf muscle

*Lv8 / Qu Quan / Spring at the Crook:* between semitendinosus & semimembranosus tendons at inner knee crease
*Ahshi Point / Medial Knee: between Sp10 & Ki10*
*Ki10 / Yin Gu / Yin Valley:* middle inner knee crease tendons (near Lv8)
*Ahshi Point / Medial Knee:* between Sp10 and Ki10 on medial knee sartorius muscle, near its knee attachment
*EP / Heading / Top Crane:* superior anterior knee at quad tendon
*Ahshi Point / Lateral Knee:* superior lateral patellar corner at vastus lateralis muscle tendon
*GB34 / Yang Ling Quan / Yang Mound Spring:* below knee where tibia attaches

## Disruption of Brain Function Review

**Front of Head Points**
*EP / Yin Tang / Hall of Impression:* between the eyebrows
*EP Yu Yao / Fish Waist:* in the middle between each eyebrow
*Ahshi Point / Middle of Forehead:* between Yin Tang and hairline
*TW23 / Si Zhu Kong / Silken Bamboo Hollow:* lateral corner of eyebrows
*GB1 / Tong Zi Liao / Pupil Crevice:* lateral corner of each eye
*EP / Tai Yang / Supreme Yang:* about 1" posterior each lateral eye corner
**Side of Head Points**
*GB4 / Han Yan / Jaw Serenity:* inside hairline at temple
*GB5 / Xuan Lu / Suspended Skull:* below GB4
*GB6 / Xuan Li / Suspended Hair:* below GB5
*GB7 / Qu Bin / Crook of the Temple:* below GB6
*GB8 / Shuai Gu / Leading Valley:* about an inch above top of ear
**Back of Head Points**
*GV17 / Nao Hu / Brains Door:* center occipital bone at back of skull
*UB9 / Yu Zhen / Jade Pillow:* finger width out from GV17
*GV16 / Feng Fu / Palace of Wind:* under GV17 at base of skull
*UB10 / Tian Zhu / Celestial Pillar:* between center and outer lower rear skull edge
*GB20 / Feng Chi / Wind Pool:* outside lower edge of cerebellum
**Face Points**
*St3 / Juliao / Great Crevice:* under each eyeball center
*St5 / Da Ying / Great Welcome:* front side of masseter muscle (visible when teeth clenched)
*St6 / Jia Che / Jawbone:* middle of masseter muscle

## Disruption of Tissue & Mechanical Function Review

**Tissue Function**
*Eyes – Ears – Nose – Throat & Neck*
**Mechanical Function**
Jaw Hinge
TW17, SI17, TW21, SI19 & GB2 from previous sections
Collarbone
*Ki27 / Shu Fu / Shu Mansion:* lower border medial clavicle plus St12, St13, Lu2, & LI16 from previous sections
Shoulder – Elbows – Arm Bones – Wrist – Hands & Fingers – Hips & Thighs
*EP Jian Qian, SI9, LI11, Lu5, Ht3, TW10, TW11 from previous sections*
*TW2 / Yemen / Humor Gate:* back of hand between little and ring finger knuckle
*SI3 / Wan Gu / Wrist Bone:* ulnar hand side between little finger and hamate bone
*St31 / Bi Guan / Thigh Gate:* where outer leg connects to hip
*GB31 / Feng Shi / Wind Market:* sides of Iliotibial (IT) band where middle finger touches outer thigh with arms at sides

Ahshi Point / Middle Anterior Quad
Ahshi Point / Hamstring Muscle Group
Knee Joint – Calf Muscles & Achilles Tendon – Feet & Ankles

## Disruption of Qi Energy Review

*GV20 / Bai Hui / Hundred Meetings:* highest head point where parietal and occipital lobes meet, and the pulse can be felt

*GV26 / Ren Zhong / Mans Middle:* under nose tip on philtrum

*CV24 / Cheng Jiang / Sauce Receptacle:* anterior face in mentolabial groove between lower lip and chin tip

*Ahshi Point / Tip of the Chin:* under CV24 at center of most prominent forward part of chin

*EP / Shang Lian Quan / Upper Spring of Integrity:* under mandible at tongue root

*CV23 / Lian Quan / Corner Spring:* between chin tip and throat

*Ahshi Point / Under Lateral Jaw (Mumps area):* at parotid gland

*Ahshi Points / Scalene Muscles:* between trachea and SCM muscles

*P6 / Nei Guan / Inner Pass:* proximal to medial wrist crease

*SI11 / Tian Zong / Heavenly Gathering:* middle scapula, 1/3 down where teres minor, teres major, & infraspinatus originate

*CV17 / Shan Zhong / Chest Center:* chest center on sternum between nipples

*St15 / Wu Yi / Roof:* in 2nd rib spaces, 2 ribs above nipple, between pec muscles

*GB22 / Yuan Ye / Armpit Abyss:* lateral body in 5th rib spaces

*GB23 / Zhe Jin / Flank Sinews:* 5th rib spaces 1" anterior to GB22

*Lv14 / Qi Men / Cycle Gate:* 6th rib spaces under each nipple

*GB 24 / Ri Yue / Sun and Moon:* directly below Lv14 in 7th rib spaces

*St19 / Bu Rong / Not Contained:* medial border of 7th rib online with xiphoid process tip

*Lv13 / Zhang Men / Completion Gate:* end of 11th rib

*GB25 / Jing Men / Capital Gate:* end of 12th rib

*CV12 / Zhong Wan / Central Venter:* midway between navel and sternum base

*CV8 / Shen Que / Spirit Gate:* the navel

*St25 / Tian Shu / Celestial Pivot:* about 2" on either side of the navel

*CV4 / Guan Yuan /Gate of Origin:* dantien area of lower abdomen

*CV6 / Qi Hai / Sea of Qi:* dantien area of lower abdomen

*CV1 / Hui Yin / Meeting of Yin:* perineum between anus and scrotum in men; anus and posterior labia in women

*GV1 / Chang Qiang / Long Strong:* between anus and coccyx

*LI4 / He Gu / Joining Valley:* between thumb and index finger knuckles

*EP Yao Tong Xue / Lumbar Pain Points:* two points on back of hand between 2nd/3rd & 4th/5th metacarpal bones

*St36 / Zu San Li / Leg 3-mile:* one hands width below patella, one finger width lateral to shinbone

*Sp6 / San Yin Jiao / Three Yin Intersection:* about a hand's width up from inner anklebone, anterior to Achilles tendon

# THE MARTIAL ARTS SYSTEM

## Chapter VI

A *System* in martial arts refers to the component parts and a methodology that make up a type or *Style* of fighting. A sophisticated martial art system is formulated and defined with a lexicon, methodology, and techniques. It uses terms, principles, and training methods that allow for refinement and the indexing of knowledge, with the capability to develop students into experts in that style of fighting and/or movement.

A martial arts style evolves in a culture as the result of environment, culture, genetics, tendencies, preferences, and even technology. This can become refined over time by teachers contributing to a knowledge base that can be organized into the learning and training framework called a "System."

Kenpo, like most modern street styles, also has sport components so students can experience some of the dynamics of fighting without the street life or death and personal consequences. Striking styles, like Boxing, Kickboxing, Savate, and grappling styles, like Wrestling, Judo, sport Jiu Jitsu, and those that combine striking and grappling, like MMA and Pankration, are practiced primarily as sport.

Many of the traditional street styles came from other cultures in another time, like the assorted styles of Chinese Kung Fu and Japanese Karate. American Kenpo is a hybrid system originally formulated and developed by the late Kenpo Grandmaster Edmund K Parker in the 1950's and 1960's. His style was based on his life experience and training in a Japanese/Chinese hybrid learned from his teacher, Professor William KS (Thunderbolt) Chow (See the *Spirit* Chapter III – History of AK).

Even though terminology and technique vary, human movement, anatomy, and physiology are known quantities, so it becomes a question of emphasis. The *Style* baseline here is American Kenpo which focuses on street defense, where another style may have a different focus, emphasize another method, or attitude, or have the same focus but with a different take.

My American Kenpo Alliance (AKA) formulation will be the outline used here to describe how a martial arts system works and is put together. Specifics will be especially useful for Kenpo practitioners, but since martial arts contain many overlapping techniques this enables other martial art styles and systems to also find useful tools and information in this text.

Regardless of style differences a punch is a punch, a kick is a kick, and a choke is a choke, so whatever it's called "when pure knuckles meet pure flesh that's pure..." whatever you want to call it.

The first step in developing a system is to determine the goals of the style, and then the system can be built to accomplish those goals. What Mr. Parker developed left a great reference for training and carrying on the methods, techniques, and traditions of his martial art system.

The Kenpo I learned originally was brilliant for its day and is still an incredibly good system, even without refinements. From my experience of 40+ years in martial arts and 30+ years teaching Kenpo full-time I have incorporated many changes to that original system, as have others, based upon several factors.

The original Kenpo system was developed in a time when most students were adult men. Techniques were developed mostly against from untrained to more one-dimensionally trained Karate or Jiu Jitsu fighters. There were also less sport fighting opportunities with minimal Boxing, Wrestling, and Judo available as ways men could learn and test their fighting skills. Since not all men had access to these *Sport Styles*, the streets became where they would test techniques and try to prove themselves, and where fighting multiple opponents required a more special skill set.

Ed Parker was a large powerful man who developed his Kenpo system based upon his life experience and perspective growing up in Hawaii, then Utah and Southern California. During those times law enforcement, military, and other tough guys took karate to learn how to fight better on the street or in their jobs. There were very few children, women, older men, or more timid men participating during those times so the training environment was designed for "tough guys" to train with other "tough guys."

A gathering of old school Kenpo Black Belts always looked to me like a biker's convention with a bunch of large burly tough guys, and a few smaller athletic stud types that could hang with those big boys, all standing around telling fight and training stories. Many trained at that time to gain an edge in their inevitable next street fight.

The Kenpo taught during that era was extremely violent with the techniques learned, in my opinion, lacking in humane flexibility should the situation call for less destruction. Society was less litigious, and with fewer video cameras, so the culture would mostly let men "duke it out."

With the original "Karate Kid" movie in 1984 a large influx of children came into Karate Schools, so Mr. Miyagi could have a good influence on them. This dramatically increased how many school's there were along with the training emphasis. More women began training during the 1990's, then adult men 40+ and more timid men in the 2000's. This new student demographic influx changed how many martial arts school's operated as business models were developed to teach the masses.

This made it necessary to adjust teaching styles, the system, and some training methods so everyone could stay safe, enjoy training, and benefit at their own pace. The original Kenpo is still there but now almost everyone can get the tools and gain the confidence inherent in martial arts training as more people's lives can benefit. Everything is relative to where someone starts so the 'tough guys' still also benefit but those who may have lived in fear can now live with more confidence and peace of mind.

Kenpo now as before is an empty-handed street defense art utilizing sophisticated methodology against one or multiple opponents with or without external weapons. The destructive capability is still there, but with a different confrontation framework and controlling techniques added for when that is sufficient to end a threat.

Like the original system, modern Kenpo is made up of the 4 primary components, *Basics, Sets/Forms, Sparring/Sport Fighting,* and *Self-Defense Techniques/Street Fighting.* Students learn these pieces in a progressive way as they move through belt ranks towards expertise and mastery.

**Basics** are the individual movements that include *Stances, Foot Maneuvers, Blocks, Parry's, Checks, Punches, Strikes, Kicks, Holds, Locks, Chokes,* etc. These are categorized here as 'Whole-Body Movements', 'Body Extension Movements', and 'Body Contraction Movements'. These individual movements are where the mental and physical understanding of how the body can be used efficiently and effectively as a weapon, while gaining an awareness of our own vulnerabilities.

Martial arts styles all use the same *Basics,* even if called by other names, referred to differently, or taught with a different emphasis. The crucial point is that universal principles of movement, body structure and leverage are followed regardless of these other factors (see the *Mind*).

**Sets & Forms** are used by many martial art styles, especially striking systems. These "movement routines" are developed by experts to teach transitions, combinations, develop muscle memory, balance, focus, and build conditioning while indexing the techniques of a system. This is also how a martial artist learns to control his or her own body in space.

Traditional martial art patterns are controversial to some who see "in the air" movement without value in "real" fighting. The long history of this training method should give the obvious answer as to its layers of value.

Sport martial arts call it "shadowboxing" where many see it as less structured. The reality is that trained fighters are rehearsing fight lessons with mental intention and purpose. Coaches have fighters practice movement patterns and scenarios for skill development, and to prepare for a fight. This imaginary fight scenario repetition develops muscle memory so correct movement can be done and applied without conscious thought.

**Sparring/Sport Fighting** are the different regulated fight games used to train and compete in what is an accepted way of fighting that is often found in "civilized" cultures, where they also provide an outlet for people who want, and perhaps need this outlet.

This type of training contains many personal growth lessons while providing relatively safe fighting opportunities without the moral, personal, or legal repercussions of a street altercation. Rules and sportsmanship also allow for repeated practice with less chance of injury or personal dispute.

The fact is that many/most street style martial artists in a civil society rarely if ever use their street techniques, unless as part of their law enforcement or military job. Since vital target practice with partners must always be controlled a false sense of security can develop without the full contact and full results of a live interaction with an uncooperative opponent.

Most street styles therefore also practice sport fighting as benefits include physical conditioning, range, timing, transitions, adaptability, mental toughness, functioning under pressure, familiarity with different fighting postures and positions, etc.

**Self-Defense Techniques/Street Fighting** involves learning and rehearsing pre-designed sequences against anticipated attack scenarios. This develops body and target awareness while allowing practice of the concepts and principles of martial arts. These pre-arranged patterns eventually give way to adaptable and spontaneous techniques as determined by the situation (see *Equation Formula* in the *Mind*).

In Kenpo, the *Basics, Sets & Forms*, and *Sport Fighting* components are learned and practiced to primarily make the *Self-Defense Techniques* better. Precise *Basics*, with body control developed by *Sets & Forms*, then experience, toughness and conditioning gained through *Sport Fighting*, all contribute to this end.

Initially there are 3 primary ranges (striking, grabbing, stand-up and ground grappling) with 8 major angles of attack and defense analyzed when learning a self-defense system (see *Clock Concept*). Mr. Parker listed 5 ranges in his teachings including *Out of Range* and *Range Manipulation* (See the *Mind, Distance & Timing*).

*Out of Range* can mean far away, perhaps in conversation, but this is a non-starter for analyzing the actual physical interaction, unless of course a firearm is involved in which case it takes on a whole new meaning. *Out of Range* can also refer to the space just outside the gap between combatants. This is practiced extensively in sport fighting as it quickly changes to *In Range* in that dynamic.

*Range Manipulation* transcends the other 3 ranges so is infused at a higher level of training. The 3 middle ranges (striking, grabbing, grappling) is where the physical fight takes place.

**Striking Range** is the distance we can reach each other with accelerated weapons, primarily the hands, feet, knees, and elbows.

**Grabbing Range** is the distance where the intention is to grab, hold, and control, although striking can also be done at this distance,

**Grappling Range** happens with opponents both standing, or both lying on the ground, or a combination of standing and lying on the ground. Grappling is where body center awareness is most easily felt as combatants interlock to control or cause damage.

The 8 major angles, or positions of defense and attack use the *Clock Concept* with lines connecting 3-9 and 6-12 making a "+" (plus) sign with 1:30-7:30 and 4:30-10:30 making an "x" (multiplication sign). This *Mathematical Symbol Concept* is part of the Kenpo lexicon.

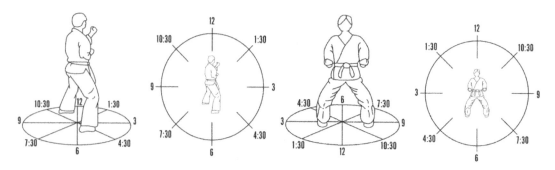

These positions can be referenced on the floor, viewed upright vertically, or around us in a 3-dimensional sphere. This provides directional references to help apply techniques, to see angles of movement, angles not defended, and potential or attacking weapons.

*Forms* practice also uses footwork to these directions as attackers in the street context can come from any of 360°, with these 8 positions as the reference angles that make understanding angles of defense and attack more mentally manageable.

With these 8 angles and 3 ranges in mind an attack can come from any combination of them by one or more than one attacker, with or without external weapons. This makes for a complex matrix of scenarios to index and practice, with each adaptable using Mr. Parker's *Equation Formula*.

These self-defense techniques can be organized and practiced by *Type of Attack, Angle of Attack,* and *Range of Attack,* among others. Contact is required but should be controlled and regulated with training partners.

The remainder of this book lists and describes these 4 major components of a *Martial Art System.* As a baseline, the *Basics, Sets & Forms, Sparring/Sport Fighting,* and *Self-Defense Techniques/Street Fighting* contained and explained here are are from my American Kenpo Alliance (AKA) system, but any martial artist or style can gain benefit from this information. Video links are also available at BarryBBarker.com as a visual reference to what is covered.

# THE BASICS OF MARTIAL ARTS

## Chapter VII

Basics are the building blocks upon which a martial arts system, or any movement-based activity, like gymnastics or dance, is built. A thorough understanding of basics with knowledge of structural alignment, movement mechanics, applications, and limitations, are a good place to start when learning any martial art.

*Intention* is critically important when it comes to movement, with Mr. Parker credited as saying "Many answers lie in a single move." For example, the motion of answering the telephone is the same as an upward elbow strike or looking at a wristwatch the same as an inward elbow strike. Many observable movement homographs like these exist.

A *Front Crossover* step as an example can be a way to maneuver closer or further away from an opponent, but could also be an inverted side stomp kick, a pushing or pulling sweep, or a way to walk up or down stairs. Remember that what differentiates similar physical motions is the mental intention, or purpose, for doing that motion.

A traditional martial art teaching style would be to isolate the individual movement mechanics of each basic. Using this method, a straight punch is be taught from a horse stance, a fighting stance is learned separately, then footwork added. This method of learning builds precision of movement and insight into each separate skill that then can carry over to when those basics are combined.

Modern sport styles by comparison tend to incorporate combination movements much earlier. For example, a Boxing jab is generally shown from a fighting stance and often with footwork, with possibly a body movement like slipping incorporated, and this may be followed with a rear hand punch. The precision is taught later for those who want to train more seriously.

Like any education, a skill is more deeply rooted when each piece is learned well first then combined later, even if sometimes it may seem tedious or boring, like learning scales on a piano. This is classical training in every discipline from martial arts to dance to playing a musical instrument, etc.

Many people do not want to take the time to learn in this classical way, so it becomes one reason for the popularity of fight-oriented fitness classes. Those interested in fitness, or even competing in fighting at a novice level, do not necessarily need to move precisely, providing their mechanics are not causing them injury.

Precise movement is important however for the serious competitive fighter and is part of the "art" in martial art. The traditional martial art formula of isolating each basic is time tested and where students learn best with an empty cup while trusting in those who have more insight into the process.

Individual basics are eventually used in combinations, simultaneously and sequentially, making for compound movements that a skilled practitioner can then connect rapidly, efficiently, creatively, and with insight. This exponentially expands someone's movement vocabulary.

Interactively, basics can be used with an opponent(s) standing, kneeling, ground grappling, or any combination of these. The basics baseline used here is my American Kenpo Alliance System, so the descriptions are primarily from this standup grappling and striking viewpoint, with an emphasis on self-defense although sport fighting is discussed throughout.

Ground grappling styles have their own base positions with methods of attack and defense not fully covered here. Grappling however is an immensely powerful knowledge asset for the "standup" martial artist to have at least a basic understanding. This helps them to stay upright or know how to get back onto their feet if on the ground.

From the street/self-defense martial art perspective staying on the feet is best with the ground avoided for many reasons, including environmental hazards, multiple opponents, and weapons.

The names used here are in English and mostly are descriptive of the motion or type of movement, versus another language's names, cultural terms, slang, or metaphoric and analogous characteristics as is sometimes used in martial arts (e.g. spinning outward hook kick vs dragon whips its tail, etc.). A few common terms are referenced where they are the more recognizable name.

Basics can be formatted in many ways but are broken down here into the 3 major groupings of **Postures & Whole-Body Movements** (Stances, Foot Maneuvers, Body Maneuvers), **Body Extension Movements** (Blocks, Parries, Checks, Punches, Kicks, Strikes), and **Body Contraction Movements** (Grabs, Holds, Locks, Chokes). All martial art movement can however be listed in one of these categories.

# POSTURES & WHOLE-BODY MOVEMENTS
## Stances – Foot Maneuvers – Body Maneuvers

Although most martial art movement involves the whole body to some degree this section covers postures and body positions used to control distance, maintain balance, or regain balance, and gain leverage. This includes methods of standing, called *Stances*, ways of moving the feet, called *Foot Maneuvers,* and ways of interacting with another person or with the ground, called *Body & Ground Maneuvers*. Video is the best way to grasp this with much of these able to be seen at BarryBBarker.com.

An important concept and principle of movement is staying within the context of our own body dimensions. *Whole-Body* basics, whether for attack or defense, are used most effectively with good balance, body control, and a foot to ground connection that is crucial for traction (See the *Mind, Balance*).

All fighting technique begins with this whole-body movement. It is used to close distance, create space, or done as a precursor to applying offensive or defensive moves. Even the act of moving the whole body can be used as a weapon as a simple shuffle forward not only closes distance but can also be used to collapse the front knee of an opponent as our knee advances, etc.

**STANCES** can seem boring to practice. They are however a necessary and important piece of the martial art puzzle. Beginners especially need to spend the time learning and practicing them until they are done correctly and without conscious thought.

The key to understanding the importance of stances is in the value of a strong solid physical foundation. This provides the balanced leverage needed for efficient, flexible, and powerful technique. Anything solid needs this type of foundation meaning stances should be taken seriously and learned well, even if they can seem boring.

Stances are places of body posture and leverage from where other movements can be effectively executed. They are developed best with an understanding of each stance's mechanics, which includes foot angles, body posture, weight distribution, applications, and transitions.

Stances are divided here into two main categories with 5 **Position Stances** and 14 **Fighting Stances** (not counting left and right sides). Most stances are learned within the first year of training and it is no coincidence that Black Belts are still doing the same stances as the White Belts, but hopefully much better.

**Position Stances** are common reference points used for class structure (*Natural & Attention*), starting positions for Set & Form practice (*Standing & Meditating*), and provides a bilateral structure that pre-loads the musculoskeletal system for upper body movement practice (*Training Horse*).

These are not fighting postures, although some common elements exist, such as feet rooted, back straight, eyes and mind fixed and focused, muscles pre-loaded, etc.

**Natural    Attention    Standing Horse    Meditating Horse    Training Horse**

The *Natural Stance* has feet about shoulder width apart with hands behind the back (hand holding wrist), or the arms hanging down by the side as one would stand naturally. The posture is relaxed, yet poised and attentive.

The *Attention Stance* has feet together, toes and heels touching, straight arms, hands tight against the sides, fingers together with thumbs slightly bent. Heels together with toes turned out at a 45° is another acceptable method common in the military that gives better balance and allows everyone to have their knees together with straight legs.

The *Standing Horse Stance* keeps the *Attention Stance* foot position, but with the knees slightly bent, and is heels and toes together. The hands are put in front of the chest with a right closed fist against a left open palm (Kenpo Karate or "The Law of the Fist and the Empty Hand"). This is the starting position for some *Movement Routines*.

The *Meditating Horse Stance* keeps the *Standing Horse* hand position except the left foot will step out about shoulder width apart parallel and pointed forward, or toes slightly inward. The knees are bent about halfway to a squat and pushed out slightly. A formal class starts and ends with this posture and it is another starting position for movement routines.

The *Training Horse Stance* keeps the same body position as the *Meditating Horse,* but the fists are pulled back to the waist with palms up, commonly called the "chamber position." This is where upper body basics are traditionally drilled in martial arts. (See *Posture,* the *Mind*).

**Fighting Stances** are the foot alignment, body positioning, and weight transfer postures towards or away from an opponent. Most are temporary or transitional positions used to set up and apply basics.

From the street style perspective, whether in a sport stance or standing naturally the different stances exists at different reference positions on the clock around us. This can also be done using the length of one foot as a template around a 360° circumference, with the other foot as a pivot point to show all the stance positions with the same reference point.

However visualized, there are 8 *Forward Fighting Stances* and 8 complimentary *Reverse Fighting Stances*, reflecting the different angle and weight distribution possibilities.

Note: Whichever leg is towards the opponent determines left or right side of that stance, but this is not universal.

*Forward Fighting Stances* are the most forward point of a stance facing an opponent. The *Reverse Fighting Stances* are the backside of a stance towards an attacker, with mental attention in that direction.

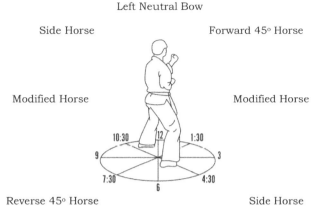

Fighting stances store potential energy for accelerated motion in different directions. These are not static postures but dynamically constructed positions with the potential for constant movement and dynamic change, even if they can sometimes look still ("like a flame that burns only when touched" - Kenpo axiom).

Fighting *Stances* covered are the *Neutral Bow / Reverse Neutral Bow; Wide Kneel / Reverse Wide Kneel; Forward Bow / Reverse Bow; Rear Bow / Modified Forward Bow; Close Kneel / Reverse Close Kneel; Cat / Reverse Cat; Front Twist / Rear Twist; Side Horse, and 45° Horse / Reverse 45° Horse.*

The *Neutral Bow Stance,* or *Fighting Stance,* is a standing posture commonly associated with Boxing. Kenpo is essentially street boxing and calls this positioning a Neutral Bow.

*Neutral* here means not favoring one side or the other, and *Bow* means bent. Mechanics include a 50/50 weight distribution, but this static number is easily misunderstood. Body weight in fighting should never be in the middle for any length of time. Boxer's call it "flatfooted" and others call it "double weighted." Whatever the name, the weight does not stay in the middle.

This posture is dynamically centered with feet and legs springloaded for explosive movement in any direction. The front toe and rear heel align towards an opponent (toe/heel line) with the feet parallel at 45° angles (not always this way in Boxing) with one foot in front and one in back. The rear foot is shifted towards the front half of the medial ball (big toe side). The legs, hips, and shoulders are also at a 45°, so the body is not completely forward or sideways, although the hands, head, and eyes are forward. The front knee covers the groin with the front and rear foot maintaining their relative alignment to prevent someone from getting behind our front foot.

Whether maintained in place or used with a *sparring bounce*, where the weight shifts from foot to foot, the potential for movement in all directions is built into the stance, giving it flexibility.

In street defense this stance is transitional as posing in a sport styles fighting stance gives a street opponent advanced warning that is best kept hidden. A variation of this stance for self-defense has a narrower basc with legs almost straight, open hands up, and palms out. This foot position would be more like a modified horse stance.

The *Reverse Neutral Bow Stance* is the same as the Neutral Bow except against a rear attacker, so the eyes, head, and hands are towards that rear opponent where appropriate defensive and offensive movements can be done (Ram and the Eagle).

The *Wide Kneel Stance* is essentially a lower Neutral Bow where the rear heel is lifted. This stance is used to change levels for a grappling takedown shot, apply the front hand to lower targets, or bob and weave (duck) under an attack (Thundering Fists). Note: When lowering the body one heel is lifted in relation to the height change to maintain balance and posture.

The *Reverse Wide Kneel Stance* is the same as the Wide Kneel Stance except the attacker is behind, so the eyes and hands are towards that rear opponent with the heel closer to the attacker up (Entangled Arm B).

 The *Forward Bow Stance,* or Bow & Arrow Stance, transfers extra weight onto the front leg. The hips, shoulders, and straightened rear knee are turned towards an opponent either square in front or turned as is comfortable for the ankle, with the rear heel on the ground.

This increases depth penetration for the rear hand while providing ground leverage into the attached rear foot. Mechanics on front and rear legs are about a 60/40 weight distribution with the front knee bent over the front toe (bow) and the rear leg straight (arrow). The grounded heel provides a structural brace (Alternating Fists) and preloads the rear legs hip flexors and glutes for forward knee acceleration (Thrusting Thumbs).

The *Reverse Bow Stance* is the same as the Forward Bow except the attacker is in back, so hands and eyes are towards them. This is often the last stance transitioned through before exiting (Twisted Wrist), or at the end of any rear sliding leg sweep (Sweeping the Leg).

The *Rear Bow Stance* shifts the weight back from a neutral bow, like a cat stance, but with the front leg straighter and the foot remaining in place. Its complimentary *Modified Forward Bow Stance* shifts onto the front foot from a *Neutral Bow Stance,* so the shoulders remain more sideways.

The *Close Kneel Stance,* or *'Ducking' Stance,* is to a Forward Bow what a Wide Kneel is to a Neutral Bow. The rear knee is bent with that heel up as needed to match the body height level adjustment as suited to the need.

Mechanics include a 70/30 weight distribution, with this stance common when applying a rear hand weapon where the rear shoulder can turn to become the front shoulder for maximum extension.

It allows for ducking (Dividing the Enemy), changing height levels for grappling (Brown 2nd Sparring #8), transitioning to a downward knee drop (Evading the Club), and provides groin coverage for checking (Twirling Fist).

Note: Turning the rear foot from a neutral bow to a close kneel stance can be done as a ground pivot as the foot ball rotates to lift the heel, which is useful for turning and shifting purposes. Another method is to quickly <u>lift</u> and turn the foot before replanting it on the ground, which is used to push or sprint forward. This method gives the rear striking hand more explosive directional focus and vibrational ground leverage.

The *Reverse Close Kneel Stance* is the same as the *Close Kneel Stance* except the attacker is behind, so the eyes and hands are towards the rear. The raised heel closer to the attacker can then be used to push off for exiting or extended for kicking (Kick into Darkness).

The *Cat Stance* transfers most of the body weight from the front leg to the rear leg. From a neutral bow, draw the front hip back square as the weight transfers. This pulls the front foot about halfway back towards the rear foot.

The static mechanics are a 10/90 weight distribution from front to rear leg, with the rear foot pointed out about 45° while sitting on that rear leg. This is how the weight shifts in transition to stepping back or prior to kicking (Parrying Grab).

The *Reverse Cat Stance* is the same as the *Cat Stance* except the attacker is behind, so the eyes and hands are towards that rear opponent over the un-weighted leg, where rear moves like stomping (Captured Arms) and sweeping (Gripping Wrist) can be done.

The *Front Twist Stance* uses the same upper body posture as the Neutral Bow, except the legs are crossed with knees together for stability and balance. The weight more heavily rests on the front leg where the foot is flat, with the rear heel raised off the ground, like a *Cat Stance* weight distribution.

*Twist* stances can be maneuvered into by stepping (Circling Club), jumping (Tripping Leg), or rotating where the momentum can be used as a weapon (Crossing Grab).

The *Rear Twist Stance* is the same as the Front Twist Stance except the focus of the attacker is in back so the un-weighted foot with heel up is towards an opponent along with the eyes and hands. This is also maneuvered to by stepping (Ascending from Death), jumping (Calming the Club), or rotating (Flashing Fist).

The *Side Horse Stance,* or *Fighting Horse Stance*, has the same alignment as a *Training Horse Stance* except it is turned sideways to put the strongest line towards an opponent. This also presents the narrowest target line, although rear weapons are more limited and it's easier for an opponent to get behind the front foot and leg.

A *Modified Horse Stance* is a *Horse Stance* with staggered feet. It can be used sideways (Twisted Wrist) or front towards an opponent (Tripping Leg).

The *Reverse Side Horse Stance,* or Fighting Horse Stance, is identical to the Side Horse, except the eyes and hands are towards the opposite leg (Shielding Fingers).

The *45º Horse Stance,* or *Front Corner Horse Stance*, moves the feet and body offline at corner angles. With a 12 starting point the feet would end whether stepping forward or back at 1:30(R)/7:30(L) or 10:30(L)/4:30(R). Stepping towards a front opponent is a way to move forward and offline simultaneously (Hand and Shield).

The *Reverse 45º Horse Stance,* or *Rear Corner Horse Stance*, is the backside of a *45º Horse Stance*. With a 12 starting point the feet would end whether stepping forward or back at 10:30(R)/4:30(L) or 1:30(L)/7:30(R). Stepping to this stance is a way to move back and offline simultaneously (Charging Tackle).

**FOOT MANEUVERS** are ways of moving the feet to close or create distance, keep an opponent in front, adjust an angle, or move to a better position. They are divided here into *On-Line Foot Maneuvers* and *Off-Line Foot Maneuvers,* with any able to be under or over exaggerated to take larger or smaller steps. The measurement template used here relates to the body's natural movement range when walking and is intended as a reference point guideline.

These are generally done from a *Neutral Bow Fighting Stance* and often termed "shuffle steps" as a general category but are broken down into specific methods here with precise and descriptive names.

**On-Line Foot Maneuvers** move forwards or backwards while facing a known opponent while covering 4 different depth distances. Those are *No-Step* (in-place), *Half-Step, Whole-Step,* and *Two-Step Maneuvers,* with any larger distance incorporating one or more of these in combination.

*No-Step Foot Maneuvers* do not travel but are done in-place. They are the *Sparring Bounce* and methods of *Switching* the feet using one of six methods. Those are *Defensive, Defensive Reverse, Offensive, Offensive Reverse, With-a-Hop,* and *Jump Reverse.* Although explained and learned mechanically they are done fluidly and quickly when utilized.

The *Sparring Bounce* either shifts the body weight from one foot to the other with the un-weighted foot making light ground contact, i.e., tapping, or both feet lightly bouncing up and down in-place. The speed and deception of other foot maneuvers are enhanced when done from this maneuver, with a whole array of fakes and feints that can stem from this motion.

The *Defensive Switch* happens by moving the front foot back first (defensive) so the two heels form the letter V, then what was the rear foot stepping forward to become the new front foot (Circling Elbow).

The *Defensive Reverse Switch* is the first of 3 reverse switches where the back is turned briefly, i.e., spinning. For this, the front foot moves back to, towards, or past (gauging distance) the rear foot toe-to-toe (defensive), then while looking over the opposite shoulder what was the rear foot then moves forward into the opposite side stance. It can be used as a position adjustment to kick (Thrusting Palm), buckle (Alternating Fist), or sweep (Cradling the Baby).

Note: When turning the back to spin around the eyes should stay parallel with the ground and are the last to leave the target yet the first to arrive on the target after turning around and is commonly referred to as "spotting."

The *Offensive Switch* is done by moving the rear foot forward, toe to toe, with the front foot, then what was the front foot will step back away to the opposite side fighting stance (Circling Elbow).

The *Offensive Reverse Switch* is the second of 3 reverse (spinning) switches where the initial step moves the rear foot forwards to, towards, or past (gauging distance) the front foot heel-to-heel (offensive), then what was the front foot can move away ending into the opposite side stance (Parting Arms).

The *Switch with a Hop* is when both feet are slightly lifted simultaneously while changing front foot to back and back to front in the air ending in the opposite stance (Sleeper). An effort to not jump too high is recommended so an opponent cannot time that switch as easily.

The *Jump Reverse Switch* is the third of 3 reverse (spinning) switches where both feet are lifted to jump but the body turns around backwards towards the opponent (Sweeping the Leg). This method can incorporate the other two methods, but with a jump while then also looking over the opposite shoulder.

*Half-Step Foot Maneuvers* travel about one-half step forwards or backwards with 3 primary methods that each have a distinct weight shift, and one with a different timing count than the other two. These are types of "shuffle steps" but more precisely are described here as *Step-Drag, Push-Drag,* and *Pull-Drag.*

The *Step-Drag* is when one foot travels a half-step away from the other foot, moving forwards or backwards, and then the other foot moves the same distance to catch up, like an accordion or slinky (Shielding Fingers). Doing this 2-count maneuver with a jab-cross would have the jab occur on the first step followed by the cross as the back-foot drags or slides forward.

Note: When shuffling forward to jab the heel of the front foot <u>does not</u> hit the ground first. The step goes directly to the ball side of the foot, unlike a normal walking step. Planting the heel before rolling onto the toe is an inefficient fighting step for this purpose.

The *Push-Drag* is different from the step-drag in that both feet move forwards or backwards simultaneously to close or create distance. This 1-count maneuver pushes the weight from one foot onto the other while traveling and is often done from a *sparring bounce.* The weighted foot pushes meaning the back-foot pushes forward onto the front foot to travel forward, and the front foot pushes onto the back foot to travel backwards.

The *Pull-Drag* is also usually done from a *sparring bounce* and happens when one foot is jumped off of and then is also the foot landed on. This is a 1-count maneuver and is essentially a skip that can be used to travel forward or backward.

This can be done off the back foot to travel forwards, where it looks like the un-weighted foot has been pulled in the maneuver's direction, hence the name. It can however also be done on the front foot as in a leaping lead hand backknuckle or a rear hand 'Superman' punch.

*Whole-Step Foot Maneuvers* are those steps that travel the full length of a fighting stances depth. The two footwork methods used to cover this distance are the *Step-Thru* and *Drag-Step.*

The *Step-Thru* is essentially a walking step from one side of a fighting stance to the other where the rear foot will step all the way forward or the front foot will step all the way back. It is used to close or create distance and often pre-loads powerful kicks.

Note: To move forward the rear foot pushes to accelerate the front foot pivot, or that front foot can pre-step to help turn the rear hip and ease pressure on the front knee when doing a *Roundhouse* or *Side Thrust Kick*, while perhaps also stepping to a new location. When moving the front foot back, momentum is created that helps the rear ball pivot. Heel pivoting would be for a specialized use.

The *Drag-Step* occurs by moving one foot to the other then moving that other foot away. To travel forward the rear foot will step forward to join the front foot before that front foot will step forward away, or backwards the front foot will step back to join the rear foot before that rear foot steps away.

The rear leg moving forward is often used to close distance and add momentum to a lead leg kick where the lead leg moving backwards creates distance and can be used for lead hand counter punching. Combining the *step-drag, push-drag,* and *pull-drag,* a skilled fighter can vary timing and distance to set-up and possibly confuse an opponent.

Note: The middle point of this maneuver is never static but more like *clacker balls* where one leg seems to launch the movement of the other. It is generally done as a 2-count maneuver but more advanced as a 1-count.

*Two-Step Foot Maneuvers* are when steps travel the length of two full stance depths. This can be done by crossing in front or behind the base foot before that base foot "steps out" to a fighting stance, yet two-steps closer or further away from where started. The two primary methods used are the *Front Crossover Step-Out* and the *Rear Crossover Step-Out*.

The *Front-Crossover Step-Out* travels from a fighting stance with the rear foot stepping forward in front of and past the front foot, like an exaggerated *drag-step*. This movement transitions through a *twist stance* with the weight shifting onto the stepping foot, so the opposite foot can then also step forward.

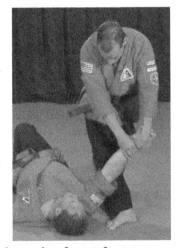

Aside from closing or creating distance this maneuvers offensive applications include applying the shin as a weapon (Returning the Gift), an inverted side kick (Deflecting Pendulum), stomp kick (Tripping Leg), Pushing Sweep (Circling Club), or Pulling sweep (Twirling Fist).

The *Rear-Crossover Step-Out,* from a fighting stance has the front foot move to step behind and past the rear foot, like an exaggerated *drag-step,* where it also transitions through a *twist stance* with the weight shifting so the opposite foot can step back. This rear crossover is often used as an exit maneuver, with the step out also able to sweep (Glancing Palm) or kick (Fatal Variation).

Note: Both crossover steps can move in the opposite direction but would travel at a slight angle due to the heel-toe alignment of a fighting stance. *Combination Methods* are ways *On-Line Foot Maneuvers* are combined to suit a situation, with the flexibility to under or over-exaggerate distance. Following are a few examples of the many ways to combine them with striking. These are often set up with a *sparring bounce*, body fakes and feints, along with rhythm and timing breaks (See *Sport Fighting* chapter).

*Push-Drag / Step-Drag (one step)*
Boxing Technique: Lead hand jab (push-drag) / lead hand jab (step) / straight rear hand punch (drag)

*Step-Drag / Step-Thru (one and one-half steps)*
Kickboxing Technique: Lead hand Jab (step), rear hand straight punch (drag) / rear leg knee, front, or roundhouse kick (step-thru)

MMA Technique: Lead hand jab (step) / rear overhand punch (drag) / change levels for a takedown (step-thru)

*Drag-Step / Step-Drag (one and one-half steps)*
Point Fighting Technique: Lead hand backknuckle or fake (drag) / lead leg wheel kick or side kick (step) / backknuckle head (step) / reverse punch ribs (drag)

KB or MMA Technique: Lead leg inside leg kick (drag rear) / lead hand punch (step down front) / 2nd lead hand punch (step front again) / rear hand punch (drag rear)

*Pull-Drag / Front Crossover Step Out (two and one-half steps)*
Point Fighting Technique: Lead leg wheel kick (pull-drag) / reverse punch as the lead foot steps down / lead hand backknuckle (front crossover) / reverse punch moving past (step out) – aka "blitz"

**Off-Line Foot Maneuvers** travel sideways or change direction while maintaining a toe-heel line towards a current or new opponent(s). Attacker(s) in the self-defense context can approach from directions around us making 4 major methods of adjustment needed. The *Side-Step-Drag travels sideways,* but the *Rear-Side Turn & Front-Side Turn* adjust 90° with the *Cover-Step* 180°. Both are further divided into offensive and defensive methods.

Note: All maneuvers are explained and taught within a normal stepping range and to a precise direction, but all are flexible to fit 360° around us. When changing direction, the focus order is mind-eyes-hands-feet as the mind must realize the threat, the eyes must see, the upper body begins to adjust, and the feet begin moving to face it.

The *Side-Step-Drag* is a method for moving left or right. Regardless of which foot is in front, when moving to the left the left foot moves first followed by the right foot moving over to realign the fighting stance. When moving right, the right foot moves first and then the left foot follows in that direction.

This can be used to sidestep an attack, adjust to a better position, or to keep an opponent in front of us. Sport fighters, in an enclosed environment like a ring or cage, often use this type of move to limit the space an opponent can move into, aka "cutting off the ring."

The *Rear Turn* as a standard *Basic* adjusts 90º to the rear/back side of the body so if the left leg were in front facing 12 then look over the left shoulder to 9, with two possible stepping options.

First, the *Defensive Rear Turn* creates space by moving the right foot away, towards 3, pivoting on the balls of the feet to face 9 in a left fighting stance. This could also be done from a right fighting stance to 12 by moving the left foot to end facing 3 in a right fighting stance.

The second is the Offensive Rear Turn to close distance, so from a left fighting stance to 12 the left foot moves towards 9 ending, with a right heel pivot, finishing in a left fighting stance to 9. This can also be done from a right fighting stance to 12 moving to face 3.

The *Front Turn* adjusts 90º to the front side of the body, so if the left leg were in front facing 12, looking to the right towards 3 would be the direction of this turn with two possible stepping options.

First, the *Defensive Front Turn* creates space by moving the left foot back towards 9 to end in a right fighting stance to 3. This can also be done with the right foot in front by moving the right foot back to 3 ending in left stance facing 9.

The second is the *Offensive Front Turn* to close distance by stepping right towards 3 to a right fighting stance. This can also be done with the right foot in front by stepping left to face at 9.

The *Cover-Step* adjusts 180º so if the left foot were in front facing 12 then this would be an adjustment method used to face 6, with one of two options.

First, the *Defensive Cover Step* creates space by moving, from a left fighting stance to 12 for example, the left foot across the 12-6 stance line, towards 3, then pivoting on the balls of both feet to face 6 in a right fighting stance. This can also be done from a right fighting stance to 12 by moving the right foot over to a 6 to end in a left fighting stance to 6.

The second is the *Offensive Cover Step* used to close distance, from a left fighting stance for example, by moving our right foot back across our stance line, towards 9, pivoting on the right ball and left heel to face 6 in a right fighting stance. This can also be done with the opposite foot in front, ending in a left fighting stance to 6.

*Combination Methods* are ways *Off-Line Foot Maneuvers* can be put together. These can also include *On-Line methods* for even greater footwork flexibility, with examples here from a left neutral bow fighting stance (LNB) to 12.

*Defensive Cover* with *Defensive Rear Turn (Defensive Rear Cover-Turn)*
Left steps forward across 12-6 & 3-9 stance lines 270° to 9 RNB.

*Offensive Cover* with *Offensive Rear Turn (Offensive Rear Cover-Turn)*
Right foot will step back across the 12-6 & 9-3 lines, 90° to 9 RNB.

*Defensive Cover* with *Defensive Front Turn (Defensive Front Cover-Turn)*
Right foot will step back across stance line, towards 9, or 90° to a 3 LNB. This is a common boxing pivot to change angles, often done with a lead hook.

*Offensive Cover* with *Offensive Front Turn (Offensive Front Cover-Turn)*
Left foot will step forward across stance line, 90° to a 3 LNB.

*Defensive Cover-Step* with a *Left Side Step-Drag*
Exaggerated left then right step over the 12-6 stance line, to a 6 RNB.

*Offensive Cover-Step* with *Right Side Step-Drag*
Exaggerated right then left step back over the 12-6 stance line, to a 6 RNB.

# BODY MANEUVERS
## Standing Evasion – Traveling Maneuvers
## Falling – Rolling – Ground Maneuvers

The ability to use the whole body simultaneously as one unit to avoid attack, close distance, or to prevent injury after tripping can be a study all its own. Four main categories covered here are *Standing Evasion, Traveling Maneuvers, Falling & Rolling Maneuvers,* and *Ground Maneuvers.*

**STANDING EVASION** is the upper body movement generally associated with Boxing. The individual moves are *Riding, Slipping, Bobbing, Weaving,* with *Turning* and *Rolling* as variations of those. All are generally done in combination or follow each other, and they contain the potential to provide counterpunch leverage from the completed motion, as used in Boxing.

*Riding* is when the head, shoulders, and/or torso move away from a striking attack to completely avoid it or to absorb an unavoidable impact. A slight withdrawal of the head or body often accompanied with a weight shift and possibly a step accomplishes this.

*Slipping* is moving the head and shoulders to the side, off the path of a straight-line attack. The weapon is often intercepted as an added layer of security, with immediate follow ups to prevent the need for additional defense (Compulsive Kneel).

From a fighting stance this is done so the weight shift to either leg brings the opposite shoulder forward. A slip to the left puts more weight on the left foot with the right shoulder more forward, where a slip to the right puts more weight on the right foot with the left shoulder more forward. This posture also preloads the body to counter punch. If the left foot is in front, then a left slip pre-loads a left punch (often a hook) and a right slip pre-loads a right punch (often a straight right).

Note: It is generally better to slip outside a straight punch. Ideally, slip right outside a left punch and left outside a right punch. This outside arm position is away from their opposite hand and on the weaker side of their muscle structure. If caught at the more undesirable inside arm position, then *Weaving* can be used to move under their arm to the better outside arm position.

*Bobbing* is when the legs bend, so the head and shoulders drop, perhaps to duck a punch. When lowering the body from a fighting stance the rear heel should be lifted, i.e., *Wide Kneel Stance,* to keep the body from being rear side heavy. This is also used to change levels for grappling, with the standing up motion used to accelerate uppercut punches, elbows, knees, etc.

*Weaving* is when the weight shifts from one leg to the other as the head forms the letter "U" by going down with the weight towards one leg then shifting the weight to the other leg before coming up. It often follows *Slipping*, as mentioned above, and is combined with *Bobbing*.

*Turning* is a type of *Riding* where the shoulders rotate away from contact using the waist (not to be confused with Foot Maneuver "Turning").

*Rolling* is a combination of *Riding, Slipping, Bobbing, Weaving,* and *Turning*, often against a flurry of punches (Look-up Boxer Nicolino Locche).

Note: *Standing Evasion,* whether individually or in combination are a refined skill that requires great timing, positional awareness, and an understanding of striking angles. This takes much practice and is best learned from a knowledgeable Boxing coach.

**TRAVELING MANEUVERS** are methods to cover greater distances than *Foot Maneuvers*. These involve explosively leaving the ground, often punching the ground with the foot ball for acceleration, to *Hop, Skip, Jump,* and/or *Leap*. They are done individually or in combination. Semantics aside, the names used here are associated with a specific movement type and dimensional body distance.

*Hopping,* sometimes called "bouncing" or "springing," is done by pushing up and down on both feet simultaneously and by alternating more weight on one foot than the other, aka "sparring bounce." This can enhance and speed up other footwork and is used to break rhythm.

*Skipping* is done when the same foot touches the ground at least two times in a row. It covers from a half-step to a full-steps distance, depending on leg explosiveness and the intended distance.

The *Pull-Drag* uses this *Skipping* maneuver, usually forwards, off the rear foot with a front leg attack (flip kick), or off the front foot to accelerate a lead or rear hand attack (e.g., Superman punch). These can be alternated and repeated to break rhythm and to close more distance.

*Jumping* involves leaving the ground with both feet simultaneously to cover one to two whole steps of distance. Moves like a jumping side kick, flying knee, lunging backknuckle, or jump spin 180°/360°/540° kicks use this maneuver.

*Leaping* is when both feet leave the ground launched by one leg. Examples are a step-thru jump spin kick or leaping onto a downed opponent (Leap of Death), or even a headfirst dive roll.

**FALLING – ROLLING – GROUND MANEUVERS** are how the body interacts safely with the ground, and how to get up from the ground if in a hostile interaction. These can be done on purpose (intentional) as in dropping under an opponent, or a dive roll to avoid danger or into an attacker's legs. They can also happen unexpectedly (unintentional) as in tripping, being tripped, or thrown.

These all presume a ground interaction from a human height level as even great technique will not help if falling out of an airplane or off a 10-story building, other than the nice chalk outline. These techniques are the difference between getting up unscathed and a trip to the hospital or worse. This is a life skill since falling also happens outside of the fighting environment.

The purpose of these techniques is to minimize damage from a falling or rolling event, as the ground is a relentless adversary. Ideally no damage is done, but the body part protection priority is first the head, then spine, internal organs, and limbs last. No damage is best but it's better to have a broken arm than a broken head.

Note: Our instinct when the body is unexpectedly accelerating towards the ground in any direction is to reach with the hands. This often results in broken wrists, so it is a tendency that needs to be trained out of and replaced with good technique where no damage is the more likely outcome.

*Falling* and *Rolling* should be learned from a knowledgeable teacher and practiced on a soft surface (mat, grass, etc.) and initially practiced as close to the ground as possible (from the knees or while sitting) then brought up to standing as confidence and skill improve. Methods to maneuver while lying or sitting on the ground and how to get up safely are covered in the next section under *Ground Maneuvers.*

**Falling** is done to any of the 3 major *Rear, Side,* or *Front* directions with two main methods practiced in martial arts. The first is used in grappling styles where throws are common and the second a result of tripping, as can happen more in the street context.

If thrown the body generally moves perpendicular towards the ground, like a helicopter landing. In this case the body contact surface should be simultaneously dispersed over a larger area and onto the more padded body parts. This method is commonly called a "breakfall," with timing and the order of contact points a key component.

To fall safely in this way the body aligns with the ground to disperse impact over a larger body surface area, and timed so the forearm(s) and possibly feet/legs hit, slap, or roll into the ground just ahead of the torso. This slows the body mass in preparation for an inevitable impact.

The other type of fall is when the body is when the body can blend or move diagonally onto the ground after tripping, more like an airplane landing. This type of fall allows for the body surface to contact the ground like a wave dispersing on the sand on a beach. This is used for *Rear Falls* and *Side Falls*, where the bent knees are then pulled towards the chest, so the torso is round which helps the body better blend with the hard ground.

Whatever the falls trajectory, the head and neck must be protected from a concussion or whiplash injury. This is done by tucking the chin, with teeth together, when falling to the *Back* or *Side*, and turned to one side when falling to the *Front*.

It is also critical that when the body hits the ground the breath is pushed out using the "reverse breath," technique (see 'Breath' in *Mind*) so the wind is not knocked out by the impact.

*Rear Falls* go to the middle of the back using either method described above, with the two arms simultaneously contacting the ground on each side of the body.

*Side Falls* can also be done at different trajectory's like the rear fall, but to one side of the back (not the lateral side of the body however) with both arms on the same side of this fall. The right-side fall would have the right arm extended lower off the hip with the left hand covering the head higher up, like a universal check. The arms are switched if falling to the left.

Note: When falling vertically (helicopter) to the side the arms make contact first then the body mass is absorbed towards the back of the scapula and lat muscles. The diagonal fall (airplane) arms contacts, the ground at thigh/hip level first and then rolls up the back to shoulder level on that side.

*Front Falls* are done face first and always use the "breakfall" method. This is one of the scarier falls to learn from standing but with good technique is very survivable. When falling forward both forearms, not palms, reach for, and attack the ground to hit and absorb the initial impact as the head is turned to one side, and all with a "reverse breath" pushing the air out.

*Dropping* is an intentional method of falling using the rear or side method either in place, traveling forward, or while moving backwards. Correct falling technique is still required but the intent uses this to purposefully attack or defend.

Offensively, this maneuver can be used to slide forward, like sliding into second base, under an opponent ending in a side fall position, but with the bottom arm higher than the head. Defensively, this maneuver is used to counter a high kick by falling under the opponent's kicking leg. In all cases an up kick into their groin, body or face can be done, or their legs attacked.

**Rolling** techniques are done in lieu of falling, where possible, as the recovery is built into most rolling motions. It is best to learn rolling close to the ground starting on the knees or sitting until the technique and confidence improve to where standing and then perhaps even diving can be done safely.

The *Forward Roll,* or *shoulder roll* in the martial arts context is designed for hard unpadded surface contact, unlike a "gymnastics" roll on a mat. For this to occur with minimal damage the ground contacts the body from the back of one shoulder diagonally down to the opposite glute muscle.

Contact to these larger padded muscle structures protects the head, neck, spine, and tailbone from ground contact. The hands and arms encircle the head to expand the surface protection area while providing a contact point to help slow the body into the roll. Whichever side the roll starts the rear shin tucks behind the front knee where it helps transition the body back to standing. A right side forward roll starts and ends with the right leg in front, and vice versa.

To stay on the ground, i.e., breakfall, at the end of a forward roll to either side, the sole of the top more forward foot is used to plant aggressively into the ground as the lower leg is bent and tucked behind the knee of that top leg. This prevents the momentum from carrying the roll up to the feet, should that be the goal.

Many Jiu Jitsu and Judo practitioners extend the bottom leg to become the more forward leg to help stop this rolls momentum. This method works fine on a mat so is an acceptable technique for those applications, but in a parking lot or on a hard ground surface the lateral malleolus of that ankle could slam into the ground where it might be shattered.

The *Backward Roll* is like the *Forward Roll* except in reverse, like watching it on rewind. From a standing position, the rear lower leg is put on the ground with foot and knee sideways, then the body to ground contact line is from one glute diagonally across the back up to the opposite shoulder, i.e., step back left, squat, rear lower leg on ground, sit onto left glute, kick right leg to roll over right shoulder. The bottom right arm would be at the chest with the top left hand reaching over the right shoulder to protect the head, both then helping to push the body up to standing.

Another version of this roll is done when sitting with the hips square where the roll is done by kicking either leg over the opposite shoulder, i.e., already sitting, or perhaps after squatting, then rolling as the right leg kicks over the left shoulder, or the left kicks over the right. This is not the roll to do from a standing fighting type stance.

The *Barrel Roll* is a specialty roll where the entire torso rolls parallel over the ground simultaneously. It can be done with or without opponent contact, or for street use this roll can be done into an attacker's legs, or while going to the ground with another body, as in countering a headlock takedown (Pinch from Death C).

**Ground Maneuvers** are how to move the body when sitting or lying on the ground and how to get up safely. These maneuvers include the *Hip Escape, Recover Position, Moving Recover Position,* and *Recover.*

The *Hip Escape* (aka "Shrimping") is done while lying flat on the ground (body in letter 'I' shape) by lifting the hips and pressing the feet (or a foot) into the ground to move the hips and buttocks while pivoting on one shoulder (body in letter 'L' shape), then adjusting to the opposite side (letter 'I') and doing it again (to letter 'L') repeating this process as needed to escape be where intended. This maneuver can also be repeated to one side over and over to move away from just that one side, where it looks more like a "Snake Crawl", i.e., slithering.

The *Recover Position* is a ground posture that provides a way to get up safely while moving away from an opponent who may be standing over us. It is used after falling or can start from a seated position on the ground. This technique minimizes exposure to kicks and punches against an upright opponent from a downed position, until able to *Recover* up to a standing posture.

Sit on one glute with that bottom leg extended, yet active to check or attack, and with the same side palm flat on the ground. The opposite foot is flat, knee bent up, with that same side arm up for defense. If in danger on the ground this position is adjusted to either side or can be alternated.

The *Moving Recover Position* or "Snail Crawl" uses the recover position to crawl along the ground on one hand and opposite foot. This is done until an opening to stand or *Recover* presents itself.

The *Recover* happens from a successful *Recover Position*, or after *Moving*, to get up from the ground efficiently and safely. With the right hand and left foot posted on the ground, for example, the body is lifted on those two points then the bottom right leg bends and slides behind and past the left posted leg and right hand, making a triangle on the ground with the hand in the middle. Then straighten up and move left foot to right then right foot away (drag step). Switch everything for the other side.

Summary Note: Like most basics, *Body Maneuvers* can be combined in limitless ways. One could *Slip* a punch, *Leap* into a *Forward Roll* (dive roll) ending in a *Side Fall* (breakfall) then adjust to a *Recover Position* and use the *Moving Recover* to create space before *Recovering* up to the feet.

## BODY EXTENSION MOVEMENTS
### Blocks, Parries & Checks, Punches & Strikes, Kicks & Balance Disruptions

These are attack and defense *Basics* where the hands, arms, feet, and legs travel with velocity away from the body, and/or return after extending. They attack and impact targets or selected weapons to intercept, damage, affect balance, and/or adjust a position.

These are the *Blocks, Parries, Checks, Punches, Strikes, Kicks & Balance Disruption* techniques that primarily engage the pushing muscles. They follow linear and circular paths singularly or in combination both simultaneously and sequentially.

Striking arts are known for these movements where body parts become accelerated projectiles with the hands and feet especially adept at forming and fitting different targets and angles, see *Contouring* in the *Mind*. Striking requires space to accelerate and extend movements, contrasted with grappling where a primary goal is to eliminate space by contracting the body.

### BLOCKS, PARRIES & CHECKS

These are methods for preventing a potential weapon from impacting its intended target. Intercepting an incoming weapon is most often done with the hands, arms, or legs to block, parry, or check, although other durable body areas are also available.

Four things can happen if someone is trying to hit you, one bad, you get hit, with the other three ways of defending. The target can be moved out of the way as was covered under *Body Maneuvers,* there is an option to attack first covered under *jamming,* and the third method uses a more durable body part to *block, parry,* or *check* a punch, strike, or kick.

**Blocking** is an impact-oriented defense done by attacking an incoming weapon at mostly perpendicular angles to intercept it in flight. This requires timing to stop the weapon or move it off its intended path by catching it before its point of contact, or by absorbing the impact on a more durable body part. Blocking is usually done with the hands, arms, or legs, although the shoulders, hips, and even the frontal lobe of the head can be used.

**Parrying** is a subtler defensive method that uses the more tactile hands to attach then redirect or ride an attack away from its intended target. The major difference between a block and a parry is the *angle of contact.* A block intercepts an attack directly, at about 90°, where a parry matches and attaches to the angle of attack to create a slight deflection past the target.

**Checking** is done against potential or anticipated weapons, whether used intentionally or unintentionally by position, pressure, control, or creating an angle that weakens the threat.

**BLOCKS** defend the unavoidable attack by impacting the weapon in flight. Karate styles originally developed these for non-sport use so aggressive arm blocking methods evolved. By comparison, sport fight blocking tends to catch and absorb impact, or hook a limb to scoop it away as a redirection.

**Arm Blocks** emphasize points of contact through the two arm rotations of inward and outward. Circling the arm inward moves through the 3 primary blocking contact vectors of inward, half-downward, and outside downward, where circling the arm outward moves through the 4 primary blocking contact vectors of upward, outward, extended outward, and inside downward.

The 5 major emphasized blocking directions in many Karate styles are *Inward, Outward, Upward, Inside Downward* and *Outside Downward*. The Kenpo *Blocking Set,* or *Star Block,* practices transitioning between these different directions and includes the *Push-Down* checking motion. If superimposed over each other, these blocks form a house that surrounds the body from top of head to bottom of groin, and even the back when the hands chamber.

Individual blocks can also have multiple variations and co-dependencies. For example, the *Outward Block* can utilize 3 different forearm rotations and the *Outside Downward Block* is generally done in combination with an opposite hand *Inside Downward Block.*

Although described here for a blocking purpose these motions help to index *Master Key Movements* of the arms where a motion can have many applications. For example, with a different intention an *Inward Block* motion could become an inward hammerfist, handsword, forearm, or elbow strike.

The alignment structure is crucial to accomplish the blocking task of not getting hit so the *Inward, Extended Outward,* and *Upward Blocks* are applied with the elbow anterior to the shoulder while aligning the humerus bone perpendicular to the attack with the hand slightly in front of the elbow to engage the tricep muscles for pushing. This creates an angle of deflection along the forearm to absorb contact and perhaps redirect an attack. This redirection can be used to unbalance, change posture, and allows for easier transitions to manipulation, and counter attacking options.

A strong attacking block successfully applied can cause pain and injury while possibly deterring an opponent, making these strong blocks especially useful for children to end a schoolyard fight.

Blocks are initially learned and practiced in traditional karate styles from a *Training Horse Stance*. This practice method helps isolate each basic from a balanced, bi-lateral, and pre-loaded body posture. This helps build whole body strength and upper body coordination. Interestingly, it also simulates the transition from the hands relaxed down by the sides to a hands up position as would be more likely to occur in a street defense situation.

When alternating blocks through the centerline, as with the *outward* and *upward* blocks, the arms cross forming an "X" or *double factor*, with the arm applying the block in front of, or outside the retracting arm. The lower *outside downward block* when combined with an *inside downward block* form a double factor that looks more like the number "4." Understanding how to use these overlaps within the scheme of blocking can add layers of sophistication to their use.

Having the blocking arm on the outside of the retracting arm helps keep it from getting trapped against the body by that other arm, and since most blocking, parrying, and checking is done with the lead or closest hand to an opponent this also translates to a fighting stance posture.

This arm overlap provides a counterbalancing motion and helps develop coordination on both body sides for simultaneous and sequential movement. Perhaps more importantly this trains the body and helps the mind find reattachment points for proprioception awareness and the reapplication of muscular strength.

When applied on a body this provides backup and reinforcement for the arms with the potential to be used offensively to trap, manipulate, and dislocate an attacking weapon caught between those blocking arms.

For example, a left inward block to the lateral elbow of a right punch together <u>with</u> a right outward block glancing thru the medial wrist (Flashing Fist), or a left inward block outside the right wrist, briefly holding, as a right outward block hits the lateral elbow (Compulsive Kneel). Both are ways to tweak the attacking limb using *double factor* blocking in this more sophisticated way.

The contact area of the forearm for blocking is from the hand to the elbow. More acceleration exists closer to the hand with more resistance closer to the elbow. The two forearm bones can be applied in four major ways as each bone can be used individually or side by side. The single bone block is where the opposite bone rides behind the applied radius or ulna bone, and the double bone block applies these bones side by side, using either inside or outside forearm. Subtle contact angle variations also exist that can be felt at different edges of the bone(s)

Each of these different blocking surfaces has advantages and disadvantages, depending on the attack vector, direction of block, body angle, and surface being blocked. These will be discussed under each individual block.

An *Inward Block* uses the hand and bent arm in front of the shoulder towards the body centerline. The hand can hammer using the single ulna bone side or be palm forward to use the medial double-bone block. These can work to passively absorb impact or more aggressively redirect a motion off its line of travel, or jam, often with both arms. The diagonal arm angle forms a wedge that can be over or under exaggerated to stop or deflect over an attack to affect balance and setup additional follow-ups.

Note: A traditional horse stance teaching method positions the fist with palm forward outside the shoulder line then rotates the hand while moving the arm inward across the centerline. This exaggeration is designed to help beginners learn hand rotation and feel preloaded power but, in my opinion, it is not good body mechanics to open the shoulder as it tracks an incorrect muscular motion for that application and can develop into an inefficient habit.

The *Inward Block* path should start with the bent elbow, hand up, in front of the shoulder, then travel forward like stabbing a knife into a tree while aligning the shoulder towards the attack. The reason for blocking is to first intercept an attack with any additional damage a bonus. Blocking should therefore move through efficient paths of motion from the beginning of training.

The sport fighting version of this *Inward Block* is more aptly called a "catch" like catching a baseball (but then dropping it). This method is used because of the snapping return of punches and then rapid follow-up combinations used in sport fighting.

In Boxing, a straight <u>left</u> punch at face height is defended with a <u>right</u> hand catch at the outside of that hand with a straight <u>right</u> punch at face height defended with a <u>left</u> hand catch at the outside of that hand. The hands do not cross the centerline to catch high punches as that would leave the face open to an opposite hand punch. Care should also be taken not to over catch as a skilled fighter will use that by faking a punch to create the opening left by the exaggerated catch attempt and then fill that gap with a successful punch.

Note: The only dangerous punch vector is where it is aligned and intended to hit, so it's best to defend by redirecting around the hand, while perhaps causing a direction change. This requires timing, but a straight punch redirected at the outside little finger knuckle drives the hand slightly downward and inward, moving it offline while cancelling the opposite hand.

The *Outward Block* has three versions, the regular *Outward Block, Outward Hooking Block,* and *Extended Outward Block*. All travel from the upper torso centerline towards the outside torso edge and are differentiated primarily by hand rotation. This rotation changes the muscular alignment of the forearm and body giving each its own value.

The regular *Outward Block* ends with the thumb side of the fist facing out with the single radius bone aligned outward into the blocking action, like when flexing the bicep muscle. This exaggerated hand rotation helps the upper arm fit tightly to the side of the body, where engaged with the lat and pec muscles form a powerful wedge.

This torso connection makes the arm structurally solid against impact and preloads the hand for a powerful extension motion with rotation, or the arm can travel away from the torso to clear a grabbing attack (Ram and the Eagle). Its use is limited however by the sensitive radial arm nerve and extensor forearm muscles vulnerability to heavy or sharp direct impact.

The *Outward Hooking Block* uses the outside forearm with the two wrist bones side by side as a lateral two-bone surface into the blocking action.

This provides more contact area and enables the wrist to arch over an attacking weapon for an added element of control (Calming the Club). This flex also engages the forearm extensor muscles to further increase the strength and durability of the contact surface.

Boxers and kickboxers often use this version of an *Outward Block*, without the wrist arch, to block punches and kicks with little adjustment. This structure is enhanced by placing the palm side of the hand on either the frontal or parietal skull bones, while tucking the chin, to provide a strong surface to absorb impact on the arms and shoulders.

The *Extended Outward Block* is a strong block that reaches out by rotating the palm forward, looks like knocking on a door. The elbow is out diagonally from the ribs with the hand slightly forward of the elbow, and the wrist slightly bent to engage the forearm flexor muscles, with the contact point at the inside angle of the ulna bone. It is used in self-defense against circular attacks (Hand of Destruction) and can be combined with the opposite arm inward to defend heavier strikes (The Nutcracker).

The *Upward Block* uses the same structural mechanics as the *Extended Outward Block* but at top of the forehead height and slightly in front. The arm ends as an angled frame around one side of the head, with the hand higher than the elbow, like an umbrella or 'A' frame roof deflects rain and snow.

It starts at the centerline, palm facing us to allow the elbow to remain down, and then the hand is rotated 180º to a palm out position at the top of the block. This motion creates a strong deflecting angle that wedges up and through a downward attack (Evading the Club) or clears a higher positioned obstacle (Blinding Vice).

Note: The Upward Block as a Horse Stance basic in Mr. Parkers Book shows the arms passing side by side. I prefer the arms cross as they pass ("X" or "double factor"). This allows for better vision, a stronger wedge angle for the arms, a two-arm reinforced support structure, along with double contact capability for defensive timing and offensive trapping.

Note: Poor body mechanics occur when the palm rotates too early causing the elbow to move away from the torso thereby losing structural integrity through the blocking path and is easily overpowered. The elbow needs to stay down to create the wedge structure needed to push up through a strong attack.

The *Inside Downward Block* is done across the body centerline, with the arm straight and most strongly applied with the palm facing out, and often used in transition to an *Outside Downward Block.*

The *Outside Downward Block,* from a training horse, starts with the bent arm in front of the stomach then travels down and out using the arms hammerfist side against a lower attack. It is often preceded by an *Inside Downward Block*, i.e., double factor, before sliding down that straight arm rotating the ulnar side of the arm into the blocking motion.

This method is used primarily in self-defense against a committed low front kick where this block redirects while hammering the attacking leg then, at least in Kenpo, often followed with a groin kick (Thrusting Palm) or strike (Rolling Fists) before their foot hits the ground.

This is not the downward blocking method used in sport fighting as a smart opponent would draw the blocking hand down with a low fake kick then kickup to the head. For sport, the better low blocks are done with the legs or a hook and parry motion using the arms against an extended straight-line kick.

Note: A specialty downward block in Kenpo is called a *Half-Downward Block* using the forearm horizontally at waist height to push down a low attack without pushing it to the side (Alternating Fists).

**Leg Blocks** are generally used to defend low kicks with the knee, shin, or thigh. The *Knee/Shin Block,* or *Knee Check*, is a common low block intending to use the knee, but often using the shin. The technique is to point the bent knee and femur bone at the incoming attack. This is the same type of structural alignment as the humerus arm bone uses when arm blocking, especially the *extended outward block*.

The foot is angled slightly behind the knee to focus the knee but forming a deflecting wedge towards the attack. The foot is flexed to engage the anterior tibialis, i.e., outer shin muscles, for extra padding.

A hard hit taken by an incoming kick against this knee angle could cause severe damage to the weapon, or at least discourage further attacks. If the knee misses, then the weapon can slide down along the padded lower leg.

Note: In Muay Thai this block is combined with a same side outward arm block, to build a wall on that side of the body. The medial corner of the elbow is ideally placed at the outside edge of the thigh for additional arm structural support. The non-blocking opposite side free hand is extended to help maintain distance.

The *Thigh Block* is also used in kickboxing against a low round kick and is where the front thigh muscles are lined up and flexed into an oncoming kick attack to jam it as the weight is put forward onto the ball side of the foot. The non-blocking side hand punches or pushes the opponent's cross shoulder simultaneously.

The purpose of this alignment and forward press is to take the attack on a more durable part of the leg than the generally intended Illiotibial band, i.e. IT band, aka "Charley Horse" area on the outer thigh. The timing and distance of this move is done to intercept the kick before it fully accelerates and focuses thereby cancelling much of the kicks power and penetration.

**Torso & Head Blocks** are specialized methods used in unique situations, including the *Shoulder Block* using mostly the lateral deltoid to absorb impact and protect the head or torso. It is common in boxing and kickboxing for a fighter to hide his chin to the inside of his shoulder with hands up to minimize the effects of head strikes.

The *Hip or Buttocks Block* is used like the shoulder block by placing this body part on the path of an incoming attack to take contact on the more durable buttocks. The legs can stay on the ground or one knee is lifted to deflect into the thigh, although hip joint contact should be avoided if possible.

The *Frontal Bone Block* uses the top of the skulls frontal bone, above the hairline, to absorb an attack. This is also the front head butt weapon surface as the neck aligns strongly at this contact point. It is often used in boxing to take an unavoidable head/face punch.

**PARRY** is a method using an upper body limb in a way that is complimentary to blocking. A block starts close to the body then travels away to intercept and challenge an attack at mostly perpendicular angles, where a parry reaches out first to attach then rides and guides the weapon past an intended target. This tends to keep an attacker's momentum moving in the direction of the attack, but missing the intended target, where it can increase countering penetration power and manipulation potential.

*Parry* directions are the same as blocks with *Inward*, *Outward* and *Upward* for higher attacks, then *Inside* and *Outside Downward* to defend lower ones. The contact point is the flexible open palm, the bent wrist as a hook, or back of hand, depending on the application. A parry is a passive action but is not soft as it takes strength and aggression to move a strong attack off its intended path.

A parry rides the attacking weapon, so this longer attachment makes it more possible to grab where other manipulations and damage can be done. The palm side parry grabs instantly (Destructive Parries) where the back of hand parry must rotate before grabbing (Broken Kneel).

Note: Parries are often combined with body maneuvers like slipping to help assure the attack misses the target and is an example of the "move the weapon/move the target" philosophy common in defensive maneuvering.

The *Inward Parry* reaches out in front of the <u>same side</u> shoulder, hand open palm out to intercept and attach to an attacking weapon then returns towards the <u>opposite</u> shoulder. This guides the attack past its intended target across our body centerline (Destructive Circles), or possibly re-applies the attack (Training the Bears).

The *Outward Parry* reaches in front of the <u>opposite</u> shoulder, hand open using the backside of the hand to intercept and attach to an attacking weapon. It guides the attacking weapon towards the <u>same side</u> shoulder past its intended target outside the body, where it could then be grabbed (Glancing Blade).

The *Upward Parry* moves out and up with the hands knife-edge intercepting then attaching to the attacking weapon before the palm flips upward to guide the attack overhead. It is often used while changing levels to duck under a high attack (Dividing the Enemy).

The *Inside Downward Parry* can be with the medial double-bone side of the forearm (Kickboxing Sparring #7) but also applied using the lateral double-bone side (Circling the Kick).

The *Outside Downward Parry* reaches in front of the opposite hip using the backside of the hand, palm open or closed. The hand is safer if closed against a front kick moving up towards the fingers, and the knuckles can strike the leg as a bonus (Deflecting Pendulum). The palm open version is common in sport fighting where it is used as a scoop (Defending Cross).

A sport redirection against a low jab for example can use a cross hand *Inward Parry* hooking over the wrist then guiding the arm down through an *Outside Downward Parry*, setting up a counter punch.

An *Inward* then *Outward Combination Parry* can use the double factor to reinforce the defense while tracking 2 of an attacker's depth zones, and possibly tweaking or dislocating his elbow joint (Destructive Circles).

**CHECKS** cover zones on our body and points of acceleration on an opponent's body to cancel and prevent potential weapons from intentionally or unintentionally causing damage, or even being used.

The *intentional* attempt is any effort done with a mindful purpose to cause harm. The *unintentional* happens accidentally and is divided into *Reflexive Responses* to contact, *Natural Reactions* to stimulus, and incidents that occur during *Movement Transitions*.

A *Reflexive Response* is how the head lunges forward to a knee in the groin, possibly applying a front head butt. A *Natural Reaction* is how the arms instinctively reach forward against an attempted takedown, possibly resulting in a finger to the eye. A *Movement Transition* is where a knee or elbow hits a target while maneuvering to another position, as commonly occurs in grappling.

Anybody around fight training long enough has examples of these *unintentional* strikes. They can also be done intentionally, with only the practitioner knowing for sure. Whatever the intention, the concept of *Checking* is designed as preemptive preventative measures of defense.

Many names and subcategories of checking exist, with many noted here, but I have organized them into 10 main types that are used to some degree in all martial arts and are a refined key component in Kenpo.

Types of Checks covered: *Position, Pinning, Pressing, Offensive, Grabbing, Structure, Angular, Balance, Environmental,* and *Gravitational*. These can be used interchangeably, sequentially, and overlapping either singularly or in combination. Checking is a fluid concept with fighting a dynamic that requires constant adjustment. In all cases, a checks purpose is to prevent potential weapons from causing harm *Intentionally* or *Unintentionally*.

A *Position Check* is when an obstacle is placed between an opponent's potential weapons and vulnerable targets or zones. A hand or leg placed in the space between potential weapons, perhaps lightly touching, and vulnerable targets can provide protection with little or no extra movement. Other terms in this category include *Area, Rebounding, Sliding, Roving, Moving, Waiters Tray, Cross-Body, Out & In Hooking.*

A free hand in space (Delayed Hand), a just used hand (Hand of Destruction), forearm (Buckling the Leg) or leg (Hand and Shield) can cover open areas while other weapons attack or defend; these can also move from one location to another (Cradling the Baby) and are as basic as having the hands up while in a fighting stance.

A *Pinning Check* attaches and holds an attacker's hand/wrist/arm after they touch, grab, hold, or are pre-positioned, often pulling it against our self. This immobilizes the attacking weapon where it can also be used to control and manipulate balance and posture.

This can be brief while simultaneously attacking the joint of an extended limb (Snapping Arm), where it may be referred to as a "trap," see *Pressing Check*. It can also be used to hold an attacker's limb after intercepting it in flight (Taming the Fist), hold one grabbing hand (Triggered Palm), or both (Fist of Aggression) against the body while the free arm attacks.

A *Pressing Check* is like a *Position Check* but more aggressively attaches to an attacker's limb(s) to immobilize by pushing it in space, or against them. This is done to feel, control, manipulate, and possibly damage. Other terms include *Trap, Collapsing, Sliding,* and *Roving.*

Examples are holding their limb in space while attacking a joint (Conquering Arm), or against a body (Glancing Palm), knee against knee (Gift of Destruction), crossing arms against each other (Cross of Destruction), moving along a limb from one location to another, i.e., *frictional pull,* to break balance (Twin Lapel Grab) or clear a limb (Snapping Arm).

The term "trap" is used in different martial art contexts but is a type of *Pressing Check* here. In sport, a hand can reach out to press "trapping" an opponent's hand in space to open a zone for another weapon to fill. This was made famous by Bruce Lee in "Enter the Dragon" where he uses his rear hand to check, i.e., trap, O'Hara's lead hand creating a backknuckle opening. A second attempt is countered with a rear hand catch setting up a re-trap into another backknuckle strike.

An *Offensive Check* utilizes force with timing to impact a surface to stop or affect movement either before their muscle structure is fully engaged, to follow a weapon back to its source, while enroute to another target, pulling into another weapon, redirecting, manipulating, breaking balance, and/or causing pain. Other terms in this category include: *Jamming, Glancing, Detaining, Ricochet, Rolling, Riding,* and *Pain Checks*.

Hitting an attacker's shoulders before he can forcefully step forward (Jamming the Tackle), getting inside the thigh/hip of a round kick (Rolling Fists), or fist (Six Hands), a pushdown bouncing up into an eye poke (Glancing Poke); the forearm glancing off an elbow joint into a straight punch (Darting Fist); intercepting then riding energy down from its intended target (Obstructing the Club), pushing one shoulder while pulling the other (Turn of Fate), pulling the hand to accelerate a knee (Destructive Gift), or punching the back of a hand to cause a weapon release (Clipping the Blade).

A *Grabbing Check* uses the hands, arms, or legs to surround one or multiple limbs, or parts of the entire body, to control, manipulate, create openings, and keep an opponent from using potential weapons. *Hugging* is a type of this.

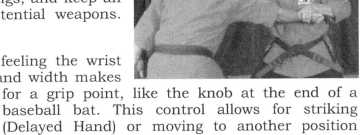

Tracking the arm while feeling the wrist get narrower until the hand width makes

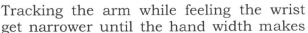

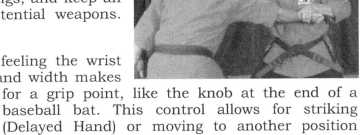 for a grip point, like the knob at the end of a baseball bat. This control allows for striking (Delayed Hand) or moving to another position relative to that arm (Turning Windmills). This can be done to one arm (Glancing Blade) or both (Begging Palms), or the legs (Defending Cross).

Other examples include wrapping an arm around an arm (Securing the Club), a headlock counter grabbing the waist (Pinch from Death B), countering a rear bear hug by hooking one foot back around a leg, or wrapping the legs around a body as in a grappling guard position.

A *Structure Check* is a reinforced frame constructed within a lock or hold to brace, control, damage, or protect an attacked joint until a release can be forced or encouraged. The "Thai neck clinch" is an example with its 3 bi-lateral contact points with hands at the back of the head/neck, forearms at the sides of the neck and elbows pushing into the front of the collarbones.

Other examples include holding an opponent's chin with one hand as that elbow and forearm lock over their shoulder as a neck brace (Crashing Elbows), or their wrist against our hip while pressing their elbow with our free arm to break balance (Hammerlock).

Defensively it can support our own joints (Entangled Arm B), "ride the storm" of a hold (Locked Horns), use the back of the crossed wrists against our forehead for neck support against a full-nelson hold (Scraping Stomp B), or grab the wrist with our free hand or clothing with the attacked hand to cancel a Kimura lock.

An *Angular Check* aligns the body in a way to avoid vital contact by stepping off angle. Examples include inside a punch (Delayed Hand) or kick (Bouncing Pendulum), outside a punch (Reversing Fist), turning the torso to avoid a kick (Circling the Kick), stepping back or forward offline from strong attacks in front (Twin Lapel Grab) or rear (Circling Elbow). It also involves moving an opponent into a checked position as with a side thrust kick to the back of his opposite leg, e.g., right kicks back of left, causing body rotation to our backside (Buckling Leg).

A *Balance Check* disrupts an opponent's center, ideally cancelling height, width, and depth simultaneously to create imbalance and vulnerability. Other terms in this category include *Manipulation* or *Cross Check*.

The hands/arms can pull (Jamming the Tackle), or push (Pursuing Panther), the feet/legs can buckle (Broken Kneel), and sweep (Untwirling Pendulum), or our entire body can crowd (Fatal Variation), bump (Dance of Death), or tilt (Tripping Leg). In sparring this can be seen grabbing an opponent's lead hand with our lead hand jerking their weight onto their front big toe. This is the entry move and root technique of the EPAK sparring system.

A *Gravitational Check* uses diagonal and downward body weight behind part(s) of our structure to settle onto an opponent's body or a part. This cancels height, affects posture, balance, and the ability to generate leverage. Other terms used in this category include *Collapsing* and *Dipping Checks*

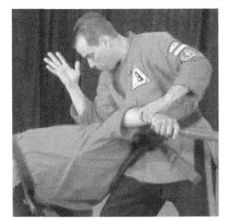

Examples include using the elbow tip(s) to press down on the back of a tackle attempt to change their energy vector (Meeting the Tackle), or on a bent opponent's spine holding them down (Crossed Arms), crashing down to bend an elbow opening the head for a strike (Fist of Aggression), pushing the head down while lifting an arm to cause rotation (Delayed Hand).

An *Environmental Check* uses an inanimate surface to pin, hold, or manipulate all or part of an opponent's body. Fighting technique uses a ring, cage, wall, tree, fence, car, or floor to do this with the floor a major environmental factor in ground grappling. Clothing is another of these.

A wall can be used as a launching platform (Turning Windmills) or to hold someone against (Crossing Fist), also the ground (Leap of Death), their clothing (Turning the Cross), our clothing (Locked Arm) can all be used to control and manipulate posture, position, and improve attacking leverage.

## PUNCHES & STRIKES

This category of *Basics* refers to methods that hit targets with accelerated body parts traveling through space as projectile weapons. These are primarily the arms using the closed hand, open hand, fingers, and elbows, or the legs using the feet and knees. They are applied along linear and circular paths of motion individually, sequentially, and simultaneously.

**Punches** hit with a closed fist using the face of the index and/or middle finger knuckles, where the fingers connect to the hand at the 3rd metatarsal, or where the fingers bend in the middle at the 2nd metatarsal. The wrist must be straight on two sides to make for the strongest structural alignment, at the back so the wrist does not bend and on the thumb side so the two large knuckles line up with the forearm bones. These hard-sharp surfaces are naturally and easily accelerated to penetrate soft and even damage solid surface targets, if properly conditioned.

**Strikes** are the upper body methods of hitting that are not *Punches*. These versatile and adaptable weapons primarily involve the hands, elbows, feet, and knees, but the head could also be used. Categories are *Closed Hand Strikes, Open Hand Strikes, Elbow Strikes, Finger Strikes,* and *Specialized Upper Body Strikes* making this a truly diverse section of *Basics. Kicks and Balance Disruptions* will have their own category.

Terms used in martial arts are not always universal and there are many formatting possibilities. The names here are uniform to this format based upon travel direction: inward, outward, straight, round, etc. by weapon shape: punch, handsword, palm, etc: and sometimes motion characteristic: thrust, whip, snap, etc.

Common or slang terms are included where that is more recognizable but, whatever something is called, a properly applied techniques effectiveness is what matters. "When pure knuckles meet pure flesh, that's pure karate and it doesn't matter how you spell it" – Ed Parker; and let me add, "what you call it."

Note: When straightening the arms or legs to extend the hands or feet as weapons it is important that the muscle structure stops a limbs extension and not the joint, as a hyperextension injury could occur. The arms tricep muscles and legs quadriceps stop the extension before the bones of those joints lock together. This takes practice and muscle control.

**PUNCHES** can involve about 270° of hand rotation making it a flexible weapon that can fit and contour onto and into many targets, and it can be applied at different angles.

Punching is common in sport fighting where the hands are reinforced and padded. Street styles also punch but without hand protection will often favor other hand striking options. The closed uncovered fist can however lessen the risk of injury to fingers, as they can become entangled in clothes or impact on an unexpected surface.

A negative of punching is that the power load, acceleration, and body mass behind a punch can often be stronger than the hand and wrist supporting the structure. A hard, durable, and perhaps moving target surface can break bones in the hand. Sport strikers will wrap and tape their hands and wrists, then wear gloves when they train and fight. Regardless, the hand is a versatile and popular way to hit.

To apply a successful punch, the hand should be tightly closed to damage the target without damaging the weapon. Other than closing all fingers at the same time there are three ways to close the fingers into a compressed fist. 1) Bend the little finger then ring, middle, and index tucking the nails into the palm; 2) Place the middle fingertip into the palm, where it naturally folds, then the other fingers; 3) Bend the index then middle, ring, and little finger. In all cases the thumb is then placed across the middle phalange of the index and middle finger to hold the fingers closed tightly in place.

When punching the wrist must be kept straight, except for the *Stiff-Arm Punch* that hinges from the shoulder. The forearm bones are the backup mass behind the fist. The tricep muscles extend the lower arm with the shoulder pushing to extend and align the body mass to apply leverage from the ground into a punch.

Karate styles practice punching initially from a horse stance with hands at the waist in the "chamber." In striking sports, the hands are up with elbows anchored near the ribs and feet aligned in a "fighting stance." The hands-up posture is practical when the combatants both have acknowledged they are fighting, as happens in sport, and sometimes street.

The horse stance posture exaggerates a transition point for punches that start with hands down, as would be more common at the start of a street fight. It also pre-loads the muscle structure to help develop bi-lateral strength, muscle memory, and coordination.

There are four major types of punches used in sport and street systems with an extra category for street use. They are *Straight, Roundhouse, Hook, Uppercut*, and an extra category called *Specialty Punches.*

**Straight Punches** are where the elbow pushes the hand away from the body, following a direct straight linear path from point of origin to point of destination. 270° of comfortable hand rotation allows the fist to be angled into a defined target boundary, generally measured in four 90° or seven 45° increments, depending on the system.

The *Inverted Horizontal Punch* is a palm up punch used at close range, often to the body (Six Hands). It is also the wrist alignment for a type of *Uppercut Punch* (Pursuing Panther).

The *Vertical Punch* is applied thumb side up and is a natural punching alignment for the wrist as it's how the arm hangs by the side. It is also the strongest wrist alignment for punching above the shoulder line as it helps maintain wrist integrity through flexion, and it fits vertically shaped targets like the groin (Locked Horns).

Some styles prefer this punch as a standard because of this strong natural alignment, although punching extension is more limited than with the horizontal punch that uses more hand and elbow rotation, along with the accompanying torso rotation to add extension, and shoulder lift for defense.

The *Horizontal Punch* is probably the most common punch. It is used often in sport fighting where it may be called a straight or reverse punch. It is applied by rotating the hand until the palm faces downward (Crossing Fist).

Notes: Internally rotating the forearm to this degree without an accompanying elbow rotation and shoulder lift, as done by Boxer's, causes the wrist bones to cross. This negatively affects the muscle structure of the forearm making the wrist weaker. This is one reason why some martial arts avoid it in favor of the *Vertical Punch*, and another reason sport fighter's wrap their hands and wrists.

This hand shape can also be "thrown" overhead using a Roundhouse, or even Hook Punch path of motion, like throwing a baseball.

The *Inverted Vertical Punch* fully rotates the hand until the palm faces out with the thumb down. It's an unorthodox punch that fits well into some targets at some angles. It can be used straight (Pinch from Death) and is the hand shape for the "overhand right" that punches into the blind angle between an opponent's front hand and shoulder into their temple or jaw (Rear Belt Grab).

Note: Between each of those four punch shapes are 45° angle punches if needed to align and fit into some targets more accurately. They are the *Inverted Diagonal Punch, Diagonal Punch,* and the *Downward Diagonal Punch* covered under "Roundhouse Punches." A low solar plexus punch fits at about 45° with palm up as an *Inverted Diagonal Punch* (Raking Fist), or slightly rotated down from vertical as a *Diagonal Punch* (Parting Arms).

**Roundhouse Punches** move forward like a straight punch, but the elbow moves out as the hand rotates to align a different punching angle. The *Roundhouse* and *Downward Diagonal Roundhouse* differentiate from a hook by hitting on the way out to a target, where a hook hits on the way back.

The *Roundhouse Punch* travels slightly inwards. For reference, if a straight punch hits the tip of the chin then the *Roundhouse Punch* hits the side of the jaw (Darting Fist).

Many boxing coaches teach a version of this punch with the hand horizontal, as a type of hook, reaching around past the hands and arms to hit the head or body with the index knuckle as the main contact point. This works well with a taped, wrapped, and gloved hand, as it adds a dimension for hitting the head and body that is difficult to defend if in close. Without hand protection however, this punch runs a risk of that index knuckle breaking on the skull or elbow. Non-sport styles can also hook back into softer rear targets like the mastoid (Twirling Fist) or kidneys (Blinding Vice).

The *Downward Diagonal Roundhouse Punch* is another punch shape where the hand is rotated between inverted vertical and roundhouse at about 45°. It hits from a high to low with a throwing motion and is no doubt the most popular bar fight punch, although the untrained may not rotate the hand.

If applied properly the knuckles are optimized on the contact surface. This punch hits at a deceptive and often uncovered blind or obscure angle ending with the elbow slightly up to get over and around an opponent's lead hand into vulnerable head targets. This punch has found popularity in MMA sport fighting where a change in levels can cause an opponent to drop his hands to defend his legs leaving his head exposed to this overhand motion flowing naturally from that grappling posture.

**Hook Punches** follow a path like a roundhouse punch but with the contact at or after the extension apex on the return side of the circle. The vertical hand shape aligns the knuckles strongly and allows for a bicep contraction, all adding power to this motion, and making it the safest angle to use without hand/wrist support (Entangled Arm B).

Note: There is some disagreement in terminology between the *Round* and *Hook* punch, and some don't even differentiate using them interchangeably. The names used here match the same type of motion as done when kicking through similar paths. *Round Kicks* hit on the way out, as does the *Round Punch,* and *Hook Kick* hits on the way back, as does a *Hook Punch.*

**Uppercut Punches** travel low to high and usually slightly away on its path to a target. The hand can be rotated to an *Inverted Horizontal* or *Vertical Uppercut Punch,* depending on distance, target, and preference.

The *Inverted Horizontal Uppercut Punch* contours under the chin and can be done closer as the narrower hand shape fits inside a tighter space.

The *Vertical Uppercut Punch* travels up and away with a stronger alignment than the *Inverted Horizontal* version and covers more depth along its path. This punch can still easily hit the mouth, nose, eyes, or forehead as the head moves away. Boxers use this punch, but an unprotected hand can experience damage at the exposed little finger knuckle and bones.

**Specialty Punches** are the unique punches used in street martial arts that fit into specific targets and pressure points. They can be delivered at various angles with different wrist rotations, and pushed from the elbow like a regular punch, or swung from the shoulder. Specialty punches covered are the *Stiff-Arm, Half-Fist, Knocking, Middle Knuckle,* and *Index Knuckle.*

The *Stiff-Arm Punch* is unique as it is applied from the swinging shoulder, and not pushed from the elbow like other punches. The weapon surface is either the face of the flat fist or the corner edge of the knuckles.

This punch is useful for hitting a lower target line (Spiraling Wrist), or up across our body to the side where a standard punch would not generate as much power (Flashing Fist).

The *Half-Fist Punch,* aka Panther Punch, uses the middle joints of the fingers, like the "knocking" punch except it's applied along a linear path. This sharp punching surface fits into narrow targets like the throat where it can be used palm up (Ascending from Death), or palm down (Pursuing Panther).

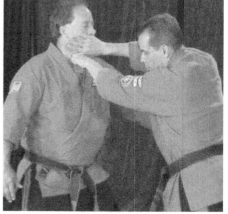

The *Knocking Punch* also uses the four folded middle finger joints, with thumb against the side for support. Its surface and motion are like knocking on a door, as the name implies.

It is applied with a circular motion to hit and glance through targets like the nerves of the inner elbow (Cradling the Baby). This punching method can be used creatively at other angles to fit other available and tender targets (Crashing Elbows).

The *Middle Knuckle Punch,* aka Dragons Head, starts as a regular fist but the middle knuckle is protruded and supported between the second joint of the index and ring fingers. The thumb is placed on top of the last middle finger joint for structural support.

This sharp pointy weapon is formed to fit or slice through small vulnerable targets. It is said the Qi of this punch travels upward, due to its applied structural alignment. It can penetrate tender body points (Ducking Dragon), slice through an eye (Flashing Fist), and can be inverted to fit into a small head target (Clipping the Blade).

The *Index Knuckle Punch,* aka Eye of the Phoenix, also forms from a normal fist as the index knuckle is protruded until the last finger joint is between the second joint of the middle finger and the thumb pad. This sharp weapon fits into the eye or behind the ear, but with minimal support on one side it is structurally weaker than the middle knuckle punch. The Qi of this punch is said to travel downwards due to its applied structural alignment.

**STRIKES** generically means "hitting" but here it refers to the variety of hitting movements that are not punching. With that in mind there are 3 *Closed Hand Strikes,* 7 *Open Hand Strikes,* 4 methods of *Finger Strikes,* 5 types of *Elbow Strikes,* and 4 *Specialized Strikes* used in street martialarts, with a few of those also used in sport.

**Closed Hand Strikes** not in the *Punch* category are the *Backknuckle, Hammerfist,* and *Reverse Hammerfist.* The backknuckle and hammerfist are legal in some sport fighting styles that allow striking.

The **Backknuckle Strike** uses the fist, except the wrist is extended slightly to align the back of the sharp knuckles onto a target. The backhand bones are generally not the focus as they would be more easily damaged.

This strike can thrust into, snap off from, whip through, or hook back into a target after traveling straight, out, in, up, or down. The 5 major types of backknuckles are *Straight, Outward (Thrust / Snap / Whip), Inward Whipping aka Hooking, Upward,* and *Downward.*

The *Straight Backknuckle* moves linear, like a vertical punch, except the wrist is arched slightly so the sharp backknuckle surface leads rather than the flatter backhand of the fist. This is an old school backknuckle that has almost been lost with the use of the more popular sport karate outward snapping version. Boxer's still legally use this slightly arched strike as a version of a jab.

The *Outward Backknuckle* applies a vertically shaped hand that hinges out from the centerline with a *Thrust* (Destructive Circles), *Snap* (Alternating Fist), or *Whip* through (Triggered Palm). It can also be applied diagonally (Ascending from Death), or vertically (Unrolling Crane).

Note: The outward whipping version of this backknuckle is legal in some full-contact fighting sports, generally after spinning footwork. This is illegal in Boxing, but MMA and kickboxing allow it, and sometimes the rules will allow for the more powerful "spinning hammerfist."

The *Inward Whipping/Hooking Backknuckle* is where the hand rotates past the head or body, then returns into a target. This motion completes the ability to hit 360° around someone's head while standing in front of them (Blinding Vice).

The *Upward Backknuckle* is virtually interchangeable with a *Stiff-Arm Lifting Punch* with the difference being the target shape and entry vector. Lifting under the chin would be a place where this backknuckle shape would be a better fit (Checking the Club).

The *Downward Backknuckle* can glance through (Thundering Fist) or crush then rebound off a target (Nutcracker).

The **Hammerfist Strike** is applied with the meaty part of the closed fist, on the little finger side of the hand, where it can *Thrust*, *Snap* or *Hook/Rake*. This hammering motion can be done in many directions and may be the most powerful hand/arm strike of the human body.

Street styles apply it inward (Shielding Fingers), outward (Darting Fist), downward (Retreating Pendulum), forward (Rolling Fists), backwards (Captured Arms), and sometimes even simultaneously (Lock of Death).

The *Inward Raking Hammerfist* is a *Hooking* motion where upon contact the knuckles rake or slice through a target, often the nose, starting at the small finger knuckle then across the other three towards the index knuckle.

The circular flow of this inward motion can be followed by another smaller orbit inward strike like an elbow (Snapping Arm) or reversed into an outward traveling motion (Raking Fist).

The *Reverse Hammerfist* uses the hammerfist hand shape but applies the index finger side of the fist. This specialized strike can rebound from (Circling the Arm), or glance through a target (Destructive Gift).

This reverse motion of a hammerfist is often done as an insert or "hidden move" within technique flow (Fatal Variation). The thumb can also be bent and placed to enhance this weapon using one (Hand of Destruction), or both hands (Thrusting Thumbs).

**Open Hand Strikes** consist of the *Palm Heel, Heel-of-Palm, Handsword, Reverse Handsword,* along with the <u>Specialty Strikes</u> *Back-of-Wrist, Back-of-Hand,* and the *Web-of-Hand,* with each able to be applied in different directions and at many angles. All are used in street techniques, with the *reverse handsword* also used in sport karate, with the *palm heel* and *heel-of-palm* also usually legal in MMA styles.

The **Palm Heel Strike** is a linear pushing movement using the base of the open hand on the palm side, with the fingers slightly bent to help draw the hands energy or Qi into the weapon surface (see *P8 / Lao Gong / Palace of Toil* Acupuncture point 'Note' under *Balance, Eastern Energetics Model* in the Body book).

Note: The version of this palm strike with the fingers bent/folded in half, like a half-fist, inhibits the Qi energy, shifting it from the palm to the joints of the folded finger joints. Slightly bent fingers also allow for more follow up options such as pokes, claws, or grabs.

This strike can be rotated 270°, like punching, to fit targets at different heights, ranges, and angles with minimal wrist stress. Using 90° increments of hand rotation, starting with palm forward and fingers down then rotating, are the *Inverted Palm, Horizontal Palm, Vertical Palm,* and *Inverted Horizontal Palm.*

The *Inverted/Fingers-Down Palm Strike* is usually applied below our own shoulder line to fit into an appropriately shaped target, like the groin (Protective Circles), or exposed joint (Evading the Club).

The *Horizontal/Fingers-Out Palm Strike* can be applied below our own shoulder line forward around the torso with one (Crushing Palm), or two hands (Blinding Vice). It can also be applied downward to a lower smaller surface target like an elbow joint (Gripping Wrist), or up under the chin (Crashing Elbows).

The *Vertical/Fingers-Up Palm Strike* is mostly used at or above our own shoulder line to the nose or chin (Thrusting Palm) and forehead (Wraparound)

to avoid joint pressure. It can also be applied downward onto targets like the back head (Thrusting Thumbs), or elbow (Gripping Wrist). This strike downward is also commonly used for board and brick breaking.

The *Inverted Horizontal/Fingers-In Palm Strike* uses the elbow angled up with the fingers rotated inward where the arm shape helps to angle around obstacles into some targets. It can be used close (Tripping Leg), or further away to high (Circling Elbow), or lower targets (Entangled Arm B).

The **Heel-of-Palm Strike** uses a circular movement to apply the palm strike hand shape, but at the medial wrist side of the hand as the striking surface. Wherever applied, the wrist remains relaxed until impact when it explosively extends to accelerate into the target.

The elbow stays slightly bent upon contact to engage the tricep muscles into the strike, while also protecting against elbow hyperextension. The 3 major directions applied are *Inward, Downward,* and *Back.*

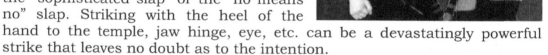

The *Inward Heel-of-Palm Strike* can be used as a type of hook applied with trunk rotation, like swinging a baseball bat. The elbow should be ahead of the shoulder to align the structure and avoid severe injury to the shoulder joint, which could occur if the shoulder were ahead of the elbow upon hard contact.

In women's self-defense classes I call this the "sophisticated slap" or the "no means no" slap. Striking with the heel of the hand to the temple, jaw hinge, eye, etc. can be a devastatingly powerful strike that leaves no doubt as to the intention.

It is used as a single movement (Destructive Circles), or in combination to sandwich with an inward elbow strike (Raking Fist). This can be staggered high and low to the temple and chin on opposite sides of the head to cause a neck tweak (Locked Horns). This motion can also be applied with straight wrists, as in slapping, generally to box the ears (Begging Palms).

The *Downward Heel-of-Palm Strike* is a powerful motion done above the waist into targets like the nose (Hooking Arms) or collarbones (Blinding Vice), or below at the spine (Crossed Arms). Dropping and settling the body weight only enhances this type of striking motion, e.g., marriage of gravity.

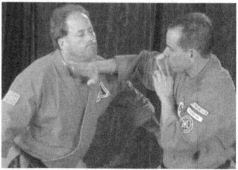

The *Back Heel-of-Palm Strike* uses a shoulder swinging motion below the waist and backwards, usually to the groin of a rear opponent (Crushing Palm).

The **Handsword Strike**, aka *Karate Chop*, uses the meaty edge of the hand on the little finger side between the base knuckle and the wrist joint. The shape of this weapon makes it useful for fitting into narrow targets, like the neck or throat. The most common motions are

*Outward, Inward,* and *Downward,* but it can also be applied backwards low.

The *Outward Handsword Strike* starts across our centerline, often set up by an inward motion. The elbow leads this strike with body torque and acceleration optimized by rotating the hand and ulnar flexing the wrist into the target.

This weapons hand shape matches the jaw line, making the neck a common target. It can be pushed forward like a jab (Taming the Fist), used with outward torso rotation (Delayed Hand), hit upward at an obscure angle (Hidden Hand), and be used against the torso (Reversing Circles).

The *Inward Handsword Strike* begins with the hand outside the centerline, often set up by an outward motion. The elbow leads then pushes this strike into the target, with palm rotation and ulnar flexing of the wrist upon impact (Hand of Destruction).

Note: Using a circular inward motion hinging off the shoulder where the elbow never reattaches to the body can result in a strained elbow, e.g., Tennis Elbow, and/or a shoulder strain when the hand meets firm resistance.

The *Downward Handsword Strike* is pushed straight down or applied after circling overhead. The straight version starts with the hand higher with palm rotated out before turning it palm-in with wrist flexion onto a target (Six Hands). The overhead strike gains momentum from the arm circling, like a throwing motion, then the elbow is bent to pull the hand down onto the target (Charging Tackle).

The *Reverse Handsword Strike,* aka *Ridgehand,* is done with an open hand like other handsword strikes except the striking surface is the meaty area between the thumb joint and wrist, or possibly the radius bone, angled to avoid the nerve. The thumb is tucked into the palm to apply this *Inward, Downward, Upward,* or the specialized *Outward Reverse* motion.

This is a type of hook used primarily by karate stylists against soft targets for self-defense, and in sport karate to various head or body targets while wearing protective equipment. The *Inward* motion can hit the necks side (Hand & Shield), or *Downward* on back of the neck (Gripping Wrist), and *Upward* between the legs (Entangled Arm B).

Note: The hand shape where the thumb is against the index knuckle, making it the contact surface, can allow that joint to be more easily damaged.
The *Inverted Outward Reverse Handsword Strike* hits with the palm up, thumb facing out (Raining Blade). It is also the hand shape seen in the Tai Chi technique "Parting Wild Horse's Mane."

Specialty Strikes are used in unique situations where they are the primary weapon that fits the application needed. Included are the *Back-of-Wrist*, *Back-of-Hand*, and *Web-of-Hand* strikes.

The *Back of Wrist Strike*, aka *Crane Hand* or *Monkey Fist*, is a specialty strike formed by flexing the wrist, so the thumb meets the four fingers as the lateral wrist angle is flexed into a target (Calming the Club).

Note: This is the opposite wrist motion of an

inward heel-of-palm strike making them complimentary reverse motion weapons.

The *Back of Hand Strike* uses the flat open hands backside, most commonly to the side of the neck as the brachial stun technique used by police, bodyguards, and bouncers where a handsword to the same target may cause severe injury or death. It can also be used back into the groin as part of a finger whip to one or two opponents (Mating the Rams).

The *Web-of-Hand Strike*, aka *Tigers Mouth*, uses the inside webbing of the hand between the thumb and index finger knuckle. It is applied in a linear manner where it fits the throat comfortably to strike (Tripping Leg), and/or grab (Securing the Club).

**Finger Strikes** are applied in 4 primary ways as determined by the hand and finger musculoskeletal structure and mechanics. They are applied straight to *Poke*, while opening to *Whip*, closing to *Claw*, or moving from side to side to *Slice*. Each of these has different applications with inherent strengths and weaknesses.

Using the fingers to strike is used mostly to attack the eyes and is in what I call the "nuclear weapon" category of offensive options. Eye attacks are great equalizers learned in street defense styles that can enable the smallest most delicate person to injure, and even stop the largest meanest person.

Finger strikes can retract quickly but can also stay on a target to press, dig, or slide to scrape tissue. Like nuclear weapons this powerful knowledge comes with responsibility as the result could be life changing. Even in training the eyes are never touched. This makes it necessary to train the fingers isometrically, or on inanimate objects, to develop the strength and coordination to apply them. In Kenpo these are indexed, sequenced, and practiced in the Finger Sets.

Poke refers to using the finger ends, and or thumb, to push or press straight into a target. This can be done using the individual digits into the eyes, the sternal notch indentation on the throat, solar plexus, or other tender body soft spots. These must be properly formed, developed, and practiced as to avoid injury. Finger pokes can be rotated 270° and formed into the *Index-Finger, 2-Finger, 4-Finger,* and *Thumb Pokes.*

The *Index-Finger Poke,* aka *Finger Dart,* is formed by bending the other 3 fingers, like steps walking up to the extended index finger, and thumb tucked on the side for support.

The *2-Finger Poke* is formed like the *Index Finger Poke* but with the middle finger extended against the edge of the index fingernail. This is the stronger of the finger pokes as the middle finger is more structurally supported on two sides. It can be used against the eyes (Glancing Poke) but is strong enough to push deep into the throats sternal notch (Returning the Gift).

The *4-Finger Poke* is shaped in two major ways. One is like a handsword with all four fingers together used like a spear, where the other leaves a small space between slightly bent fingers to fit around the nose into both eyes (Ascending from Death). This shotgun method of finger poking uses ten weapons to find the two eye targets.

The *Thumb Poke* can compliment and accompany the other finger pokes but can also be a stand-alone strike or follow another finger strike (Blinding Vice). It can be used into the eye(s) then retracted, or with the other fingers as grips to increase leverage. In sport fighting, and depending on gloves, a thumb to the eye is a real possibility where it can catch the eye from a missed punch, or perhaps be done intentionally.

Whip is a flicking movement utilizing the back of the relaxed fingers where the extensor muscles generate little muscular strength but generates a lot of speed. It can be done with any or all fingers forward (Blinding Vice), outward (Protective Parries), and backward (Mating the Rams).

Notes: Some may recall this type of strike from childhood where it was done with the ring finger, and perhaps called a "dead finger," where the thumb holds the index and/or middle finger in place. The ring finger dangles and is used to smack other kids on the head or wherever (I just heard about it).

The hand position of the backknuckle snap used in karate point fighting can be easily adapted to use this weapon for street use. These whipping or flicking finger strikes are a devastatingly fast way to attack the eyes and made famous in the movie "Kill Bill 2" where the female heroin plucks out the eye of an adversary, for "killing her Master."

Claw is the strongest application of the fingers with the *5-Finger Claw, 2-Finger Hook,* and *Thumb Gouge* used. This powerful strike can rip and tear through the eyes and other tissue with the hand straight but with fingers firmly bent with fingertips pointed slightly downward, to claw not paw. This is often applied after a *Heel-of-Palm,* so the fingernails can find the soft tissue targets more easily. A claw can also become a grab or pinch around grasped tissue.

The *5-Finger Claw* uses the nails of the four fingers and thumb to rip and tear soft tissue (Hooking Arms). It can be used through 270° of rotation to fit a selected target.

The *2-Finger Hook* is used from behind to hook into an eye (Glancing Blade), or fishhook the inside mouth corner. The forearm can also be anchored at the back of the shoulder to enhance structural leverage.

Slice or scraping with the fingernails uses a lateral side-to-side movement across vulnerable surface areas. The 4 main versions are the *2-Finger Slice, Windshield Wiper Finger Slice,* and related *Finger Splay,* plus the *Thumb Slice/Gouge.*

The *2-Finger Slice* uses the same finger shape as the 2-Finger Poke, also with the middle fingernail as the primary contact point. This slice can move laterally outward with palm down (Twins of Destruction) or inward with palm up (Turning Windmills).

The hand position for the *Windshield Wiper Finger Slice* looks like the *4-Finger Poke* except with the fingers more bent. Like the claw, this slice is often preceded by an *Inward Heel-of-Palm Strike* that attaches then acts as a pivot point for the fingers to slice *Inward* (Taming the Fist), *Outward* (Locked Horns), or back and forth through the eyes (Turning Windmills).

The *Finger Splay* is a specialized relaxed flowing raking finger strike that starts with the little finger then moves outward in a wave using the ring, middle, and index fingertips (Turning Windmills).

The *Thumb Slice/Gouge* can be an add-on off a backknuckle strike to the temple (Thundering Fists), or after a *Thumb Poke* where the nail then slices deep into the eye (Leap of Death).

**Elbow Strikes** are potentially the sharpest, hardest, and most durable striking surface per square inch on the human body. The elbow area provides the most upper body striking options with 5 striking surfaces applied mostly with a bent elbow, although part of the straight arm can also be used. Elbow surfaces used are the *Ulna Bone Tip, Tricep Muscle Base, Humerus Bone Lateral Edge, Ulna Bone Medial Edge,* and the *Elbow Crook.*

The <u>Ulna Bone Tip</u> is a sharp elbow surface that can be accelerated quickly in a small space using the humerus bones strong structural alignment. It can be applied with a partially to completely bent joint using 8 major motions. A partially bent elbow is used to align this bone for *Downward* and *Back Elbow Strikes,* or bent completely for *Upward, Upward Diagonal, Inward,* and *Downward Diagonal Elbow Strikes.* The bent elbow tip can also poke or stab with the arm positioned *Horizontal* or *Vertical.*

The *Downward Elbow Strike,* with the ulna tip, generally uses the arm bent at 45º to 90º to align the elbow tip downward, as compared to a completely bent elbow which applies the *Tricep Base,* as used in breaking. If in front, this sharp weapon penetrates quickly to affect the height zone (Meeting the Tackle) or to devastate a target (Sweeping the Leg).

The *Back-Elbow Strike* also uses the arm bent at about 45º to align the elbow tip backward, requiring only a quick arm twitch back while rotating the palm up. The hand usually remains open to apply this sharp elbow (Crushing Palm) but is sometimes closed for the flatter tricep base surface when followed by a closed hand strike (Ascending from Death). Both are effective and differentiated by target, direction, emphasis, and how much room to move the arm.

The *Upward Elbow Strike* uses the completely bent elbow with hand moving past the ear on the same side with palm towards that ear, like answering a telephone. This strike fits under a protruding target like the chin (Hooking Arms).

Note: There are different thoughts when doing an elbow strikes where the hand moves towards the body. Sport styles, with hand protection, tend to keep the hand open for relaxation and speed to tear tissue, often around the eyebrows. Street styles generally close the bare fist as the open fingers moving towards the body or face can be easily damaged on other surfaces, caught in clothing, or a poke into our own eye.

The *Upward Diagonal Elbow Strike* is between an *Upward* and *Inward Elbow,* with the hand of the striking elbow going towards the opposite ear. This strike can glance thru vertical targets like the jaw or temple, then continues through to another strike (Circling Elbow), or glances through as part of an escape (Entangled Arm A).

The *Inward Elbow Strike* is applied by bringing the hand towards the chest, like looking at a wristwatch. This is one of the body's most powerful motions applied using either the sharp tip of the ulna bone (Gift of Destruction), or the ulna forearm surface (Thrusting Thumbs).

It hits solidly into the torso (Hand and Shield) or can glance through (Cradling the Baby) into another application and can be combined with an *Inward Heel-of-Palm* to sandwich (Raking Fist) or glance through (Fist of Aggression).

The *Downward Diagonal Elbow Strike* travels inward from a high to a lower position, as the hand goes under the opposite armpit. This flows into a strong pushing motion to clear or can set up a follow up reverse elbow motion (Snapping Arm).

Note: In Muay Thai, from a hands-up position, the flow of this strike aligns so the hand clears the opponent's front hand to make space for the elbow to roll over and into a face target.

The *Horizontal Elbow Strike* projects the elbow tip forward with the arm and hand able to protect the neck, and with the option of an opposite hand support brace. The tip is used like a spear to stab into torso targets (Bouncing Pendulum), a punching arm (Twisting the Gift), or as a stand-alone strike (Unexpected Blade).

The *Vertical Elbow Strike* is applied the same as the *Horizontal Elbow Strike,* except the hand is above the elbow. This close-range strike can fit between an opponent's hands-up position, as used in Muay Thai, or in street to break balance (Falling Eagle) or create space (Entangled Arm B).

The <u>Tricep Muscle Base</u> is at the backside of the completely bent elbow around the corner from the *Ulna Tip*. It is applied with a bicep contraction and hand open for speed or closed for power, as used in brick breaking. This less sharp elbow is useful where a larger weapon surface is needed with the 4 major directions *Downward, Back, Outward,* and *Obscure.*

The *Downward Elbow Strike*, as mentioned, can also use this surface. In either application the palm is forward with the arm straight above a target and then the palm is rotated 180° to keep the arm relaxed with structural integrity, as the strike accelerates downward. The arm can drop straight down as used in brick breaking or be circled overhead first (Broken Tackle).

The *Back-Elbow Strike* with this surface is like the ulna bone tip version except the more bent arm shape can penetrate further to the rear, perhaps to create more space (Hidden Elbow).

The *Outward Elbow Strike* is done towards a side or rear attacker circling either *up & out* (Fist of Aggression) or *down & out* (Shielding Fingers), both with palm down at the point of contact.

The *Obscure Elbow Strike, or Rear Lifting Elbow,* moves up under a side or rear target. The relaxed arm lifts the bent elbow up (Captured Arms), with or without a check assist to increase force (Locked Horns). The term *Obscure* defines zones not easily seen, or blind spots.

The <u>Ulna Bone Medial Edge</u> is accelerated using an inward flapping or shoulder hinging motion. It can be applied with the sharp inside edge or the flatter forearm surface area, with care needed to avoid hitting the nearby ulnar nerve. It can be used singularly (Calming the Club) or in combination as a sandwiching strike (Blinding Vice).

The <u>Humerus Bone Lateral Edge</u> or *Chicken Wing* is when the bent elbow flaps away from the body as the hand rotates. Most of the strength and acceleration is generated from the shoulder *Inward* or *Upward.*

The *Inside Downward Elbow Strike* is done with the hand lower than the slightly bent elbow. It can be used against an opponent's extended elbow joint (Twins of Destruction) or to the side of his head (Meeting the Tackle).

The *Upward Rolling/Flapping Elbow Strike* uses the same motion but lifts the outside edge of the bent elbow joint upwards as the palm rotates down.

It resembles an upward block in front but is applied under an opponent's extended elbow(s) (Twin Lapel Grab), or chin to expose his throat (Pursuing Panther) or create space (Fatal Variation).

The Elbow Crook is at the elbow hollow at the bicep muscle base. Straightening the arm lifts it *Upward* or moves it *Inwards*. Collapsing this elbow hinge is used in the application of some grappling holds and submissions like a 'Sleeper Choke'.

The *Upward Crook-of-Elbow Strike* is like the *Upward Flapping Elbow Strike* under an opponent's chin except to the side where the arm position does not use hand rotation as it slides up the bodyline (Sweeping the Leg).

The *Inward Crook-of-Elbow Strike* is used against a wide target surface to apply heavy blunt trauma (Thundering Fists). Wrestler's use this to apply a "cross face" with this elbow hinge also closed in the application of some grappling chokes (Sleeper).

**Specialized Strikes** are other areas of the body able to be used as weapons. They include *Head Butts, Forearm, Shoulder,* and *Hip* strikes.

The Head Butt is a heavy close-range strike with an incredible weapon to target power ratio, if applied correctly. It is illegal in modern sanctioned sport fighting, but this dynamic weapon is available to street stylists. The four skull striking surfaces are the frontal bone, two parietal bones, and the occipital bone, selected for use based upon an opponent's location.

The mechanics for hitting with the head does not stem from the neck but involves the entire body from the ground up for structural support and to greatly increase the strikes backup mass. The 4 directions for applying this strike are to the *Front, Left Side, Right Side,* and *Rear.*

The *Front Head Butt* uses the frontal bone at the crown of the head just above the natural hairline, but <u>not</u> the forehead. It is aligned by slightly dropping the chin where it can be launched forward from the torso and legs into a target, usually the face (Thrusting Thumbs).

Note: This is essentially hitting someone in the face with a bowling ball, so it can be very devastating. Since the head reflexively lunges forward in response to a lower attack, like a groin strike, this potential should always be checked when striking someone low in this way, especially if close.

The *Side Head Butt* uses one of the two *Parietal Bones* on the right and left sides of the head. These are at the top lateral sides of the skull, behind the ears, but <u>not</u> the temporal bones. Since it is impossible to clearly see this weapon as it's applied, first spot the target, then launch the head strike as the head turns to align the appropriate parietal bone into that spotted target (Nutcracker).

The *Rear Head Butt* uses the occipital skull bone at the back of the head. As with all head strikes the entire body launches this weapon backwards as one unit to give it structure, weight, and power, while protecting the neck. The chin must not lift, to avoid a whiplash neck injury, while this strike is driven back into a close rear opponent, perhaps holding a bear hug (Straddling the Leg), or other close rear side attack (Scraping Stomp).

The <u>Forearm</u> as a weapon is applied as the *Ulna Bone Forearm, Radial Bone Forearm, Medial Two-Bone Forearm,* and *Lateral Two-Bone Forearm Strikes.*

The *Ulna Bone Forearm Strike* is used in blocking but also as a sharp weapon against the elbow joint (Obstructing the Club), throat (Taming the Fist), or neck (Detouring the Kick).

The *Radius Bone Forearm Strike* surface can be used against the throat as a *guillotine choke* (Turn of Fate), or to hit the chest with a leg sweep takedown (Dancing in the Dark), or to break balance (Raining Blade).

The *Lateral Two-Bone Forearm Strike* uses the outside forearm bones side by side. This solid flat surface can be used to absorb impact as in blocking (Calming the Club), but also accelerated outwards as a strike (Ascending from Death).

The *Medial Two-Bone Forearm Strike* uses the two bones of the inner arm side by side. This flat surface moves strongly inwards where it can strike/push (Turn of Fate), and even clinch (Parrying Grab). It may be more famously known for its use in football, before becoming illegal, where it was called a "clothesline tackle."

The **Shoulder** is a close-range weapon often used to create space in Boxing, disrupt balance, adjust positioning, check, or enhance a joint attack (Cross of Destruction).

The **Hip** is used like the shoulder at close range to create space, disrupt balance, adjust positioning (Retreating Pendulum), or launch throws (Locked Horns).

# KICKS & BALANCE DISRUPTIONS

**Kicks** in martial arts are a powerful method of hitting with the knees, lower legs, and various parts of the feet. The feet are especially capable of generating a great deal of acceleration and power at various heights, directions, body angles, and with a variety of weapon surfaces.

**Balance Disruptions** are methods where the legs are used to primarily attack an opponent's leg(s) to disrupt balance, often with an upper body assist. These are done with *Sweeps, Trips, Buckles, Takedowns,* and *Throws.*

**KICKS** are used in street and some sport fighting arts and, depending on angle, range, and available targets, then the knees, shins, calves, ankles, and of course the feet can be used as weapons.

There are whole martial art styles whose reputations are built upon the effectiveness of kicking, like Tae Kwon Do from Korea or Savate from France. Some are well-known for a certain type of kick, like Muay Thai's Roundhouse, Wing Chun's front/inverted side thrust/TSK kick, or Kenpo's front snap kick. Regardless of style, the effectiveness of kicking is made better with good technique developed through repetitive practice.

The three-main structural and mechanical factors for developing and applying any kick correctly are, in order of importance, *Balance, Path of Motion,* and *Foot Position.* Genetics, training, and the nuances for applying each kick are most effectively enhanced with those factors understood.

Balance occurs when we control our center to allow for dynamic structural leverage to be accelerated and applied. This is more difficult when kicking because it is done while standing on one foot. An important detail is how the body center should be above, or slightly ahead on the target side of the base foot (See *Balance* in the *Mind*). This increases the foundational leverage needed to kick with power while not pushing off from or falling into a target.

Path of Motion is the linear or circular path, or track, the kicking weapon follows to the target while optimizing balance, and the muscle firing sequence unique to each kick. More simply, Kicks *hinge* or *push.*

*Hinge Kicks* apply the foot or lower leg through straightening or bending the knee joint at the end of a kick's mechanics. This motion causes the foot to travel in a circular arc with a whipping acceleration. Straight leg kicks apply this arc from the hip.

*Push Kicks* use the hip and knee simultaneously after aligning the bottom of the foot to a target, then driving it on a linear path into full extension, or until contact is made.

Note: A *hinge* kick into extension, especially in the air or if missing the target, the quad muscle attachments need to stop the knee joint from locking (also the triceps for the elbow). Repetitive uncontrolled straightening of the knee or elbow joint will result or evolve into a joint injury.

Foot Position refers to using the best weapon surface to provide the most penetration into the target at the point of impact, while preserving the foot's structural integrity. The major parts of the foot used for kicking are the bottom, middle, two sides, back of the heel, plus the instep and ball of the foot. The knees and shins are also used.

Some styles, like Vietnamese Vo Thuat, use the toes as well. I do not teach using the toes, other than to push away at the end of a front push kick. The "knife edge" of the foot is also used but contact should be done on the bottom edge of the heel to avoid an ankle rollover injury.

Once *Balance, Path of Motion,* and *Foot Position* is understood other factors become important. Flexibility allows for different kicking motions at different heights and angles, making stretching an important training component for anyone wanting to be a "good kicker." Genetics are another factor as some are more flexible, have a better feel for balance, can generate more explosive and faster kicks, or have a dense musculoskeletal structure for heavier kicks. None of this however means that everyone can't get better at kicking from whatever genetic baseline they start.

For sport fighter's the development of proficient high and low kicks can be beneficial. For street stylists, where kicking high is discouraged, kicks are generally done to lower targets through more natural ranges of motion.

Someone exceptional at kicking could get away with high kicks in a street situation but it is risky due to lack of stretch, clothing or shoes, floor surface, cluttered or crowded room, inability to use the legs like in a swimming pool, and the unknown skill and pain tolerance of an opponent who could also catch the kicking leg. Unless the arms are tied up or otherwise unusable then kicking in self-defense should be limited to lower targets or be avoided entirely.

Kicking motions initiated to the front side of the body, whether with square or turned hips, all start by lifting the knee up in front, and usually bent. The legs, hips, and base foot can then be adjusted as needed to align different kicking motions as the foot extends to become the primary weapon.

Note: This knee-up starting position also helps conceal the intended kick until the final motion is committed. This gives an opponent less reaction time, and with the option to change the kick and/or target while the leg is in motion.

Kicks to the rear side of the body mostly start by lifting the heel up in back by bending the knee. This contraction is often followed by a pushing extension of the foot bottom towards a target.

The upper body position is also important as it is used to counterbalance kicking as part of our natural gait for control, extension, and power. This can involve leaning and/or rotating the body by exaggerating natural motions of the shoulders and hips.

When walking, as the right leg steps forward the right arm naturally swings backwards, with the opposite left arm swinging forward to counterbalance the right side. This opposite leg/hip and shoulder/arm movement happens on both sides of the body and is how human locomotion is designed. Circular kicks especially are done by exaggerating this natural motion.

Overall, there are at least 6 types of *Knee Kicks* using 4 different parts of the knee, with 29 different *Shin* and *Foot Kicks* categorized here into *Front Kicks, Inverted Kicks, Crescent Kicks, Ax Kicks, Roundhouse/Wheel Kicks, Hook Kicks, Side Kicks, Rear Kicks,* and *Stomps.*

Notes: The muscle structure of the body to apply a kick requires the hip position face the direction of the kick. Both hips are square to the front when doing a *Front, Inverted, Crescent,* or *Ax* kicks, with one hip forward for *Roundhouse, Hook,* and *Side* kick, or square to the rear for *Rear* kicks.

All kicks have variations and can be enhanced with footwork, jumping, and spinning maneuvers. Common and popular ones will be mentioned within the kick's description, otherwise the standard kick will be described.

**Knee Kicks** are a powerful weapon used at close to medium range with the knee bent 90° to about 45°, depending on leg dimension, flexibility, and the application. The 4 primary knee contact points are *Top, Point, Front,* and *Inside Angle.*

Note: Forward knee kicks are applied with ankle straight and toes ending pointed backwards as they are the last contact point to leave the ground after pushing to accelerate. This shape also helps keep the toes from hitting hard surfaces like an opponent's the shin. *Upward Knee Kicks* use more of a hip flexor and abdominal contraction to accelerate and apply force and where the ankle may end bent with toes pulled up into the motion.

Top of Knee is the part above the kneecap at the base of the quad muscles. It can be used with a 45-90° knee bend, although at 90° the toes are more exposed to incidental contact if not pointed. The 2 knee kicks using this surface are the *Roundhouse* and *Upward Knee.*

The *Roundhouse Knee Kick* is done by turning the hip over, like a *roundhouse kick* but without the lower leg extension. The hands can help brace and pull the target into this accelerating weapon or jumping can be added. It is used in Muay Thai and MMA sport fighting and in self-defense (Entangled Arm B base technique).

The *Upward Knee Kick* is done by explosively lifting the knee straight up with the intention of striking upward under a horizontal target. This knee kick is often seen in MMA against an opponent changing levels to attempt a takedown, in Muay Thai as a flying knee kick to the head, and in self-defense into a bent over attacker (Gripping Wrist).

<u>Point of Knee</u> is the sharp hard 45° wedge formed when the leg is completely flexed so the calf is against the hamstrings. This wedge aligns the large femur bone to act as a battering ram into a target and is potentially the body's strongest alignment.

This *Front Knee Kick* is done by pushing off the ground, driving the knee and hips forward into a vertical target. It can be done pulling on a neck clinch or with the same side elbow moving slightly down and back as a counterbalance. The hip push behind this application adds depth penetration and back up mass while leaning back contributes to the hips moving forward as it gets the head away from any reflexive head butt or high counter strike.

This knee strikes the torso with (Parrying Grab) without a clinch (Rear Belt Grab), and to the legs (Cradling the Baby) to damage and break balance. Street styles also use it to attack the groin (Thrusting Thumbs).

<u>Front of Knee</u> is below the kneecap at the top of the shinbone with the leg bent about 90°. This surface is applied to strike or press forward or downward as a dropping weapon. It is also the contact point when leg blocking, e.g., knee/shin block.

The *Forward Knee Kick* is a specialized type of roundhouse kick in Muay Thai where the knee is driven forward, but it can also be used to strike then press, perhaps against a wall (Conquering Arm).

The *Downward Knee Drop* is heavy and powerful as the knee is driven down onto vulnerable targets like the Achilles tendon (Lock of Death), calf (Evading the Club), or torso of a downed opponent (Tripping Leg).

Note: I often ask students "what's the best target to drop your knee onto?" Nobody seems to get this right the first time with every individual target seemingly named, but the right answer is "anywhere."

<u>Inside Angle of Knee</u> is the upper inner corner surface close to the base of the inner quad muscle and applied inward. This motion is weaker than other knee kicks, so the ankle is bent, and the toes lifted to engage more of the legs muscle structure.

This *Inward Flapping Knee Kick* is done with knee up then hinged inward at the hip joint. It is commonly used in Muay Thai from a clinch position to attack the torso, especially the floating ribs, in front of, behind, or under an opponent's elbows.

***Lower Leg & Foot Kicks*** are where kicking gets dynamic with 9 different lower leg kicks and at least 12 different lower leg and foot striking surfaces. These 9 methods in order following the muscle structure of the legs and with the hips starting in front are the *Inverted, Front, Crescent, Ax, Roundhouse/Wheel, Side, Hook, Rear,* and *Stomps* to different directions.

The 12 different striking surfaces from the lower leg down are the *Shin, Calf, Ankle Crease, Instep, Toes, Ball-of-Foot, Bottom-of-Foot, Bottom-of-Heel, Outside Heel Edge, Inside Heel Edge, Back-of-Heel,* and *Knife Edge.* These weapon surfaces will be covered as they are used to apply the various kicks.

Combined, these become at least 29 different kicks, all able to be enhanced with footwork, jumps, and spinning maneuvers. Some of the more popular enhancements will be mentioned within the kick description it applies to.

Total *Kicks* to the front: 2 types of *Inverted,* 5 *Front,* 2 *Crescents,* and 3 *Ax Kicks;* to the side: 5 types of *Roundhouse/Wheel,* 3 *Side,* and 2 *Hooks;* to the rear: 3 types of *Rear Kicks,* and 4 *Stomps* to different directions.

<u>Inverted Kicks</u> start by rotating the foot out and bending the knee where it can then be pushed forward. The 2 types of kicks using this motion are the *Inverted Roundhouse/Wheel Kick* and *Inverted Side Thrust Kick* (aka *TSK*).

The *Inverted Roundhouse/Wheel Kick* is done with either the rear leg stepping through inverting the *Roundhouse Kick* motion, or front leg inverting the *Wheel Kick* motion by pointing the knee out from that hip with the foot more inward at a diagonal. The lower leg then hinges outward accelerating the foot/ankle/shin into a leg, groin, body, or face target.

Note: The *Inverted Roundhouse* aligns to kick the front side of an opponent in a closed, L-L or R-R stance; with the *Inverted Wheel* from an open, L-R or R-L stance.

The *Inverted Side Thrust Kick* is done by lifting the rear bent leg, with the hip open and foot bottom aligned towards the target. The heel is then pushed into the torso or thigh in sport but can also be used against the knee in front (Prancing Tiger), back (Turn of Fate), or on the side (Crossing Fist) in Self-Defense Techniques.

Note: This is the least risky rear leg kick as it is virtually impossible to catch and can be done with minimal body motion. The term TSK or "thrusting sweep kick," is used in Kenpo circles to describe this general motion. It is differentiated here into two distinct kicking applications with the inverted side thrust kick pushing forward and the other a sweeping motion along the ground, covered under *Sweeps.*

<u>Front Kicks</u> are perhaps the easiest lower leg kick to learn as the mechanics do not involve hip rotation or major pivoting on the base foot. With no hip

rotation the need to counterbalance the upper body is less, although it can be useful to drop the elbow slightly on the kicking side and/or extend the hips forward.

Self-defense styles usually apply this kick to the groin or knees with sport styles favoring a pushing version of the same kick. The 5 types of *Front Kicks* are the *Stiff-Leg Lifting Front Kick, Front Scoop Kick, Upward Front Kick, Front Snap Kick,* and *Front Push Kick.*

The *Stiff-Leg Lifting Front Kick* is a leg swinging motion like punting a football. This extremely powerful motion uses the instep, ankle, or shin up into an appropriate target like the groin (Defending Cross), or a bent torso (Hammerlock). Its natural motion is easy to teach, making it a good beginners self-defense class kick.

The *Front Scoop Kick* is done at the contact point of a stiff-leg lifting front kick up into the groin, but the ankle and toes are flexed to grasp and rip through the kicked groin as the knee is bent and pulled back through the target (Checking the Club).

The *Upward Front Kick* is like the stiff-leg lifting front kick except the knee is bent first before the lower leg is extended up into a target to hit with the top of the foot, ankle, or shin before snapping back. It is applied up into an appropriate target such as the groin (Buckling the Leg) or bent over torso (Charging Tackle).

The *Front Snap Kick* is a commonly used kick in Kenpo and done primarily with the lead leg, where it is used like how a boxer uses a jab to distract, manipulate posture, and setup other options. This quick obscure weapon is often applied to the groin area (Delayed Hand), or knee (Hooking Arms).

The contact point is the ball of the foot, formed by flexing the toes up while the ankle is extended straight. This combination of pulling the toes while pushing the ankle at two different joint systems so close together can seem difficult at first but is important to this kicks success. A bent ankle will give or even collapse with heavy contact, like punching with a bent wrist.

Note: This part of the foot can be formed as the knee is lifted with the foot pushing off the ground, passing through a cat stance, or with a bent ankle that straightens as the kick is applied, more like in a *front push kick.*

This *hinge kick* travels forward so applying this linear strike using circular mechanics is done by dropping the knee slightly into the trajectory level of the foot as the leg is straightened into the target.

The reaction, distraction and postural changes from this kick can set up a barrage of follow up strikes (Hand of Destruction) and can be done more powerfully with the rear leg (Thrusting Palm).

Note: The front leg version of this kick is sometimes taught by cocking the kicking foot back next to the standing knee before kicking. This extra hamstring contraction does not help the quad muscle move the foot forward, and the foot then takes longer to reach the target by traveling backwards before forwards. The more efficient way to do this kick is to let the knee pull the foot up, passing through a 90° bend then extending the foot like a whip into the target. Besides no negative motion, the ball of foot also aligns better using this method.

The *Front Push Kick* is a popular sport fighting kick done above the waist to mostly create space by hitting then pushing an opponent away. Of course, damage can also be caused, especially if done to the face.

Note: This creating space objective is the opposite of the low *Front Snap Kick* used to keep an opponent close but out of position and hopefully bent over, as used in Kenpo.

A push kick is done by lifting the knee above the waist, foot slightly ahead with ankle and toes flexed. The hip and knee then push the foot forward until contact, where the ankle and toes are extended to add acceleration and penetration. The street application could use the toes with a sharp shoe point into the eyes, throat, or solar plexus.

This kick can also be applied with the more durable heel with less risk of injury to the smaller foot bones. This method sacrifices a little range and can stress the hamstrings more as the ankle must be strongly flexed when it is applied. Note: The *Inverted Side Thrust Kick* with the foot externally rotated is less stressful on the hamstrings for applying the heel this way.

Crescent Kicks get its name from the arc shape the leg makes when moving inside or outside. The *Inward* and *Outward Crescent Kicks* are both done to the front side of the body with the hips square and are a natural motion for the hips. This kicking motion seems natural for most people and is a kick that even someone less flexible can do at or above their waist.

The *Inward Crescent Kick* starts by lifting the bent knee slightly outside our centerline, which is lined up with the target. The lower leg is then extended at the knee and whipped inward with the hip joint where the knee then bends again to apply the inside heel edge or bottom of the foot. This kick can slap someone's extended hand or is more powerfully applied with spinning and jumping footwork (Defying the Club).

The *Outward Crescent Kick* also starts by lifting the bent knee but slightly inside and across our own centerline. The lower leg is then extended at the knee and whipped outward at the hip joint hitting with the outside edge of the heel, where the knee then bends again to retract the motion after contact. This kick can also slap someone's extended hand and be done with or without spinning footwork (Defending Cross).

The <u>Ax Kick</u> gets its name from the downward "ax" like motion it travels through towards a target after being positioned through an *Inward, Outward,* or *Straight* path. The contact surface can be the bottom or back of heel, bottom of foot, toes, or calf.

Once the leg descends below waist level onto a lower target, or to the ground, the hips are thrust slightly forward as the upper body straightens backward to engage the glute muscles, increasing leg acceleration and power, while also helping to counterbalance.

Note: The knee should not lock straight when the foot or leg hits the target as the foot will stop or slow, but the knee would keep moving, possibly into hyper-extension. The slightly bent knee can be controlled and accelerated downward without injury.

The *Inward Ax Kick* starts with the knee in front and slightly outside our centerline. The lower leg is then extended and circled inward at the hip until above the target where it then accelerates downward (Eluding Death).

The *Outward Ax Kick* is done by lifting the knee up in front and slightly inside our centerline then the lower leg is extended and circled outward, like an *outward crescent kick* except when above the target it is accelerated downward (Alternating Fists). This type of ax kick is also used in sport fighting to higher targets, and where good flexibility is needed to apply it.

The *Straight Ax Kick* is against an opponent already on the ground by lifting the knee straight up in front then extending the lower leg, like a *Front Snap Kick,* above the target then pushed down (Crossing Grab).

Note: The *Straight Ax Kick* is sometimes seen in sport and exhibition martial arts after a cartwheel or front flip. Any of the 3 ax kicks can be used on an opponent fighting from his back.

Roundhouse/Wheel Kicks are circular kicks that travel inward using the lower leg as the hip turns over. "Roundhouse" for many practitioners is the term used for this kick with either leg but here will refer to the rear leg version, with "Wheel" used to describe the lead leg kick. Generally, the rear leg is more for power and the lead leg more for speed, although footwork can enhance the power in either leg.

The 4 contact points used to apply these kicks are the *Middle to Lower Shin, Ankle Joint, Instep,* and *Ball-of-Foot.* There are also 5 major *Roundhouse / Wheel Kick* types that are named for the angle or direction applied, *Downward, Downward Diagonal, Horizontal, Upward Diagonal,* and *Forward.*

Note: Pre-steps can be used to adjust the base standing foot open prior to this kick. This helps protect the base knee and enables range and angle adjustments, while increasing power. This pre-step opens the hip flexors and adductors, preloading them into extension before accelerating them into contraction as the kick is done (see *Muscle Pre-Load* in the *Mind*). This pre-loaded hip posture can be seen in many Muay Thai fighters who carry their hips pushed slightly forward and open prior to throwing the powerful roundhouse kicks of that style.

To increase lead leg power this pre-step is taught in 3 main ways using 1-2-3-steps. A 1-step example would be the right rear leg stepping forward to about 1:30 as a step-thru to load what was the lead leg for kicking. A 2-step example would be the front foot stepping back slightly before the rear leg steps forward to pre-load for kicking. A 3-step example would be the rear leg stepping sideways and slightly forward then the front leg steps together with that leg then that rear leg steps again, step-drag-step, as the foundation for the lead leg kick. Along with timing differences, the depth of these adjustment steps varies and can look like running into the kicking motion.

Whichever leg is used the hip turns over and inward at varying degrees to align and whip the kicking leg into the target. Since one hip is turning inward the upper body on the same side counterbalances at the waist by turning that shoulder and arm outward. This is an exaggeration of the body's natural hip/shoulder gait described earlier where the arm swings back as the same side leg moves forward.

The kicking legs speed starts from the toes pushing off the ground, with the muscular power generated from the hip flexors pulling the knee towards the target, then the lower leg is extended using the quad muscles to accelerate it like a whip that upon contact pushes the whole leg, and possibly body structure, into the target.

Upon reaching a target the lower leg can either snap back by retracting the foot at the knee, as done in many Karate styles, or the entire leg could push through the target, with a 360° pivot "in the air" as taught in Muay Thai, with this full pivot done if the kick missed or glanced through its target, as solid contact would slow and eventually stop the leg and body rotation.

For the hip to turn over effectively and maintain knee integrity the heel of the base foot must move towards the target. Pivoting on the ball of this foot is done until the heel points towards the target. This protects the standing knee from twisting and adds body rotation, acceleration, and mass to this kick.

A *Downward Roundhouse/Wheel Kick* is when the knee leads the foot straight down to the ground. It can be done with the ball of foot to pin the body (Broken Kneel), or shin to drive the knee down (Reversing Fist).

A *Downward Diagonal Roundhouse/Wheel Kick* is the angle seen with the powerful Muay Thai leg kick. It extends and drops with a corkscrew motion driving the shin into the outer thigh (IT band), causing muscle/fascia cramping, aka "Charley-Horse." This makes it difficult to put  weight on that leg, taking away support and leverage (Six Hands).

The *Upward Diagonal Roundhouse/Wheel Kick* is like the horizontal version, but the angle provides other options. The rear leg is used in sport as a power kick that fits into an opening between an opponent's elbow and ribs or kicks or over his shoulder across the temporal lobe.

The wheel kick version, aka "flip kick," is used to attack the inside leg in kickboxing and MMA, often with a pre-step, or to the groin in street and Kenpo rules sparring, often with a *Pull-Drag.* The shin, ankle, foot, or toes can all be used, depending on the target (Ducking Dragon). The knee is slightly bent when doing this version as the hip primarily accelerates the foot with the knee straightening into the impact.

Note: A teaching technique to help students make this an un-telegraphed efficient kick is to put a coin on top of their own foot then try and throw it against a wall. This illustrates and assures the foot does not move backwards before going forwards.

The *Horizontal Roundhouse/Wheel Kick* uses that same motion except the body does not drop into the target but travels on a line more parallel with the floor, like swinging a baseball bat. This horizontal trajectory helps this kick align to other targets like the shoulders, head, neck, and torso (Evading the Club) or along the ground to sweep or trip (Protective Circles).

The *Forward Roundhouse/Wheel Kick* is a specialty Muay Thai kick described earlier as a *Forward Knee Kick* listed again here as it's in the *Roundhouse Kick* family, but with a unique forward trajectory.

Side Kicks can be the linear pushing *Side Thrust Kick* or circular hinging *Side Snap Kick*. In either case, the side of the hip is pointed at the target with the foot turned sideways before hitting with either the bottom or outside bottom edge of the heel.

The *Side Thrust Kick* is done by turning the hip and lifted knee over to aim the bottom of the heel at the target. The leg is then pushed straight into extension driving the heel into a target before being retracted by pulling the knee back along the same path. The elbow on the same side should be on the front half of the body so the hip can turn over more effectively and be more aligned.

This popular Karate kick is often enhanced with jumping and spinning footwork. The drag-step and rear crossover are 2-count foot maneuvers used to accelerate this kick, with the pull-drag and step-thru are efficient 1-count maneuvers.

Note: Since the hip must turn over to do this kick the back of the body can become exposed so it is used sparingly in sport fighting styles like Muay Thai where the leg can become vulnerable to a round kick or in MMA where the back can be taken if missed. It is however one of the most powerful kicking motions.

Mechanically, the hips turnover like a *Roundhouse/Wheel kick,* but the counterbalance is different. The linear foot extension is better balanced by moving the arm and shoulder of the kicking leg side inward and slightly down. This allows the body to stop rotating while projecting the bottom of the heel in a straight line towards the target.

Defensively it can be used to stop a charging opponent by cocking the knee so the bottom of the foot points at the incoming target before being powerfully extended to fill the space. Offensively the leg is lifted while slightly bent, but not overly cocked before it is launched, often into the torso.

Self-defense applications are done primarily to the knee joint and is effective to any angle around that joint. Since the hip turns to a *point of no return*, this kick is often done as a last move before exiting, with a *front crossover* (Buckling Leg), although it can be followed with a spinning motion (Snapping Arm).

The *Side Snap Kick* is also delivered from the side of the body, but the hip does not turn over. It involves the lower leg snapping out and back from the knee like a *Front Snap Kick*. The bottom outside edge of the heel is the strongest contact point of this quick kick that can buckle (Retreating Pendulum) or hyperextend a knee (Twins of Aggression).

Some sport fighters prefer this *side snap* to the *side thrust* because the cocked foot remains down before and after kicking. The leg then becomes a defensive obstacle with the foot providing groin protection and the back is not as exposed, and with its upward trajectory it is able to fit under an elbow into the ribs, but with less power and range then a fully rotated side thrust kick.

Note: The shape of the foot for side kicks should be ankle and all toes flexed up to stabilize the structure and focus the bottom of the heel. The big toe down foot position weakens the foot structure and exposes the ankle to a rollover injury.

Hook Kicks involve pulling the leg and foot back into a target with the back or bottom of the heel, or possibly the ball and toes, depending on range and intention. The 2 primary methods used are the *Outward* and *Upward Hook Kicks*.

The *Outward Hook Kick* starts by lifting the knee in front, same as all other kicks thus far, and then extending the foot across our centerline, like a missed side thrust kick, before pulling the foot and leg back behind us at the hip and knee parallel with the floor. This kick requires good flexibility to be used above the waist with 3 main ways it is applied.

The first involves pulling a straighter leg backwards through the target using the glutes, but with less knee bend. This method looks like an outward leg swing and can be effective onto an appropriate target, and applied often after spinning (Circling the Kick, base technique).

The second is done by only bending the knee to snap the heel onto then off a target. This is the *upward hook kick* motion but done parallel with the floor and used primarily to attack the torso, groin, or knee (Hidden Hand). The *Rear Scoop Kick* is arguably in this category, but I have it under *Rear Kicks* because of the exit motion after being used.

The third method uses a combination of the previous two and looks like the first version with the addition of the knee bending as the entire leg is pulled backwards, but still able to be retracted (Jumping Crane). This is the standard way taught in many karate schools and used in sport karate.

The *Upward Hook Kick* is used in self-defense against a close rear opponent by explosively lifting the heel up from the ground under and into a target then snapping the foot back down to the ground. This can be easily practiced while standing by placing the back of both hands against your own rear end, palms facing out, then alternating the heels up to kick the palm side of your own hand, like a quad stretch warm-up.

This is one of those *minor motions* that can have a *major effect* in a confrontation (See *Major & Minor Principle* in the *Mind*). It can be used against a close rear bear hug attacker where the heel can easily snap up between his legs to crush the testicles against his pubic bone (Crushing Palm). It can also be used against the torso (Hammerlock), or a bent over opponent's face (Turning Windmills).

Rear Kicks are done with the hips square backwards towards a target behind us and is primarily a street defense kick. The 3 types of rear kicks are the *Stiff-Leg Lifting Rear, Rear Scoop,* and *Rear Thrust* or *Snap.*

This is the only leg direction where the knee is <u>not</u> lifted in front to load the kick. The weapon surface can be the *Back-of-Heel, Bottom-of-Heel,* or *Calf.* The foot is vertical with toes and knee down, making it difficult to counter or catch.

The *Stiff-Leg Lifting Rear Kick* is applied by swinging the straight leg up to the rear, after prepositioning with an opponent. The contact point can vary from the *Back-of-Heel* to the *Calf*

and is a good medium-range kick if the target is too far for an *upward hook* or *rear scoop* yet too close for a *rear thrust* (Protective Circles).

The *Rear Scoop Kick* is done by bending the knee to lift the heel up to the rear under a target, like the *upward hook kick,* except the knee is then pulled forward to scrape the heel through the target with a whipping action. Targets include under the groin (Circling the Club), torso (Thrusting Thumbs), or head (Crossed Arms).

The *Rear Thrust/Snap Kick* uses the same motion, but with different emphasis. The knee is bent as the heel is lifted to the rear, aligning the heel bottom with a rear target followed by pushing the foot into that target. This is potentially the strongest kicking motion.

The *Thrust* locks out before retracting so is used to stop an approaching attacker or push away and/or end a technique sequence (Calming the Club, base technique), The *Snap* returns quickly off the target so is used more within a sequence before continuing with other movements (Kick into Darkness).

Stomp Kicks use the bottom of the heel to crush down compressing a target onto the ground. The four types of <u>Stomps</u> are *Front, Side, Rear,* and *Inverted Side,* all named by which way the toes point rather than stomp direction as some foot angles can be used in more than one direction.

The *Front Stomp Kick* is done with the toes able to point to the front (Destructive Parries) or side (Scraping Stomp).

Note: Bruce Lee famously does a leaping front stomp on his nemesis O'Hara in his classic movie "Enter the Dragon," with an unforgettably intense expression on his face.

The *Side Stomp Kick* is done with the toes turned inward, so the outside of the foot is sideways to the

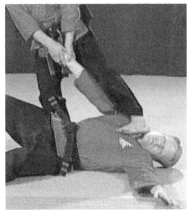

stomp's direction. It can be done comfortably to the side (Escaping Death) or the front (Fist of Aggression).

The *Inverted Side Stomp Kick* is done to the front of the body with the toes pointed outward. This is the *front crossover* step motion but used with an impact intention (Tripping Leg).

The *Rear Stomp Kick* is done only backwards by lifting the foot off the ground then forcefully stepping back and down with the heel onto a target, often the top of an opponent's foot (Crushing Palm). This motion should not go too far back but stay within the length of one foot back. This stomp was also done by Bruce Lee in "Enter the Dragon."

Additionally, this stomp can be applied after sliding the foot along the ground, with the heel up, then upon reaching a grounded target the heel is dropped to pinch and crush targets that include the groin (Hidden Hand) or collarbone (Backbreaker).

**BALANCE DISRUPTIONS** are methods used to affect a standing opponent's posture and balance either temporarily or to put them on the ground. Many of these would not be considered grappling techniques but are ways that take one or both of an opponent's legs off their base, generally using our legs to do so. The four methods covered are *Sweeps* (5 types), *Trips* (8 types), *Buckles* (2 types), and *Takedowns & Throws* (9 types).

Note: Grappling styles like Judo and Wrestling are dedicated to perfecting the variables and intricacies of getting an opponent to the ground. The techniques defined here are more for the street stylist, without a kimono and not on a matted surface, although they still can have some crossover value into sport grappling.

Sweeps are primarily used to disrupt one foot of an opponent moving it away from their other foot. This is to temporarily disrupt balance, although they could still end up on the ground. This type of technique literally moves along the floor like a broom sweeping their foot from its base position. The five main sweeps are *Front Step-Thru, Pulling, Inverted Pulling, Pushing,* and *Rear Sliding.*

Note: A sweep moves the foot, so it works best with less weight on the foot being swept, whereas a buckle bends or hyperextends the knee so is more effective with more weight on that foot. Weight must therefore often be manipulated using the upper body and hands to subtly shift an opponent's weight to apply the intended move (Twirling Fist).

The *Front Step-Thru Sweep* slides our rear leg forward along the ground, like a front step thru foot maneuver but with a slight arc like a low roundhouse kick. This motions impact lifts their heel and moves their foot, the degree of which depends on weight distribution, reactive balance, and relative leg density, along with our intention, speed, force, and any upper body assist.

Upon contact our ankle and lower shin hits, wrapping our foot around their foot and ankle to move and possibly lift their foot and leg

(Protective Parries), and it can also be done to the wrist of a posted hand (Cradling the Baby). In sport this is often used to create a timing gap or followed up with another sweep (Brown 2nd Sparring #1), but also effectively used in street arts to take an opponent completely to the ground (Twins of Aggression).

The *Pulling Sweep* starts with the front ankle and foot wrapped around the back or front of an opponent's foot and ankle bone. As our weight shifts onto our base foot for balance, the now un-weighted foot pulls their foot to or past our base foot, like a front crossover step. This can be done from an inside (Entwined Blade) or outside (Glancing Poke) leg position and is a natural follow-up to a *Front Step-Thru Sweep*.

The *Inverted Pulling Sweep* is done after rotating our foot outward into a *Front Twist Stance* to wrap our flexed foot and ankle around to grab an opponent's ankle. Our knee, foot, and ankle will then pull their foot off its base, a *step-out* foot maneuver, inside (Brown 1st Sparring #1) or outside the ankle (Clipping the Blade).

The *Pushing Sweep* is an accelerated motion utilizing the *Front Crossover Step*. It starts with both of our feet on the same side of an opponent's foot where it can then move one of their feet by hitting with the bottom of our foot to their heel (Glancing Palm).

The *Rear Sliding Leg Sweep* is a rear side motion using the back of our calf or knee to move an opponent's leg. It occurs after sliding the ball of our foot, with a bent knee and heel up, along the ground backwards until leg contact, where the heel is then pushed to the ground as the knee is straightened to accelerate the back of the leg into the sweeping motion and target.

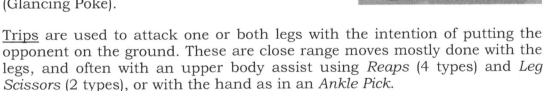

This motion can transition from a reverse cat stance (Sweeping the Leg), reverse close kneel (Retreating Pendulum), or a rear step-thru (Glancing Poke).

Trips are used to attack one or both legs with the intention of putting the opponent on the ground. These are close range moves mostly done with the legs, and often with an upper body assist using *Reaps* (4 types) and *Leg Scissors* (2 types), or with the hand as in an *Ankle Pick*.

A *Reap* is done facing an opponent using the back of our leg, usually the bent knee, hooked around to grab or post behind one of their legs. Once successfully hooked, their leg and foot are then lifted or moved off the ground by our leg, usually while holding and/or moving their upper body into the void left by their lifted foot, causing them to fall into that open area where their foot was and onto the ground.

Note: The descriptions here emphasize the back of our knee to hook the back of their knee, but some variances exist at these back-of-leg contact points. Also, a person's natural reaction when falling is to grab anything nearby to slow or prevent the fall. The closeness of these maneuvers leaves us susceptible to being pulled down, so be prepared to move to a dominant ground position, or perhaps drop a knee in a street context.

The *Reap* is a type of trip done from the inside-out or outside-in with either of our legs to either of their legs. The 4 methods to do this are *Straight-Out, Straight-In, Cross-Out,* and *Cross-In*.

The *Straight Outer Reap* is an inside-out maneuver done R-L or L-R by first placing our base foot on the ground <u>between</u> their two feet, then our un-weighted leg reaches between their legs hooking outward to the back of their knee to lift it off the ground.

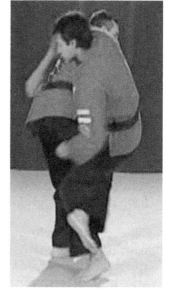

This is often done while picking up or posting their opposite leg with one hand while pushing them down with the other (Dance of Death).

This is also a common sweep after catching a kick (Defensive Takedown Sparring #2-3), and another version places our knee on the ground between their feet, with our foot behind their ankle, then pushing them over that lower leg while posting the opposite leg (Offensive Takedown Sparring #7)

The *Straight Inner Reap* circles outside-in, R-L or L-R, by first placing our base foot on the ground <u>between</u> their feet as our un-weighted leg reaches around outside their leg to hook inward. That leg is then lifted off the ground while pushing them down into the void where that lifted foot had been, then following up (Brown 2nd Sparring #5).

Note: In this version specifically, our groin is vulnerable to their knee, so our leg needs to hold their leg tightly, perhaps even hooking our reaping foot behind our own base knee. Since one of our legs ends between their legs as they hit the ground our shin or knee can easily be dropped onto their groin if for street before stepping out or sliding over to a top mount position.

The *Cross Outer Reap* is the least entangled trip as both of our feet are <u>outside</u> of their leg and our hip is behind theirs R-R or L-L, after stepping outside their base foot. Our right would reap the back of their right or, on the other side, our left against their left to take them down (Tripping Leg).

The *Cross Inner Reap* is done to the inside of their cross-side leg, R-R or L-L, so our base foot would be outside of their foot to be swept (Offensive Takedown Sparring #5), or between their legs in the case of a knee buckle (Offensive Takedown Sparring #7).

Using this motion to buckle applies the buckling foot between and behind their heel, right behind right for example, to hook and hold their foot down, then our knee pushes forward against the inside angle of their knee collapsing it and them to the ground (Scraping Stomp).

The *Leg Scissor,* or "scissor sweep" is applied in two ways, depending on relative front foot placement. If from a *Closed L-L/R-R Stance* this takedown is done one way where if in an *Open L-R/R-L Stance* it is done another. Either method requires the back of our front side hip is towards the opponent. This *Reverse Neutral Bow 'Fighting' Stance* is often setup with a pre-step and upper body feint or is formed in the air after leaping. Whatever the set up, at the point of the takedown our lead hand connects to their lead shoulder, or across their neck, to help pull them down.

The *Closed Stance Leg Scissor* done L-L, after whatever setup is applied, is done with our lower right shin posted against their anterior ankles and the back of our higher left leg against their posterior knees at the crease. The scissor motion is applied after breakfalling onto our right hip, as our left hand holds their left shoulder to slow our fall and pull them down, by rolling over from our right to left hip while using our legs to bend their knees forward and down to the ground.

Follow ups from the ground include kicking, punching, leg locks, grappling, or standing (Offensive Takedown Sparring #4).

The *Open Stance Leg Scissor* is higher on the body than the closed stance version, so if done L-R our lower right shin posts across the back of their knees, with the back of our higher left leg across the front of their hips. As we breakfall onto our right hip, with our left-hand gripping and pulling them down, we then roll over onto our left hip causing them to fall onto their back.

Follow ups from the ground include kicking, punching, leg locks, grappling, or standing (Defensive Takedown Sparring #6).

The *Ankle Pick* scoops up and holds an opponent's ankle or foot with a hand and is a popular wrestling move with many follow up options. While holding the one foot the opposite grounded foot can be tripped, the leg/hip pressed with the free arm causing them to fall backwards (Nutcracker), or the leg pulled down and around with knee pressure as in a *single leg takedown.* The held leg can also be lifted into the air to tip them over as in the Kenpo Leopard/Book Set.

Buckles bend or hyperextend the knee joint to disrupt posture and balance, with the potential to cause severe injury. This is done primarily using kicks (Thrusting Thumbs) or knees (Broken Kneel) but can also be done with the hands (Circling the Arm), or both (Shield and Punch).

The four main actions starting at the back: 1) bend the knee forwards by attacking the knee crease; 2) move the knee outwards by hitting the inside knee angle; 3) hyperextend it back to lock the knee straight by attacking the front of the knee; 4) move it inwards by hitting the outside of the knee.

Note: Striking the knee joint from any angle can cause serious and possibly permanent damage so practice with extreme caution.

The *Bent Forward Knee Buckle* is accomplished by attacking the back of knee crease, in the pocket between the tendons at point UB40, where the popliteal fossa is located. This is where the sciatic nerve splits into the tibial and fibular branches giving this target an uncontrollable nerve reflex response if struck inside that pocket with an appropriate weapon.

Methods to buckle the knee crease include the *Side Snap Kick* (Hugging Pendulum), *Side Thrust Kick* (Buckling the Leg), *Front Snap Kick* (Retreating Pendulum), *Downward Diagonal Roundhouse/Wheel Kick* (Reversing Fist), *Forward Knee Kick* (Evading the Club), and *Ax Kick* (Circling the Kick)

The *Outward Knee Buckle* happens at the inner knee joint crease, Lv8/Ki10 area, or just above the joint line at the medial thigh muscle attachment. This attack angle causes the knee to reflexively bend outwards, affecting posture and balance. It can be attacked with the feet (Hooking Arms), knees (Scraping Stomp), or hands (Entangled Arm B).

The *Locked Knee Buckle* is most effective against a straight leg, especially if their heel is planted on the ground. The most vulnerable contact point is where the femur connects to the tibia just above the kneecap in the tendons GTO. This angle of the knee can be made vulnerable by manipulating a weight transfer (Destructive Gift), pressing the knee (Straddling the Leg), or with an overpowering attack (Twins of Aggression).

The *Inward Knee Buckle* occurs with contact to the outside knee joint, usually with the foot (Hand & Shield), or knee (Twirling Fist). This could damage the medial collateral ligament (MCL) of that knee joint.

<u>Takedowns & Throws</u> are standup grappling methods used to get someone to the ground. Covered are *Takedowns* (4), *Hip Throws* (4), with the *Snap-Mare* and *Neck-Lever Throw*. These are minimal in the context of sport grappling styles like Judo or wrestling but are still useful reference points for the street stylist.

A primary strategy in street defense styles is to stay upright due to environmental considerations, multiple attackers, and possible weapons. Street style practitioners should however be aware of at least basic grappling for defensive awareness and offensive options.

The 4 takedowns covered are the *Heel Post, Lift & Trip, Double Leg,* and *Single Leg.* The 3 hip throws stem from the same base position and are the *Under Arm, Over Shoulder,* and *Waist Grab,* along with the *Snap-Mare* and *Neck Lever Throw.*

The *Heel Post Takedown* is from behind an opponent and compliments the *Lift & Trip Takedown.* It works especially well if the opponent drops his weight and widens his base to try and keep from being lifted.

If behind more to the right side then post our left foot and leg behind their left foot and legs with our right foot outside their right foot while grabbing around their waist, arms pinned or free. They are then pulled back and down to the ground by sitting to trip them over our extended left leg, into a left side fall, with their falling momentum helping pull us to a right leg step over to a top mounted position. Switch legs and position for other side.

The *Lift & Trip Takedown* is also done from behind an opponent and compliments the *Heel Post Takedown.* It works especially well if the opponent stands up tall to avoid being pulled down.

Wrap arms tightly around their waist, and perhaps arm(s), then lift their feet off the ground while swinging either of our legs inward to knock their legs out from under them while turning their torso in the opposite direction. If successful they are turned sideways in the air and then fall to the ground with us standing over them or following them to a top grappling position.

The *Double Leg Takedown* either picks up an opponent to turn them in the air before laying/slamming them down or it can drive them back and down like a tackle. Examples below are L-L.

1) Accelerating forward, our left foot will step past and outside their right foot driving and squatting as we tightly wrap our arms around their legs at the knees or under their glutes while our left shoulder impacts their ribs on their torso with our head posted on the outside. Then drag our right foot forward lifting them up and sideways in the air (i.e., football tackle), then step left forward pulling their legs outside your right hip putting/slamming them onto the ground (*step-drag-step* footwork). Follow with grappling, ground and pound, or exit (Offensive & Defensive Takedown Sparring #8's).

2) While in front yet not accelerating, common after avoiding a punch, post your feet and squat while wrapping up their legs with both arms, then lift them up and turn them sideways in the air, then put/slam them down following up with grappling or striking (Crushing Palm).

Note: The "double leg" done by wrestlers, where the front knee is driven into the mat, can be hazardous on hard surfaces so is not what is described here. The *Single Leg Takedown* for our purpose here is anytime one leg is held while their standing leg is tripped (Nutcracker), pulled down or knee levered as in Wrestling, or swept (Dance of Death). This may result from a failed *Double Leg,* a successful *Ankle Pick,* or a caught kick.

*Hip Throws* as described here consist of three variations using the same setup. For the right-side hip throw our left hand grabs their right wrist as our right then left foot will step forward turning to match the direction of their feet with our hip lower than their center and between their hips.

Our right hand and arm are then used as an *Under-Armpit Hip Throw*, around their neck to an *Over Shoulder Hip Throw*, or around their torso to a *Waist Grab Hip Throw*. Each hand and arm position sets-up a slightly different hip angle that all result in the opponent hinging over the low back and hips onto the ground (Locked Horns).

The *Snap-Mare Throw* reaches back over the shoulder with both hands to clinch around an opponent's head and neck then he is violently pulled forward and down, as in a *hip throw,* causing them to flip over or around us to the ground in front (Hidden Elbow).

Note: The safer way to practice is to drop one of our knees to the ground, on the side the training partner is flipping over, so they can roll around the shoulder without much neck pressure.

The *Neck Lever Throw* connects off a come-along hold where the cross medial wrist is grabbed as the same side arm weaves behind their elbow and up until our hand is behind their neck. Pressure into their locked elbow joint causes them to rise onto their toes, where they can be escorted away as a come along or tripped to be thrown as this pressure is applied (Twins of Destruction).

# CONTRACTION MOVEMENTS
## Grabs, Locks, Holds, Chokes

These are moves where the muscle structure surrounds to control and manipulate a target structure by collapsing around it and applying leverage. This is the primary method used in grappling where the hands, arms, and legs attach then contract around another person's body, or part(s) of their body.

Sophisticated grappling styles specialize in this aspect of fighting and are pursued to various levels of proficiency by those interested. The techniques described here are those commonly used during stand-up, clinch, and ground grappling that overlaps street and sport.

*Body Contraction Movements* are divided into the four general categories of *Grabs, Locks, Holds,* and *Chokes.* Semantics aside, the list and organization used here works for this purpose. Even though techniques of this nature can be potentially very damaging, many can be applied with a humane intention that allows for controlled regulation of force when needed. This is more difficult with striking techniques.

Sport styles use some of these to eliminate space and manipulate an opponent into a position of leverage. This is done to control, smother, joint lock, or choke, but also to cause fatigue, discomfort, misery, and pain, with the goal of winning by submission or gaining points towards a victory.

Street styles would use these techniques primarily from the standup perspective to cause mechanical dysfunction, disability, or mental unconsciousness. Ground grappling would be the last range desired in street defense as environment, multiple opponents, and non-natural weapons make it a risky choice. However, the street stylist should still learn the basics of ground grappling to at least know their vulnerabilities and how to defend until able to stand up again.

**Grabs** attach the hand(s) and fingers to body tissue for control or to cause damage and pain. **Locks** use an interlocking structure to eliminate a joints normal range of motion and then move it into a stressful position. **Holds** use the arms and legs to contain and manipulate an opponent. **Chokes** are specialized techniques against the neck and throat using the other three methods.

**GRABS** are done with the fingers and thumb in different configurations to form the *Closed Hand Grab, Hand Hooks,* and *Pinches.*

The <u>Closed Hand Grab</u> uses the fingers and opposable thumb gripping motion to clasp around an object and hold onto it. In martial arts this can include the wrist (Gripping Wrist), ankle (Straddling the Leg), head (Tripping Leg), or head hair (Lock of Death). Gripping with the hands can also be used against the muscle structure (Jamming the Tackle), and even the testicles (Nutcracker).

Note: In ancient fighting systems the testicle grab was an important offensive technique that must be defended. It is never a consideration in modern sport fighting but still exists in self-defense styles with ancient roots. Modern people are often squeamish to simulate this practice or consider using this type of technique, but it still exists.

Note: Sports like Judo and Jiu Jitsu wear a thick gi/kimono/uniform and grab extensively, as do wrestlers where hand-fighting is common although grabbing finger digits is illegal in all sport fighting. Grabbing wrists however is natural as even untrained people instinctively reach out to grab an adversary's wrists to try and control their hands.

Hand Hooks use the fingers and thumb to hang over a structure, like doing a pull up with the palm facing away or a chin up with the palms facing back. This structure can be used to grab our own wrist to secure a *Guillotine Choke* or to defend against that same choke (Locked Horns), or to fight the arm of a *Sleeper Choke* attempt (Eluding Death).

The palm and bent fingers form a cup shape that can also grab an opponent's chin to apply neck leverage, covered under *Locks*. This shape also links hands together to grip at the fingers to form the *"S" Grip,* or palm perpendicular to palm forming the *Gable Grip.*

Another type of hand hook is done with only the index and middle fingers or thumb and is commonly called a fishhook (Finger Set). It is used in street styles from behind to hook an opponent's eye (Glancing Blade) or possibly corners of the mouth (Form 4).

Pinches occur when the fingers and hand are compressed around tissue to cause damage or generate a nerve response. Pinches covered here are the *Crab, Horsebite,* and *Thumb/Index.*

The *Crab Pinch, aka Eagles Claw* or *C-Grip,* is formed by the thumb, hand webbing, and mostly the index and middle fingers making the shape of the letter "C" forming a strong combination of digits that grip around targets like the trachea, either palm down (Securing the Club) or palm up (Two-Man Set). It can also be used to press into an elbow joint when combined with a wrist grab (Hammerlock), and with the ends of these digits also available as eye pokes (Raining Blade).

Note: Patrick Swayze made this famous in the movie "Roadhouse" where he uses it to tear out an enemy's throat, to his character's regret.

The *Horsebite Pinch* uses the four fingertips, without the thumb, closed tightly into the palm with an opponent's skin squeezed between to generate a painful and reflexive nerve response. The main body areas for applying this pressure are the upper chest (Circling Parries), upper/inner thigh (Pinch from Death), upper/inner arm (Flashing Fist), and the long spinal muscles, especially over the kidneys (Locked Arm).

The *Thumb/Index Pinch* uses the two digits in its name with the thumb pad pressing against the side of the bent index finger middle joint to grab a small amount of sensitive skin. Although weaker than the *horsebite pinch* this digit positioning works better at some angles such as low and behind to an attacker's upper inner thigh (Crushing Palm).

**LOCKS** use the hands or an interlocking structure to put a joint into its extreme and locked position or apply pressure against sensitive tissue. This pressure and subsequent pain is designed to make an opponent give up, aka submit/tap out, dislocate a joint, or break a bone. Neck and limb locks are covered but hip and body locks are not. Lock categories are *Neck, Finger, Wrist, Elbow, Shoulder, Knee, Ankle,* and *Foot.*

Note: Moves that twist or stretch tendons and ligaments have varying degrees and ranges of success as pain thresholds vary, and different bodies have a variety of attachment dynamics from very flexible to extremely tight, from thin and weak to thick and strong, etc.

Neck Locks occur by taking the slack out of the neck in one of three directions. This is done to manipulate, cause pain, or severe injury by moving *Chin-Up, Chin-Down,* or *Chin-Sideways.*

The *Chin-Up Lock* can be done by reaching over or around the back of the head to grab the hair or eyes (Lock of Death), forehead (Blinding Vice), chin (Retreating Pendulum), or the thumb-index finger bar to hook the nose (Escaping Death). Whichever method is applied, the upper spine is used as a fulcrum to increase downward leverage as the hand pulls the head back and down while the chin is lifted/levered upwards.

The *Chin-Down Lock* pushes the chin into the chest and is most effectively done with body weight pressing against the back of the head. Grapplers do this when stacking someone's hips over their head, or in a *Guillotine Choke* variation where the back of the head is pressed into the lower abdomen and hips (Deflecting Pendulum). The *Full-Nelson Hold* and *Sleeper Choke* both can apply similar pressure.

The *Chin-Sideways Lock* can be done using the palm cupped under the chin to turn the head to that side as the other hand adds acceleration (Leap of Death), or the forearm and elbow hook over and behind that shoulder (Crashing Elbows).

<u>Finger Locks</u> apply pressure against this small hinge joint structure in one of six major ways, often with the opposite hand assisting. They are the *Finger Grab, Reverse Finger Grab, Finger Split, Finger Compression,* and *Cross Wrist Finger Trap.* These are indexed in the *Locking Set.*

Pressure using ulnar flexion/pushing, radial flexion/pulling, or trapping within the body structure are used to manipulate and damage. This can cause pain and injury that is difficult to ignore so these techniques are only used in street arts as finger joint attacks are illegal in all sport fighting.

These are used by bouncers and sometimes the police to control and escort an individual from one area to another. They can also be add-ons within a self-defense technique sequence where fingers can become trapped and strained intentionally or accidentally.

The key for these techniques is to tightly support the locked digit on one side to eliminate its range of motion then hyper-extend it by applying leveraged pressure against the opposite side of a nearby joint (i.e., Leverage).

The *Finger Grab Lock* is done by grabbing any or all fingers (Glancing Poke) or thumb with a cross thumb counter lock when shaking hands (Returning the Gift).

The *Reverse Finger Grab Lock* is applied by grabbing palm to palm. After gripping with thumb up or down the 1st joint is then pushed on the palm side while the 2nd or 3rd joints are pulled on the opposite side. The ground can also be used causing the opponent's fingertips to point back towards their elbow where a *Reverse Wrist Lock* could be applied (Twisting the Gift).

The *Finger Split Lock* is when at least two of an opponent's finger digits are grabbed and held in separate hands then pulled apart at the webbing, and often while pulling the fingers back into hyperextension (Locking Set).

The *Finger Compression Lock* refers to two different fingertip attacks. One is done by pressing our nail tip into the nail bed of an opponent's finger, the second to counter a rear bear hug is done by grabbing any or all fingertips then squeezing and folding them into the palm (Long Form 3).

The *Cross-Wrist Finger Trap* counters a straight wrist grab, L-R/R-L, using our body structure to trap their fingers. A grabbed right hand would be placed under our left armpit with our left radius bone and elbow crease wrapping under against the back of their fingers until our left hand is next to our left ear, with a slight torso rotation against the finger joints (Gripping Wrist).

Wrist Locks apply pressure against this joint structure where the radius bone interacts with two of the hand's carpal bones and where the ulna bone is connected via an articular disk. This flexible joint allows the hand to rotate in a circle or be moved in six major directions.

*Twisting* the wrist involves either externally rotating (i.e., supination) the hand of an opponent so their palm faces towards them called here an *Outward Wrist Lock* or the opposite direction internally rotated (i.e., pronation) into an *Inward Wrist Lock.*

*Bending* the wrist occurs when the fingers are moved towards the forearm in either direction (i.e., Flexion/Extension). Flexion towards the medial forearm is the direction where an *Outward* or *Inward Wrist Lock* is pressed or struck after aligned, or into full Extension as in a *Reverse Wrist Lock.*

*Flexing* the wrist (i.e., Radial & Ulnar Deviation) is done by moving the little finger towards the ulna bone (Desperate Fists) into a *Wrist Flex Lock.* The thumb side can be flexed towards the radius, but this motion is difficult to have an impact on most people.

Forcing the hand in these directions by *Twisting, Bnding*, or *Flexing* can be done with the torso, arms, and hands to manipulate an opponent's center and affect posture while causing pain, and perhaps damaging their wrist. Covered are the *Outward, Inward, Reverse*, and *Wrist Flex Locks,* with variations of each primarily by using the hand to grip and apply pressure. They are used in techniques and are indexed in the *Locking Set.*

Note: Countering wrist attacks is done best before effective pressure is applied by either rapidly pulling or pushing the hand away from the grip, grabbing a nearby structure for support, like clothing or another body part on us or an opponent, or using our free hand to grab and support our attacked hand, e.g., palm to palm.

The *Outward Wrist Lock* externally rotates an opponent's hand away from their centerline with two variations that *Twist* or Bend.

The Twist uses our thumb(s) to press the back little finger knuckle pushing their fingers outside their centerline, as our middle finger pulls their hands thumb side scaphoid bone as a handle. This turns the hand and little finger to point back over their same side shoulder and usually to the ground (Crossing Grab).

A Bend uses the thumb(s) to press onto the back-middle knuckle, pushing their fingers towards their centerline while pulling their middle wrist crease (Twisted Wrist), or braced against our body as a come-along or to cause damage (Thrusting Blade), or an applied key lock (Entangled Arm).

The *Inward Wrist Lock* internally rotates an opponent's hand, also with *twist* or *bend* options (Locked Horns). These use the thumb and fingers as the fulcrum to lever in the same way as the *Outward Wrist Lock*.

The <u>Twist</u> uses our thumb to push the back of their thumb or index finger joint while pulling their little finger sides pisiform bone (Unexpected Blade), or after an *Outward Wrist Lock* causing a redirection (Reversing Circles). It can also be used as a handshake attack counter (Twisting the Gift).

The <u>Bend</u> is for manipulation purposes here, as the thumb(s) apply pressure at the middle knuckle pressing towards their elbow as the middle finger(s) pull the wrist crease (Thrusting Blade) or forces them to a position where the wrist can be struck (Eluding Death).

The *Reverse Wrist Lock* forces the fingers and hand backwards into wrist extension. It can be secured with the opposite arm forming a *keylock*, or to counter a palm on our chest by trapping the hand then leaning forward and down into their finger pads (Entangled Arm B). As a come along hold it is countered by rotating the hand and lifting the elbow or extending the hand while pushing free of the grip (EPAK: Captured Leaves).

The *Wrist Flex Lock* moves an opponent's little finger into ulnar flexion, towards their own ulna wrist bone. This makes someone drop down which works best with their thumb also pointing down and with a slightly bent elbow forming the shape of the letter "Z" (Desperate Fists).

As a counter lock this is applied against either straight, R-L/L-R, or cross R-R/L-L grabs. Against a straight single or double wrist grab the hand(s) circles under-out-up over their outer wrist(s) trapping their fingers in our own ulnar flexed grip, aka crane hooks, and pressing their knuckles against our chest then applying downward pressure (Turning the Cross). Countering a cross wrist grab, R-R/L-L, is done by trapping their grip with our free hand then circling our grabbed hand under both of our hands then over their wrist to grab their radius bone before applying downward pressure (Crossing Grab).

Elbow Locks are done in one direction against the straightened joint where the humerus bone of the upper arm meets the ulna bone of the forearm. Dislocation of this joint causes a mechanical dysfunction that is difficult to ignore, with potential for not only structural damage and pain but a more significant injury due to the proximity of vital blood and nerve flow through this relatively small area.

To lock the elbow straight the forearm is secured at the wrist as pressure is applied to opposite side of the elbow joint at the base of the tricep muscle, in the notch where the bones join, at the GTO. Ground grappling styles have many options here since all limbs, the body, and floor are available for applying leverage. Those are best learned in the context of those arts.

Covered here are nine mostly standup methods of manipulation, submission, and/or dislocation, and with a few variations. They are the *Wrap-Around Arm Bar, Inverted Arm Bar, Downward Flapping Elbow Trap, Braced Elbow Arm Bar, Leg Lock Arm Bar, Over Shoulder Elbow Lock, Crossed Arm Elbow Trap, Neck Lock Arm Bar,* and *Step Over Arm Bar.*

The *Wrap-Around Arm Bar* circles over and around an opponent's straight elbow joint, grabbing it with our forearm and elbow crease, and with their medial wrist against our back armpit to apply pressure at each end (Locked Arm). This becomes a shoulder lock if they bend their elbow.

The *Inverted Arm Bar* wraps the cross-side arm under the elbow, R-R/L-L, using our elbow crease while holding their inner wrist, palm up, with our opposite hand. An upward bicep curl motion then applies pressure at the elbow simultaneously with downward pressure at the wrist (Protective Circles).

The *Downward Flapping Elbow Trap* cinches an opponent's straight elbow under one of our armpits with pressure against the joint as the held wrist is pulled in the opposite direction. It can be applied on the same side, little finger up, R-R/L-L (Spiraling Wrist), or cross R-L/L-R (Broken Gun). This motion also connects easily into a wristlock (Unexpected Blade).

The *Braced Elbow / Downward Arm Bar* starts by grabbing the back of their cross-side wrist, R-R/L-L, then welding their inner wrist to our cross hip, R wrist to R hip, etc. Rubbing pressure is then applied with the opposite forearm ulna bone to affect the GTO (Obstructing the Club), or C-Grip if the joint is further away (Hammerlock).

The *Over Shoulder Elbow Lock* starts by grabbing the cross hands inner or

medial wrist, R-R/L-L, then lifting that arms elbow joint on top of our shoulder as our opposite side R-L/L-R arm wraps over their, palm up, wrist to apply downward pressure (Entangled Arm A).

The *Crossed Arm Elbow Trap* uses an opponent's elbows against each other. If choked from behind, both wrists are grabbed then one side ducked out from under to cross their arms by attaching one arms elbow into the crease of the other (Cross of Destruction).

The *Leg Lock Arm Bar* can be done in a few ways with various leg parts. It is where our knee/leg press against the back of an opponent's locked arm simultaneously with their medial wrist posted into our opposite hip/thigh (Reversing Circles). The back of the calf can also be used (Escaping Death) or after stepping to position (Crossing Grab).

The *Neck Lock Arm Bar* used here is done while kneeling after taking an opponent down. It uses our neck to brace their medial wrist on one side

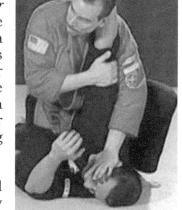

with pressure applied into their elbow joint with our opposite hand and our lifted knee, plus our extended arm braces their face, all while turning slightly into the joint (Pinch from Death B).

The *Step Over Arm Bar* is a popular ground fighting technique where the wrist is held firmly

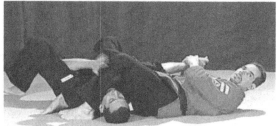

against our stomach, their thumb up, as our hip braces the back of their elbow joint and our legs hold their arm and face down, then our hips are lifted to cause a submission or joint dislocation (Pinch from Death C).

Shoulder Locks attack this ball and socket joint by twisting the arm as part of the *Braced Elbow Armbar* motion to manipulate posture (Pinch from Death) but is most vulnerable to injury with the elbow bent at 90° where the wrist is used to leverage pressure into the shoulder joint. These can be applied standing or on the ground, with us also standing or on the ground. Covered here are the *Under Shoulder/Kimura, Over Shoulder/Americana, Wraparound,* and *Double Wing Locks.*

The *Under-Shoulder / "Kimura" Lock,* named after a Japanese Jiu Jitsu practitioner who mastered its use, is done with the hand of a bent elbow <u>below</u> that arms shoulder. Pressure is applied using the *figure 4 keylock* or other methods grapplers use to place the arm into this vulnerable position.

As a standing maneuver it is used to bend an opponent forward (Deflecting Pendulum) or as a transition that takes them to the ground (Evading the Club). Once on the ground it can be used to cause shoulder damage with them lying on their side (Securing the Club) or face down (Piercing Blade).

The *Over-Shoulder / "Americana" Lock* as popularly called in Jiu Jitsu circles, is done with the hand of a bent elbow <u>above</u> that arms shoulder. Pressure is often applied using a *figure 4 keylock,* with ground fighting styles having additional methods that place and lock the arm into this vulnerable position.

As a standing maneuver it is generally used as a takedown technique (Piercing Blade) or with the opponent on the ground unable to move away from pressure where it can become a submission (Dangerous Tackle), or as a dislocation technique (Lock of Death).

The *Wraparound Shoulder Lock* is applied circling one arm over and around an opponent's bent elbow, locking their medial wrist against the back of our shoulder crease, like an *Americana Lock* or a *Whizzer* in wrestling. This can be applied over the opposite R-L/L-R arm back (Wraparound) or forwards (Securing the Club). A version of this lock can also be applied R-R/L-L facing an opponent (Taming the Fist)

The *Double Wing Lock* is a two-armed rear shoulder lock with our arms weaved either L-L/R-R through their elbow creases, aka *double chicken wing* in wrestling (Arms of Silk), or as a face down hold with their elbows locked straight (Twisting the Gift).

Ankle & Foot Locks attack the different joints in the feet and toes by twisting, over-extending, compressing, or bending them in one of five major ways. These locks are done with the opponent lying on the ground and with us standing, kneeling, or down with them.

Locking methods are the *Achilles/Calf Compression, Ankle Extension,* and *Ankle Twist.* Counters involve rotating the foot away from pressure, pulling or pushing out of the lock, possibly using the hands and other foot, or support with another structure like the hands, clothing, ground, etc. Note: Always practice these small joint locks slowly and with caution.

The *Achilles/Calf Compression Lock* is applied with the foot/ankle secured under our armpit with our forearm's radius bone wrapped around and pulling up against their Achilles tendon or calf base at the GTO with a bicep curl motion. Our opposite hand grips or *keylocks* at our wrist as our legs check their hips and free leg, then arching to increase pressure (Nutcracker).

The *Ankle Extension Lock* stretches the front ankle joint into hyperextension, separating the bones at the top of the foot. It is applied like the *Achilles/Calf Compression Lock,* except their toes are under our armpit with our forearm tight under their Achilles tendon (Dance of Death).

It can also be applied by grabbing the top of their foot in one hand then reaching over and around their leg, under their calf with the other arm, then interlocking with the forearm (Straddling the Leg).

The *Ankle Twist Lock* is applied like the *Outward Wrist Lock* using the figure '4' grip, but to the foot. It is like one version of the *Ankle Extension Lock* except used to manipulate the body. Pressure is applied by twisting the foot internally to strain the lateral ligaments of the ankle, causing them to roll over away from the pressure (Straddling the Leg).

Knee Locks forcefully hyperextend a straight knee. *Knee Bar* pressure is applied to a straightened leg at the top of the kneecap, where the femur and tibia bones are connected by ligaments, tendons, and cartilage. These will start standing using the *Squatting Knee Bar* or *Rolling Knee Bar.* Ground grapplers also have other ways to apply this lock, along with twisting the knee joint using the *Heel Hook Lock.*

The *Squatting Knee Bar* starts close against a rear attacker, where one of his feet can be seen between our two feet. Pressure is put onto his knee joint by sitting and pressing back with our rear end, watching for their heel to plant and toes to lift.

As this occurs, reach down between our legs to grab the back of their heel with both hands while sitting further back and pulling their foot forward. Their natural reaction to falling backward is to grab so turn sideways dropping one knee to the ground. Their knee ends up under and against the back of our thigh while we hold their lower leg (Straddling the Leg). This takes timing.

The *Rolling Knee Bar* from standing starts against a close rear attacker, where one of his feet can be seen between ours and is a natural follow up to a failed *Squatting Knee Bar* or as a stand-alone move. The knee between their feet drops to the ground while posting that sides hand on the ground temporarily while reaching back with the other hand between our feet to grab around the outside of their heel.

The posted hand then reaches to also grab the ankle, but inside, followed by a forward shoulder roll, on that side, as our outside calf *Ax Kicks* the back of their close knee with the in-between leg kicking up to bump their torso forwards. As they fall forward, we end with their knee joint locked against our hip while holding their ankle and locking their hips down with our legs, then lifting our hips into the locked joint (Straddling the Leg B).

The *Bent Knee Lock* is done by placing one shin into an opponent's knee crease, then bending the knee until their foot and shin are up against our stomach where pressure can be applied, separating the joint. This can be setup with a leg scissor takedown (Defensive Takedown Sparring #4).

**HOLDS** are moves where the arms and legs wrap around to contain an opponent's torso, arms, or neck. Covered are six types of *Bear Hugs* and three *Head Holds,* all from a standing position. Ground grapplers use the legs extensively to hold and control an opponent in "base positions," but these are best learned in the context of an appropriate grappling style.

Bear Hugs offensively involve using the two arms to wrap around the torso of an opponent from any direction, with the focus here on the front and rear positions. Both or one arm could be trapped in the hold or both arms could be free, but the key battle in all cases is hip position

Close attacks, for the street stylist, contain the option to use tenderizing or softening techniques to encourage the holder to release their grip. *Front (or Side)* Bear Hug tenderizing techniques include the *Front Head Butt, Forward Knee Kick,* and *Forward Thumb Strike(s)* with emphasis on making space between our hips and theirs. *Rear* side bear hug tenderizing techniques include *Rear* or *Side Head Butts, Stomp Kicks, Upward Hook Kicks, Pinches, Back Elbows, Back Hammerfists,* and groin *Grabs,* with the goal to escape or step behind to get our hips behind theirs.

The *Front Bear Hug, Both Arms Pinned* can be used to lift someone to carry or throw them down. Moving the hips back and away from their hips is how this defense starts, with the heel of our hands against the front of their hipbones or using a strike into their groin area (Thrusting Thumbs).

The *Front Bear Hug, Both Arms Free* is applied high into the armpits with double under hooks to lift and throw, or low around the waist to squeeze and arch backwards. Leg hooks can be applied temporarily with high targets struck, and with the street stylist able to gouge eyes and/or box the ears to help escape (Tripping Leg).

The *Front Bear Hug, One Arm Pinned & One Free* gives front access like the other two with the free arm able to strike or defend against a second attacker and the trapped arm available to push the hips and make space.

The *Rear Bear Hug, Both Arms Pinned* can be used to lift a person up to carry or throw them down. To defend, drop the weight while shifting the hips to one side, away from their center, while using any available tenderizing techniques to soften their grip before escaping (Crushing Palm).

The *Rear Bear Hug, Both Arms Free* can be used to lift a person up to carry or throw them down. To defend, drop the weight while shifting the hips to one side, away from their center, and using available tenderizing techniques to soften their grip before escaping (Sweeping the Leg).

The *Rear Bear Hug, One Arm Pinned & One Free* gives the same rear access as either both arms pinned or both arms free. The free arm can attack the hands, or defend against a second attacker, with the trapped arm able to pinch or strike back (Training the Bears).

Head Holds are moves where the arms are used to wrap around the neck and head to grab and control, with the potential to choke, cause discomfort, pain, damage, or submission. One each from front, side, and rear are covered.

*Front Two-Hand Clinch, aka Thai Clinch,* uses three points of contact with the forearms against the neck sides, hands overlapped at the back of their head, and both ulna bones pushing into their collarbones. Attempts to pull the head out of this structure only increase pressure (Parrying Grab).

Note: The best defense against this clinch is not to pull the head down between the elbows as an upward knee could be waiting. See the three-range process covered in the Sport Fighting chapter (Kickboxing Sparring #8).

The *Side Headlock* is a common wrestling technique, with sport rules requiring an arm be included with the head, aka "head & arm." Someone not trained tends to only grab around the neck and head leaving both arms free, making it easier to defend.

The initial street attack defense involves trying to stay on the feet while grabbing their wrist around our neck to relieve pressure. The street stylist may also need to use the free hand to defend against potential punches while tenderizing the attacker with *Pinches* and *Strikes* (Pinch from Death).

The *Full-Nelson Hold* is applied from behind where both arms slide under the armpits, then the hands press behind the head. This can apply strong leverage against the neck and is defended by placing the back of overlapped hands against our forehead for neck support while applying tenderizing moves to soften the hold (Scraping Stomp B).

Note: Wrestlers also use a "Half-Nelson" version on the ground with one arm applied to turn someone onto their back.

**CHOKES** are done with the hands, arms, and legs attacking the neck or throat to affect the air, blood, and/or the nervous system. The medical term is called *strangle* but *choke* is more commonly used in martial arts.

The blood is attacked at the carotid and vertebral arteries on the sides and back of the neck. The air is attacked at the trachea (windpipe) at the front of the throat. The nervous system is attacked at the vagus nerve, carotid sinus, and cervical spine (See *Pressure Point* chapter).

Stopping blood flow has a gradual effect on the brain where stopping the airflow is much more dramatic. Damaging the nervous system can disrupt bodily functions ranging from heart rate to blood pressure, limb function, and consciousness. Three types of *Hand* and four *Arm Chokes* are covered, with grappling systems also utilizing the legs but are not covered here.

Hand Chokes attack the neck and throat using one hand (Conquering Arm), or two (Ascending from Death), where if done correctly pressure is applied into the sternal notch, trachea, and/or carotid arteries.

The *Sternal Notch Hand Choke* stimulates the gag reflex as the fingers of one or both hands grip around the neck for leverage as one or both thumbs push into the hole between the top of the sternum and the bottom of the throat, aka sternal notch (Ascending from Death). It can also be done by poking with the fingers (Returning the Gift).

The *Trachea Hand Choke* stops the airflow using the thumb and fingers to *Crab Pinch* around the neck cartilage at the front of the throat (Raining Blade).

The *Carotid Hand Choke* is used to stop blood flow through the neck with one or both hands gripping the throat to squeeze the arteries shut (Securing the Club). Overlapping thumbs, or the thumb and fingers of one hand can push from the front with a rear support structure like the fingers, a free hand, wall, or the ground (Conquering Arm). If applied from behind the fingers would pull into this choke (Cross of Destruction).

Arm Chokes are used to attack the throat with one arm or both interlocked. Standup methods for attacking blood flow are the *Carotid Restraint* aka *"Sleeper" Choke, Arm Triangle,* and *Reverse Headlock,* with the *Reverse Forearm "Guillotine" Choke* attacking airflow.

The *Carotid Restraint / Sleeper Choke / Rear-Naked Choke* attacks blood flow through the carotid arteries on both sides of the trachea to stop blood flow to the brain. From behind, one arm slides around the neck, aligning the bent elbow crease with the front throat with the bicep muscle over one carotid artery and radius bone over the other applying pressure. Grappling styles use this and other methods to apply this choke from the ground as well.

Once in place, the choking arm is supported by the other hand reinforcing either behind their head with arms interlocked, or by connecting the hands. As the contact points are contracted the chest is expanded to eliminate space and add pressure (Turn of Fate).

The *Reverse Headlock* is done to a rear opponent where the close arm reaches up under an attacker's throat placing the radius bone against the far side of their neck as the opposite arms ulna bone is pressed against the near side, using a *Gable Grip* to connect the hands creating pressure like a nutcracker to choke, neck crank, crush, or pull their head down into a knee (Sweeping the Leg) or over into a *Snap Mare Throw* (Hidden Elbow).

The *Arm Triangle* is named because the neck is surrounded on three sides at the two carotid arteries and the back of the neck. This triangle is formed using one of their arms to choke off one carotid artery as one of our arms, or leg, forms the other two angles, with our free hand reinforcing the hold (Sleeper).

The *Guillotine Choke* is applied from in front of an opponent's head voluntarily positioned or caused to bend down. One upper arm/chest lies on the back of their neck as the lower arm is hinged around their throat placing our radius bone against their trachea, with or without their arm trapped inside. Our free hand grips the wrist of our choking arm to pull, adding choking pressure.

This can be done standing (Locked Horns) where a version places the back of their head against our lower torso greatly compounding the pressure. It can also be done on the ground with the legs wrapped around their waist from bottom guard to secure the lock and supply additional leverage into the choke (Dangerous Tackle).

# MOVEMENT ROUTINES
## Chapter VIII

These are the pre-arranged fighting and exercise patterns of martial arts. Although mostly designed to be done "in the air," i.e., without a partner, many can also be done with a partner, or onto targets. Traditional martial arts refer to these choreographed patterns as "Sets & Forms," or "Kata" in Japanese, "Poomsae/Hyung" in Korean, etc. Sport fighting calls the more free-form version of this "Shadowboxing."

Some disagreement exists at to the practical value of "in the air" movement routines. This stems from the difference between *technique-based* and *movement-based* styles. Kenpo for example originally was only technique based, i.e., without Forms, although *Sets* were used as drills and exercises.

The history of movement without a partner in martial arts is extensive and often has been hidden as exercise or dance, as in many Polynesian cultures, of which Ed Parker was a part. He obviously saw that both technique and movement practice were useful complimentary methods, as technique-based systems can benefit from movement training and movement arts can benefit from practicing movement applications.

As the story goes, in the early 1960's Ed Parker, with help from a Chinese martial artist named James Wing Woo and senior students, began implementing *Forms* into his Kenpo system. Stories vary as to who contributed what but that is not important to this discussion.

Most current and past traditional martial art systems do some version of this *in the air* movement, which speaks to its value. Modern Kenpo believes in the value of *Sets & Forms*. Some technique-based street, and most sport styles, prefer the *Shadowboxing* term.

However, whether doing individual basics, lesson related combinations, scenario-based self-defense techniques, or organized patterns of indexed motion, everybody visualizes and rehearses martial art movement without a partner. The *Shadowboxing* term comes from the sport of Boxing, but grapplers also practice rolls, falls, hip escapes, takedown mechanics, and more using this method.

A common misnomer is that *Shadowboxing* is completely free form. The reality is that fight coaches mostly work prearranged combinations and theme training when preparing fighters using this method. These and all *Movement Routines* are done with intention and purpose as random in the air movement is unproductive and wastes valuable workout time.

Pre-arranged patterns historically also help index a systems movement and technique information so that knowledge can be passed forward and refined over generations. These patterns help keep major and minor themes from getting lost in the vastness of martial arts training, or to a teacher's preference.

From a practical standpoint, the correct rehearsing of efficiently connected *Basics* with breath and intention helps the practitioner develop not only timed and coordinated and connected *Basics*, but layers of other benefits gained through rehearsing committed movement.

Well-designed and evolved pre-arranged patterns are useful since body control and movement can continuously develop with level appropriate patterns, compounding over time. Timing, posture, balance, power, footwork, visualization skills, insight, internal and external strength, flexibility, and cardiovascular endurance all benefit from this training.

Not only can "bad habits" be avoided but other important benefits can become ingrained. *Path of Motion* tracking, proper mechanical transitions within and between *Basics* categories, learning how to miss without loss of balance or injury, coordinated movement with breath and mental intention, theme and range fighting, are but some of the many benefits of motion training.

These routines are practiced for assorted reasons. For a Boxer, single opponent punching patterns are important; if for internal health then Tai Chi movements with controlled and coordinated breath provide a benefit; if for acrobatics and exercise then Wushu is beneficial; and if for self-defense, the rapid transitions, strong stances, and relentless follow-up of Kenpo have value.

Moving without another person's body mass also makes learning a new transition sequence less complicated while internalizing posture, balance, and other factors. Any movement expert would agree that it's the connecting points, or transitions, that are the most difficult; and fight coaches know that control of our own body is important to controlling someone else's.

A knowledgeable instructor, trainer, or coach will progressively increase and challenge a student with more difficult routines, combinations, and insight as they are able to handle them. The mental focus, understanding, and physical precision gained through this practice benefits those movements in other contexts as well.

Some older martial arts systems have ancient patterns with multiple themes evolved over generations and can often be quite sophisticated. Learning routines start with mechanics and in traditional martial arts are done bi-laterally either alternating sides or mirror imaging one side then the other. This helps build a balanced muscle structure and bilateral coordination.

Sport fighters however practice and fight primarily, if not exclusively, on one side to sharpen their tools with the least number of variables. Both style-influenced training decisions work in the context of their use.

In either case as a routine or combination is learned, precision is added for efficiency, breath and timing for flow, power for focus, speed for cardiovascular training, and intensity to help build fighting spirit.

Intelligently constructed routines allow for practice when no partners are available and can provide a lifetime of fitness. They can be done at different speeds and intensity levels from soft flowing Tai Chi to the hard isometric Sanchin kata to Kenpo's combination of relaxation into explosive power.

Even routines designed for a certain style can be done at another styles speed and intensity to provide some variety. However, any movement pattern that builds muscle memory, evolves body control, and develops skill with insight, regardless of style, is in this category of training.

Many of these can also be practiced interactively with partners, on pads, mitts, or bags. Sophisticated patterns never become boring as insight is endless, making them potentially always interesting and even fun.

Described and referenced here are empty-handed *Sets & Forms* from my Kenpo System, with descriptions, insight, and video links as a visual reference.

**Sets** are patterns that practice a specific type or category of *Basic. Stance Sets* practice stances, *Kicking Sets* practice kicking, etc. **Forms** combine several types of *Basics* into a martial art theme. Kenpo Form #1 uses blocks and defensive footwork to 4 angles; Form #2 uses blocks, offensive footwork and striking to 8 angles. Form 6 indexes weapon defenses, etc.

Once learned, routines are flexible and can be practiced creatively. For example, *Sets* can be overlapped to increase the coordination challenge such as doing Stance Set 1 on the right side simultaneously with Elbow or Blocking Set on the right, and/or left sides.

The primary designated purpose of moves in a *Form* can also be given other intentions, so the first step back in Kenpo Short Form 1 for example could be a foot stomp or a leg sweep, the inward blocking motion could be a hammerfist or a forearm strike, the chambering hand a back-elbow strike, etc. as many options and meanings can exist within the same motion.

Note: A martial arts myth exists about "hidden moves" in Forms. The only thing that can be hidden in movement is intention and insight. Suppressed peoples have of course "hidden" the intention of martial arts movement in dance, and smart teachers share insight with students in layers' as they are ready and worthy to receive it.

Some things can also be lost over time, be newly discovered, or rediscovered, but the creator of the pattern would have been selfish, arrogant, or just short-sited to intentionally "hide" something in a Form, defeating a main purpose for its creation. The reality is new discoveries in movement are endless.

# SETS

Sets generally practice and index a specific category of basics, although some include more complex movements and can be done interactively. Covered here are *Sets* required in my system, but there are many of these types of patterns that have been developed in Kenpo and in other styles.

The moves of each *Set* will be listed in an abbreviated fashion with intended benefits and some historical context listed as interesting and useful.

Described are 3 *Stance Sets*, 2 *Blocking Sets*, 2 *Kicking Sets*, 6 *Striking Sets* and 3 *Interactive Partner Sets*. Most can be done in the air, on targets, or with partners. The starting reference point, using the *Clock Concept*, is 12 unless another direction is noted. Starting and practice positions noted in each description are standing and training horse stances, or a fighting stance.

All can be seen demonstrated slowly while being described, then faster, i.e., "up to speed", with some on a body at BarryBBarker.com.

A smaller font size & abbreviations are used in the descriptions to save space: R = Right; L = Left; RNB = Right Neutral Bow Stance; LNB = Left Neutral Bow Stance; LFB = Left Forward Bow; RFB = Right Forward Bow; BKS = Backknuckle Strike; Simult = Simultaneous; Dbl = Double; Horiz = Horizontal; Vert = Vertical; In = Inward; Out = Outward; Up = Upward; Down = Downward; Ext = Extended; Inv = Inverted; Words "Stance" & "Strike" are left off most Basics names; w/ = with; Combo = Combination; Def = Defensive; Off = Offensive; Mod = Modified; , or - = then

## STANCE SETS

These are used to help practice transitioning from one good strong stance to another. The 3 Sets described here are practiced only in the air although other sets, or individual basics, can be overlapped to make them more challenging, interesting, and to insert applications with stance transitions.

### Benefits of Stance Sets:
- Maintaining balance through stance transitions
- Maintaining posture through stance transitions
- Learning to turn and move the hips and torso
- Learning how to shift and transfer weight
- Learning how to pivot and slide the feet
- Developing smooth and efficient stance transitions
- Building leg strength
- Indexing the major stances

### History of Stance Sets and Notes:
Stance Set #1 & 2 created by Sharkey LeCroy
Stance Set #3 attributed to Ed Parker
Note: Stance Sets 2 & 3 hand positions are not described but are on the video.

## STANCE SET #1
*Standing Horse Stance*
1. Step back to a RNB; 2. RFB; 3. R Close Kneel; 4. RFB; 5. RNB; 6. R Cat

7. Defensive Switch to LNB; 8-12 repeats moves 2-7 but with left foot in front
*Step forward to Standing Horse*

## STANCE SET #2
*Standing Horse Stance*
1. Step back L to R Reverse 45º/Back Corner Horse; 2. Adjust L foot to modified RNB
3. Shift back to L One-Legged Stance; 4. Def Switch to L Modified Horse
5. L Reverse Bow; 6. L Rev Close Kneel; 7. L Reverse Bow; 8. L Rev Neutral Bow
9. L Cat; 10. L forward to a L Forward 45º/Front Corner Horse w/L Inward Block
11. R front crossover to L Front Twist; 12. Unpivot ball/ball to RNB
13. R rear crossover to R Front Twist; 14. Unpivot front ball/rear heel to L Side Horse
15. Open front foot then step forward to Standing Horse
16-30. Step back R to repeat pattern on opposite side

## STANCE SET #3
*Standing Horse Stance*
1. Step forward to RFB; 2. RNB; 3. R Rear Bow; 4. R Cat; 5. L One-Legged Stance
6. R Rear Crossover Step to R Front Twist; 7. Unpivot ball/ball to LNB
8. Drop to L Wide Kneel; 9. Adjust to L Close Kneel/Ducking
10. LNB; 11. L Reverse Bow; 12. L Front Crossover to L Rear Twist
13. Unpivot around L heel/R ball to RNB; 14. L step thru forward to LFB
15-26. Repeat 2-12 on opposite side; 27. Unpivot R heel/L ball to LNB
28. R leaping double heel stomp to low squat Diamond Stance
29. Adjust to Concave Stance; 30. R Front Crossover to 9 low twist stance
31. Step out L to 9 LNB; 32. L Front Crossover to 3 low twist stance
33. Step out R to 12 Meditating Horse; 34-39. Hand position highlights (see video)
*Close L foot to R foot - Attention Stance*

## BLOCKING SETS
These build upon each other in the air or with a partner feeding attacks that generate the required blocks in the patterns. They can be practiced relaxed to develop speedy transitions, with dynamic tension to develop muscle tracking and build strength, with a partner rhythmically or using varied timing to build attack awareness and reaction skills.

If all the individual blocks in Blocking Set 1 are visualized superimposed bi-laterally around the body simultaneously then a house shaped framework evolves. The upward blocks are the roof, with inward blocks the front doors, extended outward blocks the upper sidewalls, downward blocks the lower sidewalls, chamber positions the back walls, and push-down checks the floor.

### Benefits of Blocking Sets:
- Develop correct structural alignment for blocking
- Transitioning from one block to another
- Developing upper body bi-lateral coordination
- Building upper body strength
- Increase leg strength while practicing in a horse stance
- Blocking awareness and reaction training
- Awareness of directions for attack and defense
- Index major blocks and blocking directions

**History of Blocking Sets:**

Blocking Set #1 attributed to Ed Parker, and often called *Star Block*
Blocking Set #2 from Jim Mitchell although I modified his original version

## BLOCKING SET #1

*Attention Stance - Step L to Meditating Horse Stance*

1. R Up Block; 2. R In Block; 3. R Extended Block (moves 1-3 done high)
4. R Down Block; 5. R Hand Chamber; 6. R Push-Down Check (moves 4-6 done low)

*"X"/double factor transition w/L hand outside:* 7-12. Repeat moves 1-6 w/L Hand
*Meditating Horse, Close L foot to R*

## BLOCKING SET #2

*From a Meditating Horse – Do 1-12 from Blocking Set #1*

13. L Up Block w/R Push Down Check; 14. L In Block w/R Chamber
15. L Ext Out Block w/R Down Out Block; "X"
16. L Down Out Block w/R Ext Out Block;
17. L Chamber w/R In Block; 18. L Push-Down Check w/R Up Block
19. R In Block w/L Chamber; 20. R Ext Out Block w/L Down Out Block; "X"
21. R Down Out Block w/L Ext Out Block; 22. R Chamber w/L In Block
23. R Push-Down Check w/L Up Block; Both hands Meditating Horse
24. Dbl Up Blocks; 25. Dbl In Blocks; 26. Dbl Ext Out Blocks; "X"
27. Dbl Down Out Blocks; 28. Dbl Chamber; 29. Dbl Push-Down Checks
30. Hands to Meditating Horse; *Close L to R; Block Set 2 Summary:*
    *Blocking Set 1, then 1-6 & 6-1 overlapped, then Both Arms simultaneously*

## KICKING SETS

These practice two and three kick combinations in the air or on targets, with each combination done not putting the foot on the ground. The kicking foot does touch the ground between combinations, although doing an entire Kicking Set with minimal ground contact can be a worthy challenge.

The three main components of kicking are, in order of importance, *Balance, Path of Motion,* and *Foot Position.* These are covered more thoroughly in the *Basics* chapter. The *Kicking Sets* practice these lessons in combinations to develop kicks with transitions, plus for repetition and exercise.

*Balance* when kicking means standing on one foot while kicking with the other. This makes one of the major lessons learned and felt as kicking the foot without moving the body center past a point of control and balance. Other important lessons include the base foot position relative to the hip rotation and applying leverage from the base foot into each kick.

*Path of Motion* is the direction the foot travels towards the target. The two paths of motion are *Linear* and *Circular,* with linear kicks pushing off the hip while circular kicks hinge off the knee. Additionally, the hips, torso, and arms will counterbalance depending on the kick.

*Foot Position* happens at the target, where the shape of the foot and ankle is important to apply force accurately without injuring the foot or related components. There are many striking surfaces on the lower leg and foot with these *Sets* focused on primarily using the ball-of-foot, bottom-of-heel, shin/instep, and back-of-heel.

**Benefits of Kicking Sets:**
- Balancing on one foot while kicking with the other
- Path of motion tracking with the legs
- Forming foot weapon shapes and transitioning from one to another
- Snap - Thrust - Hook - Whip kick transitions
- Linear to Circular & Circular to Linear kick transitions
- Low to High & High to Low kick transitions
- Front to Back & Back to Front kick transitions
- In-motion to Out & Out motion to In kick transitions
- Increased leg flexibility, strength, and coordination

**History of Kicking Sets and Notes:**
I created the two Kicking Sets described here with ideas and inspiration from a friend, fellow martial artist, and phenomenal "kicker" Mark "Crazy Legs" Burnham back in the 1980's.

Note: The path of motion plus foot and hip position are in parenthesis after the combination description.

## KICKING SET #1
*2 Kick Combinations*
*Standing Horse - Step back L to 12 RNB*
1. R Front <u>Snap</u> Kick then higher R Front <u>Snap</u> Kick, both to 10:30
    *(Circular-Circular; Ball-Ball; Hips: both front to target)*
2. R Side <u>Thrust</u> Kick then higher R Side <u>Thrust</u> Kick, both to 1:30
    *(Linear-Linear; Bottom Heel-Bottom Heel; Hips: backside of lead hip to target)*
3. R Wheel <u>Snap</u> Kick then higher R Wheel <u>Snap</u> Kick, both to 12
    *(Circular-Circular; Shin/Instep-Shin/Instep; Hips: front side lead hip to target)*
4. L Front <u>Snap</u> Kick to 12, L Rear <u>Thrust</u> Kick to 6
    *(Circular-Linear; Ball-Bottom Heel; Hips: both front then rear to target)*
5. L Side <u>Thrust</u> Kick to 12, L Wheel <u>Snap</u> Kick to 12
    *(Linear-Circular; Bottom Heel-Shin/Instep; Hips: lead hip to target)*
6. L Rear <u>Thrust</u> Kick to 6, L Front <u>Snap</u> Kick to 12, step down feet together
    *(Linear-Circular; Bottom Heel-Ball; Hips: both rear then front to target)*
Offensive Switch to a 12 LNB then repeat pattern on opposite side

## KICKING SET #2
*Two & Three Kick Combinations - Standing Horse Stance – 12 RNB*
1. R Front <u>Snap</u> Kick to 10:30, R Side <u>Thrust</u> Kick to 1:30
*(Circular-Linear; Ball-Bottom Heel; Hips: both front then back of lead hip to target)*
2. R Side <u>Thrust</u> Kick to 1:30, R Front <u>Snap</u> Kick to 10:30
*(Linear-Circular; Bottom Heel-Ball; Hips: back of lead hip then both front to target)*
3. R Out <u>Hook</u> Kick to 12, R Wheel <u>Snap</u> Kick to 12
*(Circular-Circular; Back of Heel-Shin/Instep; Hips: back then front of lead hip to target)*
4. R Front <u>Snap</u> Kick 10:30, R Side <u>Thrust</u> Kick 1:30, R Wheel <u>Snap</u> Kick to 12
*(Circular-Linear-Circular; Ball-Bottom Heel-Shin/Instep; Hips: both front then back of lead hip then front of lead hip to target)*
5. R Side <u>Thrust</u> Kick to 1:30, R Front <u>Snap</u> to 10:30, R Out <u>Hook</u> Kick to 12
    *(Note: Optional ground touch between Front & Outward Hook Kick)*
    *(Linear-Circular-Circular; Bottom Heel-Ball-Back Heel; Hips: back side of lead hip then both front then back of lead hip to target)*

6. L step-thru Front <u>Snap</u> Kick to 12, L higher Roundhouse <u>Snap</u> or <u>Thrust</u> Kick to 12, R spinning Rear <u>Thrust</u> to 12 with step-thru return to 6 and offensive cover to end, or Spinning Outward <u>Hook</u> Kick thru to 12 LNB (used by higher belts) *(Circular-Circular-Linear or Circular; Ball-Shin/Instep-Bottom or Back Heel; Hips: both front then front side of lead hip then both rear/or back of lead hip if Hook Kick at end)*
7-12. Repeat pattern on opposite side - *return to Standing Horse Stance*

## STRIKING SETS
Covered are *Elbow Set, Coordination Sets 1 & 2, Striking Set,* and *Finger Sets 1 & 2.* All can be done in the air, on targets, or with partners.

### Benefits of Striking Sets:
- Progressive muscle pre-load development and awareness
- Separate upper & lower body coordination
- Connecting different weapons on the same side of the body
- Alternating weapons from one side of the body to the other
- Using weapons on both sides of the body simultaneously
- Interactive upper and lower body coordination
- Develop weapon shape and transitions between them
- Snap - Thrust - Hook - Whip upper body transitions
- Linear to Circular & Circular to Linear upper body transitions
- Low to High & High to Low upper body transitions
- Front to Back & Back to Front upper body transitions
- In/Out, Out/In, Down/Up, Up/Down upper body transitions
- Builds upper body flexibility, strength, and coordination
- Develop reactive counters to attacks
- Interactive movement with a partner

### History of Striking and Interactive Sets, and Notes:
*Elbow Set, Coordination Sets 1 & 2* and *Finger Set 1* came from the EPAK system taught to me by Jim Mitchell in the early 1980's. Jim Mitchell created *Finger Set 2,* or "Moving Finger Set."

I modified the original *Striking Set* incorporating different hand strikes and making it more interactive. It is described as an *in the air* pattern in this first section and then again in the *Interactive Partner Sets* section with the *on-body* version.

*Two-Man Set* was handed down to me through the EPAK system, shown in Mr. Parker's "Secrets of Chinese Karate" book. It is said to be an old Hung Gar Fighting Set which I have "Kenpoized" with checks and breaks (see Advanced Two-Man Set video).

*Two-Man Locking Set* was created by me in 2004 to index the finger, wrist, elbow, and shoulder joint locking movements in my Kenpo system.

Note: Initially do these sets, especially with partners, at a steady rhythm or cadence, but at a higher level be more creative and vary the tempo to make them more challenging while still enjoying them and developing spontaneous reaction timing. Additional notes mentioned as they relate to each set.

## ELBOW SET
*Attention - Step L to Meditating Horse Stance*
*(Hand shape and Weapon noted in parenthesis)*
1. R In Elbow to 12 *(Hand Closed-Tip of Ulna)*
2. R Out Elbow to 3 *(Hand Open-Base of Tricep)*
3. R Back Elbow to 6 *(Hand Open-Base of Tricep)*
4. R Up Elbow to 12 *(Hand Closed-Tip of Ulna)*
5. R Down Elbow to 12 *(Hand Open-Base of Tricep)*
6. R Obscure Elbow to 3 *(Hand Open-Base of Tricep)*
7-12. Repeat on opposite side - *Close L to R*

## COORDINATION SET 1
*Attention - Step L to 12 Meditating Horse*
*(4 direction pattern follows "+" angles; L foot stays in place and only pivots; Rear foot steps back to change direction then thru forward to show opposite side; Punches and kicks are forward where stance is facing)*
1. Step Back R to 12 LNB w/L Out Block; 2. L Horiz <u>Thrust</u> Punch
3. LFB w/R Horiz <u>Thrust</u> Punch; 4. R Front <u>Snap</u> Kick w/L Horiz <u>Thrust</u> Punch
5. Step Back to LFB w/R Horiz Thrust Punch
6. R Front Step-thru to 12 RNB w/R Out Block; 7. R Horiz <u>Thrust</u> Punch
8. RFB w/L Horiz <u>Thrust</u> Punch; 9. L Front <u>Snap</u> Kick w/R Horiz <u>Thrust</u> Punch
10. Step Back to RFB w/L Horiz <u>Thrust</u> Punch
11. L Defensive Front Turn to 9 (R steps back): Repeat Steps 1-10 towards 9
12. L Defensive Front Turn to 6 (R steps back): Repeat Steps 1-10 towards 6
13. L Defensive Front Turn to 3 (R steps back): Repeat Steps 1-10 towards 3
14. L Defensive Front Turn to 12 (R steps back): Repeat Steps 1-10 towards 12
*Right Foot Steps Back to 12 Meditating Horse - Close L foot to R*

## COORDINATION SET #2
*Attention - Step L to 12 Meditating Horse*
*(Same "+" angles and footwork as #1; Highlight section added at end)*
1. Step back R back to modified 12 LNB w/L Out/R Down Out Blocks
2. R Out Block w/L Down-Out Block; 3. LFB w/L Up Block/R Down In Hammerfist <u>Thrust</u>; 4. Modified LNB w/R Up Block/L In Down Hammerfist <u>Thrust</u>
5. LFB w/R In Block/L Hand Chamber Position
6. R Front <u>Snap</u> Kick w/L Horiz <u>Thrust</u> Punch
7. R Rear <u>Thrust</u> Kick to 6 w/R Horiz <u>Thrust</u> Punch to 12
8. LFB w/L Up Parry/R Fingers-In Palm <u>Thrust</u> Strike to 12
9. R Front Step-thru to modified RNB: Repeat 1-8
10. L Def Front Turn to 9 (R steps back): Repeat 1-9 to 9
11. L Def Front Turn to 6 (R steps back): Repeat 1-9 to 6
12. L Def Front Turn to 3 (R back): Repeat 1-9 to 3
13. L Def Front Turn to 12 (R back): Repeat 1-9 to 12
*Highlight Section*
14. R steps back to Meditating Horse w/Dbl Out Blocks; 15. Dbl In Blocks
16. Dbl Down Out Blocks; 17. Dbl Up Blocks; 18. Dbl In Down Hammerfists
19. Dbl Horiz Thrust Punch; 20. Dbl Up Parrys; 21. Dbl Inv Horiz/Fingers-In Palm
*Meditating Horse - Close L foot to R*

## STRIKING SET
*Standing Horse with hands Chambered – Step L to Horse with move #1*
*Part 1: Linear Punching with Circular Counter Strikes (all to 12) vs Part 2 Blocks*
1. R Horiz <u>Thrust</u> Punch low *(Linear)*;
2. R Out <u>Whipping</u> BKS high *(Circular)* to Chamber

3. L Horiz <u>Thrust</u> Punch low *(Linear);* 4. L Out <u>Whipping</u> BKS high *(Circular) to Chamber;* 5. R Vert <u>Thrust</u> Punch high *(Linear);* 6. R Forward Inv Hammerfist <u>Thrust</u> low *(Circular);* 7. L Vert <u>Thrust</u> Punch high *(Linear); R to Chamber*

8.   L Forward Inv Hammerfist <u>Thrust</u> low *(Circular)*
9.   R Inv Horiz <u>Thrust</u> Punch low *(Linear); L to Chamber*
10. R In Heel-of-Palm <u>Thrust</u> high *(Circular)*
11. L Inv Horiz <u>Thrust</u> Punch low *(Linear); R to Chamber*
12. L In Heel-of-Palm <u>Thrust</u> high *(Circular)*
13. R Straight Palm <u>Thrust</u> high *(Linear); L to Chamber*
14. R In Handsword or Horiz Palm <u>Thrust</u> low *(Circular)*
15. L Straight Palm <u>Thrust</u> high *(Linear); R to Chamber*
16. L In Handsword or Horiz Palm <u>Thrust</u> low *(Circular)*
   *Part 2: Blocking then Counter Blocking vs Part 1 Punches & Strikes (most with "X")*
1.   "X", R Down Block; "X" 2. R Counter Up Block; "X" 3. L Down Block; "X"
4.   L Counter Up Block; "X" 5. R Up Block; 6. L Counter Push-Down Check; "X"
7.   L Up Block; 8. R Counter Push-Down Check; "X"
9.   L Down Out Block; "X" 10. L Counter Ext Out Block; "X"
11. R Down Out Block; "X" 12. R Counter Ext Out Block; "X"
13. L Up Block; 14. R In Palm Check; "X" 15. R Up Block; 16. L In Palm Check
   *Hands to Chamber - Highlights (double punches & strikes to 12)*
17. Step L foot next to R (Standing Horse) with Dbl Horiz <u>Thrust</u> Punches
18. Dbl Outward <u>Whipping</u> BKS bringing hands to chamber
19. Dbl Straight Palm <u>Thrust</u> Strikes; 20. Dbl In Handsword or Horiz Palm <u>Thrust</u>
   *Hands to Meditating Horse - Close L foot to R*

## FINGER SET #1
*Standing Horse Stance - Step L to 12 Meditating Horse w/move #1*
*(Isometric finger practice of pokes, whips, slices, and claws;*
*Practice on human shaped inanimate targets also useful;*
*Develops coordination & strength for moves not safely applied on training partners)*
1.   R Horiz 2-Finger <u>Thrust</u> <u>Poke</u> *(high – full arm extension)*, chamber L
2.   L Horiz 2-Finger <u>Thrust</u> <u>Poke</u> *(high – full arm extension)*, chamber R
3.   R Vert 2-Finger <u>Thrust</u> <u>Poke</u> *(middle - 3/4 arm extension)*, chamber L
4.   L Vert 2-Finger <u>Thrust</u> <u>Poke</u> *(middle - 3/4 arm extension)*, chamber R
5.   R Inv Horiz 2-Finger <u>Thrust</u> <u>Poke</u> *(low - 1/2 arm extension)*, chamber L
6.   L Inv Horiz 2-Finger <u>Thrust</u> <u>Poke</u> *(low - 1/2 arm extension)*, chamber R
7.   R over L shoulder 2-Finger <u>Thrust</u> <u>Poke</u> to 6, chamber L
8.   L over R shoulder 2-Finger <u>Thrust</u> <u>Poke</u> to 6, chamber R
9.   R hand overlaps top of L w/Double Down Finger <u>Whips</u>
10. Double Sandwich Inverted Horizontal <u>Snapping</u> Finger <u>Pokes</u> *(throat)*
11. Crossed Double Vertical 2-Finger <u>Snapping</u> <u>Pokes</u> *(eyes)*
12. R Overhand Crane Finger <u>Whip</u> high w/L Horiz Check
13. L Overhand Crane Finger <u>Whip</u> high w/R Horiz Check
14. R Underhand Crane Finger <u>Whip</u> low to 12 w/L Horiz Check
15. L Underhand Crane Finger <u>Whip</u> low to 12 w/R Horiz Check
16. L Pos Check into palm-up Parry to chamber w/R In/Out Horiz 2-Finger <u>Slice</u>
17. R Palm-up Parry to chamber w/ L In/Out Horiz 2-Finger <u>Slice</u>
18. L Inside-Down Palm-up Parry to chamber w/R In Heel-of-Palm to In /Out Windshield Wiper Finger <u>Slices</u>
19. R Inside-Down Palm-up Parry to chamber w/L In Heel-of-Palm to In/Out Windshield Wiper Finger <u>Slices</u>
20. L Inside-Down Palm-Up Parry to L In Hooking Parry to 12, becomes 6 L Rear Underhand <u>Claw</u> w/R Overhead Down <u>Claw</u> to 12
21. R Inside-Down Palm-Up Parry to R In <u>Hooking</u> Parry to 12, becomes 6 R Rear

Underhand <u>Claw</u> w/L Overhead Down <u>Claw</u> to 12
22. L Inside-Down Palm-Up Parry to L In <u>Hooking</u> Parry to 12, becomes 6 L Rear Underhand <u>Claw</u> w/R Forward Underhand <u>Claw</u> to 12
23. R Inside-Down Palm-Up Parry to R In <u>Hooking</u> Parry to 12, becomes 6 R Rear Underhand <u>Claw</u> w/L Forward Underhand <u>Claw</u> to 12

*Highlight Section to 12*

24. R hand over L, Dbl Sandwich Inv Finger <u>Thrust</u> *Pokes;*
25. Double Up Finger Flick <u>Whips;</u> 26. Double Forward Thumb <u>Gouges;</u>
27. Double Out Finger <u>Slices</u>, Claw hands down to thighs
28. R then L Inward 2-Finger <u>Hooks</u>

*Meditating Horse Stance - Close Left foot to Right*

## FINGER SET #2

*Attention – Meditating Horse Stance*

*("Moving Finger Set" contains same lessons as Finger Set 1 but with Stances & Foot Maneuvers coordinated with finger strikes; Opposite hand chambered unless noted)*

1. Step R Forward to 12 RNB w/R Horiz 2-Finger <u>Thrust Poke</u> *(high),* L Pos Check
2. L Step Forward to 12 LNB w/L Horiz 2-Finger <u>Thrust Poke</u> *(high),* R Pos Check
3. L Offensive Rear Turn to 9 mod LNB w/R Vert 2-Finger <u>Thrust Poke</u>
4. L Rear Crossover, Unpivot R heel/L ball to 3 LNB w/L Vert 2-Finger <u>Thrust Poke</u>
5. L Defensive Rear Turn to 12 LFB w/R Inv 2-Finger <u>Thrust Poke</u>
6. Offensive Switch to 12 RFB w/L Inv 2-Finger <u>Thrust Poke</u>
7. R to L then L to 12 Horse w/R Horiz 2-Finger <u>Thrust Poke</u> over L shoulder to 6
8. L to R then R to 12 Horse w/L Horiz 2-Finger <u>Thrust Poke</u> over R shoulder to 6
9. R hand overlaps L then Dbl Downward Finger <u>Whips</u> to 12
10. Double Sandwich Inverted <u>Snapping</u> Finger <u>Pokes</u> to 12
11. Crossed Dbl Vert 2-Finger <u>Snapping</u> Finger <u>Pokes</u> to 12
12. Step back to R Cat forming R Crane hand, then back to 12 LFB w/R Overhand Crane Finger <u>Whip</u>, w/L Position Check
13. Step back to L Cat forming L Crane hand, then back to 12 RFB w/L Overhand Crane Finger <u>Whip</u>, w/R Position Check
14. R Off Rear Turn, Cat transition, 3 RNB w/R Underhand Crane Finger <u>Whip</u> to 3, w/L Position Check
15. R Rear step-thru to 3 mod LNB w/L Back Underhand Finger <u>Whip</u> to 9
16. L Rear step-thru to 3 RNB w/R In/Out 2-Finger <u>Slice</u> w/L Position Check
17. R Rear step-thru to 3 LNB w/L In/Out 2-Finger <u>Slice</u> w/R Position Check
18. R step-thru forward to 12 Horse Stance w/L In-Down Palm-Up Parry to chamber, w/R In/Out Windshield Wiper <u>Slices</u> to 12
19. R In-Down Palm-Up Parry to chamber w/L In/Out Windshield Wiper Finger <u>Slices</u> to 12
20. Step R forward to 12 RNB w/L Inside-Down Palm-Up Parry to L Rear Underhand <u>Claw</u> to 6 w/R Overhead Down <u>Claw</u> to 12
21. R step back to a 9 LNB w/R Inside-Down Palm-Up Parry to R Rear Underhand <u>Claw</u> to 3 w/L Overhead Down <u>Claw</u> to 9
22. R step forward to 12 R 45° Horse w/L Inside-Down Palm-Up Parry to L Rear Underhand <u>Claw</u> to 6 w/R Underhand <u>Claw</u> to 12
23. L step-thru forward to 12 L 45° Horse w/R Inside-Down Palm-Up Parry to R Rear Underhand <u>Claw</u> to 6 w/L Underhand <u>Claw</u> to 12

*Highlight Section to 12*

24. R hand over L, Dbl Sandwich Inv Finger <u>Thrust</u> *Pokes;*
25. Double Up Finger Flick <u>Whips;</u> 26. Double Forward Thumb <u>Gouges;</u>
27. Double Out Finger <u>Slices</u>, Claw hands down to thighs
28. R then L Inward 2-Finger <u>Hooks</u>

*Meditating Horse Stance - Close Left foot to Right*

# INTERACTIVE PARTNER SETS

Among many benefits, this helps develop feel, anatomical awareness, and transitions through connected continuous movement with a live person. Interactive *Partner Sets* can also be done in the air, except *Locking Set.*

## TWO-MAN STRIKING SET

This is the applied version of the previously described "in the air" Striking Set. The *Offensive Side* starts in a standing horse with both hands in chamber, the *Defensive Side* starts in a Standing Horse. Note: Developing the double factor blocking utilizes both hands simultaneously and is the highest level for practicing the *Defensive Side* of this *Set.*

| # | Offensive Side | Defensive Side |
|---|---|---|
| 1 | R Horiz Thrust Punch low | R Down-Out Block (Dbl Factor) |
| 2 | R Out Whipping BKS high | R Up Block (Dbl Factor) |
| 3 | L Horiz Thrust Punch low | L Down Block (Dbl Factor) |
| 4 | L Out BKS high | L Upward Block (Dbl Factor) |
| 5 | R Vert Thrust Punch high | R Upward Block (Dbl Factor) |
| 6 | R Forward Hammerfist low | L Push-Down Check |
| 7 | L Vert Thrust Punch high | L Upward Block (Dbl Factor) |
| 8 | L Forward Hammerfist low | R Push-Down Check |
| 9 | R Inv Horiz Punch low | L Down Block (Dbl Factor) |
| 10 | R In Heel Palm high | L Ext Out Block (Dbl Factor) |
| 11 | L Inv Horiz Punch low | R Down-Out Block (Dbl Factor) |
| 12 | L In Heel Palm high | R Ext Out Block (Dbl Factor) |
| 13 | R Straight Palm Strike high | L Upward Block (Dbl Factor) |
| 14 | R In Horiz Palm Strike low | R In Palm Check |
| 15 | L Straight Palm high | R Upward Block (Dbl Factor) |
| 16 | L In Horiz Palm Strike low | L In Palm Check |

*Close and/or Repeat using Opposite Roles w/Partner*

## TWO-MAN (PERSON) FIGHTING SET

Partners start side by side facing 12 in Standing Horse w/Dbl Push-Down Checks in front. *Offensive Side/#1* (Karate) initiates Set by attacking *Defensive Side/#2* (Kenpo) on their right.

| # | Offensive (Karate/Hard) Side #1 | Defensive (Kenpo/Soft) Side #2 |
|---|---|---|
| 1 | Side step R to a horse w/R Out BKS at #2 nose to 3 w/L check | Step back L towards 4:30 w/L In R out parry, L punch to 10:30 |
| 2 | Def cover w/dbl Out handsword blocks, R In handsword 4:30 | L In R Out parry, L step 7:30, check R arm, R BKS w/L high check, 1:30 |
| 3 | Def cover to 7:30 Rev RNB w/Vert Out forearm block, L horiz punch | R cat w/R crane hook over punch, L hand trap elbow, R front kick to 1:30 |
| 4 | 7:30 rear bow w/R Down Out block w/L overhead check | Spin 180° to L rear bow, L chamber w/R check to 1:30 |
| 5 | 7:30 L front crossover, L check, R step w/high down BKS | L rear cross-over w/L Up block, L side snap kick #1's R ribs to 1:30 |
| 6 | Step R to L w/R push-down check, L to 7:30 w/L Inv Horiz Punch | L push down to punch, R In arm clear, L In chop R temple to 1:30 |
| 7 | R Up block circling In to LFB w/R In hammerfist to 7:30 | R foot back to 4:30 LNB w/L In elbow block, L 2-finger poke, R check |
| 8 | R foot back to 10:30 LNB w/R Out parry, countergrab wrist, L half-fist | R Out parry, counter grab wrist, L In elbow strike solar plexus at 4:30 |

| 9 | Step L to R w/R In block, R step forward behind #2 L leg at 10:30 w/R Out BKS w/L hand check | Duck to wide kneel w/R In/Up parry to BKS w/L Out handsword #1 solar plexus at 4:30 |
|---|---|---|
| 10 | R In elbow block, modified RFB w/R forward elbow #2 ribs, w/L check to back of arm at 10:30 | L cat to 4:30 w/L BKS on R elbow, R push down check, L step outside R leg w/L inv crab pinch throat |
| 11 | Ride back w/L In palm block, R horiz palm to L ribs at 10:30 | Ride back w/R In hook clears R wrist, L horiz palm strike R ribs at 4:30 |
| 12 | Lean away w/R Down-Out block to L arm followed by R side thrust kick to #2 torso at 10:30 | R arm under/L arm over kick, L rear step-thru to 4:30 mod RFB, throw leg, to dbl vert horseshoe punch |
| 13 | Turn 180° to 10:30 L rev bow w/L arm down, R arm high hands open; Moving from Hard side to Soft side | Moving from Soft side to Hard side |
| | #1: R front crossover to 12, R wrist crosses over L, step out L rolling hands forward to dbl push-down checks to begin *Defensive Side* #2: L rear crossover to 6, L wrist crosses over R, step out R rolling hands forward to dbl push-down checks to begin *Offensive Side* | |

## TWO-MAN (PERSON) LOCKING SET

This Set is only done with a partner. Start facing each other; initiate with a L-R/R-L wrist grab. Person #1 applies locks until Person #2 is manipulated, taps, or cancels pressure by supporting the structure and/or moving away from pressure.

| # | *Person #1* | *Person #2* |
|---|---|---|
| 1 | Cross-Wrist Finger Trap | Move w/Lock; pull hand out to cancel |
| 2 | Cross-Thumb Wrist Twist | Move w/Lock; support structure or bend elbow In to cancel |
| 3 | Figure '4' Wrist Lock | Move w/Lock; palm to palm support |
| 4 | Thumb Lock | Tap w/Lock; support structure to cancel |
| 5 | Inside Wrist Flex Lock | Move w/Lock; push arm straight &/or roll out to cancel |
| 6 | Inward Wrist Lock | Move w/Lock; support structure to cancel |
| 7 | Outward Wrist Lock | Move w/Lock; support structure to cancel |
| 8 | Reverse Figure 4 Wrist Lock | Move with Lock; support structure cancels |
| 9 | Upward Reverse Wrist Twist | Move with Lock; support structure cancels |
| 10 | Over-Shoulder Elbow Trap | Tap with Lock; pull joint back over from shoulder to cancel |
| 11 | Arm-Bar Come-a-long | Tap w/Lock; roll palm out to cancel |
| 12 | Downward Arm Bar | Bend w/pressure; roll limb to cancel |
| 13 | Figure '4' Arm Bar | Lift w/pressure; pull elbow to body cancels |
| 14 | Over Shoulder Americana Lock | Bend Back w/pressure; support structure or straighten arm to cancel |
| 15 | Under Shoulder Kimura Lock | Bend Forward w/pressure; grab support structure or straighten arm to cancel |
| 16 | Braced Elbow Wrist Lock | Palm to palm supports structure to cancel |
| 17 | Crossed Arm Elbow Trap | Rotate arm & bend elbow to lift out, then countergrab cross wrist |
| 18 | Countergrab wrist lock | Peel thumb, pull free |
| | Repeat opposite role or same person starting on the other wrist | |

# FORMS

*Forms* are generally more sophisticated patterns than *Sets* as they contain multiple lessons built around a major theme that reflect a style, so in Kenpo they are mostly tied into the self-defense system. The numbered Kenpo forms described here are originally from the Ed Parker American Kenpo (i.e., EPAK) system, with the *Mass Attacks* Form I teach coming later from Jim Mitchell.

As mentioned, Kenpo originally did not have forms and not everyone wanted them added, but Mr. Parker saw their value and put them into his system in the early 1960's. His "Infinite Insights-Book 5" chapter on Forms reveals some of his thoughts in the development and addition of what he referred to as "Basics in Motion."

Whatever the evolution, a Form structure was put in place and is now part of the movement development, technique indexing, and historical record of American Kenpo. Not all Kenpo schools do these Forms in the same way, so I have noted some of those differences where I know them. Changes made by Kenpo Masters through the years and over generations of practitioners can seem to add up but overall, the Form should still be recognizable, even with these different interpretations.

Many lessons are reiterated in Kenpo Forms with the style having a certain look to it, such as moving through bent knees with an erect upper body posture, head level, rapid hand combinations, sophisticated footwork and pivots, peripheral awareness of multiple opponent's, moving to and from different directions, relaxed motion timed to explode with the breath, ending where you started, etc.

Described here are 10 Kenpo Forms with major and some minor lessons as they accumulate in Form pattern sophistication, plus notes and some hopefully interesting historical context. Video access for these Kenpo Forms is at BarryBBarker.com. Not included here, but also in my system, are Weapon forms, Kung Fu forms, and a Tournament Form that I created.

Covered here are: *Short & Long Form 1, Short & Long Form 2, Short & Long Form 3,* plus *Forms 4-5-6,* and *Mass Attacks.* I gave these Kenpo Forms names many years ago so they could also have character trait titles beneficial to the martial artist rather than just an emotionless dispassionate number so those are also noted with each Form.

A smaller font & abbreviations are used in the descriptions to save space:
R = Right; L = Left; RNB = Right Neutral Bow Stance; LNB = Left Neutral Bow Stance; LFB = Left Forward Bow; RFB = Right Forward Bow; BKS = Backknuckle Strike; Simult = Simultaneous; Dbl = Double; Horiz/Hrz = Horizontal; Vert = Vertical; In = Inward; Out = Outward; Up = Upward; Down = Downward; Ext = Extended; Inv = Inverted; Words "Stance" & "Strike" are left off most Basics names; w/ = with; Combo = Combination; Def = Defensive; Off = Offensive; Mod = Modified; , or - = then

## SHORT FORM 1 (Courage)
## Major Themes & Lessons:
- Defensive footwork with blocks

- "L" pattern footwork moves away from the next opponent
- "I" pattern footwork moves away from the current opponent
- Moving with erect posture, knees bent, head level as in all Kenpo forms
- Covers the "+" angles of directional movement to 12, 3, 6, 9
- Indexes 5 arm movement directions of In, Out, Up, Down-In, Down-Out
- Single step with single block or whole beat movement timing
- Blocking with footwork using the double "X" factor where the blocking lead arm transitions outside of the chambering or retracting arm
- Looking before changing direction

**Notes:**
In a street style, like Kenpo, learning footwork adjustments to face side or rear opponents is important for dealing with the unexpected and/or multiple-attacker visual.

Double "X" factor is expanded upon later to incorporate traps, tweaks, and breaks to extended limbs. In this *Form* it is primarily a reattachment point for the arms to reapply muscular strength.

In the Kenpo #1 Forms the hand not engaged in blocking, or punching as in Long 1, is chambered as a transition counterbalance and to pre-load the muscle structure in preparation for the next motion.

Short Form 1 is done as a *mirror image* with all moves done on one side and then on the other.

Emphasis on *reverse motion* can give additional insight.

All defensive motions can also have offensive applications.

### SHORT FORM #1 (Courage)
*Attention Stance - Bow - Step Left to a Meditating Horse Stance*
1. Step back L to a 12 RNB w/R In Block
2. R rear Step-Thru to 12 LNB w/L In Block
3. R steps to Def Rear Turn to 9 LNB w/R In (X) to L Out Block
4. L rear Step-Thru to 9 RNB w/L In (X) to R Out Block
5. R adjusts Def Cover Step to 3 LNB w/R In (X) to L Up Block
6. L rear Step-Thru to 3 RNB w/L In (X) to R Up Block
7. L steps to Def Rear Turn to 6 RNB w/L In Down (X) to R Down Out Block
8. R rear Step-Thru to 6 LNB w/R Down In (X) to L Down Out Block
*Pivot on ball of R foot then step L to 12 Meditating Horse Stance*
*Repeat Pattern on Opposite Side*
*Pivot on ball of L foot then step R to 12 Meditating Horse Stance - Close L to R*

## LONG FORM 1 (Strength)
**New Themes & Lessons:**
- Builds upon ideas introduced in Short Form 1
- Offensive footwork introduced as moves #7 & #17 step towards attacker
- Single step with double movements, or half-beat movement timing
- Rear hip turn to a *Forward Bow Stance* develops rear hand transitioning
- Front hip return to a *Neutral Bow Stance* develops front hand transitioning
- Blocking while transition stepping, in move #2 thru a *Cat Stance*

- Even 2-count and odd 3-count movement rhythms introduced
- Concept of checking introduced into forms

**Notes:**
This form has three major sections. Moves #1-8 are mostly 2-count blocking and punching patterns. Moves #9-16 are 3-count blocking and punching patterns. Moves #17-30 are highlights of sequential blocking in 3-counts and multi-directional punching in 2-counts.

This is the first form where the formal salutation and greeting are used to introduce and finish a form. In 1983, after my instructor Jim Mitchell became unaffiliated with EPAK, he changed the hand order of the salutation, presumably for copyright reasons. In Ed Parker's IKKA the open hands are high then down to the right fist inside empty hand, then down to the praying hands position. Jim Mitchell reversed that order to start low and end high before closing. The reality is that hand position flow order is not seen on James Mitose's family crest from his 1947 book making it a personal preference.

**Historical Context:**
The second section of Long Form 1 (moves #9-16) I adjusted from the original EPAK version to do the block from a neutral bow, then adjust to a forward bow with a rear hand straight punch, then return to the neutral bow, repeating the block. The original EPAK form repeats the same block three times, turning the shoulders through a *Modified Neutral Bow*. I teach a full forward bow with a rear hand punch between the two blocks. This larger rotation-retraction motion is more important at this level in my opinion. The smaller modified rotation is introduced in the #2 Forms.

**LONG FORM #1 (Strength)**

*Presentation - Salutation - Greeting - Step L to a Meditating Horse Stance*
*Section 1: Even / 2-Count Section – Right side of Form starts here*

1. Step back L from 12 to RNB w/R In Block, RFB w/L Horiz Thrust Punch
2. Step back from 12 to a R Cat w/R In Block then finish R step back to LNB w/L In Block, LFB w/R Horiz Thrust Punch, odd/3-count rhythm introduced
3. Def Turn L to 9 LNB w/R In (X) into L Out Block, LFB w/R Horiz Thrust Punch
4. L rear Step-Thru from 9 to RNB w/L In (X) to R Out Block, RFB w/L Hrz Punch
5. Def Cover to 3 L Rev Bow, LNB w/L Out Elbow, mod LNB w/R Position Check, (X) L Up Block, LFB w/R Horiz Thrust Punch
6. L rear Step-Thru to 3 RNB w/L In (X) to R Up Blk, RFB w/L Hrz Thrust Punch
7. Right back thru R Cat w/L In Down (X) then R Off Rear Turn to 6 RNB w/R Down Out Block, RFB w/L Horiz Thrust Punch
8. R rear Step-Thru from 6 to LNB w/R In Down to L Down Out Block, LFB w/R Horiz Punch

*Section 2: Odd / 3-Count Section – Left side of Form starts here*

9. LNB to 6 w/L In Block, LFB w/R Horiz Punch, LNB w/L In Block

10. L rear Step-Thru to 6 RNB w/R In Block, RFB w/L Horiz Thrust Punch, RNB w/R In Block

11. Step L, R Def Rear Turn to 9 RNB w/L In (X) to R Out Block, RFB w/L Horiz Thrust Punch, then RNB w/L In (X) to R Out Block
12. R rear Step-Thru to 9 LNB w/R In (X) to L Out Block, LFB w/R Horiz Thrust Punch, then LNB w/R In (X) to L Out Block
13. Step L Def Cover to 3 RNB w/L In (X) to R Up Block, RFB w/L Horiz Thrust Punch, Then RNB w/L In (X) to R Up Block
14. R rear Step-Thru to 3 LNB w/R In (X) to L Up Block, LFB w/R Horiz Thrust Punch then LNB w/R In (X) to L Up Block
15. Step R, L Def Rear Turn to 12 LNB w/R In Down (X) to L Down Out Block, LFB w/R Horiz Thrust Punch, then LNB w/R In Down (X) to L Down Out Block
16. L rear Step-Thru to 12 RNB w/L In Down (X) to R Down Out Block, RFB w/L Horiz Thrust Punch, then RNB w/L In Down (X) to R Down Out Block

*Section 3 – Sequential Alternating Arms*
*Odd / 3-Count Blocks; Even / 2-Count Punches; Opposite Hand Chambers*

17. L step forward to 12 Horse for #17-23, L-R-L Down In Palm Down Block
18. R-L-R Down Out Palm Up Block to 12
19. L-R-L Push Down Checks to 12
20. R-L Straight Horiz Thrust Punches to 12
21. R Horiz Thrust Punch to 10:30 - L Horiz Thrust Punch to 1:30
22. R Horiz Thrust Punch to 9 - L Horiz Thrust Punch to 3
23. R then L Uppercut Thrust Punches to 12.

*Meditating Horse Stance - Greeting - Close L to R - Salutation*

## SHORT FORM 2 (Respect)
### New Themes & Lessons:

- Offensive footwork moves towards current and next opponent
- Defense that moves inside an attacking arm or kick
- First four moves repeat Short & Long Form 1 blocks, stepping forward
- Adds "X" angles of directional movement moving to 1:30, 4:30, 7:30, 10:30, making for 8 angles total, including "+" angles of 12-3-6-9
- Using the hand (i.e., weapon) closed to open and open to closed
- Using the same hand sequentially
- Using both hands simultaneously
- Checking included throughout starting with this Form
- Low kicks with upper body blocks and strikes
- Kenpo Self-defense techniques begin to be indexed
- Exaggerated transitions between techniques (rounded out in Long 2)
- Alternating format where one-side of a technique is done then the other side of that same technique, not *mirror image*, as in Short 1

### Historical Context:

There are no kicks in the EPAK version of Short Form 2 but in the early 1980's my former instructor Jim Mitchell added the front snap kicks on Thrusting Palm and Pursuing Panther, as done in those techniques. Some do the first move in *Ducking Dragon,* moves #5 & #6 in this Form, as a downward raking middle knuckle fist. This "zipper" motion is designed to reverse the channel flow of the centerline Conception Vessel Qi. This is theoretically a devastating strike, but in modern times with less natural weapon development, different clothing, belt buckles, and the theory behind this strike lost to most, I teach a straight punch to the bladder instead.

# SHORT FORM #2 (Respect)

*Presentation - Salutation - Greeting - Step L to a Meditating Horse Stance*

1. Step forward R to 12 RNB w/first 2 moves from *Six Hands*
2. Step thru forward L to 12 LNB w/first 2 moves from *Six Hands*
   <u>Transition</u>: Adjust hips & R heel out to face 10:30 in L Cat chambering both hands at R hip, L hand on top, i.e., cup & saucer style
3. Step L to 9 Mod LNB w/L Out block / R Horiz Thrust punch combo
   <u>Transition</u>: Adjust hips & L heel out to face 1:30 in R Cat chambering both hands at L hip, R hand on top, i.e., cup & saucer style
4. Step R to 3 Mod RNB w/R Out block / L Horiz Thrust punch combo
   <u>Transition</u>: Step L back towards 6, to 12 Front Twist Stance chambering both hands at R hip, L hand on top, i.e., cup & saucer style
5. Un-pivot CCW on R heel / L ball covering L to a 6 LNB, L Close Kneel w/L Up Open Hand Blocking Check / R Vert Punch, i.e., *Ducking Dragon*
   <u>Transition</u>: Step R foot back across the 6/12-line chambering both hands at L hip w/R hand on top (cup & saucer)
6. Pivot CW on R ball / L heel covering R to 12 RNB, R Close Kneel w/R Up Open Hand Blocking Check / L Vert punch, i.e., *Ducking Dragon*
   <u>Transition</u>: Turn around 180° CCW using R ball pivot to 6 L Cat w/arms crossed at chest, L on inside
7. Step L to 4:30 w/L Down block, then R side of *Thrusting Palm* to 4:30 RNB
   <u>Transition</u>: Step back to a 6 R Cat w/arms crossed at chest, R on inside
8. Step R foot to 7:30 RNB w/R Down block, then L side *Thrusting Palm* to 7:30 LNB
   <u>Transition</u>: Off Cover w/L ball pivot to 1:30 R Cat w/L In block
9. R Front Snap Kick, finish R side of *Pursuing Panther* to 1:30
   <u>Transition</u>: L Off front turn to 10:30 L Cat w/R In block
10. L Front Snap Kick, finish L side *Pursuing Panther* to 10:30
    *R step forward to Meditating Horse - Greeting - L to R Close - Salutation*

## LONG FORM 2 (Honor)

### New Themes & Lessons:

- Builds upon ideas and techniques introduced in Short Form 2
- 4-Count movement rhythms (2 & 3 count introduced in Long 1)
- Quarter and eighth-beat timing introduced
- Builds upon Short 2's first 8 angles with Long 1 "Section 3" highlights
- Rotating twist stances added
- Subtle rounded out transitions between techniques

### Notes:

Moves in this form can be explained using quarter and eighth count beats / rhythms / cadences. Timing variations covered in this Form are quarter-quarter-quarter-quarter, quarter-quarter-quarter-eighth-eighth, and eighth-eighth-quarter-quarter-quarter. Rhythm claps to the different cadences when teaching this form is a way to help students gain this insight.

The palm-up, palm-down, and push-down checks used in moves #11-12, #13-14, and #15-16 match the same movements done towards the end of Long Form 1, with the first two done in opposite order.

**Historical Context:**

I changed move #7 in the 1990's to an offensive turn to match the same move in Short Form 2 and help align better to starting point at Forms end. I teach moves #15-16 from a rotating twist stance, as shown to me by my then instructor Ernest George Jr. in the 1990's. Some do a *Forward Bow Stance*, as I was taught originally by Jim Mitchell.

Jim Mitchell changed moves #15-19 in the early 1980's to step forwards to 1:30 then back from 1:30 two times instead of three, as in the EPAK system.

## LONG FORM #2 (Honor)

*Presentation - Salutation - Greeting - Horse Stance ready position*

1. Step forward to 12 RNB w/first 4 moves of *Six Hands* R side
2. Step-Thru forward to 12 LNB w/first 4 moves of *Six Hands* L side
3. L Off rear turn 9 Mod LNB w/L Out Block / R Horiz Punch combo, L then R Horiz Punches, L Vert Snap Punch w/L Side Snap Kick combo to 9
4. R Off Cover 3 Mod RNB w/R Out Block / L Horiz Thrust Punch combo, R then L Horiz Punches, R Vert Snap Punch w/R Side Snap Kick combo to 3
5. L Off Rear Turn / Cover to 6 LFB into R side of *Rolling Fists*
6. R Off Cover step to 12 RFB into L side of *Rolling Fists*
7. L Off Rear Cover / Turn to 4:30 LNB w/L Down Out Block into high L In Hooking Punch or BKS, LFB w/R Horiz <u>Thrust</u> Punch, L Horiz <u>Thrust Punch</u> <u>w</u>/R Front <u>Snap Kick</u> combo, step forward to RNB w/R Vert <u>Snap</u> Punch
8. R Off Rear Turn to 7:30 RNB w/R Down Out Block up into high In Hooking Punch or BKS, RFB w/L Horiz <u>Thrust</u> Punch, R Horiz <u>Thrust Punch w</u>/L Front <u>Snap Kick</u> combo, step forward LNB w/L Vert <u>Snap</u> Punch
9. L Front Crossover to 1:30 Front Twist w/L Inv Vert high Thrust Punch w/R Hand low check, then step out R to 1:30 w/R Up Forearm strike at chin height, then L 2-Finger Poke throat followed by R-L Vert 2-Finger Poke eyes
10. R Front Crossover to 10:30 Front Twist w/R Inv Vert high Thrust Punch w/L Hand low check, step out L to 10:30 w/L Up Forearm strike at chin height, R 2-Finger Poke throat, L / R Vert 2-Finger Poke eyes
11. L Rear Crossover to 10:30 Front Twist w/L Inside Down Palm Up Block, unpivot ball / ball to a RNB w/R Vert Snap Punch
12. R Rear Crossover to 10:30 Front Twist w/R Inside Down Palm Up Block, unpivot ball / ball to LNB w/L Vert Snap Punch
13. R back w/Def Front Turn to 1:30 LNB w/L Inside Down Palm Down Block circling inside and up to L Out Block, L Uppercut Snap Punch
14. L Rear Step-Thru to 1:30 RNB w/R Inside Down Palm Up Block circling inside and up to R Out Block, R Uppercut Snap Punch
15. R ball/ball Front Rotating Twist to 1:30 w/L Push Down Check, step out to 1:30 LNB w/L Out Down Elbow, L Down Heel Palm Claw
16. L ball/ball Front Rotating Twist to 1:30 w/R Push Down Check, step out to 1:30 RNB w/R Out Down Elbow, R Down Heel Palm Claw
17. RFB to 1:30 w/L Horiz Thrust Punch, chambering R hand, L Counter Grab adjusting to 1:30 RNB w/R In Forearm Strike
18. R rear Step-Thru from 1:30 LNB w/L Overhead Down Elbow Strike
19. L rear Step-Thru 1:30 RNB w/R Overhead Down Elbow Strike

*Highlights*
Step L forward to 12 Horse Stance w/L In Elbow Strike / R In Palm Strike
Sandwich, Dbl Out Elbow Strikes to 3 & 9, R-L Up Elbows to 12
*Meditating Horse - Greeting - L to R Close - Salutation*

## SHORT FORM 3 (Peace & Justice)
**New Themes & Lessons:**
- Indexes Self-Defense Techniques against grabs and holds
- Only other *mirror image* Kenpo form, along with Short Form 1
- First form to start with feet together
- 6 front attack techniques, 6 rear attack techniques, 1 side attack
- Multiple opponent's attacking sequentially and overlapping
- Lock, trap, and break applications observed in Form movement

**Notes:**

The right side of Short Form 3 has no 9 attack and the left side no 3 attack.

The second side of this mirror image Form closes right foot to left.

### SHORT FORM #3 (Peace & Justice)
*Presentation - Salutation - Greeting - Attention Stance - Ready Position*
1. Step R forward to 12 w/R side *Twins of Destruction* up to R forearm strike
2. R 12 Cat extending arms w/Dbl Finger Pokes, Step R Side *Crashing Elbows* ending with R Hammerfist Thrust in LFB to 7:30
3. R to L step, Off Cover 3 RFB w/R Out Block / L In Elbow combo (EPAK: *Twirling Elbows*), L steps to 1:30 LFB w/R In Elbow to L chamber, i.e., cup & saucer
4. Cover to 7:30 w/R side *Circling Elbow* ending in a 7:30 R Reverse Bow
5. R ball/ball Front Rotating Twist to 7:30 to R side of *Crossing Grab*
6. R side of *Scraping Stomp* facing 10:30 with attacker behind at 4:30
7. Step forward R w/R side of *Turning the Cross* to 10:30 (Extension version)
8. L step-thru forward to L 10:30 Close Kneel w/Dbl In Hammerfist vs L arm side headlock from 1:30, 4:30 RFB w/L Straight Palm Thrust (*Lock of Death / Escaping Death* combo, or EPAK: *Lock of Death*)
9. L rear crossover to 4:30 w/R arm out, then rolling behind back into Hammerlock hold, un-pivot to L on R heel / L ball 180° CCW to LNB w/R side of *Locked Arm*; then after R leg knee kick to 10:30 step down R w/feet together
10. Step L forward to 10:30 w/R side *Crossed Arms* to 1:30 Horse
11. R side *Arms of Silk,* moves L ending in 1:30 Horse Stance
12. R step forward to 1:30 Cat w/ R side *Conquering Arm* ending in 1:30 RNB
13. R Rear Step-Thru vs R shoulder to R hip tackle, L In Hooking BKS head, grab hair to anchor chin up, Half Fist throat (EPAK: *Cutting Huggers Throat*)
*Step R Forward to Mediating Horse Stance - Close L to R*
*Repeat 1-13 on opposite mirror image side - Greeting - Close R to L - Salutation*

## LONG FORM 3 (Persistence)
**New Themes & Lessons:**
- Builds upon grab/hold technique theme introduced in Short Form 3
- Continues idea of multiple opponents attacking sequentially & overlapping
- Adds simultaneous attacks from multiple attackers

**Notes:**

Footwork pattern follows the letter "I" shape, starting at one end, travelling to the other, then returning to the original starting location.

On #25-26, Desperate Fists, I teach having the same hand (right) on top for each side so on #25 the right hand is a straight vertical thrust punch and on #26 it is an Outward BKS on the other. This indexes 2 arm clear options for that technique (my video different as I made change after video was shot).

---

# LONG FORM #3 (Persistence)

*Presentation - Salutation - Greeting - Attention Stance - Ready Position*

1. R side *Twins of Destruction* to 12, back to Attention Stance
2. L side *Twins of Destruction* to 12, back to Horse Stance
3. Dbl Finger Flicks to 12 into R side *Crashing Elbows* from 6; ending in 7:30 LFB
4. Shift to 1:30 RFB, vs L cross shoulder grab, w/R In Parry, out circle L Armpit to trap and Leg to buckle; RFB to 3 w/L palm push (EPAK: *Dominating Circles*)
5. Adjust to 12 Horse w/both fists ext low, inside out Dbl Down BKS counters wrist grabs, pulling both hands to chamber, Dbl Finger Pokes to 12, step out L for L side *Crashing Elbows* from 6, ending in 4:30 RFB
6. Shift to 10:30 LFB, vs R cross shoulder grab, w/L In Parry, out circle R Armpit to trap and leg to buckle; LFB to 9 w/R palm push (EPAK: *Dominating Circles*)
7. Adjust to 12 Horse w/both fists ext low, inside out Dbl Down BKS counters wrist grabs, pulling both hands to chamber; Dbl In Crane Hooks counters rear bear hug, shows finger compression lock, step R to L w/hands crossed at chest, R on inside, then step back R for R side of *Parting Arms* to 12
8. R foot forward to L, Off Switch, w/hands crossed chest height, L hand on inside, then step back L for L side of *Parting Arms* to 12
9. R Rear Step-Thru into R side *Glancing Poke* to 12
10. L Rear Step-Thru into L side *Glancing Poke* to 12

*(Note steps in moves #9-10, & then #11, move to back end of this forms "I" pattern)*

11. R Cat transition back to 12 Horse w/R In Armpit Trap to 3, Inv Horiz Snap Punch; then L In Armpit Trap, L Inv Horiz Snap Punch to 9, i.e., *Conquering Arm*
12. From 12 Horse Stance, R Out Armpit Trap to 3, R Out BKS; then L Out Armpit Trap, L Out BKS to 9, i.e *Wraparound*
13. Dbl *Conquering Arm* to 3 & 9, Dbl In Armpit Traps, Dbl Inv Horiz Snap Punches
14. Dbl *Wraparound* to 3 & 9, Dbl Out Armpit Traps, Dbl Out BKS
15. Front Rotating Twist Stance L vs L-L cross wrist grab into L side *Crossing Grab* to 12 up to R Down Elbow Strike, step back R to 12 Horse Stance
16. Front Rotating Twist Stance R vs R-R cross wrist grab into R side *Crossing Grab* to 12 up to L Down Elbow Strike, step back L to 12 Horse Stance
17. Pivot L heel open / R ball to 7:30 L Front Twist Stance, R step forward to 7:30 RFB w/Ext Dbl 4-Finger Pokes, RNB w/R Up Elbow, R Down Heel Palm Claw (EPAK: *Wedging Arms*), step back R to 12 Horse Stance, unpivoting on L heel
18. Pivot R heel open / L ball to 4:30 R Front Twist Stance, L step forward to 4:30 LFB w/Ext Dbl 4-Finger Pokes, LNB w/L Up Elbow, L Down Heel Palm Claw (EPAK: *Wedging Arms*), step back L to 12 Horse Stance, unpivoting on R heel
19. R step to 10:30 into R side *Blinding Vice*, R step back to 12 Horse Stance
20. L step to 1:30 into L side *Blinding Vice*, L step back to 12 Horse Stance
21. R side *Arms of Silk*, retrace steps towards 3 w/R Out BKS, to 12 Horse Stance
22. L side *Arms of Silk*, retrace steps towards 9 w/L Out BKS, to 12 Horse Stance
23. *Scraping Stomp* to R In Hook/Side Snap Kicks low to knees, then L In Hook/Side Snap Kicks low to knees
24. *Scraping Stomp* ending, L grabs R wrist under R armpit, then L step to 12, RFB to 6 w/R Out Elbow, Def Switch as R grabs L wrist under L armpit, then R step to 12, LFB to 6 w/L Out Elbow (EPAK: *Repeated Devastation*)
25. R Front Rotating Twist to 12 R side *Desperate Fists* w/R hand on top, step to LNB-LFB w/simult R Vert Thrust Punch high/lead hand out BKS low
26. L Front Rotating Twist to 12, L *Desperate Fists,* R hand <u>still</u> on top, step to LNB-LFB w/R hand BKS high/L rear Vert Thrust Punch low to 12

*Step Left Forward to Meditating Horse Stance - Greeting - Salutation*

## FORM 4 (Tenacity)
### New Themes & Lessons:
- Indexes Self-Defense Techniques against punches and kicks
- Continuous motion form
- Defending punch/kick attacks from blind angles
- Defending while on the knees
- Simultaneous kicks with punches/strikes
- Jumping combination kick introduced into forms, i.e., "Chicken Kick"

### Notes:
This is the longest Kenpo form with at least 20 defined Self-Defense Techniques, each done on both sides. The next longest Kenpo Forms, Short & Long Form 3 & Form 6, by comparison have 13 Self-Defense Techniques.

Form 4 contains all major components of the Kenpo style covering 8 major directions against multiple opponents sequentially and simultaneously. This Form uses forward and reverse motion flowing 3-dimensionally with unique footwork transitions into explosive rapid-fire hand combinations.

Form 4 is full of technique relationships towards category completion:
- Protective Parries & Darting Leaves - Kick/Poke same & opposite sides
- Unrolling Crane & Reversing Circles - Low/High alternating Blocks using reverse motion
- Broken Kneel & Flashing Hands - Back & Forward transitioning through Twist Stances
- Cradling the Baby & Protective Circles - Collapsing/Expanding Circles
- Thundering Fists & Flashing Hands - Same stance transitions applied at different ranges
- Dancing in the Dark & Untwirling Pendulum - Adjusting to different ranges of a kick/punch attack
- Parrying Grab & Circling Parries - Same and Alternating side parries
- Turning Windmills Indexes Coordination Set 2 & Finger Set 1
- Defending Cross & Nutcracker - Moving back/forward against a kick attack & standing/kneeling defense against a kick attack
- Prancing Tiger & Shield and Punch - Circles up/out & in/down
- Six Hands & Twirling Fist - Pushing vs Pulling punch attack defense
- Twirling Fist & Flashing Hands - mirror image patterns

### Historical Context:
I changed the footwork transition to techniques #22 & #23, *Thundering Fists & Untwirling Pendulum* in the early 1980's, with Jim Mitchell's approval. I was competing at that time and the original EPAK version puts your back to the judges for moves #23-38, making the footwork on #39 & #40 also different. This change stuck at our school at that time and is how I teach this Form; my students would introduce it as "Form 4 modified" in competition so to hopefully not lose points from traditional EPAK judges.

## FORM #4 (Tenacity)

*Presentation - Salutation - Greeting to Attention Stance*

1. Protective Parries R side to 12, ending w/R In Elbow to 1:30
2. Step back R 12 Horse w/R Back Elbow/L Over R Shoulder 2-Finger Horiz Poke to 6, R 2-Finger Horiz Poke to 12 w/L low Back Handsword to 6, L Up Elbow to 12 w/R low Back Hammerfist Strike to 6
3. L In/R Out snapping Blocks to 9 & 3, L/R Inv Horiz Snap Punches to 9 & 3, Concave Stance to 12 collapsing crossed arms in front followed by Dbl Out into Down Claws closing R foot to L
4. *Protective Parries* L side to 12 ending w/L In Elbow to 10:30
5. Step back L to 12 Horse w/6 L low Back Elbow/R over L shoulder 2-Finger Horiz Poke, L Horiz 2-Finger Poke to 12 w/6 R low back handsword, 12 R Up Elbow w/6 L low Back Hammerfist
6. R In/L Out snapping Blocks to 3 & 9, R/L Inv Horiz Snap Punches to 3 & 9
7. Adjust to 1:30 R Cat w/L Open Hand Check, R Front Snap Kick w/R Vert 2-Finger Poke (EPAK: *Darting Leaves*), step R back, 10:30 LNB
8. L Cat to 10:30 w/R Open Hand Check, L Front Snap Kick w/L Vert 2-Finger Poke (EPAK: Darting Leaves), step L down ending with feet together
9. Step back R, 10:30 mod LNB w/L side *Unrolling Crane* ending w/L high BKS
10. Adjust L foot back, Def Front Turn, to 10:30 Mod LNB w/R side *Unrolling Crane* ending w/R high BKS
11. R rear crossover, un-pivot L heel / R ball to 12 R side *Broken Kneel* ending w/L on top Piggy-Back Punch to 3
12. L Rear Crossover, un-pivot R heel/L ball to 12 L side *Broken Kneel* ending w/R on top Piggy-Back Punch to 9
13. Step R to 12 Front Twist w/R Ext Out Block, step out L to 12 w/L In Block & R side *Flashing Hands* to R Forward Handsword Strike
14. Step L to 12 Front Twist w/L Ext Out Block, step out R to 12 w/R In Block & L side *Flashing Hands* to L Forward Handsword Strike
15. Step L w/R side *Cradling the Baby* to 9, ending w/R In Elbow Strike, as a sandwich w/L In Heel-Palm
16. L Rear Crossover unpivot 180° R heel/L ball to 3, step L for R side *Cradling the Baby* to R In Elbow, sandwiching w/L In Heel-Palm
17. Adjust L to 10:30 Cat, then R side *Protective Circles* w/R groin grab followed by high L snapping BKS (original EPAK version)
18. L Front Crossover, Twist Stance, to 4:30 w/R In Elbow smash, step out w/L side *Protective Circles* w/L groin grab then by high R snapping BKS (original EPAK version)
19. R Rear Crossover facing 7:30 Front Twist Stance w/R Down Out Parry then L In Parry, step R to 7:30 RNB to R side *Dancing in the Dark* up to 1:30 Front Twist
20. Unpivot to 1:30 L Cat, L Rear Crossover, Front Twist w/L Down, R In Parry, step out L to 1:30 w/L side *Dancing in the Dark* to 9 Front Twist Stance
21. Step out L to 9 w/L In Block, R side *Thundering Fists* ending w/L Spinning Out BKS to 9 Front Twist
22. Step out R to 3 w/R In Block, L side *Thundering Fists* ending w/R Spinning Out BKS to 3 Front Twist
    *(Footwork adjustment here different from original EPAK version)*
23. Step L back to 1:30 RNB, w/L In-Down Palm Up Block, R Rear Crossover w/R Down-Out Block, un-pivot toe-toe w/R side *Untwirling Pendulum* ending in Front Twist Stance to 1:30 w/R Up 5-Finger Strike
24. L Rear Crossover, 10:30 Front Twist, w/L Down-Out Block, un-pivot toe toe w/L *Untwirling Pendulum* ending in Front Twist to 10:30 w/L Up 5-Finger Strike
25. Step R to 1:30 w/R side *Reversing Circles up* to R Out Handsword Strike
26. Step L to R, then L to 10:30 w/L side *Reversing Circles* up to L Out Handsword

27. Step L back to 1:30 RNB w/R Universal Check, R side *Parrying Grab* up to R Front Snap Kick
28. Step R back, 10:30 LNB w/L Universal Check, L side *Parrying Grab* up to L Front Snap Kick
29. L back to 3 RNB w/R In Parry, R side *Circling Parries* up to R Inv Horiz Punch
30. Def Cover to 9 LNB w/L In Parry, L side *Circling Parries* up to L Inv Horiz Punch
31. Adjust to 12 Horse Stance w/highlights from R side *Turning Windmills*: R Up Parry/L Forward Inv Horiz Palm, circle arms to L Up Block/R low In Hammerfist into R Up Block/L low In Hammerfist, into R In Block, R Out/In Horiz 2-Finger Slices, R Out Finger Splay
32. Highlights from L *Turning Windmills*: R In Hooking Clear to Chamber, L In Block, L Out/In Horiz 2-Finger Slices, L Out Finger Splay to L In Hook to Chamber, then Dbl Down Finger Flicks, Dbl Vert 2-Finger Pokes, Dbl Out Thumb Rips, Dbl Up Little Finger Pokes
33. R back to 12 LFB w/R side *Defending Cross* up to R Stiff-Arm Lifting Punch
34. L Step-Thru back to 12 RFB w/L side *Defending Cross* up to L Stiff-Arm Punch
35. Drop onto L knee w/R side *Nutcracker* to 12 ending w/R Uppercut Punch
36. Switch w/hop to R knee w/L side *Nutcracker* ending w/L Uppercut Punch
37. Stand up to L Cat Stance w/R side *Prancing Tiger,* to 3 ending w/R Out Snap BKS/R Side Snap Kick combo into 12 R Cat Stance
38. L side *Prancing Tiger* up to L Out Snap BKS/L Side Snap Kick combo to R One-Legged Stance w/both hands "cup & saucer" at L Chamber
39. Step L, 12 Forward 45° Horse w/R Out block/L Horiz Thrust Punch into R side *Shield and Punch,* end w/R Side Snap Kick, hands "cup & saucer" at R chamber
40. Step down R to Forward 45° Horse Stance to 12 w/L Out Block/R Horiz Punch combo into L side *Shield and Punch,* ending w/L Side Snap Kick
41. Step down L then forward R, Def Switch to 12 RNB w/R side *Six Hands,* w/move #5 a RFB w/L Handsword slicing down thru neck, RNB w/L Up-In Heel-Palm / R Down-In Heel-Palm crossing R under L, R Rev Bow w/R Obscure Handsword
42. R step, 12 Twist Stance transition then L to LNB w/L side *Six Hands* w/move #5 LFB w/R Handsword slicing down thru neck, LNB w/R Up-In Heel-Palm/L Down-In Heel-Palm crossing L under R, L Rev Bow w/L Obscure Handsword
43. L step, 12 Twist Stance transition w/L Ext Out Block then R side *Twirling Fists* up to R In Handsword Strike/L Hand Check, i.e. holding "two bowls of rice"
44. R step, 12 Twist Stance transition w/R Ext Out Block then L side *Twirling Fists* to L Front Crossover Pull Sweep as L hand pushes head into R face Punch
45. Closes w/R Pull Sweep behind L knee then step out R, L Pull Sweep until foot touches R knee, step L to 12 Meditating Horse Stance.
*Greeting - Salutation - Bow*

## FORM 5 (Determination)
### New Themes & Lessons:
- Taking an opponent to the ground is indexed on every technique
- Techniques utilizing various body fulcrums and manipulation methods
- Height adjustments moving down then up is used extensively
- Using the ground as a compression surface

**Notes:** All but two techniques in Form 5 move outside the attacking arm. *Falling Eagle* moves inside the arm but outside the foot, with *Skipping Tackle* (EPAK: Hopping Crane) as a stomp-kick sequence or *Charging Tackle* to an opponent on all 4's, or a sweep inside cross-side leg then side kick inside same side leg, or an outside leg sweep to the cross-side leg.

Kenpo movement and *Forms* generally emphasize that the head and body remain level with an erect posture while moving. The takedowns indexed in this form utilize down and up movement repeatedly, accounting for the powerful Dropping/Settling principle discussed in the *Mind*.

This Form is unique by starting in the middle of the Kenpo greeting, from the low praying hands position, then ending with the fist inside open hand before moving through the high empty hand position before closing.

**Historical Context:**
In the first technique, *Protective Parries* against a side overhead or high punch, for category completion defends using the rear hand across the body to engage under and outside the punch, although the other hand is closer. As a body technique I engage the close hand first rather than reach to pick up the attack. I have done it both ways but currently teach in the Form the traditional way, although in my own video I do it the other way.

I add an upward reverse hammerfist strike in *Circling the Arm* before the leg sweep, which is my habit on a body.

For the neck tweak in *Jumping Crane,* I brace the shoulder with my rear hand as my lead hand holds the chin, rear hand lower than lead hand, although some Kenpo practitioners place the rear hand higher, presumably both hands holding the head.

Form 5 is said to be one of two empty-handed Kenpo Forms created solely by Ed Parker, with Form 6 being the other.

## FORM #5 (Determination)
*Presentation - Salutation - Greeting to Prayer hand position*
1. Right side *Destructive Parries* against 9 attack *(R hand picks up first punch)*
2. Left side *Destructive Parries* against 3 attack *(L hand picks up first punch)*
3. Right side *Dance of Death* against attack from 12 *(R foot moves back)*
4. Left side *Dance of Death* against attack from 6 *(L Cat then L foot moves back)*
5. Right side *Leap of Death* against attack from 9 *(R Out Parry from Twist Stance)*
6. Left side *Leap of Death* against attack from 3 *(L Out Parry from Twist Stance)*
7. Right side *Backbreaker* against attack from 4:30 *(L foot back, R foot forward)*
8. Left side *Backbreaker* against attack from 7:30 *(R foot back, L foot forward)*
9. Right side *Skipping Tackle* / EPAK: *Hopping Crane* to 12 *(see 'Notes')*
10. Left side *Skipping Tackle* / EPAK: *Hopping Crane* to 12 *(see 'Notes')*
11. Right side *Sleeper* against attack from 6 *(spin around to R Cat)*
12. Left side *Sleeper* against attack from 12 *(R Step-Thru back to L Cat)*
13. Right side *Brushing the Club* against attack from 6 *(Defensive Switch to RNB)*
14. Left side *Brushing the Club* against attack from 12 *(Defensive Switch to LNB)*
15. Right side *Falling Eagle* against attack from 9 *(untwist from R foot back)*
16. Left side *Falling Eagle* against attack from 3 *(untwist from R foot forward)*
17. Right side *Circling the Arm* against attack from 1:30 *(untwist 7:30 to 1:30 R Cat)*
18. Left side *Circling the Arm* against attack from 7:30 *(Def Cover 1:30 to 7:30 L Cat)*
19. Right side *Jumping Crane* against attack from 12 (from R Rear Crossover Step)
20. Left side *Jumping Crane* against attack from 12 *(from L Front Crossover Step)*
*Last technique ends in 12 Horse Stance w/R Fist Inside Left Open Hand*
*Finish greeting, Salute, Close*

## FORM 6 (Perseverance)
**New Themes & Lessons:**
- Indexes knife, club, and gun Self-Defense Techniques
- The weapon hand is continually accounted for
- Hands move and connect in a continuous flow of motion

**Notes:**
The "Knife Defense Formula" covers seven attack angles with 4 quadrant thrusts, 1 forehand, 1 backhand, and 1 overhead attack. Form 6 covers six of those seven attack angles, with only the backhand attack missing (Piercing Blade).

There are 2 overhead Club attacks and 1 Club poke, but no forehand or backhand Club attacks. However, those inside and outside arm positions are addressed in other Form 6 Knife techniques and extensively in previous Forms.

Inside and outside arm position against front and rear threatening Gun are covered, but with no under or over Gun defenses.

Some Kenpo practitioners start both sides of the first technique *Glancing Blade* (EPAK: Glancing Lance) off angle to 1:30 then 10:30, but I originally learned them and still do them both to 12 as Techniques and in this Form.

*Unexpected Blade* releases the knifehand grip in the Form, presuming the knife has been dropped, inserting a downward claw with that hand. When applying that as a technique I prefer to continue holding the wrist to control that hand, which may still be holding the knife.

*Clipping Blade* in the traditional technique and in Form 6 uses the free hand to reach under the defending hand to grab the groin. When applying as a technique I prefer an eye poke as it is closer and not obstructed by my other arm.

*Capturing the Club* has two upward inward overhead circling club strikes into the attacker's face, with the first lifting his head then the second with the leg sweep and back heel-of-palm strike into his groin. Some only do one of these strikes.

**Historical Context:**
Form 6 is said to be one of two empty-handed Kenpo Forms created solely by Ed Parker, with Form 5 being the other.

### FORM #6 (Perseverance)
*Presentation – Salutation - Greeting*
*Inverted Close to Standing Horse with Double Push Downs in Front*
1. R side *Glancing Blade* against attack from 12 *(repeat open to Dbl Push Downs)*
2. L side *Glancing Blade* against attack from 12
3. R Cat to 3 starts R side *Unexpected Blade*
4. LNB to 9 starts L side *Unexpected Blade*

5. R rear crossover then untwist to 1:30 starts R side *Clipping the Blade*
6. L rear crossover then untwist to 10:30 starts L side *Clipping the Blade*
7. L rear step-thru to 12 RNB starts R side *Thrusting Blade*
8. R rear step-thru to 12 starts L side *Thrusting Blade*
9. L offensive rear turn to 9 starts R side *Raining Blade*
10. R offensive cover step to 3 starts L side *Raining Blade*
11. L offensive front turn to 12 starts R side *Capturing the Club*
12. R step out from twist stance to 6 starts L side *Capturing the Club*
13. R step out from twist stance to 12 starts R side *Circling the Club*
14. L step out from twist stance to 6 starts L side *Circling the Club*
15. L-R chicken knee to 3 R side *Brushing the Club* (*EPAK: Escaping the Club ending*)
16. R-L chicken knee to 9 L side *Brushing the Club* (*EPAK: Escaping the Club ending*)
17. L front rotating twist stance to 12 starts R side *Entwined Blade*
18. R front rotating twist stance to 12 starts L side *Entwined Blade*
19. R offensive front turn to 3 starts R side *Capturing the Gun*
20. L offensive cover to L Cat to 9 starts L side *Capturing the Gun*
21. R rear rotating twist stance to 4:30 starts R side *Broken Gun*
22. L rear rotating twists stance to 7:30 starts L side *Broken Gun*
23. L rear step-thru into L front rotating twist to 1:30 starts R side *Defying the Gun*
24. R rear cross unpivot to 10:30 then R front rotating twist starts L *Defying the Gun*
25. R front twist stance to 3 starts R side *Twisted Gun*
26. R rear cross, L back together then R forward to RNB starts L side *Twisted Gun*

*Highlights*
*Left cross step back then right steps out to Horse Stance with R then L Glancing*
*Blade hands followed by R then L Twisted Gun opening hands - Salute - Close*

## MASS ATTACKS FORM (Fortitude)
### New Themes & Lessons:
• Indexes Self-Defense Techniques against multiple opponents

### Notes:
This is the only Kenpo form with techniques done only on one side. The technique order is as listed on my systems 1st Degree Black Belt "Two-Man technique" requirements.

### Historical Context:
There was another version of Mass Attacks I learned in the early 1980's and told was from the Tracy Kenpo system. Jim Mitchell replaced that with this version that indexed our systems Two-Man Techniques.

### MASS ATTACKS (Fortitude)
*Salutation with Inverted Close to Standing Position facing 12:00*
1. R side *Flowing Hands* against side 3 & 9 shoulder grabs
2. R side *Bear and the Ram* faces 3 against front 3 punch & rear 9 grab
3. R side *Fingers of Wisdom* faces 12 against side 3 & 9 shoulder grabs
4. R side *Ram and the Eagle* against front 12 punch & rear 6 collar grab
5. R side *Courting the Tiger* faces 12 against side 3 & 9 wrist/arm grabs
6. **L side** *Dividing the Enemy* faces 3 against front 3 punch & rear 9 approach
7. **L side** *Mating the Rams* faces 12 against side 3 & 9 shoulder grabs
8. R side *Training the Bears* faces 12 against front 12 punch & rear 6 bearhug
9. R side *Opposing Palms* against front 12 & rear 6 collar grabs
10. R side *Grouping the Enemy* against front 12 punch & rear 6 approach
*R to L Close – Salute*

# SPORT FIGHTING

## Chapter IX

Sport fighting refers to competitive games of fighting. These are done against a single opponent and are generally matched by perceived skill level. Full-contact games are also divided into weight divisions, and by gender. Combatants compete with rules designed to fit that games type of fighting. This develops a specific skill set while having a method to decide winners and losers all while protecting the competitors and helping maintain civility before, during, and after the fight.

Sport fighting competitors train with the intention "to fight" and then voluntarily show up for that purpose, where street stylists train hoping "not to fight." A sport fight takes place in a controlled environment with a referee to regulate the action, judges to help determine the outcome, and medical personnel nearby should anyone become injured.

Boxing and wrestling are popular sport fighting styles in Western culture with Eastern/Asian martial arts styles adding kicks/knees/elbows/open hand attacks to their striking arts like Karate from Okinawa & Japan or Muay Thai from Thailand, and submissions to their grappling styles like Chin Na from China or Judo and Jiu/Ju Jitsu from Japan. Together these Western and Eastern styles have been combined into the hybrid known as Mixed Martial Arts or MMA.

Sport fighting competition can be appealing to the masses as everyone it seems wants to see a good fight, and many people will pay to see one or an entire show of them. Different fight sports have been popular at various times in Western culture, with Boxing the main spectator fighting sport for decades until the rise in popularity of MMA.

There is a breed of person who likes to fight and has the durability to do so. For them, the opportunity to train and fight without the legal, moral, or retribution issues associated with street fighting can be appealing. Sport fighting can also be a liberating and maturing experience that helps release frustration, anger, or aggressive tendencies. Some gain recognition and even money as professional fighters.

Most street styles practice sport fighting to various degrees to help attain the many lessons and benefits of live interaction. One of, if not the major lesson of sport fighting is working against an uncooperative opponent in a spontaneous environment. Prearranged movements and sequences always done with control on a cooperative partner has limitations. Vital target attacks such as eyes, throat, and groin always must be controlled and regulated for safety when training.

This can give a false sense of security to the street stylist as applying vital target techniques on a live, moving, unpredictable, uncooperative, determined, perhaps durable, and possibly trained opponent who is fighting back could and no doubt would prove more difficult.

Additionally, non-sport styles that only practice reactive defensive fighting techniques often don't learn how to initiate an attack, even though sometimes a preemptive attack may be needed. Discovering the incredible amount of conditioning required for sport fighting can also be enlightening and humbling.

Another benefit for the non-sport stylist who competes, or at least spars, in one or more sport fighting styles is in seeing the postures, strengths, and weaknesses of other approaches to fighting. Knowing only street techniques without knowledge or experience with the postures, strengths, weaknesses, and strategies of a Boxer, Kickboxer, Wrestler, Jiu Jitsu practitioner, or MMA fighter is foolish, and potentially dangerous.

Insight gained can help the street stylist choose the right technique against a skilled opponent in a real confrontation by helping recognize postural attitudes and tendencies that can telegraph what someone may know, and perhaps not know. This can help to avoid a trained opponent's strengths while knowing where and how to attack their weaknesses.

Additional sport fighting lessons like functioning under pressure, not quitting, dealing with adversity, fighting with and through injuries, taking a hit, and all the personal growth that takes place when under duress are invaluable to any martial artist. It can also be fun, is less dangerous than street fighting, and a great way to build camaraderie while probably making some lifelong friends.

Sport fighting is also where martial artists should be fighting. Street fighting is way too dangerous physically, morally, emotionally, and legally so should be avoided if possible. Besides all that, some of the toughest yet most humble people are sport-fighting athletes as the activity builds character, confidence, and focused determination.

Owning a sport fighting gym along with a Karate school for many years has given me many insights into several different sport-fighting worlds, from the fast timing and distance game called Karate Point Fighting to the multi-range powerful 8-weapon kickboxing system of Muay Thai, or the efficient "sweet science" of Boxing and the powerful grappling art of Jiu Jitsu.

Those experiences are shared here in discussions on *What Smart Fighters Know, G.R.E.A.T., Tips for Sport Fighters, The Elements of a Champion,* and the *Fighter's Preparation Guide.* It has also helped me to develop the *Sport System for Street Stylists* offered to my Kenpo students to help them become more well-rounded practitioners.

# WHAT SMART FIGHTERS KNOW

## How to **NOT** Get Hit or How to Minimize the Damage
Step 1: Accept it is desirable to <u>not</u> get hit in a fight
Step 2: Know it is possible to <u>not</u> get hit in a fight
Step 3: Make it a goal to <u>not</u> get hit in a fight
Step 4: Expect to not be phased <u>when</u> you get hit in a fight

Minimize any damage with good timing by moving (ride, slip, etc), jamming, blocking / catching a hit on a more durable surface area. This includes punches and kicks to the shoulders and arms, even punches to the crown of head, or kicks to the bent knee/shin or quadriceps, etc.

## Where to Look While Fighting (3 Major Opinions)
**Eyes:** The thought is that by looking into someone's eyes we can read their intentions better, psyche them out, &/or be better able to deceive them. Looking into the eyes makes fighting more personal for sure so is more likely to occur in a fight where it is personal, like a street fight.

Some negatives are that the opponent could be the smarter fighter who is reading your intentions and deceiving you; or who might look scary and intimidating thereby psyching you out; or perhaps they are someone you know who is able to break your concentration. If the eyes are the "window to the soul" then this method is not for everyone against everyone.

**Throat:** This method fights the mechanical structure and not the "soul" since looking at someone's throat is not as personal. Observing the throat allows for upper body torso movement to be more easily seen as the shoulders move on either side telegraphing the body's intention.

**Sternum:** This is like looking at the throat with the idea that looking lower makes it easier to pick up hip movement for kicks and footwork. This along with shoulder movement also helps to see changes in body height level.

Bottom Line: Experiment and find what works for you.

## Eye Focus and the Minds Visual Intention
**Black Dot vs White Dot Focus:** Black Dot focus is represented by the

 black dot on the white background. White Dot focus is represented by the white dot on the black background.

Note: The illustrations depicted here are the same exact size but may appear different as image contrasts can create an illusion.

In looking at the black dot the eyes can tend to notice the white around it.

This is peripheral or overall awareness. In looking at the white dot the eyes can tend to be drawn more into the white dot. This is pinpoint focus for precise accuracy and pinpoint contact, i.e., "aim small, miss small."

In fighting there is a need for both as overall peripheral awareness, or Black Dot Focus, that looks at the throat yet sees the shoulders move, but when hitting a target, like the throat, a more refined momentary and pinpoint focus is used that looks directly at the target when hitting it.

**Eyes Wide Open Looking:** Whether training or competing, an opponent needs 100% visual attention with wide-open eyes. A posture that allows for a complete visual picture is preferred. Also, avoid getting distracted by looking at family, colleagues, or other observers.

In street-defense, these wide-open eyes also need an awareness of environmental obstacles, available resources, other attackers, and nearby hazards.

## How to Breathe
**Nose and/or Mouth Breathing:** The *IN,* or Inhalation breath, should be drawn through the nose using quick and short bursts to bring focused air into the lungs as respiration increases. Use the reverse breath technique with the *OUT,* or exhalation breath, done through the nose or mouth.

The exhalation breath through the nose is done in short bursts, with exhalation through the mouth able to release more air volume. The use of these depends on the size and duration of a movement. The mouth can also make definitive noises and sounds that release internal pressure, while possibly causing a mental distraction, and can even be intimidating.

**Out-Breath Should Match Movement:** A small move gets a small *Out* breath, where a bigger move gets a bigger *Out* breath. Old school Boxing coaches teach this *Out* breath through the nose, causing a tight diaphragm contraction while protecting the clenched jaw and maintaining skull integrity, as mouthpiece technology was often primitive or not available.

Multiple quick bursts of air also reflect the smaller movements of combination punching as compared with bigger movements like kicks or takedowns where an *Out* breath through the mouth may be more appropriate, as in a football tackle. Modern mouthpieces allow for both.

## Theme Training / Sparring / Fighting
Training time should be used to improve some part of your fight game, adding to the whole. Unless a coach/instructor is having you work on a specific theme, have one for yourself. The options are limitless but can include offense/defense; specific weapons or setups, footwork & evasion; techniques & timing, bad position drills, etc. Practice and train with a developmental purpose in mind.

## Game Planning an Opponent
You would need to know who you are fighting and have a way to study them for this to apply, although just knowing who the coaches, instructors, or trainers are can give many coaches quite a bit of insight.

Put any ego aside and be honest to analyze this without bias or fear. Start with the end in mind, like neutralizing their great round kick for example by determining strategies and tactics to minimize or neutralize this or their other strengths, while setting up your own.

Important considerations to objectively evaluate include: Their strengths vs your weaknesses & your strengths vs their weaknesses; these can be further broken down into physical strength, cardio/endurance, skill at various ranges, experience, and durability.

## Respect Your Opponent
Perhaps you will like everyone you spar or fight against but that is not mandatory. You must however respect their potential to cause harm, the same as a street punk challenging you in a parking lot or a drunk at the bar. Everyone with intention to hurt you is dangerous and that needs to be respected in fighting for several reasons.

1) Everyone is potentially dangerous if they are trying to fight you so don't underestimate or take anyone lightly - believe in yourself but respect an opponent's potential to do harm.

2) Disrespect breeds more disrespect and makes fighting more personal. For sport this makes it even more dangerous than it already is because animosity generates extra effort to push the boundaries of rules and etiquette. This creates an opportunistic add-on mentality with a tendency to insert illegal moves or apply dirty fighting tactics. Mutual respect tends to make people fight fairer, even in some street encounters.

3) In training and competition an opponent is helping us with our own personal growth by giving us an opportunity to test ourselves, practice, improve technique, and perhaps provide an outlet for aggression and a desire to fight. They should be appreciated for what they are giving us, even while still trying to defeat them.

# G.R.E.A.T. / Tips for Sport Fighters
## Gap - Rhythm - Evasion - Angles & Accuracy - Tempo & Timing

I developed this acronym for a seminar series I held for MMA fighters in 2009-2010. It seemed to me that once everyone had a ground game most MMA fights became standup fights so the lessons and timeless ideas from Karate fighters and other striking styles would be useful.

At that time, I had noticed some MMA fighters with traditional martial arts striking backgrounds, like George St. Pierre, Lyota Machida, and Anderson Silva were using these ideas successfully. All were durable enough for the MMA full-contact world of fighting and had good ground games, so their other acquired stand-up skill set could be utilized to often give them an edge.

They often dominated opponents with timing and distance techniques that I knew from Karate Point Fighting. Others recognized, learned, and began training in these techniques of set point timing, gap control, body language reads, pacing methods, rhythm, tempo, and timing changes, etc. This improved the overall skill level of MMA fighters and lead to more competitive fights, especially at the higher levels.

It is after all sport fighting, so as much as some fans want to see a brutal street fight with vicious knockouts or grueling submissions the reality is a fighter's objective is to WIN THE FIGHT by one of the accepted methods, which includes by decision. The following methods and ideas help achieve that objective of victory however it occurs.

## GAP
*The Art of War by Sun Tzu - Regarding Physical Territory (i.e., The Gap)*
"A place of vulnerability that is accessible to both the warlord and his enemies. Maintenance of this territory is advantageous to the owner because it may afford a factor of slight control. An invader is easily seen coming into view. It is always an area of contention and is hardly defensible without mortal combat. It is a place of no permanent control. Seek to avoid this place."

**Definition:** "Gap" is the distance between us and an opponent with "Range" a weapons end point after closing that Gap. Different fight games use different Gap baselines making for different Range options:

*Grappler* = Connected, touching, hand fighting, manipulating
*Boxer* = ½ step away; hand distance for fast powerful punching combos
*Kickboxer* = 1 step away; leg distance for combining kicks with punches
*Karate Fighter* = 1½ steps away; just outside the range of all weapons
*MMA* = All distances depending on matchup, strengths, and fight dynamics

**Terms, Applications & Techniques:**
*Controlling and Maintaining the Gap* with footwork and body movement.

*Dynamic Range Control*: In-range vs out-of-range; all the way-in attacking or all the way-out countering/escaping/assessing); teasing the range/gap or mongoose/snake technique

*Lead Hand Antenna* or feeler to maintain desired space and for setups

*Observing* stance, weight shift & posture to control, influence, manipulate

*Stance Setups*: Closed stance (lead side setup, front leg vulnerable); Open Stance (outside foot position, rear side setup, front leg vulnerable)

*Closing the Gap* (footwork timing, distance tricks, alignment illusions)

*Patience*: Setup, pull the trigger - trust your training

## RHYTHM
**Definition:** Regular movement, flow or beat with the objective in fighting to change it in a way that makes an opponent guess, hesitate, become flat-footed, and/or confused.

**Terms, Applications & Techniques:**
*Fake:* Causing an opponent to change their position by changing our position or timing, and perhaps creating an opening.

*Broken Striking Rhythms:*
Full Beat extends to hit target

¾ Beat extends until defended then pushes through to target

½ Beat extends the weapon (hand, elbow, foot, knee) partially to draw a reaction, then that weapon or another adjusts to extend into an open target

¼ Beat shoulder or hand fake/twitch followed by same side weapon (L shoulder fake, L punch) where a punch launches off the fake, or after returning from fake; or opposite side weapon (L shoulder fake, R punch) where the shoulder or hand fake return motion launches the other shoulders weapon

Note: Boxers especially also tilt their body with these rhythm setups.

*Broken Footwork Rhythms:* Lead step (step-drag shuffle), lead jump/skip (Superman punch), double tap (in-place or moving), knee lift (with or without pull-drag), rear drag (hide behind front foot), switch feet/sides, stutter steps, stop & go

*Odd & Even Attack Rhythms:* Be unpredictable and hard to read by constantly changing attack rhythms, otherwise "smart" fighters will read then pick you apart. Rhythm reads can also be used to set up an opponent and requires observing posture, noticing body language, tendencies, and natural reactions to your different body rhythms

Odd count rhythm: L Jab-R Punch-R Kick, (1, 3, 5 moves, etc.)
Even count rhythm: L Jab-R Punch-R Gauge Step-L Kick, (2, 4, 6 moves, etc.)

## EVASION
**Definition:** The techniques and practice of <u>not getting hit</u>, or even touched. This is the art of not being still, as it's always harder to hit a moving target

**Terms, Applications & Techniques:**
*Control the gap* for spacing/distance and to see what is open with enough time to notice and react to what is coming

*Body Movement* to avoid power angles using ride, slip, bob, weave, etc.

*Foot Maneuvers* (on & offline): Move in-out-sideways-angle-circle step and combined footwork (if *in-range* keep head, body, & feet moving)

*Weight transfer* is knowledge of your own foot-to-foot weight shift, and being able to use different rhythms to change it up; and observing how an opponent's weight shifts, where it is, and where it's going

*Manipulate* (push-pull-turn) an opponent to create space; the front hand can help to measure and keep distance

*Regroup* when necessary and know when to give up on an attempt or position, i.e., cut your losses

*Unavoidable Contact* should be minimally damaging by taking hits on more durable body areas, like round kicks to a bent lifted knee/shin or engaged quad, punches & kicks to shoulders & arms or even the crown of the head.

## ANGLES
**Definition:** The alignment of feet and body parts to achieve the desired results. Whether adjusting our self, or causing an opponent to move, the body and weapon alignment angles are critical to success as nobody can cover every part of themselves simultaneously.

**Terms, Applications & Techniques:**
*Our Body & Weapon* positioning for optimal alignment

*Opponent's Body & Weapon* positioning of feet, weight, posture, and weapon

*Angle Changes* using footwork

*See "With" Your Weapons,* as the weapons perspective is different than the eyes, seeing angles and targets the eyes perspective may miss

*Feint:* Changing position to attack an existing opening

## ACCURACY
**Definition:** Precise alignment and location or targets where natural weapons can attack with intention to have a desired effect and achieve a result. See the *Pressue Point* chapter to clarify points and locations.

Note: Targets get missed so plan on more than one move, i.e., combinations. Remember "Quantity has a Quality all its own." Keep fighting, keep working!

**Terms, Applications & Techniques:** Legal sport fighting targets are:

**Head / Neck:**

*Chin:* 4 vectors: <u>front point</u> or straight angle causes head to snap downward; <u>underneath</u> or uppercut angle causes head to snap back; <u>left</u> and <u>right sides</u> or round/hook angles to turn the head suddenly. These angles result in a neck compression, whiplash, disorientation, or disrupted equilibrium causing dizziness or unconsciousness.

*Nose:* 3 vectors: <u>tip of nose</u> or philtrum below are a straight angle knockout/revival point target; <u>left</u> and <u>right</u> sides round/hook angles. These can all result in discomfort, blood flow, watery eyes, blocked sinuses, headache, and mental distraction.

*Jaw & Jaw Hinge* attacked using mostly round/hook angles: Facial nerve (CNVII) trauma at the jaws masseter muscle (St7) disrupts sensation to one side of face and is mentally disconcerting. Jaw hinge trauma behind the ear lobe (SJ17) can cause severe stabbing pain, and a dislocated jaw.

*Mastoid* attacked using mostly round/hook angles: further behind the ear (GB20), is an illegal target in sport fighting but often hit residually, or on purpose but never admitted to, can cause an equilibrium disruption due to its location near the cerebellum, or even an immediate knockout.

*Temple:* Thinner skull bone area above and slightly forward of the ear. Trauma can result in concussion, dizziness, and unconsciousness.

*Neck:* 8 vectors, 5 legal in sport fighting can cause physical and mental dysfunction. The legal ones starting in front are the throat or trachea, Guillotine choke; 2 carotid arteries, Sleeper choke; 2 SCM muscles covering the carotid sinus and vagus nerve, Muay Thai shin kick). Illegal sport neck vectors are in the back at the 2 mastoids and cervical spine.

*Eyes & Eyebrows:* Getting hit in the eyeball is very disconcerting or with a cut above the eye, especially at the bony outer eyebrow corner (GB1), allowing blood to flow down into the eye resulting in a sport fight stoppage.

**Torso:**

*Sternum:* straight in trauma between the nipples (CV17) negatively affects the Qi, and with it the fighting spirit.

*Solar Plexus:* straight or up trauma to the xyphoid process, extending down off the sternum base (CV16), affects the diaphragm muscle making inhalation difficult, or wind knocked out. To find on a clothed opponent draw a mental X on them from each of their shoulders to their opposite hip then hit the middle.

*Floating Ribs:* round/hook angles to these less stable unattached structures at the lower part of the rib cage (Lv13/GB 25) are easier to damage than the other ribs that are attached to the sternum, and they give closer access to the blood-filled liver & spleen internal organs.

*Liver:* on the right side is where painful organ trauma also weakens the legs.

*Spleen:* on the left side is where organ trauma causes severe pain.

### Legs (especially their front leg):
*Side of Hip:* trauma to the iliac crest (St31) or just below causes severe sharp disabling pain, or hip pointer, that can prevent or make it painful to move the leg away from the body's midline.

*Iliotibial Band:* Impact or damage to the legs on the side halfway between the knee and hip (GB31) causes inability to put weight on that affected leg.

*Inside Knee:* Just above and behind the inner joint crease (Lv8). Impact causes the knee to reflexively bend outwards affecting balance and creating vulnerability to a follow-up attack.

*Outside Knee:* Behind the outer knee crease (UB39). Impact causes the knee to buckle inward creating vulnerability to a follow-up attack.

*Inside Ankle:* Just above the inner anklebone close to Achilles tendon (Sp6) is a vulnerable leg sweep angle to disrupt balance.

*Outside Ankle:* Above the outer anklebone back towards the Achilles tendon (GB39) is another good leg sweep and balance disruption point

### TEMPO
**Definition:** The rate of movement

### Terms, Applications & Techniques:
Changing the speed of movement using the body, weapons, and footwork to disrupt an opponent's timing and rhythm, and even cause them to speed up or slow down. Options are slow/fast, tense/relaxed, or any combination.

They are used to cause confusion, hesitation, and frustration while creating openings that set up an opponent by making it more difficult for them to read, prepare, and react to motion coming at them.

A weapon moving towards a target generally causes that target to be defended. This opens other targets, so tempo control gives the ability to attack an alternate target while in route to a previous target. This tempo control allows for angular adjustments, so a weapon can be redirected then accelerated into a new target, see *Broken Rhythm.*

Another tempo application is accelerating a weapon into a target. The greatest force upon impact is generated when a weapons speed is increasing <u>as</u> it reaches a target. This occurs from proper mechanics, progressively increasing muscular acceleration, momentum, backup mass, leverage, and mental intention timed and focused with the breath.

## TIMING

**Definition:** A coordinated movement that occurs when intended.

**Terms, Applications & Techniques:**

*Set Point* involves reading an opponent's foot movement, weight transfer, and body positioning by observing their weight shift, and especially the <u>how</u> and <u>when</u> of their front foot stepping to know <u>when</u> to apply an attack.

This concept recognizes body weight must be shifted onto the front foot, *Set Point*, for an accelerated powerful movement forward to take place. This leaves a moment of vulnerability <u>as</u> the weight is being shifted to the front foot, but just <u>before</u> it fully settles.

This subtle observation is best trained with slow drills that isolate this vulnerable moment with a timed hit/tap/touch of some type that can eventually be sped up to where it can be noticed and timed at full speed.

It's also important to know how to disguise your own *Set Point* against a similarly aware and trained fighter.

Openings can also be timed using a fighter's own unique body and limb rhythm. Observing an up and down bounce in someone's lead hand for example can be timed and exploited. *Broken Rhythm* and *Tempo* changes can be used to help exaggerate these tendencies allowing for them to be anticipated and used to setup an attack.

Note: Inside and outside ankle sweep points can also be done using set point to apply an effective sweep just before a step is completed by kicking and hooking the ankle with our foot/ankle/shin hitting subtly to lift and pull to misplace their foot, and then follow up.

*Timing* is everything! Nothing works without it!
This applies physically, practically, financially & metaphorically.

# TIPS FOR SPORT FIGHTERS

These are a few random observations that apply to sport fighters specifically, with some crossover value to all martial artists.

**COMPETITION MAKES YOU BETTER!** If you train in a sport style then try and compete, and if you train in a street style find a sport format you can compete in or at least spar with, in a competitive way.

**LIKING TO FIGHT IS NOT ENOUGH. YOU MUST LIKE TO TRAIN!**
Reasons to "like" training include:
1. The feeling of getting totally exhausted
2. The camaraderie of training with others of a like mind
3. How you feel and look after you clean up
4. You like being healthy and fit

**DO NOT HURT TRAINING PARTNERS! TRAINING IS NOT FIGHTING!**
Reasons to NOT hurt training partners include:
1. They may be your family or friends
2. If you hurt them you will have one less training partner
3. If you are too dangerous to train with then no one will train with you
4. A tougher training partner may hurt you

**LEARN TECHNIQUE BUT APPRECIATE IT IS NEVER-ENDING!**

**FIND YOUR OWN FIGHTING STYLE!**

**REMEMBER: THESE ARE GAMES OF FIGHTING!**
Learn the rules; understand the strategies and tactics; matchups make fights; train & fight to WIN THE GAME.

**PATIENCE!**
You DO NOT have to win in the first minute or the first round. Plan, train and prepare mentally to go the distance while fighting hard and smart the entire time. Take a knockout or submission if it comes but otherwise earn the decision and the victory!

**CONTROL YOUR EMOTIONS!**
Emotion, especially from anger, tires the body and distracts the mind. Some fighters need to not like a person they are fighting where others don't need for it to be personal. Find what works for you but control your emotions.

**BE HUMBLE AND POLITE IN LIFE!**
Fighters are generally humble nice people who do not walk around with a chip on their shoulder. A punk reputation is not good for building a fan base, for business, or in personal day-to-day interaction with family and other people in your community. Leave a good legacy when done.

# ELEMENTS OF A CHAMPION

## Motivation / Heart / Drive

*(The decision to compete, the discipline to train, the determination to win)*

Requires no conditioning - Requires no technique

Requires no experience

Coaches and mentors can be helpful, but are not mandatory

## Lifestyle

*(Sleep, Rest & Recovery, Thoughts, Liquids, Food)*

Requires discipline to avoid poor choices

(See Fighter's Preparation Guide)

## Conditioning

*(Endurance, Strength, Flexibility)*

Requires motivation to train - Requires some technique

Requires no experience to develop - Coaching helpful but not mandatory

## Fighting Technique

*(Individual Techniques, Transitions, Combinations, Insight)*

Requires motivation to learn - Conditioning useful but not critical

Requires no experience to start learning

Guidance highly recommended

## Coaches - Instructors - Teachers - Trainers

*(Saves trial and error, with many things never figured out alone)*

A must to attain higher levels of skill

The best of these will only work with motivated, and some only talented

people, which you must demonstrate and not just talk about

## Fighting Experience

Requires the previously listed factors to get experience

Requires knowledge of how to avoid injury while gaining experience

Technique is reinforced, adapted, and improved upon with experience

## Luck, Fate, Chance, God's Will, etc.

Natural talent - Genetics - Opportunity

# FIGHTER'S PREPARATION & TRAINING GUIDE

I developed this guideline when some of my Kenpo students wanted to compete in amateur kickboxing back in the early 1990's. I designed it for 3 two-minute rounds of amateur kickboxing, but it can be modified for other fight games and time structures or used as a framework to develop a customized fight prep workout regimen.

It helped us at that time as we used this format and did not lose any fights. I eventually turned my fighters over to a professional kickboxing coach, as my longterm passion was not in that area, but the information formulated at that time is useful and adaptable, so it is put here as a baseline for anyone competing or considering competing in fighting, where of course expert guidance would be recommended.

Note: There is an entire science to "making weight" that is especially important to know for any full-contact fight game but is not covered here. Expert advice is absolutely needed to do this safely.

The three perspectives I used in my guide were:
**Internal Preparation:** What goes into the body; nutrition & environment
**Mental Preparation:** What goes in the mind; how to think, thoughts
**Physical Preparation:** Sport specific workout; fitness & lifestyle

## I.  INTERNAL PREPARATION
## A.  Nutrition
1.  Protein and Carbohydrates
    a. Protein supplement and food: chicken & fish best
    b. Whole grains, fruits, veggies, legumes, pastas for carbohydrates
2. Lots of water and drinks to replace lost electrolytes
    a. Stay "hydrated" before, during & after training
    b. No carbonated drinks *(Coke, Pepsi, etc.)*
    c. No alcohol or caffeine
    d. No Smoking *(duh)*
    e. No candy, pastries, etc.
    f. Juices are good but better from a juicer
## B.  Environment
1.  Stay away from sick people
    a. Wash your hands and face often, especially nose and mouth
2.  Get plenty of fresh air
    a. Practice controlled breathing techniques with movement
3.  Get plenty of rest and sleep
    a. Do not stay out late
4.  No sex at least 1-week before a fight. It is not about testosterone level

## II.  MENTAL PREPARATION
## A.  Visualization
1.  See the entire event through its completion at least once each day
    a.  You wake up that morning

    b.  See yourself warming up before the fight
    c.  Dominating your opponent
    d.  Getting applause and adulation from family and friends
    e.  Going home that night healthy and content with your effort

**B. Know why you are fighting**
1. Focus on one or more reason(s) to fight
    a.  Competition and growth experience, or testing yourself
    b.  Family & friends
    c.  Your school, gym, or team
    d.  Pride & honor
    e.  You just like it
    f.  Impress people or someone specific in the audience
    g.  Money, perhaps not the best reason
    h.  You decide, but find at least one good motivating reason to fight

**C. Do not fight with your emotions - Fight Smart!**
1. Take care of business patiently and methodically taking knockouts or stoppages only if they come
    a.  Your opponent stands between you and your reason(s) for fighting
    b.  Do not be afraid to hurt your opponent, within the rules
2. Save emotions for extra reserve strength, courage, & determination

**D. Strategy**
1. Know the rules of the event/competition/fight
    a.  Allowable ways to win: decision, knockout, or submission?
    b.  What are legal targets and weapons?
    c.  What is illegal & what are the penalties?
    d.  What are the standing counts & what constitutes a stoppage, etc?
2. Do not let yourself get scouted
    a.  Show what you do not do well if being watched
    b.  Show what you will not be throwing if being watched
    c.  Make your best stuff not as effective if being watched
3. Speak, think, and train good habits
    a.  Be anxious - not nervous or scared
    b.  Be confident - not cocky or arrogant
    c.  Show respect for an opponent - not fear
    d.  Take advantage of any opportunity to put doubt in his mind
    e.  Attack with specific targets in mind
    f.  Finish stronger than you start, during each round and at fights end
    g.  Be humble in victory
    h.  Never doubt your purpose, intent, or resolve
4. Pace yourself mentally, physically & emotionally
    a.  Peak on *Fight Night!*
5. Keep your personal life in order
    a.  Do not get distracted - stay focused

**III. PHYSICAL PREPARATION**
**A. Make time to train - you <u>MUST</u> be in shape**
1. Train 2 - 3 hours / day; 6 days / week; take one day off to recover
    a.  Try to train during the time of day you are scheduled to fight
**B. Injury prevention**

1. Tape up &/or pad weak points like wrists, ankles, previous injuries, etc.
2. Warm-up before heavy training
3. Use liniments to develop and heal feet, hands, shins, forearms, etc.
4. Get a medical expert's opinion when/if injured

**C. 2-Hour Workout Routine** *(For 3 two-minute rounds of amateur KB)*
As is, in sections, varying time on each, or change the order
1. Warm-up - about 5-10 minutes
   a. Loosen up – Actively move through each joints range of motion
   b. Light static stretches through lower & upper body muscle groups
2. Endurance / Cardio - about 30-40 minutes *(any single or mix)*
   a. Run 3 miles (1 mile for each round – Std & often done early morning)
   b. Run twelve 40-yard sprints (4 per round - alternate run, jog back)
   c. Jump rope 3 two-minute rounds, with 30-second rest between
   *(Increase speed towards the end of each round - expect to finish strong)*
3. Strength - about 30-40 minutes
   a. Range of motion & sport specific resistance training
   b. Heavy bag &/or pads w/16 oz gloves - 3 two min rounds, 1 min rest.
   *Theme Training* recommended, for example:
   Rnd 1 = Straight Punches & Kicks
   Rnd 2 = Circular Punches & Kicks
   Rnd 3 = Combo Punches & Kicks *(Everything)*
   Rnd 4 = Push yourself an Extra Round
4. Contact Training/Body Toughening - 10-15 min *(Dress how you will fight, use gradual body toughening drills to slowly build the body and mind for heavy contact)*. Torso, legs, shoulders, and arms.
5. Shadowboxing - 10-15 minutes - 3 two min rounds with 1 min rest Fight and defeat an imaginary opponent in the ring: Spend time on footwork and cutting off the ring, getting out of the corner, relax & flow naturally while *Theme Training,* or using your entire skill set
6. Sparring - 10-15 min *(light & relaxed)* - 3 two min rounds, 1 min rest Put your tools together - do not get hurt & do not hurt training partners *Theme Training* recommended, for example:
   Rnd 1 = Offense (punch/kick, kick/punch, high, low & angles)
   Rnd 2 = Defense (move, jam, block, push, clinch, cover-up)
   Rnd 3 = Integrate offense w/defense
   Rnd 4 = Push yourself an extra round using all tools
7. Flexibility & Relaxation - As time is available
   a. Cool down, stretch, and rehydrate
   b. Rest, discuss & socialize w/colleagues
   c. Get any therapy work done (hot tub, massage, etc.)
   d. Look forward to your next training session

# SPORT SYSTEM FOR THE STREET STYLIST

The *Sparring System* presented here is one I developed over many years and is a multi-fold reinvention of the original EPAK, or Ed Parker American Kenpo, coded sparring system I had learned back in the early 1980's. That system is from another time and was/is missing many 1-1 fighting components and concepts that limit its use as a sport fighting system.

Important lessons not covered in that sparring system include angular footwork, broken rhythm, advanced gap and timing concepts, fighting at different ranges, and counter fighting techniques. Other than a couple street-worthy techniques it is not useful for most people as a sport fighting system.

The only move I kept from that original EPAK sparring system is what I see as the root technique called "B1a," although I use a different code to describe it. This is taught left to left where our front left-hand grabs/traps the opponent's front left wrist pulling their arm forward, down, and to the side, essentially putting their weight onto their front big toe, as our rear right-hand punches them in the head/face through the space created.

This creating an opening while canceling dimensional zones is an important fight lesson as the neutralization of height, width, and depth is a useful and sophisticated concept. Although an illegal technique in Sport Karate, and difficult to do if wearing Boxing or MMA gloves, it is an excellent street-oriented entry technique that teaches valuable lessons.

Using codes, like B1a, to define the techniques was a great idea but it was incomplete, so I expanded it to include all footwork, kicks, punches, and blocks, and added codes for body maneuvers, clinch work, takedowns, sweeps, and grappling, then symbol codes for timing and rhythm lessons. Every range is incorporated here so street style students can get exposure to all the major Sport Fighting games as they progress through the system.

This is a progressive sparring system divided over 10 ranks from Yellow Belt to 1st Degree Black Belt. The ranks start with hand then kick techniques separate followed by combining those into Karate first contact or *Point Fighting* techniques, then ranks covering *Muay Thai Kickboxing*, *Western Boxing*, 2 Ranks of *Jiu Jitsu* ground fighting (1 position / 1 submission), 2 Ranks of mixed *Judo/Wrestling* takedown fighting (1 offense / 1 defense/countering), then *Mixed Martial Arts* or MMA.

Along with this technique exposure I recognize and tell students it is best to learn these sport styles from experts in those styles, and I have supplied that to my students with a sport fighting gym for many years. I also encourage them to participate more fully, where they have an interest or some special talent.

Regardless of if the interest and/or training opportunity is there, this sport fighting style awareness is beneficial to becoming well-rounded in martial arts.

Sport fighting has several understandable components. Strikers use *Fight Attitudes, Fighting Side, Hand Positioning, Contact Levels, Impact Ranges, and Weapon/Target Variables.* Grapplers use variations of those with *Base Positions* along with transitions and ways to win by pin, submission, or on points. All use *Objectives-Strategies-Tactics* making for a sophisticated matrix of sport fighting analysis factors and personal style options.

Fight Attitudes are *Offense* and *Defense*, with *Counter Fighting* a component of *Defense*. While engaged in fighting, opponents are either attacking, being attacked, alternating between the two, attacking simultaneously, or looking at each other figuring out what to do next.

*Offensive* techniques involve initiating an attack, with *Defensive* techniques either reactive to avoid and minimize damage or proactive to apply counter fighting techniques. Whether from training habits or instinct it is good to have avoided an attack, but it is better and a higher skill level to defend then attack back, or counter-fighting.

*Counter-fighting* sets an opponent up to react in an anticipated way that is then instantly countered. There is nothing wrong with just not getting hit, and the reality is sometimes that is all you can do, but it's a more sophisticated level of fighting to set up an opponent for a counter-fighting technique. Some of these are contained in my Sport Fighting System at each range of fighting covered.

Fighting Side or relative foot position are the standup base positions done when facing an opponent. Either can have left or right foot more forward, matching up in a *Closed Stance* (L-L/R-R) or an *Open Stance* (L-R/R-L) with an opponent.

The first 3 lists/ranks described in this chapter alternate between these two *Fighting Side* positions to familiarize students with these different foot and body postures. Boxing and Kickboxing lists are taught left to left (L-L) to simplify the possibilities students can "freestyle" how they prefer.

There are definite thoughts, opinions, and strategies for using this foot placement dynamic. Some fight coaches and even styles prefer fighters pick one side to fight from, then not vary from that regardless of the opponent. Other fight coaches and some styles encourage fighters to switch their feet for various strategic, tactical, and positional reasons.

An example of this is the Boxing tactic against an *open stance* fighter (L-R/R-L) where the effort is to have the front foot to the outside of the opponent's front foot. This outside foot position gives the rear hand an advantage in range, body alignment, and leverage into power while staying away from the opponent's rear side power. This makes the relative location of the front foot a battle within a boxing match, or other stand up fight.

Hand Positioning for striking arts consists of 4 major static or moving hand placements, depending on type of fighting, range, and personal preference.

Both hands could be up, or both hands could be down, or the front hand could be higher than the rear hand, or the rear hand could be higher than the front hand. Like with *Foot Position,* different coaches, fighters, and sports tend towards the method(s) they prefer, and all can justify what they prefer and why.

Contact Levels depends on the sports purpose and is often different in training. Karate point fighting is a light-medium contact stop and go game, although Karate in-school sparring is generally practiced continuously. Amateur Boxing is often like a point competition but with continuous scoring, with the professional Boxing game more power oriented, although both often train much lighter, especially to the head.

Impact Ranges are a key factor influenced by the sports objectives and is divided here into *Contact Range, Penetration Range* and *Manipulation Range.* Karate Point Fighting range is further away than Kickboxing, which is generally further away than Boxing, which is further away than Grappling. Controlling this range, distance, or gap between fighters is critical to success in these different fight games.

The *gap* is a no-man's land between fighters at the edge of their weapons. It can be a dangerous, contentious, and competitive place where offensive and defensive moves are often set up. There are very real distances a martial artist should know and understand as to where different sport styles can apply their best techniques.

In Karate Point Fighting that gap is about 1½ steps away, see *Foot Maneuvers,* in Kickboxing it shortens to about 1 step, in Boxing to about ½ step, and in Grappling the fight starts when combatants connect. In MMA it can vary and is influenced by the match up and game plan as contrasted with an opponent. In all cases this *gap* opens and closes as part of the fight dynamic.

Weapon/Target Variables are determined by the fight games rules, objectives, and equipment. Karate Point Fighters wear foam dipped vinyl gear with face hits discouraged and front hand body hits not counted; Kickboxers may or may not be able to clinch, knee, elbow, or kick the legs depending on the sanctioning; Boxers aren't ever allowed to elbow or trip; Grapplers are not supposed to strike and have an assortment of competitive variations with Folkstyle,Ffreestyle and Greco-Roman Wrestling, plus Judo, and Jiu Jitsu all with different rules.

## SPARRING CONCEPT OVERVIEW SUMMARY
### Fight Attitudes:
1) *Offense / Offensive Fighting* are attacking techniques used to initiate a fighting action. Generally, the bodyweight shifts forwards with this attitude and, depending on the fight game, can involve punches, kicks, knees, elbows, takedowns, and submissions.

2) *Defense / Defensive & Counter Fighting* moves are done to protect against offensive techniques with the two methods being defending and counter-fighting. Generally, the bodyweight is initially shifted away or off angle with this attitude to avoid an offensive attack, then hopefully defended by applying a counter fighting technique.

The three ways to defend a striking attempt are to move the target out of the way (body and foot maneuvers); intercept the attacking weapon (blocks, catches, parries, checks); or preempt the attack by jamming the weapon before it accelerates (checks and/or preemptive striking).

*Counter Fighting* means defending an opening we created as bait or an enticement for someone to attack in a certain way, which we anticipate to then apply an offensive move to counter that attack.

**Fighting Side:**
1) *Closed Stance* or same side lead - left to left (L-L) or right to right (R-R) with opponents having their same foot in front towards each other.

2) *Open Stance* or opposite side lead - left to right (L-R) or right to left (R-L) with opponents having a different foot placed in front towards each other.

Note: Boxing terminology calls a fighter with their left foot in front *"orthodox"* and one with their right foot in front a *"southpaw."* Entry angles, tactics, and strategies can all be affected by these foot position dynamics.

**Hand Positioning:**
1) *Both Hands Up* with elbows down; palms facing each other like a Boxer or rotated forward like in traditional Muay Thai are often the choices, or even with the palm sides put on the forehead as sometimes seen in MMA.

One of the negatives of this posture from the street, and some Point Fighting rules, is that the groin is exposed depending on relative foot placement.

2) *Front Hand Low / Rear Hand High* is a popular point fighting posture, and the posture of choice for some Boxers like former heavyweight champions Larry Holmes and George Forman. These arm positions cover the ribs and even groin without much movement while allowing the lead arm to rest as the lead shoulder and rear hand defend.

The lead hand jab from this posture travels up from a blind lower angle so it can be deceptive and difficult to pick up. A negative would be the head could be harder to protect with just the one hand up.

3) *Front Hand High / Rear Hand Low* is also popular among many Point Fighters, but used by others as well, as it allows for the front hand to be a range feeler to block or jam an attack and obstruct vision.

Having the rear hand low more easily defends the inside angles to the body and groin to round attacks while being able to attack from a low trajectory outside an opponent's peripheral vision (also like with the front hand low).

4) *Both Hands Low* requires good body movement to make this work (Research Boxer 'Nicolino Locche' as he is most credited with this movement style). Former Boxing champion Muhammad Ali made this style famous, often carrying his hands low daring an opponent to try and hit his head, which he would often move then counter punch. Ali also used his lead hand masterfully from this position applying punches from every conceivable angle.

This hand position presents a deceptive trajectory with both hands at the outer edge of an opponent's downward peripheral vision. The temptation to look down can break eye and mental focus, along with posture, plus the arms are resting while perhaps giving the illusion of not being prepared.

**Contact Levels:**
1) *No-Contact* means not touching intended targets but focusing just short of hitting. This focused "in the air" type of fighting is how strikes to the head and face were allowed in American Karate Tournaments through the late 1960's and early 1970's although not always adhered to, and often called the "blood and guts" era of Karate Sport Fighting. This was before hand protection was worn, and full-contact body shots were allowed, so this focused punching method allowed for full power face and head bareknuckle punches.

Other Karate competitions, especially outside the U.S., still compete with full-contact body fighting and controlled headshots (Research Kyokushin 100-Man Kumite). Most U.S. Karate tournaments require full gear with either no or light head contact, especially in kid's divisions, and with various degrees of body contact accepted.

2) *Semi-Contact* or *Light-Contact* means touching targets but not penetrating or forcing the target to move because of the contact. There are many degrees of touch contact depending on the combatants, the fight game involved, and whether training or competing.

Note: What is "semi-contact" to one person may be "full-contact" to another so participant's need to agree for training and might need supervision to maintain that agreed upon level of contact.

3) *Full-Contact* means it is acceptable to hit as hard as possible with the intention to cause unconsciousness, physical body damage, or otherwise make someone unable to continue, or want to quit. This level of contact occurs when competing in Boxing, Kickboxing, and MMA.

Note: As mentioned, many times levels of contact are mixed in training. Light contact to the head with full contact to the body or any variation that allows fighters to accomplish the goals of a training session.

**Impact Ranges:**
1) *Contact Range* is that distance where the target surface area can be touched by our weapons. Most Karate Point Fighting is done at this range of impact, with Muay Thai often having a "play fighting" mentality in training that lends itself well to this safer range of contact.

Boxing coaches also use this range for movement-oriented sparring and in competition by telling fighters "just touch him" to stay busy, determine range, prevent attack, and setup combinations.

2) *Penetration Range* is the distance, usually in full-contact fighting, where the striking intention is to penetrate tissue and move part of an opponent's anatomy. This is hitting with "bad intentions" and is acceptable in a full-contact competition where striking is allowed.

3) *Manipulation Range* is the distance where two, connected opponent's, maneuver to move each other into an unbalanced and vulnerable position. Although someone can be manipulated with striking this context involves grappling techniques such as clinches, locks, holds, or pins designed to control an opponent's actions by pushing and pulling them into a bad position, or set them up for another maneuver.

**Weapon/Target Variables:**
Depending on the fight game, and whether standup or grappling, weapons include hands, feet, elbows, knees, interlocking movements, throws, trips, and sweeps. Targets can include head, face, neck, body, limbs, and joints, with many targets illegal: including eyes, groin, back of head or body, finger digits, etc. Base positions, other than the standup ranges covered earlier include standup clinching, or on the ground mount, guard, side mount, etc., plus other positions used in sport Wrestling.

**Combinations and Variations:**
Unlimited combinations can then evolve using *Fight Attitudes, Fighting Side, Hand Positioning, Contact Levels,* and *Impact Ranges,* with any number and type of *Weapon/Target Variations.* These are affected by the rules of the fight game or are agreed upon in training where the term "freestyle" is often used to describe non-rehearsed sparring (fighting).

Combining components makes for a staggering number of variables and is a good reason for training in different sport styles to develop these individual skill sets. Take a 2-move hand combination for example then imagine 3-4+ move combinations.

2-Move Hand Combination Possibilities:
- *Closed* or *Open* Stance
- Any of 4 *Hand Positions*
- Any *Offensive, Defensive or Counter Fighting Attitude*
- Any of the 3 *Contact Levels*

- Any of 3 *Impact Ranges*
- Various *Weapons/Target Variables* at different angles and heights. An example are the 4 ways to apply a 2-move hand combination: 2 front hand moves; 2 rear hand moves; front hand then rear hand; rear hand then front hand. This of course does not include fakes, feints, rhythm breaks, tempo changes, etc., or the many target choices

## Objectives, Strategies, and Tactics:

These become even more important at higher skill levels of fighting, especially in competition with a known opponent.
*Objective*: Our ultimate goal (winning the fight)
*Strategy*: A plan of action (how to reach the *Objective*)
*Tactics*:    How the battle is fought (ways to achieve a *Strategy*)

If the *objective* is to win a sport fight a *strategy* against a powerful puncher might be to kick their front leg until they can't put weight on it, with a *tactic* the setups that create the opportunity to kick that leg, while avoiding their punching power. These concepts are timeless in the history of personal and group warfare and should not be ignored. Those who are victorious at the highest level use them. See the *Mind* for a more complete discussion.

## Sport Fighting System

The *Sport Fighting System* described here addresses all fighting ranges and runs parallel at each level with my Self-Defense System for street defense. It is a coded system that, like written music, is shorthand that eventually can give way to improvisation for those versed in the related movements.

The first three ranks (Yellow-Orange-Purple) are dedicated to Karate "first contact" or Point Fighting range, although this is usually practiced in the school as continuous sparring rather than the stop-n-go version done at Karate tournaments. This is the type of sparring I would recommend for beginners and definitely use with children or anyone new, or maybe averse to contact training and/or fighting.

The gap in this fight game operates about 1½ steps away from an opponent, with the primary lesson of learning how to control distance, to hit and not get hit, plus the invaluable timing and distance lessons important for any striker. As a sport it is generally a lighter contact game, so it is safer for everyone to get live fighting experience against different opponents, and it doesn't require weight divisions or more precise matchups as needed for a full-contact fighting competition

The next two ranks (Blue-Green) move closer into the power striking games of Kickboxing and Boxing. Students should have a good sense of timing, distance, and defense at this point, so the contact level can increase.

Kickboxing operates at about a 1 step gap, with techniques taken mostly from Muay Thai and its aggressive attack attitude, power oriented striking, devastating leg kicks, and clinching techniques.

Boxing operates at about a ½ step gap. The stances and movement of Boxing are similar to Kenpo (i.e., street boxing), aside from only using the punching knuckles to hit, where Kenpo uses every part of the hand.

The next two ranks (Red-3rd Brown) go to the ground to learn grappling, with takedowns purposely put off a few ranks until students know what they can do if on the ground. The grappling techniques learned represent a beginner level in Brazilian Jiu Jitsu and are broken down into *position* then *submission* grappling.

The next two ranks (Brown Belt 2nd & Brown 1st) operate after closing the gap to practice takedowns using techniques from Wrestling, Judo, and Karate. This is a powerful range of fighting, like ground grappling, where a standup fighter without knowledge is very vulnerable. Special thanks here to one of my Kenpo Black Belts and Brazilian Jiu Jitsu Black Belt Dave Arnold for adding submission endings to these takedown lists as his 4th Degree Black Belt Project.

Those going to Black Belt 1st Degree in my system would have been exposed to every sport fighting range so they can then begin to combine styles into Mixed Martial Arts, aka MMA techniques. This transitioning and mixing of ranges and styles teaches important lessons, with this style's unique bonus of learning how to fight with our back against a cage or wall.

**How to Use this Sport Fighting System**
Safety is paramount when training in fighting so equally important is that practitioners agree upon the style and fighting components before they start. This guideline can come from an instructor, coach, or be agreed upon between training partners, and may have to be supervised.

Working on technique should be differentiated from freestyle fighting, and that from competitive sparring and/or competition. In training this must be done with awareness of the physical dynamic between participants, and their relative skill level as someone at a higher-level should not take advantage of someone at a lower skill level.

For example, if someone is not familiar with takedown defenses then a more skilled person should not use those in freestyle if training with that person. They can instead focus on improving another part of their game or teach the training partner so they can adequately and safely defend themself. In this way both are challenged, and neither is frustrated, or becomes injured.

Training is most beneficial when it is challenging yet safe, with the bonus that it can be done more often and for longer periods of time. This allows for more experience to be gained while limiting injuries, and possibly even personal animosities. This is better for everyone and is even fun.

I also encourage *Theme Training* at all levels where the focus can be more limited. This helps to absorb concepts and principles better while gaining experience of a component element in the middle of the chaos.

*Theme Training* examples include *offense/defense, hands only, kicks only, hands vs kicks, lead side only, rear side only, bad position drills, clinch work, takedowns,* and *various ground positions.* This could also be style specific by just doing *Point Fighting, Boxing, Kickboxing, Stand-Up Grappling, or Ground Grappling.*

Following are the *Sparring System Codes* and then the *Sparring Lists* for my "Sport Art for Street Stylists" by rank. Many of the techniques can be done much faster than the time it takes to read the code so don't be surprised if a technique code takes longer to read than to do.

Each belt ranks "Sparring List" describes the *Major Theme* covered, *Sport Fighting Style* practiced, primary *Stance & Hand Position, Contact Levels,* and allowable *Impact Ranges* for competition use. *Offensive & Defensive Counter Fighting Themes* are followed with *Notes,* then the coded *Offense Techniques* and *Defensive Counter Fighting Techniques* are listed with a brief written description.

Most can be seen demonstrated and explained at BarryBBarker.com.

# SPARRING SYSTEM CODES
### (Listed Numerically or Alphabetically)

## Symbols
Underlined = <u>LEFT</u>
- = Timing Space (Then)
; = Or
( ) = Optional Move/s
/ = Simultaneous Move (With)
\> = Move forward
< = Move Backwards
{} = Optional Feint or Fake
**Feint** = Changing our position to attack an existing opening
**Fake** = Causing opponent to change their position or timing creating an opening

## Foot Maneuvers
1 = In Place Stance Change
2 = Step
3 = Drag
2/3 = Push-drag or Pull-drag
4 = Front Crossover
5 = Step Out
6 = Rear Crossover
7 = Step- Thru
8 = Switch Feet
9 = Back -Side Side-Step
10 = Open-Side Side-Step

## Sweeps & Takedowns
11 = Pulling Sweep
12 = Step-Thru Sweep
13 = Rear Leg Sweep
14 = Cross Outer Reap
15 = Straight Outer Reap
16 = Scissor Sweep
17 = Cross Inner Reap
18 = Straight Inner Reap
19 = Rear Heel Trip
20 = Double Leg
21 = Single Leg
22 = Lift & Trip
HT = Hip Throw

## Abbreviations
Inv = Inverted Move
Ju = Jumping Move
Sp = Spinning Move
Up = Upward Move

## Body Maneuvers
Bo = Bob
Ri = Ride
Ro = Roll
RcP = Recover Position
Rc = Recover to Stand
Sl = Slip
Tu = Turn
We = Weave

## Blocks, Checks & Traps
AG = Arm Grab / Hold
AT = Arm Trap
CLR = Clearing Move
CT = Catch w/Hands
DIB = Down-In Block
DOB = Down-Out Block
EB = Extended Block
IB = Inward Block
KB = Knee/Shin Block
LC = Leg Catch / Trap
OB = Outward Block
PD = Push-Down Block
SCP = Scoop Block
TB = Thigh Block
UB = Upward Block

## Punches & Strikes
BKS = BackKnuckleStrike
CR = Cross Punch
HK = Hook Punch
JB = Lead Hand Jab
OH = Overhead Punch
RP = Reverse Punch
RHS = ReverseHandsword
RHP = RoundHousePunch
UP = Uppercut Punch

## Kicks
FK = Front Kick
FPK = Front Push Kick
FSK = Front Stomp Kick
KN = Knee Kick
OHK = Outward Hook Kick
RK = Rear Kick
RHK = Roundhouse Kick
SK = Side Kick
TSK = Inverted Side Kick
*(Thrusting Sweep Kick)*
WK = Wheel Kick

## Position Grappling
AD = Arm Drag
BG = Bottom Guard (Full)
BHG = Bottom Half-Guard
BMT = Bottom Mount
BR = Bridge Rollover/Upa
BSMT = Bottom Side Mount
CAC = Cross Arm Control
CL = Clinch
CLC = Clinch Counters
DE = Defend Position
GSS = Guard Scissor Sweep
HBP = Head-Body Push w/HE
HE = Hip Escape
KS = Knee on Stomach
Pass = Any Top Guard Escape
PO = Push Off (w/hands)
RH = Rear Guard w/Hooks
ShP = Shoulder Push
SUS = Sit-up (Push) Sweep
TB = Take Back
TG = Top Guard (Full)
THG = Top Half-Guard
TMT = Top Mount
TSMT = Top Side Mount

## Submission Grappling
AB = Arm Bar (w/Arms)
AM = Americana Lock
ATC = Arm Triangle Choke
BKL = Bent Knee Lock
FAL = Foot/Ankle Lock
GL = Guillotine Choke
GP = Ground & Pound
HH = Heel Hook
KB = Knee Bar
KL = Kimura Lock
LT = Leg Trap Submission
LTC = Leg Triangle Choke
OMA = Omaplata Lock
RAB = Reverse Arm Bar
SAB = Step-Over Arm Bar
SC = Sleeper Choke
Sub = Any Submission

### *Go to BarryBBarker.com for Sparring System Videos*

# Poway Kenpo Yellow Belt – HAND POINT SPARRING

**Major Themes:** Punching & hand striking techniques; Moving in and out of range; Trapping techniques to clear opponent's front arm and create openings; Free Sparring using hands only

**Sport Fight Style:**  Point & Continuous
**Stance Position:**  Closed Stance (Left-Left for this list)
**Hand Position(s):**  Both Hands Up
**Contact Level(s):**  No Contact to Light (Touch) Contact
**Impact Range(s):**  Contact Range

**Offensive Themes:** Point/touch contact sparring distance for hands; Punching & striking head (high) and body (low) targets; Attacking inside and outside opponent's lead arm; Using various parts of the hand to punch & strike at different angles; Linear & circular striking methods; Trapping with front and rear hands; Seeing targets from the weapons perspective, as if they had eyes.

**Counter-Fighting Themes:** Covering the centerline; Using hands to block, catch, hook, and jam; Countering hands with hands.

**Notes:** Offensive attacking techniques can be done with or without footwork and with or without traps, depending on distance and available targets; Defensive counter-fighting techniques can be done by defending then attacking, or simultaneously by defending while attacking.

## *OFFENSIVE ATTACKING TECHNIQUES*:
**1. (AT)JB2-3**
*Lead hand jab (or RHS/Hk) to head w/optional inside arm trap &/or shuffle step*
**2. (AT)BKS2-3**
*Lead hand BKS to head w/optional outside arm trap &/or shuffle step*
**3. (AT)2-RP3**
*Rear hand body punch w/optional jamming trap check to lift elbow &/or shuffle*
**4. (AG)2-RHS**
*Rear hand RHS (or RP) to head w/optional arm trap/grab (EPAK B1A) &/or shuffle*

## *DEFENSIVE COUNTER-FIGHTING TECHNIQUES*:
**5.  vs JB2-3  =  IB-RHS or JB**
*Jab countered w/rear hand catch & lead hand counter*
**6.  vs 2BKS-3  =  UB; EB-1RP**
*BKS countered w/lead hand block & rear hand low RP*
**7.  vs 2-RP3  =  DOB-JB**
*RP countered w/low cross down-out block/parry & lead hand counter Jab*
**8.  vs RHS  =  EB-1RP**
*RHS countered w/lead hand high extended block & rear hand counter RP*

# Poway Kenpo Orange Belt – FOOT POINT SPARRING

**Major Themes:** Kicking techniques w/footwork; Moving offline and away to counter kicks; Free-sparring using feet only; Free-Sparring using hands & feet from the first two lists

**Sport Fight Style:** Point & Continuous
**Stance Position:** Open Stance (L-R described below)
**Hand Position(s)** Both Hands Up / Front Hand Low / Rear hand Low
**Contact Level(s):** No Contact to Light Contact
**Impact Range(s):** Contact Range

**Offensive Themes:** Applying kicks from an open stance; Sparring distance for legs or kicking range; Kicking head (high) and body (low) targets; Applying most major linear & circular kicking methods; Using various parts of the foot to appropriate targets; Using footwork to align and set up different kicks.

**Counter-Fighting Themes:** Defending kicks from an open stance; Offline maneuvers to avoid kicks; Deflecting kicks using hands and arms; Using kicks to counter kicks.

**Notes:** Techniques here can also be practiced by reversing offense/defense roles to practice from the opposite stance; Each offensive technique can also be applied from a closed stance using footwork and target adjustments, as noted under base description; Each defensive technique can use hand and arm checks to open more space and give more time for counter; Each defensive technique could be adapted to fit a closed stance attack with footwork and target adjustments but not covered in the notes here.

## OFFENSIVE ATTACKING TECHNIQUES:
1. **10-FK**          *Lead L leg front kick, after moving R foot to an inside angle*
                      *If Closed Stance (L-L) move L to inside angle w/R front kick*
2. **10-6-RK-4-5-9**  *Lead leg rear thrust kick, after moving L foot to an inside angle*
                      *If Closed Stance (L-L) rear leg step-thru (i.e., spin rear kick)*
3. **4-WK-6-5**       *Lead leg wheel/round kick to head or leg, after front crossover*
                      *If Closed Stance (L-L) same footwork with kick to front side targets*
4. **3-SK-3-5**       *Lead leg side thrust kick after drag step or rear crossover forward*
   **or 6-SK-4-5**    *If Closed Stance (L-L) same technique applies*

## DEFENSIVE COUNTER-FIGHTING TECHNIQUES:
5. **vs 7FK**   = **9-RK**    *Counter front kick w/rear thrust kick, after offline step*
                              *Optional DIB inside front kick, w/offline steps*
6. **vs 10-6-RK** = **10-7-FK** *Counter rear kick w/front kick, after an offline step*
                              *Optional DOB outside rear kick w/offline step*
7. **vs 4-WK**  = **10-SK**   *Counter wheel kick w/side kick, after an offline step*
                              *Optional IB &/or EB inside wheel kick w/offline step*
8. **vs 3-SK**  = **7/9-WK**  *Counter side kick w/wheel kick, after an offline step*
                              *Optional DOB &/or DIB to side kick w/offline step*

# Poway Kenpo Purple Belt – HAND & FOOT POINT SPARRING

**Major Themes:** Combining hands & feet; Front & rear hand leads; Fakes, feints, broken rhythm, using initial move to create target openings; Hands followed by feet; Feet followed by hands

**Sport Fight Style:** Point & Continuous
**Stance Position:** Closed Stance (Left to Left for list)
**Hand Position:** Any or add Alternating Front or Rear Hand Low/High
**Contact Level(s):** No Contact to Light Contact
**Impact Range(s):** Contact Range

**Offensive Themes:** 2-hand and 2-kick combinations; Lead hand-rear hand; Rear hand-lead hand; Lead kick-lead kick; Hand-kick combinations such as Lead kick then lead hand or Lead hand then lead kick; Front foot lead step; Rear foot lead step; Jump/skip leads; Fakes & feints; Broken rhythm; Spinning moves.

**Countering-Fighting Themes:** Countering feet with hands; Countering hands with feet; Moving backwards with kick counters; Countering a blocked kick; Stalling a kick for more time to counter.

**Notes:** This list contains the major techniques and tools used in competition Point Fighting. Even though only 8 techniques are listed there are actually 18 techniques contained, not including the many fake, feint, and broken rhythm variables available.

## *OFFENSIVE ATTACKING TECHNIQUES*:
**1. {BKS}2; JuBKS; -RP3; -RHS3**
*Front hand lead BKS w/lead step or jump & optional rear hand RP/RHS (i.e., "Superman" punch)*
**2. {RP}; -4BKS-(WK)5RP; -7RHS**
*Rear hand lead RP, step w/BKS, optional WK, step w/RP (i.e., Calif. Blitz), or RHS*
**3. 2/3{SK}-2BKS3; 2BKS-3-SK; <7BKS**
*Pull-drag SK then BKS; step BKS drag then SK; lead SK (or fake to spin) then BKS*
**4. 2/3{WK}; 2/3{SK}; -WK (-RP4-5)**
*Two circular kicks (WK), or linear (SK)/circular (WK), to optional hand followup*

## *DEFENSIVE COUNTER-FIGHTING TECHNIQUES*:
**5. vs BKS2-3 = 10/EB-BKS; -WK; -InvRP**
*Offline step w/lead BKS also blocking, &/or WK, InvRP, individually or combination*
**6. vs RP-7 = <2-SK (4BKS-5RP)**
*Move back w/timed SK, then optional follow up*
**7. vs 2/3SK = <2PD->BKS2/3; <UB-UpFK**
*Push leg down-counter w/hands, or lift leg up w/groin up-kick counter*
**8. vs 2/3WK = 9(IB)RP (-7RP)**
*Inside off angle step w/L check & R punch*

# Poway Kenpo Blue Belt – MUAY THAI KICKBOXING

**Major Theme:** Kickboxing techniques, concepts, and rhythms
**Sport Fight Style:** Muay Thai Kickboxing (8 Weapon fighting system)
**Stance Position:** Closed Stance (Left to Left for list)
**Hand Position(s):** Both Hands Up
**Contact Level(s):** Light to Full Contact
**Impact Range(s):** Contact to Penetration & Manipulation Range

**Offensive Themes:** Odd and even attack rhythms; Body rotation alternating punches & kicks; Front hand lead setup; Rear hand lead setup; Three power round kick angles, to legs, torso, head; Clinch control; Knee attacks; Moving from striking range into clinch range; Moving from clinch range out to striking range.

**Counter-Fighting Themes:** Defending outside & inside leg kicks; Defending body & head round kicks; Jamming defense; Moving attacker's weapon offline; Clinch counters; Simultaneous defense w/offense.

**Notes:** These techniques should also be practiced on Thai Pads; Elbows are not included here, although an important part of Muay Thai, they are difficult to control in sparring and most Western competitions don't allow them, plus Kenpo students use elbows extensively in other areas of training.

## *OFFENSIVE ATTACKING TECHNIQUES*:
**1. 2{JB}-CR3-7FPK; RHK; [CL]KN**
*Front hand leads-Rear hand follows-Rear leg kicks (Odd count rhythm)*
**2. 2{JB}-CR3-7/10-FPK; RHK; [CL]KN**
*Front hand leads-Rear hand follows-Gauge Step-Front leg kicks (Even count rhythm)*
**3. CR-RHP-9RHK-CL-KN-KN-7PO-RHK**
*Rear hand leads-Front hand follows-Rear leg kicks-Clinch-Knees-Push-Kick*
**4. CR-7CR-FPK; RHK; [CL]KN** (can insert same #3 ending starting opposite side)
*Rear hand leads-Front hand follows w/step thru-into any rear (L) leg kick*

## *DEFENSIVE COUNTER-FIGHTING TECHNIQUES:*
**5. vs Low RHK (L or R) = KB-9RHK or 10RHK; TB/CR; <6>5CR-(RHK)**
*Knee/shin block, or Jam w/thigh, or Move leg back-Punch &/or kick follow-up*
**6. vs High RHK(Body) = AT/LC-CLR-RHK; AT-CLR-RHK**
                 **(Head) = OB/AT/LC-CLR-RHK; OB/AT-CLR-RHK**
*vs Under elbow kick: Wraparound arm trap catch leg-clear & follow-up*
*vs Above elbow kick: Out block/catch leg w/opp hand over/under-clear, follow-up*
**7. vs FPK = 9SCP &/or DIB or 10 DIB or DOB-Punch/Kick or any follow-up**
    **vs FPK = 9SCP &/or DIB or 10 DIB or DOB-Punch/Kick or any follow-up**
*Move sideways-clear kick w/scoop or brush outside or inside leg then follow up*
**8. vs CL-KN (R/L) = Chest/Chest; Shoulder Wedge; Neck Tilt; Elbow Tilt**
*Chest/Chest = Get under elbows, clinch waist & cancel by pulling close, head up*
*Shoulder Wedge = Dip lead shoulder between elbows-reach up counter clinch*
*Neck Tilt = Head against yours/down: Rear hand to back of neck-Front hand under elbow-Push up w/pull down (their shoulders vertical) duck out w/step*
*Elbow Tilt = Head up: Rear hand over elbow-Front hand under elbow-Push up w/pull down (their shoulders vertical) duck out w/step*

# Poway Kenpo Green Belt – WESTERN BOXING

**Major Theme:** Western Boxing Techniques and Concepts
**Sport Fight Style:** Boxing (the "sweet science")
**Stance Position:** Closed Stance (Left to Left for list)
**Hand Position(s):** Both Hands Up
**Contact Level(s):** Light to Full Contact
**Impact Range(s):** Contact Range to Penetration Range

**Offensive Themes:** Using 4 primary boxing punches in combinations (L-R, L-L, R-L, R-R); Punching at different heights in combinations (high-high, low-low, high-low, low-high); Using an opponent's defense to setup our offense; Punching off a miss; Off-angle punching; Power punching off body torso movement.

**Countering-Fighting Themes:** Head & body movement; Catching head high punches (L catches R/R catches L); Countering off a catch; Countering off head movement; Following the return motion of a punch with a counter punch.

**Notes:** Boxing techniques and combinations should be practiced on hand mitts, w/footwork moving around, and while measuring w/the front hand to keep space and feel distance. Move around, like in a Boxing ring (not just back and forth).

## OFFENSIVE ATTACKING TECHNIQUES:
**1. 2JB-3CR-HK-UP; CR**
*LRLR: extended long punches followed by close punches*
**2. 2{JB}-(9)HK-CR-UP; HK**
*LLRR: Jab draws catch to open for hook counter & follow-ups*
**3. 2/3{CR}-OH-UP-HK**
*RRLL: CR draws catch to open for overhand right counter & follow-ups*
**4. 2-3{CR}-HK-HK-CR; UP**
*RLLR: Rear hand miss closes distance for body hook counter & follow-ups*

## DEFENSIVE COUNTER-FIGHTING TECHNIQUES:
**1. vs JB = Sl/CT/JB; CT-PD-CR; Sl-UP or Sl10/7HK-CR**
*Snapping Jab: L Catch/Slip/Ride-Counter Jab (staggered or same time)*
*Lower or Lazy Jab: R Catch top of hand-skip over w/R straight punch*
*Lunging or Measuring Jab: (slip outside w/uppercut under arm to chin, or Step outside w/L hook thru ribs-then CR to face*
**2. vs CR = 9CT-CR-(HK); Ri/Tu/Sl-CR; Sl-Bo-We-HK**
*Outside arm: Catch/Slip L - R Punch) to body*
*End of hand: Ride/Slip R - R Punch) to head*
*Inside arm: Ride/Slip/Bob/Weave-L Hook) to head*
**3. vs HK = OB-JB or CR; Sl-Bo-We-CR**
*Block with Counter jab or straight right (staggered or same time)*
*Slip Left-Bob-Weave R-Straight R counter punch*
**4. vs UP/UP = CT-CR or CT-JB; Ri-2JB-3CR**
*Catch with same side hand, counter with cross or jab*
*Ride back-move forward with counter punching*

## Poway Kenpo Red Belt – POSITION GROUND GRAPPLING

**Major Theme:**    Position Grappling Base Postures and Transitions
**Sport Fight Style:** Brazilian Jiu Jitsu
**Body Position:**    Top/Bottom: Guard (Full & Half)
                         Mount (Front & Rear) - Side Mount
**Hand Position(s):** Various
**Contact Level(s):**  Grappling Contact
**Impact Ranges(s):** Manipulation Range

**Offensive Themes:** Establishing grappling base positions before attacking; Familiarity w/attacking from major top & bottom base positions; Using base positions for control; Using base positions as transitions to initiate a different &/or better base position.

**Defensive Themes:** Establishing base position to begin a grappling defense; Familiarity w/defending from major top and bottom base positions; Manipulating opponent's base positions to setup counters; Transitions to a different base position; Recognizing and moving from a bad position or posture.

**Notes:** This list divided into top & bottom base positions as offense & defense exist from all. The 4 top position techniques connect as one technique. The 4 bottom position techniques are done as stand-alone maneuvers. Freestyle ground grappling is safest starting from the knees.

### *TOP POSITION TECHNIQUES*:
**1. TG-DE-Pass-THG-DE**
Defend top Guard, Pass to top Half-Guard
**2. THG-DE-Pass-TSMT**
Defend top Half-Guard, Pass to top Side-Mount
**3. TSMT-KS-TMT-DE**
Defend top Side-Mount, Pass to top Mount
**4. TMT-DE-CAC-TB-RG**
Defend top Mount, Control arm, Turn to rear Mount or Guard

### *BOTTOM POSITION TECHNIQUES*:
**1. BG-DE (AD/GSS/SUS-TMT)**
*Defend bottom Guard; Arm drag to take back; Scissor-Sweep or Sit-Up Sweep to Top Mount*
**2. BHG-DE (HBP/AD-TB; HE-BG; BR-TMT)**
*Defend bottom Half-Guard*
*Push head &/or body or arm drag w/hip escape to move out &/or take back*
*Hip escape to pull trapped leg out to bottom Guard*
*Trap, bridge, & roll - Pass to top Mount*
**3. BSMT-DE (HBP; HE-BG-DE-GSS/SUS-TMT)**
*Defend bottom Side-Mount (on side of back w/elbows at hip and neck or armpit)*
*Push head &/or body w/hip escape to move out & away to knees*
*Hip escape to replace one leg to bottom Guard, sweep to top Mount*
**4. BMT-DE (BR-TG or HE-BG)**
*Defend bottom Mount, Bridge to top Guard or hip escape to bottom Guard*

# Poway Kenpo Brown Belt 3rd – SUBMISSION GROUND GRAPPLING

**Major Theme:** Submission Grappling
**Sport Fight Style:** Brazilian Jiu Jitsu
**Body Position:** Top/Bottom: Guard (Full & Half)
Mount (Front & Rear) - Side Mount
**Hand Position(s):** Various
**Contact Level(s):** Grappling Contact
**Impact Ranges(s):** Manipulation Range

**Offensive Themes:** Familiarity with major chokes and locks from top and bottom grappling base positions; Connecting submission techniques; Base position transitions to apply submissions.

**Defensive Themes:** Familiarity defending submission attempts from major top & bottom base positions; Transitioning to another position to avoid a submission attempt.

**Notes:** This list divided into top and bottom base positions as offense and defense exist from all; Each base position maneuvered into where multiple submission options can be practiced; Listed submissions can be practiced individually or connected sequentially. Freestyle ground grappling is safest starting from the knees.

## *TOP POSITION TECHNIQUES:*
**1. TG-Pass-TSMT-LT/AB; LT/AM; AB; ATC; SAB *(Near Arm Attacks)***
*Pass top Guard to top Side-Mount: Submission options - Leg trap Armbar / Leg trap Shoulder Lock / Figure 4 Armbar / Arm-Triangle / Step-Over Armbar*
**2. TG-Pass-TSMT-AM-AB-KL-SAB *(Far Arm Attacks)***
*Pass top Guard to top Side-Mount: Submission options - Americana Lock / Figure 4 Armbar / Kimura Lock / Step-Over Armbar*
**3. THG-Pass-TMT-AM/SAB; CAC-TB-RG-SC**
*Pass to Top-Mount: Submission options - Americana Lock; Cross-Arm-Control, turn to take their back, Sleeper Choke*
**4. TSMT-KS-TMT-AM; KL; SAB**
*Knee-on-Stomach to Top-Mount: Submission options - Americana / Kimura / Step-Over Armbar*

## *BOTTOM POSITION TECHNIQUES:*
**1. BG-GL-KL-ATC-RAB-OMA-LTC**
*Bottom Guard: Submission flow options - Guillotine; Kimura; Arm-Triangle Choke; Reverse Armbar; Leg-Triangle Choke; Omaplata Shoulder Lock*
**2. BHG-CAC-HE-TB-RG/SC or BR-THG-TSMT-ATC**
*Bottom Half-Guard, Cross-Arm Control, Hip-Escape to take back-Sleeper Choke; Bridge to top Half-Guard, move to top Side-Mount, Arm-Triangle Choke*
**3. BSMT-HE-BG-GSS/SUS-TMT-Sub**
*Hip escape to bottom Guard, Any Guard sweep to Top-Mount, Any submission*
**4. BMT-BR-TG-Pass-TSMT-Sub**
*Bridge to Top-Guard, Pass to top Side-Mount, Any submission*

# Poway Kenpo Brown Belt 2nd – OFFENSIVE TAKEDOWNS

**Major Theme:** Attacking with Sweeps & Takedowns
**Sport Fight Style:** Judo - Karate - Wrestling
**Body Position:** Any Stance Matchup (L or R slightly forward)
**Hand Position(s):** Various
**Contact Level(s):** Standup Grappling Contact
**Impact Range(s):** Manipulation Range

**Offensive Themes:** Techniques 1-4 attack outside leg & body; Techniques 5-8 attack inside leg & body; Technique pairs 1-2, 3-4, & 5-6 use the same setup respective to the other; Setting up Sweeps & Takedowns w/Punches & Strikes; Following up Sweeps/Takedowns w/Strikes &/or Submissions.

**Notes:** The defensive theme is to follow-up after an ititial offensive attack is 'Countered'. Takedown openings are determined by opponent's initial or adjusted foot position, so if their stance is narrow, it's easier to get outside/behind or if wider then inside/front; Extra benefit's include improved awareness of vulnerability to sweeps and improved falling skills.

## *OFFENSIVE ATTACKING TECHNIQUES:*

**1. JB-3CR-12-Sp13-RHK; FK; SAB; FAL; vs Countered = 5-13; SC**
*Jab-Cross-Step thru sweep: (standing SC option) L spin sweep-RHK, FK, FAL, SAB*
*Vs Countered: Drag L Sweep R 13 far leg or Standing Sleeper Choke*

**2. (8)7RHK-11-2-3-19; 22 -TMT-RP-FK; SC; AM; vs Countered = 5-13; SC**
*RHK lead leg, Pull sweep (standing SC option)-Rear Heel Trip or Lift & Trip-Strike &/or Sub*
*Vs Countered: Drag L Sweep R 13 far leg or Standing Sleeper Choke*

**3. 2BKS3-14/RHS-RP; SC; FAL; HH; vs Countered = SC**
*BKS with lunging Step-Drag outside his front foot (feint), (standing ATC or SC option)*
*Cross outer reap front leg w/high forearm push-Strike &/or Submission*
*Vs Countered: SC*

**4. 2/10BKS-16/AT-(RHP)-(RHK); BKL; TB-SC; vs Countered = UpFK-RcP-Rc**
*BKS with lunging Step-Drag outside front foot (feint), (standing ATC or SC option)-grab lead shoulder into Scissor Sweep Takedown-Strike &/or Sub*
*Vs Countered = Up kick from ground then recover to feet*

**5. 2/3WK/BKS-18(17)-TMT-RP-RP-FK; AM; SAB; vs Countered = GC; 20; 21**
*Pull-Drag Wheel K groin/inside leg w/L Cross-Body check: Drag L>R Straight Inner R Reap Takedown (or L cross inner) to Top Mount-L Punch face-L foot on ground w/R Punch-TSK-exit; &/or American lock or Step Over Armbar submission*
*Vs if Countered = Guillotine &/or Takedown*

**6. 2/3WK/BKS-15-RP; FAL; TB-BKL; vs Countered to Guard = PO-FK; DE**
*Pull-drag Wheel Kick groin/inside leg w/L Cross-Body Check-drag to L Straight Outer Reap Takedown-Vert Punch groin; &/or Ankle Lock submission*
*Vs if Pulled into guard = Push off before held-Kick or defend position*

**7. 2JB-3CR-7/17-3RK; KB; FAL; HH; vs Countered = HT; 15**
*Jab-Cross-R step between feet: Cross Inner Reap (buckles knee)-Rear Kick groin*
*Vs Countered = Hip Throw; L knee to ground w/R foot behind L Leg-Push/trip over*

**8. FK-Bo20(21)-TSMT-RP-TSK; AM; KL; ATC; SAB; vs Countered = TB-19; PO**
*Front Kick taps lead knee: Change levels-Dbl or Sgl Leg Takedown to Top Side Mount-L foot on ground w/R Vert Punch face-TSK-exit; &/or Submission*
*Vs if Countered = Take their back-Rear Heel Trip to Top Mount; Push off & kick*

# Poway Kenpo Brown Belt 1st – DEFENSIVE TAKEDOWNS

**Major Theme:** Defending Strikes with Sweeps & Takedowns
**Sport Fight Style:** Judo - Karate - Wrestling
**Body Position:** Any Stance Matchup
**Hand Position(s):** Various
**Contact Level(s):** Standup Grappling Contact
**Impact Range(s):** Manipulation Range

**Counter-Fighting Themes:** Techniques 1-3 defend against circular kicking attacks; Techniques 4-5 defend against straight line kicking; Techniques 6-8 defend against hands; Counter fighting strategies & tactics to set up sweeps & takedowns; Countering kicks by dropping under; Catching & trapping kicks.

**Notes:** The offensive theme here are the follow-ups after the initial sweep or takedown is countered. Other training benefits include vulnerability awareness of extending the limbs to strike and improved falling skills.

## *DEFENSIVE COUNTER-FIGHTING TECHNIQUES:*

**1. vs High RHK = Dr-FK-LG11-AK; FAL; Dr13; vs Countered = BG; RcP-Rc**
*Drop w/ Up-Kick groin, bottom foot hooks far ankle/L hand grabs near ankle (Lock option), Inverted Pull-Sweep w/L Push-Kick Takedown, Ax-Kick, Back-Roll to feet; Ankle-Lock Submission; Drop Spin/ Outward Leg Sweep*
*Vs if Countered = Pull Guard, Recover Position-Recover*

**2. vs OHK; RHK = OB/AT-LC-15-RP; FK; FAL; BKL; vs Cntrd = 19-22; 20-21**
*Catch & hold L side circular body or head Kick, R Straight Outer-Reap Takedown, Punch/ Kick groin; &/or Ankle or Knee-Lock Submission*
*Vs if Countered = Takedown to Top-Mount*

**3. vs WK; SpOHK = OB/AT-LC-15-RP; FK; FAL; BKL; vs Cntr = 19-22; 20-21**
*Catch & hold R side circular body or head Kick, L Straight Outer-Reap Takedown, Punch/ Kick groin; Ankle &/or Knee-Lock Submission*
*Vs if Countered = Takedown to Top-Mount*

**4. vs 5FPK = Ri/DOB-3-14/RHS-TSK; FAL; HH; vs Cntrd = 19-22; 20-21**
*Scoop-Block outside kicking leg, Cross Outer-Reap w/L Strike to Takedown; Ankle-Lock &/or Heel-Hook submission*
*Vs if Countered = Takedown to Top-Mount*

**5. vs 7FPK = Ri/DOB-12-13-TSK; FAL; KB; TM-AM; vs Countered = SC**
*Scoop Block outside right kick, L Step-Thru-Sweep, R Spinning-Outward-Sweep, w/ Strike; Ankle &/or Knee-Bar Submission*
*Vs if Countered = Sleeper Choke*

**6. vs Hand Blitz = Dr16-AK; RHK; BKL; FAL; vs Countered = UpFK-RcP-Rc**
*From reverse Stance, drop under attack w/ Scissor-Sweep Takedown, Ax/Round-Kick; Bent-Knee &/or Ankle-Lock Submission*
*Vs if Countered = Up Kick from ground, Recover Position, Recover*

**7. vs 2BKS3 = Sl/IB-7-19, 22-TMT-RP-TSK; Any Sub; vs Cntrd = TB-SC**
*Slip outside BKS, Step thru behind (standing Sleeper option), Heel-Trip or Lift & Trip Takedown, plant L foot w/R Punch face, R TSK-exit; &/or any Submission*
*Vs if Countered = Move behind, Sleeper Choke*

**8. vs 2JB-3CR = Sl-Bo/We-20, 21-TSMT-RP-TSK; Any Sub; vs Cntr = TB-SC**
*Avoid punches, Step R behind w/ Dbl or Single-Leg Takedown to Top-Mount, R foot on ground w/L Vert Punch face, L TSK-exit; &/or any Submission*
*Vs if Countered = Move behind, Sleeper Choke*

# Poway Kenpo 1st Black Belt - MMA

| | |
|---|---|
| **Major Theme:** | Mixed Martial Arts (MMA - Pankration) |
| **Sport Fight Style:** | Striking with Grappling & Submissions |
| **Body Position:** | Any |
| **Hand Position(s):** | Various |
| **Contact Level(s):** | Light to Full Contact |
| **Impact Range(s):** | Contact-Penetration-Manipulation Range |

**Offensive Themes:** Create combinations based upon mixing range & weapons; Changing levels from high to low & low to high; Establish base position after a takedown; Ground & pound to set up submission.

**Counter-Fighting Themes:** Defending tackles w/strikes; Defending punches w/takedowns; Establishing base position after being taken down; Defending while braced against a cage or wall.

**Notes:** Many offensive & defensive techniques from the other ranges can be applied. Techniques avoided are striking techniques that expose the back to a grappling clinch & takedown technique.

## *OFFENSIVE ATTACKING TECHNIQUES:*
**1. Takedown-Establish Base-Ground & Pound-Submission**
*Shoot & takedown to base-Striking on ground before Submission*
**2. Boxing-Takedown-Establish Base-Submission**
*Boxing range-Change levels for takedown to base-Any Submission*
**3. Kickboxing-Takedown-Establish Base-Submission**
*Kickboxing range-Change levels for takedown to base-Any Submission*
**4. Clinch-Takedown-Establish Base-Ground & Pound-Submission**
*Clinch range-Any takedown to base-Striking on ground before Submission*

## *DEFENSIVE COUNTER-FIGHTING TECHNIQUES:*
**1. vs Tackle = (8)UpKN(UpKN); <Punches; Sprawl-TB; GC; GP Submission**
*Up Knee Kick face; move back while Punching; Sprawl, Guillotine or take his back; Ground & pound into Submission*
**2. vs Punch Attack = Bo/We-20, 21-TSMT-TMT-GP-Submission**
*Avoid Punches-Change levels-Takedown to Top position-Ground & pound into Submission*
**3. vs Kick Attack = CT-12(15)-GP-Submission**
*Catch Kick/Leg-Any Takedown-Ground & Pound into Submission*
**4. vs Back to Cage/Wall = Widen Base; Turn & Drop Hips; Head Push; Arm Wrap; Ankle Pick, Hook Leg; GC; Turn him to wall-Strike &/or Submission**
*Legs wide apart; Turn & drop hips; Push his head down, Overhook (whizzer) his arm; Ankle Pick to trip; Hook his leg w/your leg; Guillotine Choke; Quickly turn & pin him to wall; Apply any Striking &/or Submission*

# SELF-DEFENSE SYSTEM

## Chapter X

These are the Self-Defense Techniques (i.c., Street Techniques) that constitute my American Kenpo system. This chapter covers all those techniques, using my naming structure and as they evolved at my school over 35 years. However, Kenpo practitioners from any source can find great value from the insight contained in this chapter, where all the techniques are written out, and by seeing them taught and demonstrated at BarryBBarker.com.

Everything covered up to this point, from *Anatomy* to *Pressure Points*, *Basics* to *Sets*, from *Forms* to *Sport Fighting* are there to help the Kenpo practitioner become better at these Self-Defense Techniques, as this is where the martial art *Concepts and Principles* are stored and illustrated.

The late Kenpo Master Edmund K Parker formulated his original American Kenpo System of techniques at the root of what is here. It is presented sometimes as originally learned and other times with modifications and changes implemented by me and others over my 35+ years teaching Kenpo.

The goal of Kenpo technique practice is to develop effective self-defense skill that is adaptable to any situation and that can be applied extemporaneously. This is done through repetitive practice of choreographed Self-Defense Technique sequences that illustrate the Concepts and Principles of applied interactive movement while utilizing every weapon, target, angle, range, position, against every type of attack.

Through scenario rehearsal, Kenpo practitioners gain interactive movement experience and knowledge along with contact training to build physical and mental toughness, target depth perception, and weapon focus. This weapon/target awareness grows and refines over time and is an extremely valuable benefit of Kenpo technique training.

Every weapon, method, and target are available in this type of fighting, including the legal and especially illegal targets of sport fighting. Kenpo practitioners try to get good at attacking these illegal targets especially, using various methods. Since these are "street techniques" they can be very vicious and violent with lots of "dirty fighting" moves.

There are also less violent options contained here. The original EPAK system I had learned did not offer many humane choices but, teaching in a different time, I have added many controlling options throughout my system. The viciousness is still there if needed but opportunities exist to use more restraint if and when that would be more appropriate.

Kenpo is a fighting style where we try to remain standing, which is how we should prefer to be in a street environment altercation. The original EPAK system consists of only one technique done lying on the ground (EPAK version of "Dangerous Tackle"). Otherwise, all Kenpo techniques start and end with us standing and the opponent either driven away or lying on the ground as we exit.

The reality of course is that we could fall or be taken to the ground in battle and have an opponent standing over us or be down grappling with us. Grapplers want to eliminate space where the striking and street defense goal would be to create space, with a goal to stay on or get back to our feet. If we end up grappling, whether top or bottom, our goal is to stand back up.

The potential to finish a street fight with ground grappling and submissions exists for sure but it must be done quickly as other opponent's, obstacles, and hazards may lurk nearby. The EPAK Kenpo system does not directly address these positions but many of the concepts and principles used in standup Kenpo can also be used on the ground.

To address this within my Kenpo system I have filled gaps in the *Tackle* technique formula, updated the *Arm Choke* defenses, added essential elements to the *Bear Hug* formula, and developed a *Ground Option* on several grabbing and punching techniques. This allows for the application and practice of these ideas in the curriculum and gets them out of the realm of theoretical and conceptual analysis, or just taught as a seminar topic.

*Ground Option* variables occur after being fully mounted with their hips above ours, or halfway mounted with one leg out, aka half-guard. These dominant ground positions are the most difficult to defend and escape from. If mounted it's important to keep our hips under theirs, perhaps with elbows posted against his knees, so that lifting our hips can disrupt their balance and keep them from sitting on our chest. Moving (i.e., *Hip Escape* Basic) and bumping the hips then helps in the effort to escape and counter.

Note: This is street so dirty fighting can and should be used. Moves most grapplers would not be defending are fingers to the eyes, cupping the ears, press and rub the sharp knuckles or elbows into tender points, groin grabs, pinching sensitive skin areas, finger digit manipulation, etc.

Even though Kenpo is a standup fighting system with the goal to be on our feet, this type of interaction does not begin in a neutral bow or "fighting stance." Those are all transitional stances used after a fight is <u>not</u> avoided.

The pre-fight street stance is the more natural position with the feet slightly staggered, probably with both hands' up palms forward in a "let's not fight" or "I don't want to fight" posture. This is best done positioned to one side of an opponent's centerline, and if possible, in an *Open Stance* with our most forward foot outside their most forward foot. This narrows their attack choices while moving away from their rear side power and gives better access to getting behind them (i.e., taking their back).

This preparatory position, while probably talking and assessing, is important. Since <u>not</u> wanting to street-fight should in fact be the case, then standing in this non-threatening yet ready posture serves some very practical purposes. It shows an adversary and witnesses that we really don't want to fight, and it can make a potential threat underestimate or be unaware of our position's capabilities, not to mention witness accounts of the interaction later. The technique knowledge from this chapter could then be applied if needed.

Techniques in the martial art school format, where they are learned by rank, has multiple attack themes at each belt rank. For example, my schools first rank has wrist grabs, body grabs, pushes, punches, bear hugs, a kick, and a club attack. This attack assortment at each level is done because if only one group attack variables were taught before moving on to the next, like all wrist grab techniques together, it could be years before a student would learn defenses against some other type of attack. But they are formatted differently in this chapter as is best for practicing once known.

### Format
With endless "what ifs" in techniques an attack variety is initially the most useful. Once all technique variables for a type of attack are known it becomes more useful to practice them by *Technique Grouping* or *Theme*. These can be categorized by the response using *Family Groupings* and *Master Key Movements,* or organized by attack characteristic using *Range, Angle, Relative Body Position, Type of Attack,* and/or *Severity of Attack.*

These methods allow the "what-if" variables to be seen together and techniques practiced that have similar reference points. This leads to faster position recognition and adjustments into a free flow of appropriate use movement without preconception.

**Family Groupings** are variables that exist throughout as an attacker's intention in moving their arms and hands towards us could be to *grab* and control, *push* to make space, or accelerate as projectiles to *strike.* With a *range* adjustment those arms can also become *Hugs, Holds, Locks,* or *Tackles.*

A progressive analysis then evolves where *Grabbing Range* could involve hands grabbing wrists *straight* (Gripping Wrist), *cross* (Crossed Grab), *2-on-1* (Darting Fist), *double in front* (Begging Palms) or *rear* (Crossed Arms) or become body grabs with variables such as *pushing* (Twin Lapel Grab), *pulling* (Fist of Aggression), or holding *in-place* (Grabbing Hair).

*Punching/Striking/Kicking Range* techniques can be organized by where our feet and body are located relative to an attacker's feet and arms after our initial reaction (what I call the "Oh S**t" move) or while in the flow of dynamic interactive movement.

There are 8 lower and upper body standing base positions when interacting with another person. Knowing these variables speeds up position recognition so we can move more efficiently and effectively. They are:

Closed Stance Positions (L-L or R-R)
Lower body inside lead foot / upper body inside arm (Six Hands)
Lower body inside lead foot / upper body outside arm (Cradling the Baby)
Lower body outside lead foot / upper body inside arm (Falling Eagle)
Lower body outside lead foot / upper body outside arm (Compulsive Kneel)

Open Stance Positions (L-R or R-L)
Lower body inside lead foot / upper body inside arm (Hand of Destruction)
Lower body inside lead foot / upper body outside arm (Crossing Grab)
Lower body outside lead foot / upper body inside arm (Securing the Club)
Lower body outside lead foot / upper body outside arm (Hand and Shield)

Punch defenses alone can put us *inside* (Delayed Hand), *outside* (Flashing Fist), *under* (Protective Circles) or *over* (Shielding Fingers) an attacker's arm. Kick Defenses can end up in similar relative positions *inside* (Thrusting Palm) or *outside* (Buckling the Leg) a kicking leg or hip. *Bear Hugs, Holds, Locks,* and *Tackles* also contain many variables.

**Master Key Movements** refer to motion with potential for multiple applications. Circling the arm *inward* or *outward* (i.e., "wax on-wax off") as indexed in Kenpo Short Form 1 where the *inward* and *outward downward blocking* motions use the arm in one direction, and the *upward, outward, inside downward blocks* use it in the other.

"Many answers lie in a single move" applies here as focusing the outward arm circle motion in the upward direction could be used to *Block/Parry* (Protective Circles), *Check* (Ducking Dragon), *Punch* (Pursuing Panther), *Forearm Strike* (Twin Lapel Grab), *Palm Strike* (Triggered Palm), *Elbow Strike* (Twisted Wrist), etc.

This goes to Intention as an *inward* arm circle motion could be focused as an *Inward Block* (Crossing Fist), *Hammerfist* (Fist of Aggression), *Elbow Tweak* (Glancing Palm), *Body Manipulation* (Crossing Grab), *Check* (Destructive Gift), *Clear* (Ascending from Death), etc.

**Range** is the distance between an opponent and our self from where different **Angles** (*Clock Concept*)**, Relative Body Positions** (*Sport Fighting*), **Type of Attack** (*Basics: Striking, Grabbing, Grappling*), and **Severity of Attack** (*analyzed through Mr. Parkers 'Web of Knowledge' Concept*) all stem from.

**Severity of Attack** categorizes techniques as Mr. Parker described by "degrees of difficulty when handling an attack" and he illustrated in his "Web of Knowledge." He organized *grabs* first as the least difficult to defend, with *weapon* and *multiple attacker* defenses as the most difficult (See Mr. Parker's books).

My analysis includes *Range* in the formulation to determine organizational order as I have found it better to sort techniques first by *range,* or furthest out to closest in, then organize those by *Severity of Attack.*

This just means that in my analysis *Weapon Attacks* are after *Punches & Strikes* but before *Tackles & Takedowns*. The *Range* used to attack with a knife or club is like a punch/hand strike, but a threatening gun more at grabbing distance. Many techniques are interchangeable at this distance with knife/club defense ideas often similar to punch/strike and vice versa.

These many ways of organizing techniques provide a variety of indexing options with similar reference points. Additionally, individual basics and sections within techniques are interchangeable as a piece of one can be *Grafted* into the flow of another. This is a continual and necessary reality of spontaneous unrehearsed interactive movement. These techniques provide knowledge of where those transitions can effectively take place.

The following write-ups contain more detailed information, hidden moves, and insight than would have been possible to put in my videos at BarryBBarker.com, so use them together. Note: All techniques are explained and demonstrated on one "standard side", but all can be done on either side as indexed in Kenpo Forms.

Note: The Kenpo "standard side" mostly puts the right leg in front. Kenpo is considered a right-handed system with the heritage of this street fighting method putting that side forward. Whether evolved from most people being right-handed so the stronger and more coordinated side leads or moving to empty-hand fighting after losing a weapon, or the difficulty a "southpaw" gives many people, Kenpo technique primarily puts the right side in front.

Western sport fighting by contrast predominantly puts the dominant hand in the rear, using the less-dominant front hand to set it up. These different fighting concepts and paradigms both have proven merit. The street fight however must end fast and is therefore applied without the "round" mentality of sport fighting.

Note: In my Kenpo system, beginner's and intermediate level students learn part of each technique, with Brown and Black Belts learning the entire or complete technique. Those working on 2nd and 3rd Degree Black Belt learn the endings or "Extensions" to the previously learned Beginner and Intermediate Level techniques.

The descriptions here therefore consist of the entire technique but note where any would stop for lower belt students then continue for advanced students as (Extension Begins Here). Italics and parentheses are used where moves are different between the base technique and its extension, or to point out something extra, to differentiate, or list a body organ or pressure point.

Even though these techniques are based upon Ed Parker's American Kenpo (EPAK) techniques, many have minor or major changes from the original as I had learned them from Jim Mitchell in the early 1980's, and there are some new ones, with a few combined into one technique.

Note: I do not use the EPAK or Tracy systems coded names. Jim Mitchell initiated this change in 1983 and I found it less confusing for students so in my descriptions a "fist" is not a "mace" and "arms" are not "twigs", etc.

However, in the write-ups and on my video site I have listed the original EPAK name in *(parenthesis)* next to the name I use. There is also a Cross-Reference Chart with my Poway Kenpo names alphabetically listed but with the EPAK and Tracy Kenpo names alongside for people more familiar with those naming formats. Thank you to one of my Black Belts, Dr. John Hippen, for putting all that together for me.

The Kenpo *Self-Defense Technique* formula generally starts by defending an attack in a way to neutralize the attempt and avoid us being injured, while positioning us favorably and putting the attacker in a vulnerable position by disrupting their balance and posture, taking their center, and not giving it back, while hopefully causing them physical pain and mental distraction.

Strikes, manipulations, and controlling movements are then inflicted to progressively break them down until they are no longer able to cause harm. Lastly is to exit safely using the most efficient angle and method, while maintaining environmental awareness.

## Practice & Safety
These Kenpo *Self-Defense Techniques* contain a wealth of information that every martial artist can benefit from knowing, regardless of style. It is imperative however that they are practiced safely as many dangerous and potentially lethal moves are contained in them.

When practicing on training partners some weapons and methods are not fully utilized, with some targets never hit, and some moves never fully finished. However, many targets can and should be hit to varying degrees, depending on the partner, to influence and assure technique success.

Bodywork on a live person is still vital to learning, with cooperative partners important for practicing. This allows striking moves to be practiced strong and hard with focused yet controlled contact where nobody becomes injured. Full contact hitting is practiced on inanimate objects or protected targets as hitting with correctly formed, aligned, and focused weapons is also important. Manipulation and takedown techniques are often able to be more fully utilized in practice.

The target focus guideline I use to help students develop striking control at full speed and power is a maximum 2" away from a target for beginners, 1" for intermediate, and ½" maximum for Brown and Black Belts. Partners must react in an anticipated way to allow completion of these pre-arranged and formulated technique sequences with many targets contacted to various degrees to effectively bend, turn, move, or manipulate them so the next movement will align as designed in the technique being practiced.

All targets and weapons can be modified for safety if hard contact training or demonstrating. Examples: use the flat of the elbow instead of the tip; kick the upper inner thigh instead the testicles; extend a powerful side thrust kick past the knee; tap the temples, forehead, or slide the finger pads across the eyebrows instead of poking or scraping the eyes; etc. Instruction from someone knowledgeable and experienced is always the best way to learn this.

When you are the training partner (i.e., dummy) give partners a realistic reaction to a successfully applied move, but always protect yourself as accidents can happen. Examples: lift your shoulders to protect the back of your neck; check your own vital targets like the armpit; protect your joints; bend and ride with contact. Wear appropriate protection (i.e., mouthpiece, groin cup). Hands or mitts can be held to protect some targets as *rebounding* is important to many follow-ups. Solo training on a rubber dummy or heavy bag is also useful, as is practicing in the air (i.e., Shadowboxing).

Note: The traditional Karate Gi provides an air pocket to help absorb impact and gives the preparatory awareness to receive contact, with the Karate Belt not only representing rank and keeping the jacket closed but it can also be a support structure for the low back and torso through strenuous efforts.

The following Kenpo Self-Defense Techniques are categorized by *Range* then *Severity of Attack* with sub-categories such as *Handshake Attacks* together in the *Hand, Wrist and Arm Grab Attacks* section, etc. Each section is arranged in a logical and progressive practice order to help build upon the theme. Contained are 143 Kenpo Self-Defense Techniques divided and sub-divided into the following categories:

**Hand, Wrist, & Arm Grab Attacks:** *Two-Hand* and *One-Hand Wrist Grabs from the Front, Handshake Grabs,* plus *Hand & Wrist Grabs from the Rear.*
16 Self-Defense Techniques total.

**Body, Neck, & Head Grab Attacks:** *One-Hand* and *Two-Hand Grabs from the Front, One-Hand Grabs from the Side,* and *Grabs from the Rear.*
16 Self-Defense Techniques total.

**Pushing Attacks:** *One-Hand* and *Two-Hand Pushes from the Front.*
8 Self-Defense Techniques total.

**Punch & Strike Attacks:** *Inside, Outside,* and *Underneath Arm Defenses.*
32 Self-Defense Techniques total.

**Club, Knife, Gun Attacks:** 10 *Club,* 8 *Knife,* and 4 *Gun*
22 Self-Defense Techniques total.

**Kick & Kick/Punch Combination Attacks:** *Inside Straight Kick, Inside Round Kick, Outside Straight Kick.*
17 Self-Defense Techniques total.

**Tackles & Takedowns:** *Off-Line* and *On-Line Tackle Defenses.*
6 Self-Defense Techniques total.

**Hugs/Holds & Locks:** *Front Bear Hugs, Rear Bear Hugs,* and *Locks.* 16 Self-Defense Techniques total.

**Multiple Attackers:** 10 *Two-Man/Person* Self-Defense Techniques total.

*A smaller font & abbreviations are used in the descriptions to save space:*
R = Right; L = Left; NB = Neutral Bow; FB = Forward Bow; BKS = Backknuckle Strike; RHS = Reverse Hand Sword/Ridgehand Strike; CW = Clockwise; CCW = Counter Clockwise; Inv = Inverted; Horiz = Horizontal; Vert = Vertical; Simult = Simultaneous; Def = Defensive; Off = Offensive; w/ = with; , = then; Dbl = Double; In = Inward; Out = Outward; Up = Upward; Down = Downward; Ext = Extended; Rev – Reverse; Mod – Modified; Words "stance" & "strike" left off most names; Combo = Combination.

### Kenpo Self-Defense Technique Cross Reference Name Chart
*Page #'s are where Technique Write-Up is found in this Red "Body" book*

| # | Poway Kenpo Names | | EPAK Names | Tracy Kenpo Names |
|---|---|---|---|---|
| 1 | Alternating Fists | Pg263 | Alternating Maces | Japanese Sword |
| 2 | Arms of Silk | Pg301 | Wings of Silk | Silk Wind |
| 3 | Ascending from Death | Pg256 | Heavenly Ascent | The Wedge |
| 4 | Back Breaker | Pg272 | Back Breaker | Eagle Claws |
| 5 | Bear and the Ram | Pg307 | The Bear and the Ram | Eagle Pin |
| 6 | Begging Palms | Pg249 | Begging Hands | Anvil |
| 7 | Blinding Vice | Pg257 | Blinding Sacrifice | Darting Serpent |
| 8 | Bouncing Pendulum | Pg289 | Swinging Pendulum | Chopping the Log |
| 9 | Broken Gun | Pg286 | Broken Rod | Turning the Flame |
| 10 | Broken Kneel | Pg295 | Destructive Kneel | Sowing the Seeds |
| 11 | Broken Tackle | Pg289 | Broken Ram | Encircling Arms |
| 12 | Brushing the Club | Pg279 | Brushing the Storm | Startled Cat |
| 13 | Buckling the Leg | Pg291 | Buckling Branch | Blocking the Kick |
| 14 | Calming the Club | Pg280 | Calming the Storm | Calming the Storm |
| 15 | Captured Arms | Pg299 | Captured Twigs | Japanese Strangle Hold |
| 16 | Capturing the Club | Pg280 | Capturing the Storm | Spinning from the Sun |
| 17 | Capturing the Gun | Pg285 | Capturing the Rod | Uncovering the Flame |
| 18 | Charging Tackle | Pg294 | Charging Ram | Encircling Arms |
| 19 | Checking the Club | Pg278 | Checking the Storm | Evasion |
| 20 | Circling Elbow | Pg258 | Circling Wing | Crash of the Eagle |
| 21 | Circling Parries | Pg275 | Circling Fans | Whirling Leaves |
| 22 | Circling the Arm | Pg271 | Circling the Horizon | Shaolin Warrior |
| 23 | Circling the Club | Pg283 | Circling the Storm | Crashing Elbows var. |
| 24 | Circling the Kick A | Pg288 | Circle of Doom | Circle of China |
| 25 | Circling the Kick B | Pg288 | N/A | N/A |
| 26 | Clipping the Blade 1-2 | Pg283 | Clipping Lance & Storm | Cobra and the Mongoose |
| 27 | Compulsive Kneel | Pg272 | Kneel of Compulsion | Eagle Miss |

| 28 | Conquering Arm | Pg254 | Conquering Shield | Advancing Phoenix |
|---|---|---|---|---|
| 29 | Courting the Tiger | Pg305 | Courting the Tiger | Knee Sweep |
| 30 | Cradling the Baby | Pg270 | Gathering Clouds | Parting the Waves |
| 31 | Crashing Elbows | Pg299 | Crashing Wings | Circling Elbows |
| 32 | Cross of Destruction | Pg259 | Cross of Destruction | Bridge |
| 33 | Crossed Arms | Pg252 | Crossed Twigs | Shackle Break |
| 34 | Crossing Fist | Pg268 | Attacking Mace | Kenpo Shield |
| 35 | Crossing Grab | Pg246 | Crossing Talon | Crossing Talon |
| 36 | Crushing Palm | Pg298 | Crushing Hammer | Rising Elbow |
| 37 | Dance of Death | Pg271 | Dance of Death | Dance of Death |
| 38 | Dancing in the Dark | Pg293 | Dance of Darkness | Brushing Wind |
| 39 | Dangerous Tackle | Pg296 | Encounter with Danger | Falling Rock |
| 40 | Darting Fist | Pg250 | Darting Mace | Cobra and the Mongoose |
| 41 | Defending Cross | Pg288 | Defensive Cross | Sweeping Winds |
| 42 | Deflecting Pendulum | Pg291 | Deflecting Hammer | Blocking the Kick |
| 43 | Defying the Club | Pg280 | Defying the Storm | Bending Reeds |
| 44 | Defying the Gun | Pg286 | Defying the Rod | Uncovering the Flame |
| 45 | Delayed Hand | Pg265 | Delayed Sword | Delayed Sword |
| 46 | Desperate Fists | Pg250 | Desperate Falcons | Crossing the Lock |
| 47 | Destructive Circles | Pg273 | Circling Destruction | Cyclone |
| 48 | Destructive Gift | Pg248 | Broken Gift | Gift variation |
| 49 | Destructive Parries | Pg276 | Destructive Fans | Spinning Hammers |
| 50 | Detouring the Kick | Pg289 | Detour from Doom | Chopping the Log |
| 51 | Dividing the Enemy | Pg307 | Parting of the Snakes | Chinese Junk |
| 52 | Ducking Dragon | Pg259 | Short Form 2 | Short Form 2 |
| 53 | Eluding Death | Pg304 | N/A | N/A |
| 54 | Entangled Arm A | Pg247 | Entangled Wing | Breaking the Sword |
| 55 | Entangled Arm B | Pg247 | Bow of Compulsion | Eagle Miss |
| 56 | Entwined Blade | Pg284 | Entwined Lance | Chinese Fan |
| 57 | Entwined Fists | Pg274 | Entwined Maces | Crossing the Mountain |
| 58 | Escaping Death | Pg304 | Escape from Death | Japanese Stranglehold |
| 59 | Evading the Club | Pg278 | Evading the Storm | Evasion |
| 60 | Falling Eagle | Pg254 | Falling Falcon | Drawbridge |
| 61 | Fatal Variation | Pg266 | Fatal Cross | Bridging the Gap |
| 62 | Fingers of Wisdom | Pg305 | Snakes of Wisdom | Sweeping Branches |
| 63 | Fist of Aggression | Pg255 | Mace of Aggression | Covering Talon |
| 64 | Flashing Fist | Pg268 | Flashing Mace | Whirling Warrior |
| 65 | Flashing Hands | Pg268 | Flashing Wings | Flashing Wings |
| 66 | Flowing Hands | Pg306 | Falcons of Force | Flowing Hands |

| 67 | Glancing Blade | Pg283 | Glancing Lance | Striking Mace |
|---|---|---|---|---|
| 68 | Glancing Palm | Pg260 | Glancing Salute | Rocker |
| 69 | Glancing Poke | Pg245 | Glancing Spear | Bending the Limb |
| 70 | Grabbing Hair | Pg253 | Clutching Feathers | Eagles Beak |
| 71 | Gripping Wrist | Pg246 | Gripping Talon | Pushing the Circle |
| 72 | Grouping the Enemy | Pg308 | Gathering of the Snakes | Whirling Warrior |
| 73 | Hammerlock | Pg252 | Flight to Freedom | Passing the Horizon |
| 74 | Hand and Shield | Pg273 | Shield and Sword | Crossed Swords |
| 75 | Hand of Destruction | Pg266 | Sword of Destruction | Japanese Sword |
| 76 | Hidden Elbow | Pg257 | Obscure Wing | Japanese Stranglehold |
| 77 | Hidden Hand | Pg258 | Obscure Sword | Broken Staff |
| 78 | Hooking Arms | Pg263 | Hooking Wings | Sweeping Arm Hook |
| 79 | Hugging Pendulum | Pg292 | Hugging Pendulum | The Serpent |
| 80 | Jamming the Tackle | Pg296 | N/A | N/A |
| 81 | Jumping Crane | Pg270 | Leaping Crane | Springing Tiger |
| 82 | Kick into Darkness | Pg276 | Thrust into Darkness | N/A |
| 83 | Leap of Death | Pg282 | Leap of Death | Leap of Death |
| 84 | Lock of Death | Pg303 | Grip of Death | Headlock |
| 85 | Locked Arm | Pg251 | Locked Wing | Locking Arm |
| 86 | Locked Horns | Pg302 | Locking Horns | Headlock |
| 87 | Mating the Rams | Pg306 | Marriage of the Rams | Folding Wings |
| 88 | Meeting the Tackle | Pg296 | Intercepting the Ram | Encircling Arms |
| 89 | Obstructing the Club | Pg279 | Obstructing the Storm | Crossing the Sun |
| 90 | Opposing Palms | Pg306 | Grasping Eagles | Chinese Junk |
| 91 | Parrying Grab | Pg274 | Snaking Talon | Crossing the Mountain |
| 92 | Parting Arms | Pg262 | Parting Wings | Flashing Daggers |
| 93 | Piercing Blade | Pg284 | Piercing Lance | Tumbling Clouds |
| 94 | Pinch from Death | Pg303 | The Grasp of Death | Headlock |
| 95 | Prancing Tiger | Pg267 | Prance of the Tiger | The Lotus |
| 96 | Protective Circles | Pg275 | Circles of Protection | Winding Limbs |
| 97 | Protective Parries | Pg275 | Protective Fans | Long 4 |
| 98 | Pursuing Panther | Pg267 | Short Form 2 | Short 2 |
| 99 | Raining Blade | Pg285 | Raining Lance | Whirling Thorn |
| 100 | Raking Fist | Pg255 | Raking Mace | Striking Asp |
| 101 | Ram and the Eagle | Pg307 | Ram and the Eagle | Whirling Blades |
| 102 | Rear Belt Grab | Pg259 | Menacing Twirl | Turning the Flame |
| 103 | Retreating Pendulum | Pg292 | Retreating Pendulum | The Serpent |
| 104 | Returning Club | Pg282 | Returning Storm | Dance of the Mongoose |
| 105 | Returning the Gift | Pg249 | Gift in Return | Gift variation |

| 106 | Reversing Circles | Pg291 | Reversing Circles | Long 4 |
|-----|-------------------|-------|-------------------|--------|
| 107 | Reversing Fist | Pg273 | Reversing Mace | Double Spear |
| 108 | Rolling Fists | Pg289 | Long Form 2 | N/A |
| 109 | Scraping Stomp A | Pg302 | Scraping Hoof | Heel Hook |
| 110 | Scraping Stomp B | Pg302 | Twirling Sacrifice | N/A |
| 111 | Securing the Club | Pg281 | Securing the Storm | The Scorpion |
| 112 | Shield and Punch | Pg270 | Shield and Mace | Attacking the Wall |
| 113 | Shielding Fingers | Pg266 | Shielding Hammer Raining Claw combo | Double Asp |
| 114 | Six Hands | Pg266 | Five Swords | Five Swords |
| 115 | Skipping Tackle | Pg295 | Form 5 | Form 5 |
| 116 | Sleeper | Pg292 | Sleeper | Sleeper |
| 117 | Snapping Arm | Pg261 | Snapping Twig | Snapping Twig |
| 118 | Spiraling Wrist | Pg300 | Spiraling Twig | Spiraling Wrist |
| 119 | Straddling the Leg | Pg300 | Squatting Sacrifice | N/A |
| 120 | Sweeping the Leg | Pg301 | N/A | N/A |
| 121 | Taming the Fist | Pg269 | Taming the Mace | Passing Wind |
| 122 | The Nutcracker | Pg290 | Bowing to Buddha | Kneeling Tiger |
| 123 | Thrusting Blade | Pg284 | Thrusting Lance | Locking the Gate |
| 124 | Thrusting Palm | Pg287 | Thrusting Salute | Blocking the Kick |
| 125 | Thrusting Thumbs | Pg298 | Thrusting Prongs | Knee Lift |
| 126 | Thundering Fists | Pg271 | Thundering Hammers | Thundering Hammers |
| 127 | Training the Bears | Pg308 | Reprimanding the Bears | Covering the Moon |
| 128 | Triggered Palm | Pg260 | Triggered Salute | Aiming the Spear |
| 129 | Tripping Leg | Pg298 | Tripping Arrow | Reaching for the Moon |
| 130 | Turn of Fate | Pg262 | Twist of Fate | Parting the Reeds |
| 131 | Turning the Cross | Pg249 | Fatal Cross | Bridging the Gap |
| 132 | Turning Windmills | Pg276 | Circling Windmills | Long 4 |
| 133 | Twin Lapel Grab | Pg255 | Twin Kimono | Kimono Grab variation |
| 134 | Twins of Aggression | Pg261 | N/A | N/A |
| 135 | Twins of Destruction | Pg256 | Destructive Twins | Two-Headed Serpent |
| 136 | Twirling Fist | Pg274 | Twirling Hammers | Reversing Hammers |
| 137 | Twisted Gun | Pg285 | Twisted Rod | Covering the Flame |
| 138 | Twisted Wrist | Pg251 | Twisted Twig | Attacking Temple |
| 139 | Twisting the Gift | Pg248 | Gift of Destiny | Chinese Thumbscrew |
| 140 | Unexpected Blade | Pg283 | Unfurling Lance | Chinese Fan |
| 141 | Unrolling Crane | Pg290 | Unfurling Crane | Drums of Manchu |
| 142 | Untwirling Pendulum | Pg293 | Unwinding Pendulum | Checking the Tide |
| 143 | Wraparound | Pg258 | Obscure Claws | Hidden Fist |

***Go to BarryBBarker.com for Reference Videos***

# HAND, WRIST, & ARM GRAB ATTACKS

Attacker grabs hands, wrists, and/or the arms with their hands in various ways and from different directions. The initial control and manipulation attempt is always countered in a way that borrows any force they give, causes a release, relieves pressure, and/or traps their hand(s), while checking our self against their potential follow up with an awareness to affect their body position, posture, and balance.

The presumption with any one-handed hand grab attack is that the opponent's opposite hand will be striking in some way. The initial move therefore must immediately defend that possibility by putting something in the way, moving to a safer angle, and/or affecting their posture and balance, while hopefully causing them simultaneous pain. Once the attack is effectively neutralized then offensive follow-ups will be more successful.

## ONE-HAND WRIST GRABS FROM THE FRONT
GLANCING POKE (*Glancing Spear*) Pg 245
GRIPPING WRIST (*Gripping Talon*) Pg 246
CROSSING GRAB (*Crossing Talon*) Pg 246
ENTANGLED ARM A (*Entangled Wing*) Pg 247
ENTANGLED ARM B (*Bow of Compulsion*) Pg 247

## HANDSHAKE ATTACKS
DESTRUCTIVE GIFT (*Gift of Destruction*) Pg 248
TWISTING THE GIFT (*Gift of Destiny*) Pg 248
RETURNING THE GIFT (*Gift in Return/Broken Gift*) Pg 249

## TWO-HAND WRIST GRABS FROM THE FRONT
BEGGING PALMS (*Begging Hands*) Pg 249
TURNING THE CROSS (*Fatal Cross*) Pg 249
DESPERATE FISTS (*Desperate Falcons*) Pg 250
DARTING FIST (*Darting Mace*) Pg 250
TWISTED WRIST (*Twisted Twig*) Pg 251
LOCKED ARM (*Locked Wing*) Pg 251

## HAND & WRIST GRABS FROM THE REAR
HAMMERLOCK (*Hammerlock/Flight to Freedom*) Pg 252
CROSSED ARMS (*Crossed Twigs*) Pg 252

## ONE-HAND WRIST GRABS FROM THE FRONT
**GLANCING POKE** (*Glancing Spear*)
**Right to Left Straight Wrist Grab from 12**

1. Lift L hand palm to you, R reaches under grabs back of his R thumb base, turn his thumb down (*Cross Thumb Wrist Twist releases grip & affects posture – Cross Wrist Finger Trap from Gripping Wrist interchangeable here*), R back (12 LNB).

2. L rev bow sliding your L hand out from his grip (*possible finger tweak*) under your R armpit w/R hand around to his medial wrist.

3. LNB pulling his R wrist to L Out elbow his R ribs (*or face if his arm drops or shorter opponent*), L hand lifts outside his R elbow to check.

4. R hand on L *(hands stacked on his R arm)*, mod LNB pushing arm down to his groin *("glancing poke")*, LFB w/R 4-finger eye poke *(shifts his weight back)*, L checks R arm.

5. L arm across his chest *(optional R-R wrist grab)* w/gauge step R *(4:30 RFB)*, L front crossover sweep R leg *(4:30 front twist)* pushing him high w/L *(unbalance or to ground)*.
Extension Begins Here

6. Un-pivot CW *(L heel/R ball)*, possible R wrist hook w/your L arm *(hyper-extends elbow against your L side)* to 9 R rev Cat circling R arm over his head *(or out whipping BKS thru R kidney)*, R rear spinning leg sweep thru back of R leg w/R In heel palm his chest driving him onto his back at 10:30 *(ending in 10:30 LFB)*.

7. R down round ball kick solar plexus *(or best available)*, front crossover out exits to 6.

## GRIPPING WRIST *(Gripping Talon)*
### Left to Right Straight Wrist Grab from 12

1. R hand and wrist under your L armpit wrapping L arm under his L hand *(your L radius bone against his knuckles)*, hinge your L hand up to your L ear *(Cross Wrist Finger Trap w/R forearm & bicep muscle – Cross Thumb Wrist Twist from Glancing Poke interchangeable here)* turning your shoulders slightly against his finger joints *(your L)* affects his posture and possibly injures his fingers.

2. L countergrab his L wrist stepping R forward inside his L foot *(12 R side horse)* w/R Out elbow *(possible finger rip)* into his L rib cage.

3. L rear crossover step outside his L foot *(12 rear twist stance)* w/R outward whipping BKS thru his groin or solar plexus.

4. R rev cat, R rear sliding leg sweep *(12 R rev bow)* inside his L knee w/R radius side wrist strike his R mastoid hooking over the back of his neck pulling him down in front.

5. As his head is forced down from the previous sweep and neck strike do a right upward knee kick into his face (timed with head movement).

6. R front crossover to 4:30 w/R down palm strike onto the back of his R elbow anchoring his R wrist to your R hip then exit towards 3.
Extension Begins Here

6. L rear crossover (9 front twist) still w/L wrist in L hand as R reaches over his head to hook his chin, anchor R forearm over his neck and upper back.

7. Un-pivot to 9 LNB w/R hand/arm pressure turns his head over his R shoulder *(face down to face up)*, his weight falls back, step thru back L *(9 RFB)* pulling his back against top of your R thigh/knee, L-R In down hammerfist his L then R collarbones.

8. Offensive cover L to 6 LFB *(your L)* w/R horiz palm strike under his chin to drive his head and back onto the ground in front of you.

9. (Kicks connect in bouncing manner) R inv TSK throat/chin, R front stomp stomach, R step over his body next to L hip w/L down knee drop on sternum (or collarbone).

10. Cover L w/R down knee onto solar plexus, R front crossover his body exit 4:30.

## CROSSING GRAB *(Crossing Talon)*
### Right-to-Right Cross Wrist Grab from 12

1. *(Fake Handshake can setup)*. L pins back of R grab, pull *(if resisted, R elbow bends)*, R hand outside over R wrist *(countergrab wristlock)*, down pressure drops him.

2. Whether or not a successful wristlock, step R to 3 RFB w/L In forearm to back of his R elbow holding his R wrist against your R hip *(his L hand to the ground from pressure)*

3. Step L forward placing your knee/shin against his R hip *(possible knee strike)* w/L Out elbow to his R temple *(skip if bent too low)*, L underhand heel palm his R jaw hinge.

4. Hook and grab his chin wL then drop your left elbow down onto his upper spine while pulling up on his chin *(fulcrum)* to turn his head *(tweaking his neck)*.

5. Slide L elbow down his spine then L overhead down elbow on back/spine *(mid-thoracic)*, L down heel palm strike onto the base of his skull *(GV16, UB10, or GB20)*.

6. L hand grabs over L side of his head/neck, still holding his R wrist in your R hand, adjust to LFB pulling him into R front knee kick into best available face/head target.
Extension Starts Here

7. After knee kick step back w/Down pressure on his R elbow joint w/L hand *(pulling him forward)* then L hand joins R grabbing back of his R hand for an out wristlock.

8. L rear step-thru to 7:30 w/Out wristlock throw sending him to his back *(7:30)*, R step over his body w/down ax kick to his solar plexus *(stops him from rolling out of wristlock throw)* then R foot on ground over in front of his stomach.

9. Apply pressure to his R elbow w/L down knee drop onto his neck.

10. Bounce off cover CCW, rotate his wrist out, drop your R knee on his chest pulling his R elbow around against your L shin *(possible break)*.

11. Re-grab his R hand with your two hands rotating it inward so his R elbow faces your R hip as your L foot then steps over his head.

12. Front rotating twist *(CW)* traps R wrist at L hip as R leg rotates into his R elbow.

13. R back over his head *(possible head stomp)*, L rear step thru to exit.

## ENTANGLED ARM A *(Entangled Wing)*
### Right Figure 4 Wrist Lock from 12 - Loose

1. Immediately check your wrist pressing your L palm into your R palm for support *(and possibly your forehead against your own hand)* against the lock.

2. Lift R elbow between his two arms *(R Up diag elbow)* to above his R collarbone stepping forward RNB, side of your head pins his L forearm to your R elbow crook cinching down his arm *(trapping his arm)*.

3. Reach over his arms with your L hand to grab the meaty base of his thumb *(thenar eminence)* with a L rear crossover outside of his left foot.

4. Un-pivot *(L ball, R heel)* to 12 L side horse turning his L hand palm up over your R shoulder *(over shoulder elbow lock)* locking down his medial wrist w/your R elbow crease w/L back elbow to his L kidney *(palm up, moving him behind and to your R side)*.

5. L grabs his R wrist, R out elbow strike to his sternum *(palm down)*.

6. R front crossover to 3 w/R in forearm strike to his R elbow to exit.

<u>Extension Begins Here</u>

6. Hold his L wrist w/L hand for entire technique *(be aware of his L elbow)*, slide your L foot next to your R adjusting to R rev cat w/R downward outward BKS into his groin.

7. R rear sliding leg sweep to 10:30 *(4:30 LFB)* inside his L knee w/R up lifting BKS to his nose, R hand over L side of his neck *(neck lever)*.

8. Force his head down onto R then L up knee kicks *(chicken knee)*, step down L near R foot pulling R hand out under his L arm w/R forearm against back of his L armpit.

9. R rear sliding leg sweep thru inside R knee pushing back of his L armpit w/R forearm *(causing him to bend)*.

10. Your L hand turns his L palm up *(his L elbow points back towards your R hip)* as your R hand grabs over his R shoulder to pull his arm towards you w/R forward step thru using R thigh *(or hip)* to break his elbow as you step forward to exit towards 6.

## ENTANGLED ARM B *(Bow of Compulsion)*
### Right Figure 4 Wrist Lock from 12 - Tight
*(Our palm could face us or towards the opponent)*

1. Check your wrist w/L palm to R *(or back of hand if rev lock)*, possibly w/forehead against your hand for additional support. *(Optional attack & counter from EPAK version: W/R hand extended to check advance he attempts to apply rev finger or wristlock)*.

2. In either case step forward between his feet to 12 RNB w/R forward vert elbow into his solar plexus *(create space)*, drop down pulling R hand and arm down out of hold.

3. Shift L *(R rev wide kneel)* w/R In vert hook punch inside his R knee *(Ahshi Point)*, shift R w/R out whipping BKS to same point on L knee still checking his arms w/L.

4. R up rev handsword his groin reaching L over L side of his neck.

5. Your right hand joins your L around the L side of his head then stand up *(or jump)* with a L roundhouse knee to his forehead or temple.

<u>Extension Begins Here</u>

4. Another right inward vertical hook punch to his right medial knee.

5. Stand up w/R out raking knuckle strike thru R side of his nose adjusting to a RFB w/L inv horiz palm *(fingers in)* strike to his sternum.

6. RNB w/R In hammerfist slicing thru the left side of his nose followed closely by a left outward two finger slice across his left eye.

7. Continue circling R arm back thru chamber then R In elbow thru his L jaw w/L In heel palm his R jaw *(sandwiching effect or hit his right temple with L to tweak his neck)*.

8. Use rev motion from w/R Out *(slightly obscure)* elbow strike thru his chin followed by R Out heel palm R side of his jaw that becomes a R outward claw thru his face.

9. L In heel palm to R jaw into L In windshield wiper finger slices thru his eyes then checks down his body line as R hand circles overhead and weight shifts back.

10. From 12 R rear bow R front scoop kick his groin w/R down heel palm claw thru eyes and nose circling R hand until it up in front of your R shoulder, L hand checks.

11. As your weight settles forward to a 12 RNB *(after the scoop kick)* R inverted horizontal palm strike *(fingers in)* to his sternum *(Ren17)* or over his Heart *(potentially lethal targets done this way so practice carefully)* then right rear step thru to exit.

# HANDSHAKE ATTACKS

*(Overlap & press thumb pad across top of their 2nd thumb joint to apply painful force)*

**DESTRUCTIVE GIFT** *(Gift of Destruction)*

**Right Handshake from 12**

1. L step *(or hop)* forward outside his R foot *(10:30)*, R knee kick his groin or R thigh pulling his R hand to your R hip *(CW hand rotation)* striking *(or checking)* back of his R elbow w/L In palm strike.

2. R foot forward inside his R foot, your R knee buckles his R knee *(1:30)* while your L hand pins his R arm to his side with a R In elbow his sternum.

Extension Starts Here

3. Adjust L foot back off angle to 10:30 R close kneel w/L In heel palm thru his R jaw hinge then L In windshield wiper strike and slice.

4. R hand follows L w/R Out raking hammerfist strike thru his R jaw *(still in R close kneel)* w/L Out heel palm to his Ltemple *(neck tweak)*.

5. Adjust to a RNB with a right inward hammerfist strike glancing thru the left side of his nose (these 4 strikes happen close together).

6. In the same motion adjust to a rev RNB *(hip shift)* dropping your weight slightly w/R down diagonal hammerfist onto his solar plexus.

7. Right toe to left into left spinning side thrust kick to the front of his left knee then left front crossover towards 4:30 to exit.

**TWISTING THE GIFT** *(Gift of Destiny)*

**Right Handshake Grab from 12**

**Opponent Not Punching**

1. Grab back of his hand w/L, step L outside his R foot *(toe out)* rotating his hand internally, his R elbow lifts, and weight shifts to his R heel.

2. R step to 10:30 *(toe in)* ducking under his R arm twisting his wrist more *(L elbow checks R lat muscle keeping his elbow 90° & up)* w/Up Rev Wrist Twist *(he's on his toes)*.

3. Left rear step thru toe out to 10:30 causing him to walk backwards into a wall or proceed to move #4 except with takedown to 10:30.

**Opponent Punching with Opposite Hand**

1. L grabs back of hand, R forward between his feet w/R forward horiz elbow his L arm to stop punc. Hit other targets if he is not punching.

2. L rear rotating twist *(L heel/R toe)* turning his R hand internally and up ducking under R elbow *(Up rev wrist lock)* moving hand from front of your R shoulder to front of L *(L elbow at his R lat muscle keeps arm 90° as R grip adjusts R middle finger presses palm side of his R little finger palm joint & w/L middle finger pulling pisiform hand bone)*.

3. R toe to L *(toes in)*, step back L toe out to 7:30 *(off switch w/cover step)* twisting and lifting against his wrist *(he walks backwards)*.

4. Time his backward movement, R foot behind him *(R rev cat)*, R rear sliding leg sweep behind his R leg or both *(only one in training)* trips to the ground.

5. R hand holds grip, follow him to ground *(adjust where he lands)* w/R down knee drop R ribs *(Liver)* drives his R elbow to ground, bend, and twist hand CW.

Extension Begins Here

6. Stand R pulling his R hand up twisting CW as L hand slides down to push his R elbow as legs help turn him over *(on his stomach with his R arm in your right hand)*.

7. R step over his body w/L knee drop on his back holding him down w/back of his R wrist in pocket of your R hip while L hand picks up his L wrist.

8. Place back of his L wrist in pocket of your L hip, turn L w/inside of your knees outside his elbows *(opponent is face down with his arms lifted behind his back with you straddled over him controlling his wrists with your hands)*.

9. Move forward as needed to lock his arms in place, sit on his back *(opponent on stomach w/two arms straight up behind his back in pockets of your hips w/your knees pressing against his elbows w/his palms up while holding and pressing his wrists towards his head as desired for control or to cause damage).*

**RETURNING THE GIFT** *(Gift in Return)*
**Right Handshake Grab from 12**
1. Grab back of his R hand w/L, your fingers down grabbing his hand.
**Opponent Not Punching**
Pull his hand up level w/your R shoulder extending his arm, L steps forward *(12 side horse)* outside his R arm w/L up flapping elbow *(as R drops)* striking under his R elbow.
**Opponent Punching with Opposite Hand**
Step forward L outside his R leg *(your head outside his R shoulder)* to a 12 L close kneel jamming his R hand w/your two hands into his groin.
2. R rear cross 10:30 *(R foot outside his R)*, unpivot *(L heel/R ball)* moving his R arm overhead from front L shoulder to front R, R rev Cat behind R leg *(10:30 R cat)* his elbow higher than his hand w/your R elbow against his R scapula or spine *(arches him back)*.
3. Your two hands pull his R arm down w/R rear sliding leg sweep thru back of his R leg or both *(one leg in practice)* slamming his back to the ground at 10:30, your R hand releases to chamber *(your L holds his R wrist)*.
4. Gauge as needed to jam your L shin against his R elbow dropping R knee on his R rib cage *(Liver)* w/R down 2-finger vert poke to throat *(sternal notch)*.
Extension Begins Here
5. Your R hand mirrors your L holding his R wrist. #6-11 kicks connect in a sequence bouncing off the targets building in intensity.
6. Right inverted side stomp kick onto his throat.
7. Right side stomp kick onto the top of his right hip, thigh, or knee.
8. Right inverted side stomp kick into the pocket of his right shoulder.
9. Right downward heel stomp kick onto his solar plexus.
10. R foot then steps over his body turning w/R down knee drop onto his sternum (L close kneel to 9) pulling his R elbow around your L shin.
11. Pivot L open, R shin kick his R elbow, R front twist, shin braces R elbow as both hands pull his wrist (breaks elbow), L toe to toe switch exit to 10:30.

# TWO-HAND WRIST GRABS FROM THE FRONT

**BEGGING PALMS** *(Begging Hands)*
**Two-Hand Double Wrist Grab from 12**
1. Step back L 12 mod RNB clapping palms together, lift between his grip w/dbl Out hooking checks over wrists pulling your elbows to sides and him slightly forward off balance *(counter grab in extension)*.
2. R Cat w/R then L front snap kicks *(Chicken kick in extension)* his groin/lower abdomen to LNB with Universal Check.
Extension Starts Here
3. Step forward from L front kick to 12 modified LNB w/dbl inward palm slap *(ear box)* to both of his ears immediately clinching his neck *(Thai clinch style)*.
4. Right rear crossover to 10:30 then L rear sliding leg sweep thru the front inside angle of his R knee cranking his head down to face you.
5. R hand slides to back of his head *(both hands hold his head on same side)*, L front knee his face step to 6 turning R *(spinning)* looking over R shoulder.
6. R stiff leg lifting kick between his legs *(or side thrust his knee)* w/R Up rev heel palm his nose; R front crossover step out exit to 6.

**TURNING THE CROSS**
**Two-Hand Double Wrist Grab from 12**
1. Step back L to 12 mod RNB jerking your arms down and slightly back *(pulls him forward off balance)* moving to dbl In hooking checks over his wrists *(optional wrist flex lock in ext)* clears his arms as your hands go to chamber.
2. Push drag forward with a dbl horiz palm strike to his floating ribs.
Extension Starts Here

2. Push drag forward w/dbl vert middle finger fist snapping strikes into 6th rib spaces under each nipple (Lv14).

3. R crossover L w/dbl BKS his temples, use his face as a track to slide your hands back towards your chest until space to do crossed dbl 2-finger eye poke.

4. R cross grab his R trapezius muscles (or clothing), forearm under his chin w/L arm cross grab his L trapezius muscle (or clothing) for crossed arm choke.

5. Step forward L (off switch) R lifts his chin as L pulls L shoulder forward to turn him until back to you (&/or move yourself around), R hand hooks his chin as L forearm checks his back shoulder line as your R steps back to a LFB.

6. R front knee kick his lower spine then L front knee his middle spine, chicken kick (2nd knee optional and/or R TSK back of his R knee w/#7.

7. L side thrust kick (or R TSK) back of his R knee, L pushing R shoulder, R pulling chin over R shoulder (neck tweak), L front crossover exit towards 6.

## DESPERATE FISTS
### Two-Hand Double Wrist Grab from 12
1. Circle hands CW, R step back to 12 LNB w/L checking his right (possible grab) pushing it over his left while chambering your right hand.

2. Right straight vertical punch to nose or sternum.

<u>Extension Starts Here</u>

1. Circle hands CW bringing back of his R hand to your R hand grabing the webbing sliding your L hand to his elbow pinning back of his R hand to your chest (wrist flex lock) gauging as needed to force him down to his knees.

2. Gauge L foot forward w/R In elbow to nose, R front knee his solar plexus, R step back offline as L grips back of his R elbow (C grip), R wrist in R hand.

3. Offensive cover step to a 6 RFB driving him down onto his face.

4. Step L over R shoulder (possible glancing heel kick head) toe-in above his R shoulder as L feels for elbow crease, step back R above his L shoulder bending his elbow until R hand behind his back (Hammerlock) holding wrist and elbow driving L knee down on his R scapula, both hands pulling up on his arm dislocating shoulder.

5. R down knee back of his neck w/R down palm his R scapula.

6. Stand w/R glancing heel kick thru inside (medial) angle of his R scapula followed by R down stomp kick onto that same target.

7. Hop off previous stomp to your L foot followed by R down stomping rear kick to back of his neck, then R front crossover exit to 7:30.

## DARTING FIST (Darting Mace)
### Two-Hand Grab to Right Wrist from 12
Note: The grip of this attack could be with space between wrists (Option A) or overlapped with no space between wrists (Option B). This determines whether the grabbed hand moves up between their hands or outside their right wrist.

1. L foot forward to 12 LNB lifting R hand up between his wrists (A) to your R shoulder trapping inside his R wrist w/L In forearm strike his R elbow joint (scissoring effect), or (B) R hand up outside their R wrist countergrab w/L Inward forearm strike.

2. Glance thru back of his R elbow w/vert thrust punch his R temple (or palm face).

3. L half down block his arms, LFB w/R vertical thrust punch to his sternum.

4. R front step-thru transitioning thru R cat (optional R front knee to groin) w/L obscure handsword strike (goes under your R hand) to throat as R hand chambers.

5. Complete step-thru to a 12 RNB with a right straight palm strike to his face (best available target) with a left-hand position check.

<u>Extension Begins Here</u>

6. L front crossover forward (front twist stance) circling R hand to forward down hammerfist onto his R ribs (appendix area) while L hand checks his right arm.

7. Un-pivot (L heel/R ball) LNB w/L In heel palm his L jaw (or mastoid) R to chamber.

8. Use the previous strike as a catalyst, rotating L front twist w/R vert hook punch thru L temple into R In elbow down thru his L jaw into R forward hammerfist to his groin (3 strikes in one down settling motion). L hand check could be applying a face claw.

9. Un-pivot to LNB w/R obscure elbow under chin holding his chin w/R hand L uppercut punch (or single knuckle punch at Ren23).

10. Weight to R *(12 L rear bow)*, L front scoop kick thru groin, switch w/hop R front push kick solar plexus *(chicken kick)* clears him away, step forward or back to NB.

## **TWISTED WRIST** *(Twisted Twig)*
### *Right Outward Wrist Lock from 12*
1. Half down block top of his thumb joints pulling heel of R palm to your R chamber (levers out of hold). If lock secured support palm to palm before levering out.
2. RNB forward w/R elbow up under chin, L position check his R arm.
3. Keep check shifting heels to opponent (R mod horse) w/R back elbow solar plexus.
4. R rev bow, R back hammerfist groin. 7:30 Front crossover out to RNB facing him.
Extension Begins Here
3. L rear crossover to R rear twist to 1:30 *(outside his L if in front)* w/R downward elbow strike onto his sternum *(CV17)*.
4. Transition thru R rev Cat w/R rear sliding leg sweep thru inside angle of his L knee w/R back hammerfist his groin and L palm his neck/collarbone crease then checks.
5. As he bends from the sweep R up lifting punch his nose, R arm under holds his throat and neck *(rev headlock)* w/L hand, grabbing your R to cinch choke opposite side.
6. Pull his head down *(turn his face towards you)* w/R then L chicken knee kicks to his R temple then L foot back *(R close kneel to 7:30)*.
7. Un-pivot to 4:30 horse w/snap-mare head throw flipping *(drop R knee to ground and pull training partners over)* him over *(or around)* your R shoulder until he is on his back with his head between your legs and his feet away.
8. Circle R arm overhead, drop R knee on his R collarbone w/R overhead down hammerfist back under his chin *(your R arm path between your own legs)* to 10:30.
9. Bounce off previous knee to 1:30 w/L down knee drop onto his L collarbone w/L inv vert punch down onto his nose.
10. Bounce up turning CCW in the air landing on your L outside his R shoulder at 10:30 w/R down roundhouse kick onto his solar lexus.
11. Right front crossover sweep kick thru his face exiting towards 4:30.

## **LOCKED ARM** *(Locked Wing)*
### *Right Inward Wrist Lock from 12*
1. R arm rolls w/hold as you step forward R CCW in front of his R (toe in) to rev RNB, turning your R arm behind your own back *(Hammerlock)* w/L rear step thru to 12 rev LNB crashing your L leg into front of his R knee w/L Out elbow then claw thru his face.
2. Wrap L arm around his R elbow *(possibly between his arms)* w/wraparound arm bar turning your shoulders R *(12 mod RNB)* pulling him around you slightly.
3. Before his weight steps step back R *(to 10:30)* 4:30 RFB dipping L shoulder down in towards your R leg w/force against his R elbow *(levering him around and down in front)*.
4. Circle R arm to overhead down heel palm on his spine sandwiching body w/R Up knee to his chest *(sandwich could also be face/back of head or throat/back of neck)*.
Extension Begins here
5. From knee step forward w/R vert elbow thru R side of his neck, hooking over to grab his chin *(or front of his L shoulder)* w/L reaching over his body grabbing his L hip bone *(or clothing or a meaty area of his lower torso)*.
6. Pull him into L front knee his R ribs, step back L RFB pulling and anchoring your arms turning him over *(from face down to face up)* onto your R knee putting your L knee on the ground *(watch his L arm as he flips over if unable to check previously)*.
7. L down claw his face circling R arm overhead down hammerfist his sternum as L holds him on R knee *(if L arm was not trapped previously adjust L hand accordingly)*.
8. Step forward L foot to R w/R forward vert elbow to L side of his neck pushing him off of your R knee onto his back *(face up w/his head at 6 you are standing next to his L)*.
9. Step R towards his head w/R Out whip BKS under his chin, drag L foot up (step drag) w/L down knee onto best available torso target w/L palm under his chin (or face).
10. Bounce up off his body landing w/L down foot stomp onto his throat (your R foot above his head) then exit to 6 w/L TSK thru his face.

# HAND & WRIST GRABS FROM THE REAR

**HAMMERLOCK** *(Flight to Freedom)*

### Right Reverse Arm Lock from 6

1. Step back L *(6 L rev NB)* into his R knee w/L back underhand heel palm his groin, rebound L Out elbow his face while R hand counter grabs his R wrist behind your back.
2. Pivot R foot open *(on your heel)*, step L to 1:30 w/optional R side thrust kick into front of his R knee or ribs *(in Extension toe to toe switch with arm whip, no kick)*.
3. L toe to R lifting R hand up w/L, grab above back of his R elbow w/L, R back *(7:30 LNB completes Off switch)* his R wrist palm against R hip w/L hand holding his R elbow.
4. R Up front kick his chest or groin, R step *(12 RFB)* w/down armbar driving him down onto his face where he is held in place.

<u>Extension Begins Here</u>

4. Follow R Up front kick w/L Up front kick *(chicken kick)* his chest holding wrist, weight settles forward to 7:30 LNB w/L down forearm onto his R elbow joint.
5. *(Crossing Grab)* L Out elbow R temple, L back underhand heel palm his R jaw hinge, hook his chin, drop your L elbow *(neck tweak)*, L arm down along spine, L overhead down elbow spine, L down heel palm R mastoid, grab his head, R knee face.
6. After R knee step back down w/down pressure holding the back of his R elbow while continuing to hold his R wrist in your R hand.
7. L rev close kneel w/L up hook kick chest, L front crossover dragging him to 1:30 w/R up hook kick his groin *(or solar plexus)*, step out R, L up hook kick solar plexus or face *(3 up hook kicks dragging him)*, L crossover to front twist *(rear twist to opponent)*.
8. Step out R to 1:30 LFB levering him face down w/armbar pressure, L front crossover thru the back of his head *(TSK)* exiting to 1:30.


**CROSSED ARMS** *(Crossed Twigs)*

### Two-Hand Double Wrist Grab from 6

Note: This control and compliance specialty attack has two wrists grabbed from behind then jerked down and back causing a weight shift towards the heels and down then rolled over face down arms behind back. The first move in defense establishes base so may require a step back. Short Form 3 steps forward so is also in standard technique.

1. Step L forward towards 1:30 *(R reverse bow to 7:30)* grabbing his two wrists from underneath in your hands pulling him forward and slightly sideways off balance.
2. Hold wrists turning back to 7:30 RNB w/R Out elbow his face throwing his R arm over and down across his L to cancel him *(L hand holds his L wrist behind your back)*.
3. R hand releases his wrist circling a R overhead downward elbow to his upper spine *(probably between his shoulder blades)* then pushdown w/R elbow.
4. Release L wrist *(behind your back)* then circle L arm overhead *(gauge L foot as needed)* adjusting to 9 RFB w/L overhead down elbow his low spine *(probably L4-L5 forces his hips down)* then push down to cancel *(both elbows pressing his spine down)*.
5. L Up knee his R ribs w/dbl down heel palm his back *(L hand strikes his L kidney, possible skin pinch w/R strike onto his R rhomboid muscle)*.

<u>Extension Begins Here</u>

6. R front knee kick then R front snap kick inside his L knee, step forward to 9 RNB w/R forward vert elbow his R jaw hinge *(push)* hooking R hand over his neck *(pull)*.
7. Turn 180° L to 9 R rev close kneel holding his head down w/R hand then R rear scoop kick thru L side of his face, R toe to L *(spin CCW)*.
8. Spin L rear sliding leg sweep inside angle of his R knee at 6 w/universal check at R shoulder to keep upright *(possible L back underhand heel palm groin w/R palm to face)*.
9. L foot to 10:30 LFB L hand holding his L shoulder *(fingers in)* w/R straight palm thru his R mastoid *(push)*, hook over back of his neck *(pull)* pulling him into R front knee to his face chambering R hand.
10. Weight settles to 9 RNB w/R inv palm to his R jaw hinge *(stay connected)* your L hand pushing forward down against his R shoulder.
11. Continue pushing his face back, up and around *(him looking up and over his L shoulder)* as L foot slides *(L off rear turn then cover to 12)* pushing back of his head to the ground w/R hand *(L hand at his R shoulder)* dropping your R knee on his Liver.
12. Right TSK thru his face while crossing out towards 12 to exit.

# BODY, NECK, & HEAD GRAB ATTACKS

Attacker uses hands to grab the torso, shoulders, hair, or neck, with pushing, pulling, or holding energy. If attacked with a one-hand grab presume they are punching / striking with their free hand.

Keys to defending this type of attack involve pinning the grabbing hand(s) to the attacked surface in a way that makes their fingers, wrists, and elbows vulnerable while riding with or interrupting their attacking energy. This is done while avoiding any striking motion, beginning to control and manipulate their body center, and hopefully causing them some pain and mental distraction.

### ONE-HAND GRABS FROM THE FRONT
GRABBING HAIR *(Clutching Feathers)* Pg 253
CONQUERING ARM *(Conquering Shield)* – plus Ground Option Pg 254
FALLING EAGLE *(Falling Falcon)* – plus Ground Option Pg 254

### TWO-HAND GRABS FROM THE FRONT
FIST OF AGGRESSION *(Mace of Aggression)* Pg 255
RAKING FIST *(Raking Mace)* – plus Ground Option Pg 255
TWIN LAPEL GRAB *(Twin Kimono)* Pg 255
ASCENDING FROM DEATH *(Heavenly Ascent)* Pg 256
TWINS OF DESTRUCTION *(Destructive Twins)* Pg 256
BLINDING VICE *(Blinding Sacrifice)* Pg 257

### ONE HAND GRABS FROM THE SIDE
HIDDEN ELBOW *(Obscure Wing)* Pg 257
WRAPAROUND *(Obscure Claws)* Pg 258
HIDDEN HAND *(Obscure Sword)* Pg 258

### GRABS FROM THE REAR
CIRCLING ELBOW *(Circling Wing)* Pg 258
CROSS OF DESTRUCTION *(Cross of Destruction)* Pg 259
REAR BELT GRAB *(Menacing Twirl)* Pg 259
DUCKING DRAGON *(Short Form 2)* Pg 259

### ONE-HAND GRABS FROM THE FRONT
**GRABBING HAIR** *(Clutching Feathers)*
***Left Hand Hair Grab from 12***
1. Grab and pin his L hand tightly to your head w/your L hand *(your L thumb in thumb/index webbing of their R hand w/your middle finger between their ulna and pisiform bone)* as you step back L to a 12 R close kneel stance chambering your R hand.
2. Without hesitation adjust to a RNB extending his arm breaking his balance w/Out ulnar wrist flex lock to his L wrist *(cancels his potential R punch)* w/R vert thrust punch to his ribs *(middle finger fist in Ext pressed into his L armpit at Ht1 or middle ribs at GB21/22)*.
3. R Out block inside his L arm becoming ext out block clears his arm squaring his body, gauge forward as needed to R close kneel w/L invert horiz punch to solar plexus.
4. RNB w/R In hammerfist his L temple, jaw or nose as L hand checks their R arm.
Extension Begins Here
5. Continue thru previous target adjusting L foot forward to 12 R rev close kneel w/R back hammerfist strike to his groin *(Left hand checking or possible palm strike)*.

6. R rear scoop kick up thru his groin, bounce R foot off the ground then R rear thrust kick into his abdomen to drive him away, R front cross exiting to 6.

**CONQUERING ARM** *(Conquering Shield)*
*Left Hand Choke against wall from 12*
   1. *(Back against wall)* Open L foot, slide R foot to L *(10:30 R cat)*, L traps inside L wrist *(C grip)* w/R In forearm strike *(In block)* outside L elbow *(timing like hands clapping)*.
   2. Hold L wrist as R arm slides thru L elbow extending above his L arm *(possible R punch face)* w/R front snap kick inside R knee *(use wall to brace for kicking leverage)*.
   3. *(Small finger can be rotated up to expose elbow joint but not in practice)* Settle weight from kick to 10:30 RNB *(marriage of gravity)* w/R down elbow bending *(or on side of elbow)*.
   4. R Up elbow chin, R down heel palm nose, claw eyes *(L hand holds L wrist)*.
   5. R hand his L wrist Out to your R *(squares his body)*, L palm *(regular, horiz, fingers in, or punch)* sternum or solar plexus.
Extension Begins Here
   5. Continue holding L wrist w/L collapsing his L elbow w/R forearm.
   6. RFB w/L In Elbow chin, L knee to groin stepping down L next to R.
   7. Cover step back R pulling his L arm while pushing his throat w/L forearm driving his back into the wall followed by L knee to groin or forward knee pinning torso to wall.
Optional face to wall: R arm hooks under his L elbow & armpit *(Kimura Lock)* moving L foot back along wall, cover L driving his head into wall, R arm out of hold, R palm low spine pushing his hips against wall, R knee low spine, step down R moves 8-11 to back of body.
   8. Step down from L knee moving L w/R In stiff-arm punch face/head.
   9. Step R w/L uppercut punch chin/head followed by L knee to inside L thigh *(or R if behind)* stepping L down w/L down elbow onto top of sternum or spine *(if face to wall)*.
   10. Gauge R foot to L w/L Up elbow chin, L rear sliding leg sweep inside R knee *(in front or L knee if behind sweeping leg along wall)* w/L back hammerfist to groin or kidney.
   11. L rear crossover to 12 *(front twist)*, un-pivot *(R heel / L ball)* w/L Out raking hammerfist thru nose, R In raking hammerfist temple, unwinding into R side thrust kick sternum or spine *(if behind)* pinning him to wall, cross out to exit.

**Ground Option:** If Mounted w/L one-hand extended arm choke at neck or lapel pressing into floor. L traps inside L wrist w/R In block outside L elbow (hyper-extending). R slides over then down collapsing their elbow, R Out handsword R side of neck, reattach to arm w/L knee to tailbone *(pull him forward)*, R foot posts outside his L ankle, bridge rolls them over putting you in Top Guard, use tenderizing or ground & pound to escape *(Closed Guard: elbow-punch-palm strike/press inner knees & groin, pinch tender skin areas, heel palm bladder, knee tailbone, Open Guard: elbow-punch-palm legs, knee on groin or side, kick inner legs, crossover knee drop on legs, etc)*.

**FALLING EAGLE** *(Falling Falcon)*
*Right Hand Grabs Left Front Shoulder from 12*
   1. L pins R hand & wrist to L shoulder, step forward outside his R foot *(10:30 RFB)* w/R forward vert elbow *(or palm)* up into his R armpit *(shift his weight towards his R heel)*.
   2. Rotate hips L *(CCW)* to 6 LFB forearm pushing his shoulder while pulling back & down against his R wrist tripping him over your R leg onto his back with his head at 6.
   3. R counter grab back R wrist covering R *(CW)* w/L down heel palm back of R elbow.
   4. Slide L hand up to grab his R wrist next to your R hand *(resembles L handed batters grip)* lifting L knee up above his face, L side thrust *(stomp)* kick down onto his jaw while pulling up on his arm, then L foot to your left at 4:30.
   5. Countergrab back R wrist w/L, twist CCW w/R inside down heel palm back R elbow.
   6. Slide R hand up to grab R wrist w/your L hand *(resembles R handed batters grip)*, open L foot to 4:30, R side of leg kick thru back of his R elbow, R Up heel hook thru R kidney, R down ball kick onto solar plexus *(all while holding his R arm w/your hands)*.
   7. Rotate R foot CW w/R inv side stomp kick on his throat pulling up on his R arm.
   9. Step over his body above his L shoulder throwing his R arm down to your L followed by L inv sweep kick *(TSK)* thru his face as you cross out and exit towards 7:30.

**Ground Option:** If Mounted w/grab attack applied pin R wrist w/L & post L foot outside his R ankle, lifting hips to bridge w/possible R knee strike or push tailbone, w/R hand push to R shoulder rolling him over ending in Top Guard, use tenderizing or ground & pound to escape *(Closed Guard: elbow-punch-palm strike/press inner knees & groin, pinch tender skin areas, heel palm bladder, knee tailbone, Open Guard: elbow-punch-palm legs, knee on groin or side, kick inner legs, crossover knee drop on legs, etc).*

# TWO-HAND GRABS FROM THE FRONT

## FIST OF AGGRESSION *(Mace of Aggression)*
### Two-Hand Lapel Grab Pulling from 12
1. *(Optional L 2-finger In eye rake thru R eye in Ext)* Pin both hands w/L pinning check *(L hand grabs his L hand as L forearm & wrist trap his R arm to your chest)*, step forward RNB borrowing force *(leg check, knee buckle, stomp)* w/R In raking hammerfist L side of nose to R half down block on arms *(R arm collapses outside angle of L elbow joint, LI11).*
2. As head comes forward *(watch for unintentional head butt)* R In elbow thru L jaw.
3. Use reverse motion w/R snapping Out elbow his face *(depends on where he is looking so hit best available target, just not the teeth).*
<u>Extension Begins Here</u>
4. From Out elbow R Out handsword R side of neck *(R carotid or SCM muscles).*
5. Slide R arm down his centerline *(cross body check)* adjusting to 12 RFB w/L vert thrust punch to his sternum *(over your L check).*
6. L step thru front snap kick his groin then steps forward turning L CW *(left toe in).*
7. Continue to turn CW w/R spinning rear thrust kick to best available body target to clear opponent, R front crossover step out towards 6 to exit.

## RAKING FIST *(Raking Mace)*
### Two-Hand Lapel Grab Pulling from 12
1. (Optional L 2-finger In eye rake thru R eye in Ext) Pin both hands w/L pinning check (L hand grabs his L hand as L forearm & wrist trap his R arm to your chest), step forward RNB borrowing force (leg check, knee buckle, stomp) w/R inv horiz snap punch stomach.
2. Circle R hand over his L arm w/R In hammerfist thru L side of his nose into R half down block across top of his arms (strike outside corner of their L elbow crease at LI11).
3. R Out handsword strike R side of his neck (moves #2/3 figure 8 motion in the air).
4. Dbl down In hook clear thru inner forearms (frictional pull) knocks hands off lapel.
5. Push drag forward as needed with R In elbow w/L In heel palm (Extension can stagger St5 & Tai Yang affecting neck) thru to universal check.
<u>Extension Begins Here</u>
6. L hand pivots to L In 2-finger eye slice (R modified NB transition) on way to L cross body check while R arm circles to R inward heel of palm strike (RNB) his L temple.
7. R hand pivots into windshield wiper slices across his eyes, shift back to R rear bow w/R down claw thru eyes w/R front scoop kick his groin, R straight arm behind R hip.
8. Step forward to 12 RNB w/R stiff-armed lifting punch up glancing thru his nose.
9. Circle arm up CW to R In handsword L side neck *(pushes head down and to his R).*
10. L short roundhouse kick *(or knee)* across his nose, exit back to RNB.

**Ground Option:** Mounted w/both hands on neck or lapel, L pins both arms, R hook punch ribs, R hammerfist thru nose & down so forearm collapses their L elbow *(optional Out handsword neck then reattach)*, post L foot outside their R heel, lift hips to bridge &/or drive R knee to push tailbone trolling over ending in Top Guard, use tenderizing or ground & pound to escape *(Closed Guard: elbow-punch-palm strike/press inner knees & groin, pinch tender skin areas, heel palm bladder, knee tailbone, Open Guard: elbow-punch-palm legs, knee on groin or side, kick inner legs, crossover knee drop on legs, etc).*

## TWIN LAPEL GRAB *(Twin Kimono)*
### Two-Hand Lapel Grab Pushing from 12
1. *(Optional L 2-finger In eye rake thru R eye in Extension)* Pin check his hands w/L *(your L grabs over his L, your L forearm and wrist trap his R arm to your chest)* absorbing push stepping back L offline to R rev 45o horse w/R Up forearm strike *(looks like up block)* to L elbow joint *(if elbows are bent do R inside down elbow outside his left elbow).*
2. 10:30 R close kneel w/R Out whip BKS thru solar plexus or groin circling arm up.

3. 10:30 RNB w/R In raking hammerfist thru nose then down to clears arms.

4. R obscure handsword *(or elbow)* up into his throat then universal check.

<u>Extension Begins Here</u>

5. L 10:30 front crossover, R hand slides down checks arms w/L palm under chin.

6. R Up knee kick to groin chambering R w/L left cross body check.

7. R forward to RNB w/R Up rolling forearm strike lifting his chin.

8. Gauge R foot towards 3 *(toes out)* w/R outward heel palm claw to his R jaw.

9. In same flow L pushing sweep *(or Rhouse kick)* inside his L ankle w/L inv horiz palm strike *(fingers in)* thru his R jaw hinge ending with your L toe in *(spinning CW)*.

10. Continue spinning R to R Up stiff leg lifting rear kick into his groin w/R rear Up lifting heel palm under his chin, R front crossover step out towards 4:30 to exit.

## ASCENDING FROM DEATH *(Heavenly Ascent)*
### *Two-Hand Choke Pushing from 12*

1. Step back L to 12 R rev bow w/R inward armpit trap clearing his arms down *(possible hand & finger tweak between your right shoulder & neck)*.

2. Adjust to a 12 RNB with a right outward elbow strike thru his nose.

3. Modified RNB w/R outward whipping BKS thru the right side of his jaw.

4. 12 RFB w/L straight palm under chin *(possible 4 finger eye poke)*, R chambers.

5. Adjust to RNB w/R snapping inv horiz half fist his throat *(or inverted snap punch his stomach)* while L hand checks his arms *(caution with throat strikes)*.

<u>Extension Begins Here</u>

6. R rear step thru to 12 L cat grabbing his wrists w/both hands pulling him off balance.

7. L front kick his groin, R front kick his solar plexus *(chicken kick)* L holding his R wrist cocking R straight arm behind your R hip.

8. R step forward *(opponent bent over)* w/R stiff-armed lifting punch up thru his nose.

9. R down dropping BKS on his nose *(#8/9 are up/down motions)*.

10. In the same arm flow do a R In hammer fist thru L side of his nose.

11. Left rear crossover to a R rear twist stance to 12 with a R outward BKS *(#10/11 are diag in/out, figure 8 motions)* to R side of nose *(or R Out forearm to R side neck)*.

12. R rev cat, R rear sliding leg sweep inside his L knee w/L position check *(possible palm strike or 4-finger poke)* w/R back heel palm his groin, grab testicles w/R hand grip.

13. Rip his groin with your R hand *(followed by possible R rear scoop kick)* then R front crossover step out and thru towards 6 to exit.

## TWINS OF DESTRUCTION *(Destructive Twins)*
### *Two-Hand Choke from 12*

1. R vert horseshoe punch *(R hand inv horiz punch under his L arm to solar plexus w/L overhead punch above his R arm into his nose)* while stepping forward to a 12 RNB.

2. R rear bow, L pushes his R arm down as R/lifts his L arm, step R to 1:30 RFB w/R In/L Out dbl factor parry outside L arm *(clears, possibly tweaking his L elbow)*.

3. L Out 2-finger slice his L eye then grab <u>inside</u> his L wrist, weld back of his wrist against L hip w/L step to 9 LFB w/R inside down elbow against his left elbow.

4. Step R inside his L foot *(12 RNB between feet)* w/R Out BKS solar plexus or groin.

5. L rear crossover outside his L foot, snaking R hand up under his L armpit behind his neck *(neck lever hold)* continuing to hold his L wrist at your L hip *(his palm up)*.

6. 12 R rev cat *(him behind your R shoulder)* R rear sliding leg sweep thru inside angle of his L knee w/down pressure to back of his neck *(neck lever throw)* causing him to flip onto his back, ending face up inside of your L foot w/his feet at 6 *(your L hand holds neck hook to complete throw, but still works if he rolls over w/feet to your R at 9)*.

7. R front crossover, your L knee pin his R arm *(or his neck if sideways)* checking his legs w/L arm, R down BKS his groin, or vert punch his solar plexus *(depends on body position & preference)*, then stand and cross out towards 4:30 to exit.

<u>Extension Begins Here</u>

7. After throw step R to 7:30 *(outside R shoulder)* w/L down knee to his L collarbone.

8. Bounce off knee jumping and turning L *(CCW)* landing L next to his R side *(where your R foot was)* w/R down roundhouse shin kick between his legs to his groin, R down knee drop onto his stomach with R half fist strike into his throat.

9. Stand up from knee drop w/R front glancing heel kick under his chin then *(after lifting your R knee)* R down heel stomp onto his face.

10. Jump forward towards 12 above his head onto your R foot w/L rear thrust kick back to 6 on top of his head *(cervical compression, caution in training)*.

11. From previous kick bring L toe to R followed by a low right outward hook kick thru his left temple and around to a LNB above his head.

12. Right round ball kick his R temple, R toe to L *(CCW spin)* into L rear sliding heel stomp onto his R collarbone then right front crossover step out towards 12 to exit.

**BLINDING VICE** *(Blinding Sacrifice)*
**Two-Hand Choke from 12**

1. Wedge your 2 hands/arms up between his arms w/dbl horiz 2-finger pokes to his eyes *(also creates space between his arms and backs him up)*.

2. Clear his arms out and down, step forward to 12 modified RNB w/dbl horiz palm strikes thru floating ribs *(your hands end behind his back – optional front head butt)*.

3. R Cat w/dbl In hooking BKS thru kidneys *(pulls him forward, optional R front knee groin & head butt)*, hands up dbl out blocks between his arms *(checks before next move)*.

4. From R Cat dbl Out finger flicks, dbl Out thumb gouge his eyes.

5. Step forward to modified RNB w/dbl down heel palms onto his collarbones grabbing his shoulders *(thumbs into scalene muscles optional)*.

6. Step drag back pulling him forward and down releasing grip circling dbl In roundhouse punches sandwiching his two temples.

7. Collapse both forearms In *(In flapping vert elbow)* sandwiches both his jaw hinges, clinch your hands around his neck *(Thai clinch)*.

8. R Up knee kick his face supporting his head w/two hands, step down to RNB pushing his neck down to the floor, exit towards 6.

Extension Begins Here

9. After Up knee kick invert R hand palm pressing against L side of his jaw *(your fingers pointed down)* grabbing R side of his head w/your L hand moving L foot back off angle slightly *(6 off cover)* R pushing in and up, L pulling back and down causing him to look and turn to his R until back to you *(12 reverse RNB w/his back against yours)*.

10. *(Lethal, crippling move, use extreme caution in practice and careful judgment in real life)*. Drop to R knee pulling his head down so back of his neck strikes across the top of your R shoulder *(probably breaking his neck)*. Clear him off then stand up, exit to 6.

## ONE HAND GRABS FROM THE SIDE

**HIDDEN ELBOW** *(A = Obscure Wing; B = Sword & Hammer extension)*
**Left Neck or Cross Shoulder Grab from 3**

1. L hand position check over R shoulder, step R to 3 *(12 Horse)* w/R back elbow strike into opponent's solar plexus.

2. Right back hammerfist strike to his groin.

3. Right obscure elbow strike under his chin.

Extension Begins Here

2. Gauge L foot to R w/R back hammerfist strike to his groin.

3. R rear sliding leg sweep thru inside L knee *(1:30 LFB)* w/R Up lifting forearm chin

**Option A**

4. R arm up grabs his throat securing grip w/L hand *(reverse headlock)*.

5. Pull head down onto R-L Up knee kicks *(chicken kick)* into his face, L foot then steps back to 1:30 R close kneel stance still holding his head tightly in your two arms.

6. 10:30 horse pulling head down *(snap mare)* flipping him over R shoulder *(practice R knee on ground, around shoulder)* onto back, his feet away and head between your two feet.

7. L TSK his face at 1:30 leaping up and around CCW landing L next to his R side w/R down roundhouse kick his solar plexus.

8. Right TSK thru his face while crossing out towards 4:30 to exit.

**Option B**

4. *(Neck grab missed from Option A or just prefer this version)*. R rear scoop kick thru his groin, front crossover step to 10:30 *(4:30 RNB towards opponent)*.

5. Drag L foot to R *(Drag Step)* in leaping fashion w/flying R Up knee kick lifting his face and straightening him up then step R toe to L to spin CCW.

6. L spinning rear or side thrust kick best available body target to clear opponent followed by a R front crossover step out exiting towards 10:30.

## WRAPAROUND
### Left Hand Close Shoulder Grab from 3
1. L hand position check covers face w/R arm circle up back over behind his L arm wrapping and trapping his L elbow joint stepping forward to 12 LFB.
2. RNB towards opponent w/R Out snapping BKS to his solar plexus or groin.

Extension Begins Here
1. L hand position check face w/R Out elbow followed by R Out claw his face then wrap over and back behind his L arm trapping his L elbow joint *(reinforce grip w/L hand)* then step forward left to 10:30 ending in a 4:30 right reverse bow.
*2. Optional Submission End: Step back R to 10:30 lifting elbow w/wrist pressure back (behind your R shoulder) takes him down, Americana lock standing or mounted.*
2. Standard Ending: Hold arm w/cover step towards opponent *(4:30 RFB)* w/L palm strike thru his chin then *(crane)* hook outward around the left side of his neck.
3. Use neck hook to pull him to L front knee kick to stomach or groin w/R Out BKS whip thru solar plexus or ribs, L to chamber *(R hand up behind him w/L knee in air)*.
4. L foot back to 4:30 RFB w/L straight palm thrust to his forehead w/R In hooking BKS thru back of his neck *(causes whiplash)* as your R hand goes under your L armpit.
5. 4:30 RNB, rebound R hand off your body w/R Out handsword throat, L position check.

## HIDDEN HAND *(Obscure Sword)*
### Left Hand Shoulder Grab Pulling from 4:30
1. Drop weight slightly, look, slide R foot back *(outside his L foot if in front)* pinning his L hand w/L using his pull *(Borrowed Force)* to pivot towards him to a 4:30 RNB w/a R obscure handsword strike *(hidden hand)* up into his throat.
2. Left front snap kick his stomach or groin then step back to a RNB.

Extension Begins Here
2. As previous handsword snaps back towards your L shoulder do L front kick to groin followed by R front kick inside his R knee *(chicken kick)*, turns his body to his R.
3. Settle R foot between his feet w/R Out hammerfist thru his L collarbone *(possibly catching nose on path)* turning his torso back to his L then chamber for next move.
4. Right vert thrust punch to his R shoulder rotating him to his R.
5. L rear crossover outside his L foot towards 7:30 *(R rear twist)* w/R Up elbow under chin, R down elbow top of sternum, R back hammerfist his groin *(in rapid succession)*.
6. Un-pivot L CCW *(R heel/L ball)* to 6 LNB w/L back elbow to his L kidney at 1:30.
7. Step R behind him to 1:30 LFB grabbing his shoulders *(like Backbreaker)*.
8. R front knee kick tailbone pulling shoulders back & down putting him on knees.
9. Step forward to a RFB shoving him forward and down onto his stomach.
10. L rear crossover *(inside his R leg sweeps his legs apart)*, R rear sliding heel stomp his testicles *(R rev bow)*, R front crossover *(optional TSK or stomp his L heel)* w/7:30 exit.

# GRABS FROM THE REAR
## CIRCLING ELBOW *(Circling Wing)*
### Two-Hand Choke Pushing from 6
1. Absorb rear push *(opening R foot)* step L to 1:30 *(7:30 R rev bow)*, cover 180° to 7:30 RNB circling R arm back over his R arm *(out armpit trap)*.
2. Adjust to a 7:30 RFB with L four finger poke to his eyes.
3. RNB to 7:30 w/R Up elbow under chin while L hand checks outside his R arm.
4. R rev bow to 7:30 *(clear his R arm towards his L hip)* w/R back hammerfist to groin *(R knee pushes his R leg to create opening if needed)*. Cross out to end.

Extension Begins Here
5. R back to L *(def switch)* as R hand slides down his R arm to grab his R wrist, step L forward w/L down forearm his R elbow *(his wrist welded to your right hip as he bends)*.
6. R front knee kick his R ribcage *(Liver)* then step back.
7. L foot back *(def switch)* feeding back of his R hand to your L hand, R step forward w/R down BKS the back of his neck.
8. R Up elbow lifts his head while still controlling his right wrist at your hip.
9. R step back to 12 pulling back of his R elbow w/R hand *(arm bar moves him to 12)*.
10. Cover step to 12 RFB switching your hands so R holds his R wrist and L slides to his R back elbow, lever his arm until he is face down pinning his R arm flat to ground.

11. Left front stomp kick onto his right elbow then step left over it.
12. R rear sliding heel stomp his neck after sliding around his R arm, cross out exit.

## CROSS OF DESTRUCTION *(Cross of Destruction)*
### Two-Hand Choke In-Place or Pulling from 6
1. Reach back each of your hands grabbing each of his stepping L to 9 *(12 horse)*. Note: The thumb joints are grabbed where some like to rotate the palms up to expose his elbows to the shoulder tops; my preference pins their L thumb webbing tight to the neck then turning out into that joint causing a dislocation *(be careful in practice)*.
2. R cat 3 *(his L thumb joint dislocated in ext)* lifting ducking under his L arm, crossing L onto crook of his R elbow *(crossed arm elbow trap)*.
3. R front snap kick inside R knee, 3 RNB driving R shoulder down onto his crossed elbows, bracing his L wrist and pushing his R wrist *(causing an elbow dislocation)*.
Extension Begins Here
4. Hold L w/L rear crossover to 6 w/R down outward BKS whipping thru his groin.
5. R rev cat circling R arm out overhead, R rear sliding leg sweep thru inside L knee w/R overhead down hammerfist or inv hook BKS his R mastoid driving his head down.
6. R front knee kick up into his nose still holding his L wrist in your L hand while your R arm circles up and CCW in front of you.
7. From knee kick, R front crossover to 10:30 *(4:30 rear twist)* w/R down out hammerfist strike to his L jaw hinge while pulling his L wrist with your L hand.
8. Right rear scoop kick thru his groin then cross out to 1:30 to exit.

## REAR BELT GRAB *(Menacing Twirl)*
### Left Hand Belt Grab Pulling from 6
1. Drop your weight slightly looking over R shoulder sliding R foot back *(careful of their foot)* as hands transition thru L chamber *(cup & saucer style R on top)* then un-pivot *(R ball / L heel)* to a 6 RNB with a R downward outward block clearing his arm(s).
2. 6 RFB w/L straight palm heel under chin *(possible extended to 4-finger eye poke)*.
3. L-R chicken knee kick his groin, step forward to 6 RNB w/R cross body check
Extension Begins Here
3. From chicken knee kick step forward to 6 RNB w/R In inv horiz palm strike *(fingers in)* thru his L jaw hinge *(turns his face R)*.
4. Gauge L foot behind your R thru a 10:30 R cat w/R outward claw thru his face, R outward hook kick thru the inside of his left knee.
5. With R foot in the air from previous kick R front snap kick inside his R knee w/L hand check as R hand chambers.
6. Settle weight to 4:30 RNB w/R Up rolling forearm under chin followed by optional downward elbow strike on top of his sternum or collarbone.
7. R close kneel stance w/R down whipping BKS strike glancing thru L collarbone.
8. Stand up RNB with R inv hook punch *(hairpin)* thru his L temple.
9. R rev bow w/R rear scoop kick thru groin, front crossover step-out exits to 12.

## DUCKING DRAGON
### Right to Left Cross Shoulder Grab Pulling from 6
1. Drop weight slightly, look over L shoulder, slide L foot back *(careful not to trip over their lead foot)* as your two hands transition thru R chamber *(cup & saucer style left hand on top)* then un-pivot *(left ball / right heel)* to a 6 LNB.
2. L close kneel *(ducking)* w/R vert punch *(middle knuckle punch in Ext)* to his urinary bladder *(between navel & pubic bone)* w/L arm cross body check against his chest.
3. Stand up w/R front or knee kick best centerline target, step back to 6 LNB.
Extension Begins Here
3. Catch his face w/L Out claw as he bends, grab around the L side of his neck w/R hand.
4. R front knee kick his groin turning his face to his R w/your hands *(neck tweak)*.
5. Step back R to 10:30, weight to R leg *(L rev bow)*, R slides down L arm to grab his L wrist pushing inv middle finger fist into tender point behind his L ear lobe *(SJ17)*.
6. Holding this position L wheel shin kick inside his L knee *(causes slight buckle)* then L toe to R *(spinning)* letting go of wrist and tender point.
7. Turn CW w/R spin kick *(stiff leg lift, side thrust, out hook or crescent kick)*, crossing out towards 12 to exit facing opponent at 6.

# PUSHING ATTACKS

Attacker is reaching for, or successfully pushes the torso with one or two hands from the front. This can be done as a touch, shove, or more explosive jolt that hits. Punch & Strike defenses have crossover value in this category.

A push can be with one hand to the straight or cross shoulder causing the body to turn, and where force is borrowed then applied to the opposite side. A centerline one-hand or two hand push up high or low can cause a step back, but where those arm(s) can be trapped or both arms moved to the same side, down, or apart outward while deflecting the pushing energy.

Note: A push from the rear must be seen to be defended so this angle is a non-starter and side pushes can be easily adapted to using these front push techniques.

## ONE HAND PUSHES FROM THE FRONT
TRIGGERED PALM *(Triggered Salute)* Pg 260
GLANCING PALM *(Glancing Salute)* Pg 260
SNAPPING ARM *(Snapping Twig)* Pg 261

## TWO HAND PUSHES FROM THE FRONT
TWINS OF AGGRESSION Pg 261
PARTING ARMS *(Parting Wings)* Pg 262
TURN OF FATE *(Twist of Fate)* Pg 262
ALTERNATING FISTS *(Alternating Mace)* Pg 263
HOOKING ARMS *(Hooking Wings)* Pg 263

## ONE HAND PUSHES FROM THE FRONT
**TRIGGERED PALM** *(Thrusting Salute)*
***Right to Left Straight Shoulder Push from 12***
1. L pins R push hand at back of wrist crease absorbing push *(borrowed force)* stepping forward R to 12 RNB w/R straight palm heel thrust up under his chin.
2. Hold wrist w/R down handsword bending and hooking his R elbow crook *(LI11)* pulling down across towards your R hip *(cancels height, width, depth & potential L punch)*.
3. With no loss of motion right inward elbow strike thru his nose.
4. Using reverse motion optional R Out elbow thru his R temple, R Out whipping BKS thru R jaw *(one whipping motion)* until your R hand is at your R chamber position.
5. Right inverted horizontal punch into his solar plexus or Liver.
<u>Extension Begins Here</u>
5. L rear crossover to 12 R rear twist w/R snapping uppercut punch under his chin.
6. Transition thru R rev cat to R rear sliding leg sweep thru his inside L knee *(to 1:30)* w/R back hammerfist his groin w/L hand position check *(possible palm or finger strike)*.
7. Gauge L foot, R front step thru knee kick inside of his R knee *(nerve junction)* at 9 *(buckle)* w/R Out elbow snapping back towards 3 to his R temple, keep moving to exit.

**GLANCING PALM** *(Glancing Salute)*
***Right to Right Cross Shoulder Push from 12***
1. R pins R push hand at back wrist crease, absorbing push *(borrowed force)* stepping forward L outside his arm *(forward 45o horse)* w/L In forearm to back of R elbow joint as R traps his R wrist. The angle these push/pull vectors meet the wrist & elbow can be adjusted and regulated to do more or less damage.
2. L reverse bow scissoring his R elbow between your two arms.

3. Ideal Phase: he steps L foot; gauge L foot between his two feet to 1:30 w/R chamber, pushing his R arm into his own groin w/L hand. If R step, step L outside his R instead.
4. LFB w/R straight palm glancing thru chin, hook & hold around R side of his neck.
5. Pull him forward into R knee kick to groin *(R thigh or ribs if R leg in front.*
6. Step forward *(1:30 RNB)* w/R In elbow his face *(R overhead down elbow spine if he bends)*, w/possible knee buckle against his R knee while checking his R arm w/L hand.
<u>Extension Begins Here</u>
7. From R In elbow L rear crossover step to 1:30 w/R Out vertical BKS to his nose.
8. R rev cat, R rear sliding leg sweep thru inside L knee w/R back hammerfist his groin and L 4-finger eye poke.
9. Kick/sweep thru back of his R heel moving his foot towards 6 w/R outward elbow strike to his sternum *(Ren17)* tripping him to the ground then cross out to exit.

## SNAPPING ARM *(Snapping Twig)*
### *Left Hand Push to Sternum from 12*
1. L step back *(12 RNB)* absorbing push trapping his L wrist crease w/L hand *(L In finger slice thru right eye on way to trap in Ext)* turning your shoulders to absorb the push extending a R upward lifting palm heel strike under his left elbow joint.
2. Pivot R palm to hook over his L elbow crook *(optional R In finger slice thru L eye on way to hook in Ext)*, pulling and sliding towards his wrist *(frictional pull)* to 12 RFB w/L Out handsword to the L side of his neck *(your R hand passing thru R chamber)*.
3. Adjust to RNB w/R In raking hammer fist strike thru his nose as your left-hand checks *(left outward finger slice thru his left eye following the hammerfist in extension)*.
4. Step drag forward (12 modified RNB) circling hands In to sandwich his face w/R In elbow *(his L side)* & L In heel palm *(his R side)* w/R under L armpit to universal check.
<u>Extension Begins Here</u>
5. L front crossover to 12 *(front twist)* dropping low w/R forward hammerfist strike to his groin with the left hand checking high *(possible face claw)*.
6. Stand up w/R obscure elbow under his chin un-pivoting to LNB w/R Out face claw, L palm strike his sternum to create space and position him for next series of strikes.
7. LFB w/R horiz palm to his L floating rib *(or R In hammerfist his L Kidney if L arm in way)* cocking a L hand palm up in front of your right shoulder
8. LNB w/L Out hand sword strike L side of his neck, R hand chambers.
9. Pivot on L heel open to 10:30 w/R In inv horiz palm strike *(fingers in)* his left jaw hinge.
10. R step thru R side thrust kick thru his R knee *(inside angle or straight into locked joint)*, R front crossover exit to 6, or L spinning Out hook kick his head ending in a RNB.

# TWO HAND PUSHES FROM THE FRONT
## TWINS OF AGGRESSION
### *Two-Hand High Push from 12*
1. Step back L to RNB w/R In block outside his L arm *(L Out parry first in Ext counter grabs and holds his L wrist)* shifting to your L foot *(L reverse bow)*.
2. R side snap kick his front knee.
3. Open R foot, L step thru front snap kick groin to 12 LNB w/universal check.
<u>Extension Begins Here</u>
4. Still holding his L wrist in your L hand step forward from L kick to 10:30 LFB w/R *(fingers in)* palm strike L side of his face *(turns his face R)* thru to R Out hook around R side of his neck as L pulls his L arm *(shifts his weight, causing him to turn slightly)*.
5. R step thru sweep kick thru back of his L lower leg pulling his head w/R causing sweeping him onto his back behind you face up.
6. Look over L shoulder, L sliding heel kick the L side of his head.
7. Look over R shoulder, drag L foot to replace R foot *(drag step)* in a leaping fashion ending wR front stomp kick down onto his groin then step off between his legs.
8. R front rotating twist w/L down knee drop on L thigh w/R down vert punch his urinary bladder w/L hand cross body check to guard against his potential right kick.
9. Stand up un-pivoting then rotate L to a L close kneel stance to 10:30 with a R downward knee drop onto the same thigh target.
10. Stand up gauging your R foot towards his feet then L front crossover sweep kick thru the top of his left ankle as you exit.

**PARTING ARMS** *(Parting Wings)*
**Two-Hand High Push from 12**

1. Absorb push stepping back R (12 modified LNB) w/dbl Out handsword blocks inside to separate his two wrists.

2. Adjust to LFB w/R horiz palm *(or R inward handsword strike)* to his left floating rib *(Spleen side)* with left hand palm up in front of your right shoulder for next move.

3. LNB to 12 w/L Out handsword L side of his neck, chambering R hand.

4. 12 LFB w/R vert punch *(middle finger fist in extension)* his sternum *(Ren17)*, L hand slides down his arms and bodyline *(cross body check)*.

Extension Begins Here

5. As his head comes forward R In 2-finger slice across his L eye *(still in LFB)* then LNB w/L inward handsword strike to the R side of his neck *(SCM Muscles)*.

6. Shift back to L cat followed by L then R front snap kicks *(Chicken kick)* to his groin and solar plexus while your R hand circles behind you and overhead.

7. Settle R foot forward to 12 rev RNB 12 *(cross 12 line to set up moves #8-10)* w/R In down hammer fist strike thru L side of his nose.

8. Keep moving forward w/L rear crossover to 12 circling R arm to R Out snapping BKS to his right temple.

9. Un-pivot 360° *(R heel/L ball)* to 12 LNB w/L Out whipping BKS to his left temple.

10. R step thru front snap kick groin w/L cross body check and R hand chambers.

11. R foot forward to 12 RNB w/R inv horiz half-fist punch to throat. No cross out here as opponent should be moving away.

**TURN OF FATE** *(Twist of Fate)*
**Two-Hand High Push from 12**

1. Step back L absorbing push *(12 modified RNB)* with a double outward hand sword block up between and separating his two pushing hands.

2. Transition thru a right cat stance with a right front snap groin kick.

3. Option A: Attacker had stepped with his right foot to push you:
Step forward from kick 12 *(RNB)* w/R palm strike his L shoulder as L hand slides down to pull his R upper arm across in front of R hip *(turns him around into Sleeper Choke)*.

Option B: Attacker stepped with his left foot and/or was difficult to turn:
Step forward from kick w/R palm strike his L shoulder as your L slides down to pull his R arm across in front of R hip but stepping L forward to 12 *(gauge as needed)* covering to 6 RNB behind him *(same position as A into Sleeper Choke except you step behind him)*.

4. Regardless of direction after A or B successfully completed L inv thrusting side kick *(TSK)* to back of L knee *(buckles his knee and cancels his height)* then step back to the previous stance and strongly apply the sleeper choke while pulling him back and down.

5. After choke, offensive cover step w/R forearm *(clothesline)* across his throat driving him onto his back *(in Ext hook and hold his L wrist w/L hand causing his to turn face down)*, shuffle forward w/R down vert face punch *(hop, drop, pop)*.

Extension Begins Here

6. Gauge forward *(drag step)* following him to ground w/R hand *(C grip)* at back of his neck pushing his face onto the floor w/R down knee drop on his L kidney *(6 L close kneel)*

7. Stand up, holding his L wrist, R inv side stomp onto his neck *(cervical)*.

8. Bounce off and over his body outside his R hip w/R down knee drop *(4:30 L close kneel)* his middle back *(thoracic spine)* as your R hand joins your L holding his L wrist *(your hands face the same direction holding his right wrist like a pull up)*.

9. R inv stomp kick glancing thru his L elbow stepping to a R front twist to 4:30 *(his elbow wedged where your R calf and L shin cross)* pulling his L wrist up *(breaking his L elbow)*.

10. Left foot then steps out and R foot back thru moving towards 4:30 to exit.

**ALTERNATING FISTS** *(Alternating Mace)*

**Two-Hand Low Push from 12**

1. Step back to 12 RNB w/R half down block on top of his forearms.
2. Adjust to a RFB with a right vertical thrust punch into his sternum.
3. RNB w/L check to his arms w/R Out snapping BKS his R temple.

<u>Extension Begins Here</u>

1. L back *(12 RFB)* w/R half down block his forearms w/L vert thrust punch sternum.
2. RNB w/L check his arms w/R outward snapping BKS to his right temple.
3. RFB w/L vert thrust punch thru his L shoulder *(begins to turn him)*.
4. L front or round kick to inside L knee *(turns him further)* then L foot to R *(toe to toe)*.
5. Continue turning CW w/R spinning Out ax kick *(calf against back of his knee)* buckling his R knee to ground *(ending with R foot just inside his L knee on the ground)*.
6. Step R foot to L *(toe to toe)* looking over L shoulder w/L spinning Out hook kick thru his face spinning out to a RNB facing opponent at 1:30.

**HOOKING ARMS** *(Hooking Wings)*

**Two Hand Low Push or Attempted Bear Hug from 12**

1. Step back L then to R cat w/dbl In hooks over and inside his two wrists to separate them using frictional pull to disrupt his balance.
2. R front snap kick his groin circling your R arm overhead w/L hand position check.
3. 12 RNB w/R In raking hammerfist thru his left temple *(or left side of his nose)* then down across your body towards your left hip while your left hand checks his right arm.
4. Circle R hand up next to your L shoulder *(3 & 4 make a figure 8)* then R outward whipping BKS thru his R temple to chamber maintaining L check against his R arm.
5. Step forward R w/R upward elbow strike under his chin then drag your L foot forward *(completes step drag)* w/R down overhead heel palm to bridge of his nose.

<u>Extension Begins Here</u>

6. Gauge L towards 3 to R Cat facing 10:30 w/R Out claw thru his face and eyes moving your left hand to grab the outside of his left elbow.
7. Chamber R w/R Outward hook kick to the inside of his left knee.
8. With R leg in the air, R front snap kick inside his R knee circling R arm overhead.
9. As weight settles to a 10:30 RNB R down hammerfist his L kidney *(holding his left arm in your left hand to open this target)*.
10. Shift your weight L to R rev close kneel, R rear scoop kick groin cross out exit to 6.

# PUNCH & STRIKE ATTACKS

Attacker is trying to punch or strike with an upper body weapon following a straight, cross, or round path. This section divides them into *Inside Arm Defenses, Outside Arm Defenses,* and *Underneath Arm Defenses.*

For reference these techniques step to an *Ideal Phase* location, but a different angle may and perhaps should be taken to better establish alignment for efficient technique completion (i.e., strong line/weak line).

Most Kenpo punching technique defenses were designed against the step-thru Karate punch launched where the same side foot ends in front. This puts the attacker's right foot in front with a right punch and left in front with a left punch. This large, committed motion could then be defended with an aggressive blocking or parrying motion and makes the earlier described end foot location and relative hand position a part of technique formulation.

This is still useful for that type of follow-thru punching motion, but the original EPAK system did not directly address the quick returning jab or rear hand power punch thrown as a Boxer or other sport fighter would use them. Even though we should not be engaged in this sparring posture in street defense an opponent could position them self in this way to attack, or we could end up in this posture during a prolonged fight.

To address this, I modified several Kenpo techniques to defend against this sport punch possibility. Using an initial defense like those used in sport fighting accomplishes this, and then the street technique can be grafted in from there (See *Depth Zones*).

The first goal is to defend, so as not to get punched in the face, then quickly convert to the street tactics of Kenpo. This intercepting of the fist can be enhanced by hammering the nose on the way, hitting the nerves in the wrist, adding the other hand to hit the bicep, collapse the arm, or tweak the elbow, etc., but the punch must be defended. Kicking the groin is often the next move in many Kenpo techniques as punchers tend to square up to hit with power.

Note: There is also the real possibility of a sport type fight in a street context, depending on combatants and the environment (e.g., "guys duking it out"). However, caution is recommended in this playground type fight scenario as generally when someone starts losing the rules start changing or disappearing. This is a main reason why there are referees in sports.

## INSIDE ARM DEFENSES
DELAYED HAND *(Delayed Sword)* Pg 265
SIX HANDS *(Five Swords)* Pg 266
FATAL VARIATION *(Fatal Deviation)* Pg 266
HAND OF DESTRUCTION *(Sword of Destruction)* Pg 266
SHIELDING FINGERS *(Shielding Hammer/Raining Claw)* Pg 266

PURSUING PANTHER *(Short Form 2)* Pg 267
PRANCING TIGER *(Prance of the Tiger)* Pg 267

## **OUTSIDE ARM DEFENSES**
CROSSING FIST *(Attacking Mace)* Pg 268
FLASHING FIST *(Flashing Mace)* Pg 268
FLASHING HANDS *(Flashing Hands)* Pg 268
BROKEN KNEEL *(Destructive Kneel)* Pg 269
TAMING THE FIST *(Taming the Mace)* – plus Ground Option Pg 269
CRADLING THE BABY *(Gathering Clouds)* Pg 270
JUMPING CRANE *(Leaping Crane)* Pg 270
SHIELD AND PUNCH *(Shield and Mace)* Pg 270
THUNDERING FISTS *(Thundering Hammers)* Pg 271
DANCE OF DEATH *(Dance of Death)* Pg 271
CIRCLING THE ARM *(Circling the Horizon)* Pg 271
COMPULSIVE KNEEL *(Kneel of Compulsion)* – plus Ground Option Pg 272
BACKBREAKER *(The Back Breaker)* Pg 272
REVERSING FIST *(Reversing Mace)* – plus Ground Option Pg 273
DESTRUCTIVE CIRCLES *(Circling Destruction)* Pg 273
HAND AND SHIELD *(Shield and Sword)* Pg 273
TWIRLING FIST *(Twirling Hammers)* Pg 274
PARRYING GRAB *(Snaking Talon)* – plus Ground Option Pg 274
ENTWINED FISTS *(Entwined Maces)* Pg 274
CIRCLING PARRIES *(Circling Fans)* – plus Ground Option Pg 275
PROTECTIVE PARRIES *(Protective Fans)* – plus Ground Option Pg 275

## **UNDERNEATH ARM DEFENSES**
PROTECTIVE CIRCLES *(Circles of Protection)* Pg 275
TURNING WINDMILLS *(Circling Windmills)* Pg 276
DESTRUCTIVE PARRIES *(Destructive Fans)* Pg 276
KICK INTO DARKNESS *(Thrust into Darkness)* Pg 276

## **INSIDE ARM DEFENSES**

**DELAYED HAND** *(Delayed Sword)*
***Right Straight Punch from 12***
1. L back to 12 RNB *(Ext steps back off angle to 10:30)* w/R In block inside R wrist *(extension adds left outward parry that counter grabs his right wrist)*.
2. R cat *(Ext rotates his R wrist out to disrupt his posture)*, R front snap kick his groin.
3. Weight forward *(marriage of gravity)* to 12 RNB w/R Out handsword R side of neck.
<u>Extension Begins Here</u>
4. From previous strike hook R hand over back of his head *(C grip)* still holding his R wrist in your L hand, push his head down lifting his R hand up and sliding your L foot back to turn him around backwards then down onto his back *(about 4:30)* continuing to hold his R wrist in your left hand as your right hand slides out to the chamber.
5. Follow him down w/R down dropping vert punch to his face and R knee onto his Liver *(R floating rib)* while tweaking his R elbow around your L shin.
6. Stand up w/R front heel kick thru R side of his chin then straight down ax kick back into his L jaw, drop your L knee across his neck/collarbone *(low front twist)* checking his legs w/L arm and optional R down vert thrust punch into his solar plexus.
7. Left toe eye rake while stepping over his face to exit.

**SIX HANDS** *(Five Swords)*
***Right Roundhouse Punch from 12***
  1. Step R forward to 12 RNB jamming attack w/R In hammerfist R bicep *(Golgi Tendon Organ, GTO reflex strike, & possible nose rake on way in Ext)* w/L ext block inside R wrist.
  2. R modified RNB w/R outward handsword strike to the right side of his neck.
  3. RFB w/L palm under chin *(Ext adds L 4-finger eye poke)* while right hand chambers.
  4. RNB w/R invert horiz snap punch solar plexus *(or Spleen)* while L hand positions in front of your R shoulder *(his left shoulder)*.
  5. As he bends forward adjust L foot back to 10:30 RFB w/L Out handsword L side of his neck that hooks over back of his neck pulling him into range *(L handsword slices thru below his neck in Ext w/R Out whipping BKS thru groin)*, R handsword up R ear.
  6. RNB w/R down handsword back of neck as L hand slides to check his L shoulder.
<u>Extension Begins Here</u>
  5. Same footwork as base technique with a L out-down slicing handsword to neck ending with L hand below his head.
  6. RNB to 10:30 w/R down handsword onto then slicing thru back of his neck *(ends below his neck)* w/L Up heel palm up thru R jaw *(these motions together tweak his neck)*.
  7. Drag L foot to R *(R rev cat)* w/R obscure handsword slicing up thru past his throat w/L hand position check at his L shoulder *(your back is slightly towards opponent at 12)*.
  8. R down vert punch thru L jaw w/R stiff leg lifting rear kick into his groin *(or R rear sliding leg sweep inside his L knee)*, R toe to L *(spinning CCW)* looking over L shoulder.
  9. Jump turn L w/L down ax kick to back of neck or R round shin kick L leg, exit.

**FATAL VARIATION** *(Fatal Deviation)*
***Right then Left Roundhouse Punch Combo from 12***
Note: Use "Unrolling Crane" without the kick as a complimentary L-R Round Punch technique.
  1. Step back or forward *(depending on range and timing)* to 12 RNB *(entire technique done to 12)* w/R In block inside R punch and left-hand check or assist with blocking.
  2. RFB w/R ext out block inside L punch w/L vertical thrust punch into his face.
  3. RNB w/R inward handsword strike to the left side of his neck while left hand checks.
  4. Circle R hand back to yourself as L circles up and in w/L front crossover *(front twist)* settling w/R inv horiz palm forward to his sternum w/L In heel palm R temple.
  5. L windshield wiper slice thru his eyes to L cross body check *(possible pinch to his L pec muscle)* into a right front knee kick into his groin while chambering your right hand.
  6. Step forward to R rev NB *(R foot crossing 12 line slightly to set up ending)* w/R upward rolling forearm strike under his chin.
  7. L rear crossover w/R side thrust kick to his chest, front crossover step-out exiting to 6.

**HAND OF DESTRUCTION** *(Sword of Destruction)*
***Left Round Punch from 12***
  1. Step back L to 12 RNB *(Ext steps back off angle to 1:30)* w/R ext out block inside his L wrist w/L hand position check *(Ext with possible L palm strike to his sternum if in range)*.
  2. Transition thru a R cat stance with a R front snap kick into his groin or R crease.
  3. Settle weight forward *(RNB)* w/R In handsword L side of his neck *(SCM muscles)*.
<u>Extension Begins Here</u>
  4. Modified RNB with L outward handsword to his L carotid artery *(St9)*.
  5. L rear crossover to 1:30 *(outside his L foot if in front)* w/L inv horiz palm *(fingers in)* thru his L jaw hinge followed by R In elbow thru same target or L temple *(3-4-5 rapid fire)*.
  6. Transition thru R rev cat, R rear sliding leg sweep thru inside angle of his L knee w/R back underhand heel palm into his groin and a possible left four-finger eye poke.
  7. R front crossover 7:30 w/R Out thumb strike R jaw hinge *(SJ17 or R eye)*, 7:30 exit.

**SHIELDING FINGERS** *(Shielding Hammers/Raining Claw)*
***Left Roundhouse / possible Right Uppercut Punch Combo from 12***
This technique combines Shielding Hammer & Raining Claw from the EPAK System so an opponent could throw a R uppercut punch after the L roundhouse.
  1. Step back L to 12 RNB *(or 1:30 line)* w/R ext out block *(possible out raking hammerfist)* inside L wrist w/L hand position check *(possible L palm strike his sternum if in range)*.

2. R step forward w/R In hammerfist to L side of his nose *(or temple)*

3. L forward *(completes step drag)* w/R forward horiz elbow to sternum *(or solar plexus)*. Note: This is where a half downward block would have been inserted to pick up an uppercut punch follow-up as done in EPAK Raining Claw.

4. L palm strike catches his face *(modified RNB)* then claws down becoming a cross body check across his shoulder/chest line and arms.

5. RNB w/R uppercut punch under his chin, or forward vertical BKS his nose, or inverted half fist his throat.

Extension Begins Here

6. L front crossover *(front twist)* w/R forward hammerfist strike into is groin w/high L hand position check *(possible palm strike and/or 4-finger eye poke)*.

7. Stand up with a right obscure elbow strike under his chin.

8. Un-pivot *(L heel / R ball)* to L side horse w/L inv horiz palm strike *(fingers in)* to his sternum *(adjusts his distance)* while shifting your weight to R foot.

9. L side thrust kick best available torso target *(clears him away)*, L front crossover exit.

## PURSUING PANTHER
### Left Lead Roundhouse Punch from 12

1. Step back L to 12 RNB *(Ext steps back off angle to 1:30)* w/R ext out block *(Ext w/R Out raking hammerfist thru nose on way to this block)* to inside L wrist w/L hand position check *(extension with possible left palm strike to his sternum if in range)*.

2. Adjust to R cat w/L inward block to that same arm *(double block)*

3. Right front snap kick to his groin.

4. As weight settles forward to RNB, R upper cut punch under his chin that rolls thru and up *(right rolling forearm lifts and holds his chin up)* with left hand chambering.

5. Left half-fist punch into his throat. *(Caution: potential lethal move)*

Extension Begins Here

5. L rear crossover to R rear twist to 1:30 w/R downward elbow strike on top of his sternum or collarbone *(left hand is position check on this move in extension)*.

6. R rev cat into R rear sliding leg sweep thru inside angle of his L knee w/R back hammerfist strike into his groin *(left hand checking or striking)*.

7. RNB *(pivot towards him on both heels)* w/R horiz elbow into his solar plexus.

8. Modified RNB with a right outward heel of palm strike lifting his chin.

9. RFB with a left horizontal half fist strike to his throat *(trachea area)*.

10. L step thru front knee kick his groin chambering L w/R cross body chest check.

11. Settle your weight forward to LNB with a left straight palm strike to his nose.

11. Right step thru front push kick to his solar plexus to clear him away.

## PRANCING TIGER *(Prance of the Tiger)*
### Right Body Hook Punch from 3

1. Step back R *(12 L cat)* w/R inside forearm block w/L push down check *(possible elbow tweak)* against his R arm and wrist, respectively. Your L hand then grabs R wrist.

2. R obscure elbow under his chin followed by R outward claw thru his face.

3. L TSK his R knee w/R In hammerfist thru his nose *(possibly right bicep)*.

4. Switch your feet w/R side snap kick *(chicken kick style)* inside his L knee w/R outward snapping BKS his R temple.

5. R front crossover to 9 *(possible R leg sweep)* to front twist w/R outward two finger slice thru his right eye while pulling his right wrist in your left hand.

6. Spin L thru L rev close kneel, L rear sliding leg sweep thru front inside angle of his R knee *(opens his stance)* with a L back heel of palm strike into his groin.

7. Cover to 1:30 LFB facing him circling R arm overhead, R Up knee kick sternum w/R overhead down hammerfist his upper spine *(sandwiches his body)* as L circles overhead.

8. L Up knee kick his body w/L down hammerfist to his spine *(sandwiching his body)*.

9. L front crossover to 7:30 w/L downward palm strike onto the back of his neck driving him to the ground then exit in that same direction.

# OUTSIDE ARM DEFENSES

**CROSSING FIST** *(Attacking Mace)*
**Right Crossing Punch from 12**
1. Step back to 12 LNB w/L In block outside R punch, grab over R wrist, chamber R.
2. Adjust to a 12 LFB with a R horiz thrust punch into his R rib cage.
3. As he moves away from punch R hand joins L to hold his R wrist, pull him into R front kick into same target *(or Roundhouse his stomach or TSK front knee as in extension)*.
<u>Extension Begins Here</u> *(Extension presumes a wall to your right)*
1. Slip outside R punch w/L In parry outside R hand grabbing back of his R wrist while stepping forward L to 12 LFB w/R horiz thrust punch *(or In elbow if too close)* to R ribs.
2. As he moves away from punch slide R hand back and under his right arm grabbing inside his R wrist *(both hands holding his R wrist)* turning his palm up *(affect posture)*.
3. Pull him into a right TSK down onto his right knee.
4. Step R towards 3 *(wall location in extension)* to RFB w/L inside down forearm strike to back of his R elbow *(still holding his right wrist in your right hand)*.
5. L step thru forward w/L knee to back of his R knee w/L Out BKS his R ribs *(Liver)*.
6. Continue holding R wrist in R hand placing L hand on back of his R elbow *(C grip)*, step drag forward using L knee to drive his R knee into wall as L hand pushes his medial R arm flat against wall *(front of his body should be pressed tightly against the wall)*.
7. Push off his body L toe to R looking over R shoulder *(spinning R)* followed by a R side thrust kick to best available rear body target *(R knee, R kidney or back of his neck)*.
8. Right front crossover step out towards 9 to exit.

**FLASHING FIST** *(Flashing Mace)*
**Right Crossing Punch Stepping Thru from 12**
1. Step back *(or forward, depends on range)* to 12 LNB w/L In block outside R punch as R arm cocks next to R ear *(in Ext this move glances thru inner R wrist scissoring his R elbow)*.
2. Pivot L foot open *(heel pivot)*, R step thru outside R foot to 10:30 w/R vertical hook punch *(middle finger fist strike in extension)* thru his right eye.
3. Adjust stance to turn and focus L to 4:30 w/L Out BKS *(or hammerfist)* under his R arm into his R kidney or ribs as R hand checks his R arm.
4. R feeds his R arm to you L grabbing from inside *(L inside / R outside, possibly pinching his inner arm &/or bicep muscle)*, pull down on his arm *(cancel his height)* dropping to 4:30 L wide kneel as R hand slides outside R hip *(L still holds his R arm)*.
5. Adjust to L close kneel w/R whipping overhead punch up thru his nose.
6. Use circular momentum of previous punch over your head to help turn 360° R *(R heel / L ball)* ending w/R cross body check over your R shoulder towards him at 4:30.
<u>Extension Begins Here</u>
6. Using momentum of punch over your head turn 180° R to R rev cat *(R cat to 10:30)*.
7. R rear sliding leg sweep thru back of R leg w/R down heel palm *(or hammerfist)* his sternum *(regulate strike or he doesn't fall)* ending in 10:30 LFB whim in front of you.
8. In same flow before he falls adjust to 10:30 LNB w/L In heel palm *(or hammerfist)* up into his middle spine holding him up briefly with your left hand.
9. Adjust to 10:30 LFB w/R down heel palm *(or hammerfist)* onto his sternum *(#7-9 are 3 quick hand strikes)* sweeping and driving him down to the ground onto his back.
10. R inv side stomp onto his face, R back to 10:30 LNB, L rear step thru exit to 4:30.

**FLASHING HANDS** *(Flashing Wings)*
**Right Crossing Punch Stepping Thru from 12**
1. L In block outside R punch stepping forward or back depending on range to 12 LNB.
2. L close kneel *(w/R knee check)* w/R In elbow thru his R rib cage *(your right elbow behind his right shoulder)* with a left-hand check to his right arm at the elbow.
3. R arm up then R Out elbow followed by R Out handsword both glancing thru the back of his neck, maintaining right knee and left-hand checks.
4. Keep shifting R to R close kneel to 3 *(L knee checks his R)* w/L fingers-in palm strike thru his right jaw hinge as your right-hand slides down his right arm to check.
5. L hand follows R hand down his R arm to maintain check as R hand circles up, L close kneel *(your R knee checks his R)* w/R In handsword his nose philtrum or throat as your left-hand checks to his right elbow *(shift his weight back)*.

6. Gauge R foot then L front push sweep back of his R ankle *(spreads his base)* then step back, gauge R foot back to R cat *(3 behind him)* w/L cross body check across his shoulder line as your right-hand chambers.

7. Step forward *(still behind opponent)* to 3 RNB w/R horiz palm thru back of his R jaw hinge then hooking his chin with your right hand.

8. Immediately adjust back to R cat as you pull back against his chin hooking your right forearm over his right shoulder *(takes the slack out of his neck and levers him back)*.

9. R Up knee kick to his middle spine while anchoring his head and neck backwards.

10. With R knee still in the air R side thrust kick back of his R knee pulling his chin over his R shoulder as L hand posts the back of his R shoulder *(tweaks his neck)* then right front crossover step out towards 10:30 to exit.

### BROKEN KNEEL *(Destructive Kneel)*
#### *Right Crossing Punch Stepping Thru from 12*

1. L In parry outside R punch, step L forward, L close kneel w/R Out parry *(dbl factor)*.

2. Counter grab inside R wrist w/R, attach back of his R wrist to your R hip w/step drag to 3 R close kneel *(past his R foot)* as L knee buckles back of his R knee *(his knee on ground)* w/L inv palm, L bicep strike *(compounding strikes)* thru his right elbow joint.

3. Adjust L to 12 L close kneel w/L Out whipping BKS thru R ribs w/R In heel palm claw thru face, hands to L chamber *(L on top)* w/R knee drop on R calf or Achilles tendon.

4. Hop to 3 R close kneel w/piggyback punch to lower spine *(make him arch back)*.

5. L Out crane hook R side of his neck hooking throat as R hand hooks *(grabs)* his R wrist *(R elbow tweaked against your body)*, L knee kick middle spine, step back to 7:30.

6. Move L w/R In down hammerfist strike onto his sternum *(driving him onto his back)*.

7. In same flow R down roundhouse ball kick onto his solar plexus pinning him to ground, then front crossover step-out towards 6 to exit.

### TAMING THE FIST *(Taming the Mace)*
#### *Right Crossing Punch Stepping Thru - 12; Wall at 6*

1. L In parry catches outside R, L step forward to 12 close-kneel w/R In raking hammerfist thru nose to R half down block his R elbow crease *(inward folding arm trap bends his right arm and shifts his weight to the back of his right heel)*. Option to wrap R arm over his right elbow then back to his front to manipulate, or after move#2)

2. R Out handsword his neck then grab top of his R trapezius muscle as your left hand grabs the back of his right hand *(prep for outward wrist lock)*.

3. Step back L *(10:30 R close kneel)* pulling him forward onto his toes, cover L lifting R forearm under his chin to push his throat w/an Out wrist lock throwing him backwards into the wall as R forearm presses his trachea and L hand slams his R thumb into wall.

4. Follow his momentum with right front knee kick to his groin.

5. Step R back *(LNB facing wall at 6)* w/L horiz palm to R ribs *(Liver)*, R position check.

6. Defensive switch to a 6 RNB with a R straight palm strike up under his chin *(and/or 4-finger strike into his eyes)* driving that back of his head into the wall.

7. R down claw his face w/possible forward vertical elbow strike into his sternum then into a right inward elbow strike to his left rib cage, with a left-hand position check.

8. RFB w/R outward BKS to his right temple and L vertical punch to his solar plexus.

9. Angle change L foot back to 4:30 R close kneel w/R back hammerfist his groin and L In heel of palm R jaw hinge *(or temple)* pivot to In windshield wiper slice thru his eyes before hooking outward around the back of his neck.

10. Adjust to a RNB while pulling his head down at the neck with a R upward forearm strike under his chin that then wraps up around his throat *(reverse headlock)*.

11. Pull his head down turning his face towards you w/R Up knee to his R temple, R front crossover to 12 holding his neck *(for safety grab training partners shoulders)*.

12. L toe to R levering his neck at chin & back of head *(shoulders in practice)* turns him back to you, R step back to 12 slamming him to his back, L rear crossover out exit to 12.

**Ground Option:** While mounted against R punch or R cross collar choke L pins R hand w/R In raking hammerfist thru nose to collapse R elbow crease, R Out handsword R side of neck then grabbing neck or clothing to pull forward and down as L foot posts outside his R heel lifting hips to bridge &/or R knee to tailbone rolling him over ending in Top Guard, use tenderizing or ground & pound to escape *(Closed Guard: elbow-punch-palm strike/press inner knees & groin, pinch tender skin areas, heel palm bladder, knee tailbone, Open Guard: elbow-punch-palm legs, knee on groin or side, kick inner legs, crossover knee drop on legs, etc).*

### CRADLING THE BABY *(Gathering Clouds)*
**Right Crossing Punch Stepping Thru from 12**
1. L In parry outside R punch stepping L towards 10:30 to modified horse stance w/R inward knocking punch glancing thru his right medial elbow nerve *(SI8)*.
2. Step drag R to 3 R close kneel w/R Out handsword R kidney as L knee hits and checks outside his R knee.
3. Step drag L to 10:30 close kneel w/R In elbow thru then behind his R rib cage as your R knee hits and checks inside his R knee.
4. R front step thru towards 10:30 pushing his R knee *(moves his lower body back)* w/R Out elbow pushing his upper back *(moves his upper body forwards)* bending him to 6.
5. Quickly bring R foot to L *(def reverse switch)* then L rear sliding leg sweep thru inside of his R leg *(his right hand braces the ground to avoid falling face first into the floor)*.
6. L front step thru sweep kick thru R wrist *(his supporting arm)* causing him to fall onto his stomach, in the same motion L toe to R *(spinning R)* to R rear thrust kick down onto his right kidney, then front crossover step out towards 7:30 to exit.

### JUMPING CRANE *(Leaping Crane)*
**Right Crossing Punch Stepping Thru from 12**
1. Jump L to L 1-legged stance w/L In parry catching outside R punch w/R inward knocking punch thru his right inner elbow *(SI8)*.
2. R side snap kick back of his R knee *(buckles him to his knee at 1:30)*.
3. Step forward *(1:30 RNB between his feet)* w/R down BKS to low spine *(arches back)*.
4. R In elbow sandwiching w/L inward heel of palm strike his neck *(GB20s)*.
5. Reach over his L shoulder w/R grabbing his chin, L posts at back of his L shoulder, RFB pulling your R to your R ear as L holds and braces his L shoulder *(neck tweak)*.
6. Still holding shoulder adjust to RNB w/R inward handsword strike to the back of his neck then grab the top of his two shoulders *(holding both shoulders with your hands)*.
7. Shift back *(R rear bow)*, R front scoop kick thru his groin, L front snap kick low spine *(chicken kick)*, R front stomp his R calf *(or Achilles)* as L hand holds his R shoulder.
8. Step off his calf forward L then R *(both end outside his R leg w/weight on your R foot)* followed by L Out hook kick back into his sternum *(or face)* causing him to fall onto his back at 7:30 then step forward w/L looking over your R shoulder at opponent.
9. Drag step, rear crossover, or leap towards opponent ending w/R side thrust kick (or stomp) onto his face, then right front crossover towards 4:30 to exit.

### SHIELD AND PUNCH *(Shield and Mace)*
**Right Crossing Punch Stepping Thru from 12**
1. R Out parrying block R to R punch stepping L foot forward off angle to 12 L forward 45o horse w/L horiz thrust punch (hits & pushes his R kidney/hip *(bracing punch check)*.
2. Moves #2-4 flow together as inward overlapping circles. R down hammerfist R low back *(kidney area)* circling your L hand up to check back of his R shoulder.
3. L hand pushes his R arm down as R hand circles up to In heel palm claw his face.
4. L checks his R shoulder, drop to L wide kneel w/R downward outward handsword strike to the back of his right knee at 3 *(buckles his knee)*.
5. Stand up w/R side snap kick to back of his L knee while your L hand pulls down on his right shoulder *(both his knees should be buckled to the ground)*.
6. Now behind step between his legs to RNB w/R In handsword R side of his neck.
7. RFB w/L In handsword L side of his neck *(sandwiching w/R hand)*, clinch his neck *(hands on chin)*, lever his chin up w/forearms anchored at upper back *(him looking up)*.
8. L knee kick middle spine, step outside his L foot, R front knee kick his spine, cross step behind your L *(L front twist to 4:30)* holding his chin *(shoulders in training)*.

9. Un-pivot to LNB turning his head over his R shoulder *(shoulders in training)* turning him over face down, R front snap ball kick his face then step back to exit.

## THUNDERING FISTS *(Thundering Hammers)*
### Right Roundhouse or Hook Punch from 12
1. Slip R, duck under punch *(bob)* to L rev wide kneel letting his arm travel over your head w/L hand checking your head. EPAK version & Form 4 against a R crossing punch
2. Shift L *(possible step)* to 10:30 L wide kneel *(weave)* outside R hip w/R forward stiff-arm punch to groin *(or R forearm solar plexus)*, L cocked by L ear *(R knee check R knee)*.
3. Stand up w/R elbow up vertically checking outside his R armpit shifting R to R wide kneel w/L down hammerfist to R kidney *(L knee checks outside his R knee)*.
4. Place L hand to check the back of his R shoulder shifting L to L wide kneel w/R downward hammerfist onto the back of his neck *(your R knee checking his R knee)*.
5. Step back L to RNB circling your R arm inside and up *(possible In hammerfist his R bicep or L temple)* ending w/your R hand in front of your L shoulder.
6. Push drag towards opponent w/R down whipping BKS thru back of his neck *(chambering your R hand)* as your L hand continues to hold and check his R shoulder.
7. Shuffle forward as needed w/R inv palm strike to R side of his jaw as your L hand pushes his right shoulder *(turning him CCW until his back is facing you)*.
### Skip to move 10 for Option 2
**Option 1:** *(if opponent is your size or smaller)*
8. After opponent turned around gauge back pulling him back down until his back is lying on your R thigh.
9. L then R downward hammerfists onto his L then R collarbones.
**Option 2:** *(skip moves 8-9 if opponent too big, you lose control or just prefer this option)*
10. R rear step thru towards 6 pulling back against his chin with your hands slamming the back of his head and body onto the ground in front of you at 12.
11. L foot inside out then L side stomp his sternum, L TSK face w/crossover exit to 6.

## DANCE OF DEATH *(Dance of Death)*
### Right Boxers Cross Punch from 12
1. L In parry catches his punch, L step forward to 12 LNB outside his R arm, L close kneel w/R underhand rev handsword his groin *(L hand checks outside his R elbow)*.
2. R obscure elbow under his chin, then place back of R hand outside his shoulder at armpit to prevent Guillotine w/pull guard counter, as L reaches down to pick up back of his R knee *(your knees aligned between his)*, R outer reap takedown trips him down to his back *(you in horse stance to 10:30 whim on his back w/both legs up outside of your hips)*.
3. Still holding his R leg w/your L arm *(possible ankle or calf compression lock)* R Out whipping BKS thru inside of his L knee followed by R down inv vert punch his groin as your R knee drops onto the inside of his left thigh *(left wide kneel stance)*.
4. Your R hand slides to his R heel as your L slides to top of his toes, cover w/ ankle twist turnover flipping him over onto his stomach *(you are in a 1:30 RFB)*.
5. L front crossover stomp kick onto his low back *(lumbar)* letting go of his R leg *(1:30 RFB)* then jump over him to R foot outside his R hip *(towards 4:30)*.
6. L side snap kick R kidney, L sliding stomp sliding to ground tight against R side *(can pinch clothes &/or skin)*, L close kneel drops w/R down handsword back of neck *(cervical)*.
7. R front crossover stomp kick onto his middle back *(thoracic)* moving towards 10:30 then jump off to L foot above his L shoulder w/R rear thrust kick down onto L pocket of his neck *(or skull)* then right front crossover towards 10:30 to exit.

## CIRCLING THE ARM *(Circling the Horizon)*
### Right Punch Stepping Thru from 12
1. L In parry catches outside his R punch stepping forward L to 45o horse stance to 12.
2. R foot then steps forward to 1:30 R cat as L checks outside his R elbow circling your L hand inside and up to a R vertical thrust punch into his nose.
3. Step R forward behind his R foot to 1:30 RNB w/R inward elbow strike to his ribs as left hand maintains check now holding outside his right shoulder.
4. Drop down to L knee w/R down out hammerfist back inside angle of his R knee *(buckles and opens his knee)* followed by R upward reverse hammerfist up into his groin.

5. Circle R hand out and up *(possible R BKS thru his R knee)* followed by In Dow heel palm his sternum w/R rear sliding leg sweep thru back of his R leg, L hand pulls him down onto his back pinning him to ground w/both hands *(you still on one knee)*.

6. Plant R foot near your L knee then stand up w/optional L glancing heel kick thru his R rib cage turning R w/a jump spin motion ending w/R rear thrust kick down onto his face then right front crossover towards 4:30 to exit.

**COMPULSIVE KNEEL** *(Kneel of Compulsion)*
**Right Crossing Punch Stepping Thru from 3**
*The 6 Depth Zone lines (dz) covered in this technique.*

1. L In parry outside his R punch *(dz1)*, R step outside his R foot w/R Out parry outside his right elbow *(dz2)* together possibly tweaking his elbow.

2. Grab his R shoulder *(dz3)* w/R hand, step forward L toe to R behind grabbing his L shoulder *(dz5)* w/L, step back R *(offensive reverse switch)* ending in 7:30 LFB pulling him back onto his heels controlling his centerline *(dz4)*.

3. R step thru side snap kick back of his L knee (dz6) pulling his R shoulder back and down while pushing his L shoulder forward (rotates him around and down to his L knee).

4. Settle R foot forward between his legs *(RNB behind him)* w/R In elbow his R mastoid w/L inward heel-of-palm to his L mastoid or jaw hinge *(sandwiching his head)*.

5. Gauge R foot into a L spinning outward hook kick thru his head.

<u>Extension Begins Here</u>

5. Grab and hook back of his neck w/R bringing L toe to R inverting your L hand to grab R wrist *(your L palm up)* pushing his hand behind his back *(hammerlock position)*.

6. Step back R *(completes off switch)* to 4:30 pulling him down onto his face dropping L knee on his R kidney *(R close kneel to 4:30)* w/R down palm strike to R scapula.

7. Stand up *(gauge R as needed)* w/L Out ax kick to L side of neck/collarbone *(1:30)*.

8. Gauge L foot as needed, R down knee back of neck/upper spine *(1:30 L close kneel)*.

9. Bounce up off previous knee switching in the air over his head landing w/L down knee drop onto back of his neck/upper spine *(1:30 right close kneel)*.

10. Stand up sliding your R ankle to support his neck, front rotating twist L connects L ankle w/his head *(his neck against R ankle and head against your L locking his neck)*.

11. L rear step thru tweaks his neck to a RNB *(use extreme caution in practice)*.

**Ground Option:** While mounted or in Half-Guard L In parry, R Out parry vs R punch grabbing R shoulder w/R hand, L knee tailbone *(drives body weight forward)* as L hand reaches to grab over L shoulder *(hair, chin, or clothing)*; either post L foot outside R heel then bridge to roll over L shoulder to top position *(them possibly on side)* or Hip Escape L from underneath driving them face first into floor, use tenderizing or ground & pound to escape *(Hip Escape: Take back; Closed Guard: elbow-punch-palm strike/press inner knees & groin, pinch tender skin areas, heel palm bladder, knee tailbone, Open Guard: elbow-punch-palm legs, knee on groin or side, kick inner legs, crossover knee drop on legs, etc)*.

**BACKBREAKER** *(The Back Breaker)*
**Right Punch Stepping Thru from 3**

1. L Iin parry outside R punch, step R outside his R foot w/R outward parry outside his R elbow together possibly tweaking his elbow.

2. Grab R shoulder w/R, step forward L toe to R behind grabbing his L shoulder w/L, step back R *(off rev switch)* to 7:30 LFB pulling him to his heels controlling his centerline.

3. R knee kick middle spine, step back to LFB pulling him back onto your L thigh.

4. Cradle around L side of his chin *(optional L thumb gouge L eye)* causing him to look up to his R while your R hand cocks by your R ear.

5. Right downward handsword strike across the side of his nose.

6. Dbl down BKS thru two collarbones *(flair your elbows out then rotate palms up while flapping your elbows down to accelerate)*.

7. Circle hands inward grabbing under his chin, L rear step thru guiding his head back and down *(possible face claws)* slamming and pinning him to the ground.

8. R Out rotating side of heel kick his R jaw hinge *(moves his head)*, R toe to L *(spinning L)*, L rear sliding heel stomp onto his R collarbone, front crossover towards 1:30 to exit.

**REVERSING FIST** *(Reversing Mace)*
**Left Lunging Jab or Step Thru Punch from 12**

1. Step back L offline to 12 rev NB w/R In parry outside L punch then left outward parry *(double factor)* at the back of his left elbow *(possible elbow tweak)*.

2. Countergrab L wrist w/L, pull his weight to his L foot w/R Out BKS L ribs *(Spleen)*.

3. Right downward wheel kick to buckle the back of his left knee to ground.

<u>Extension Begins Here</u>

4. R foot outside his L calf, L rear crossover over his L between his legs with a R downward outward hammerfist onto his L collarbone.

5. Un-pivot to your L *(R heel / L ball)* w/L Out BKS R mastoid, chambering your R.

6. Grab his collar *(hair or L shoulder)* w/L adjusting R foot around to 7:30 LNB *(L def rear turn)*, LFB w/R horiz thrust punch to middle spine *(T7 at lower scapula border)*.

8. Grab his shoulders w/both hands, R front knee kick his low spine followed by a right inverted side stomp down onto the back of his left Achilles tendon *(or calf)*.

9. Step thru back R pulling him back down to his back, L TSK thru face w/exit to 1:30.

**Ground Option:** While mounted or Half-Guard, R In parry, L Out parry vs L punch grabbing his L shoulder w/L hand, R knee tailbone drives body weight forward as R hand reaches to grab over R shoulder *(hair, chin, clothing)*; either post R foot outside L heel then bridge to roll over your R shoulder to top position *(them possibly on side)* or Hip Escape R from underneath driving them face first to floor, use tenderizing or ground & pound to escape *(Hip Escape: Take back; Closed Guard: elbow-punch-palm strike/press inner knees & groin, pinch tender skin areas, heel palm bladder, knee tailbone, Open Guard: elbow-punch-palm legs, knee on groin or side, kick inner legs, crossover knee drop on legs, etc)*.

**DESTRUCTIVE CIRCLES** *(Circling Destruction)*
**Left Lunging Jab or Step Thru Punch - 12**

1. R In parry outside his L hand, L Out parry back of L elbow *(possible elbow tweak)*, step forward R to 12 RNB *(behind his L foot)* w/R Out whipping BKS thru L ribs *(back of your L hand still attached checking outside his L elbow)*.

2. L steps behind your R *(R close kneel to 9)* w/L In heel palm his L temple *(In Ext: hook & grab chin anchoring L forearm behind L trapezius muscle, no slack in neck)* R at R ear.

3. RNB w/R straight palm to L mastoid *(neck tweak in Ext can damage the neck)*.

4. Grab both shoulders *(square him up and control his weight shift)* shifting back to R rear bow w/R front scoop kick thru his groin, R side snap kick back of L knee *(buckle)*.

5. Step forward to 3 RFB w/dbl palm strikes his back driving him face first to ground.

<u>Extension Begins Here</u>

5. Step forward to 3 RNB R knee into tailbone pulling his shoulders *(him onto knees)*.

6. L front crossover outside L leg/hip pushing him forward down to floor with your two hands dropping R knee onto his tailbone *(pins his hips to the ground)*.

7. Stand up, R front stomp kick lumbar spine *(R foot parallel moving up his spine)*.

8. Standing on his back, L front crossover w/L inverted side stomp down between his shoulder blades onto his thoracic spine *(3rd spinal section as you move up his back)*.

9. Jump off his back landing on L foot outside his L shoulder w/R down knee drop across his neck *(Cervical Spine, 4th spinal segment up his back)* w/possible R downward palm strike to the back of his head *(your right foot is outside his right shoulder)*.

10. Jump or bounce off previous knee turning 180° CW in the air *(switching your feet)* landing R outside his L shoulder w/L front stomp his head *(or neck)*, step back L to exit.

**HAND AND SHIELD** *(Shield and Sword)*
**Left Crossing Punch Stepping Thru from 12**

1. R In parry outside L punch, stepping R forward to 1:30 *(12 R forward 45o horse)*.

2. R close kneel to 1:30 *(check L knee angle at 10:30 w/your L knee)* w/L Out parry to his left elbow *(elbow tweak in extension)*, R hand chambers.

3. Step drag L to 9 *(L off front turn)* to L close kneel *(R knee checking his L knee)* w/R In rev handsword to R mastoid *(GB20)* maintaining L arm check against his left elbow.

4. Pull his neck w/last strike shifting R *(off front turn)* to 12 close-kneel w/L In elbow to left ribs *(if his L arm up)* or forehead/temple *(if his L arm down)*, R checks L elbow.

5. L rear crossover to 4:30 *(10:30 front twist)* checking back of L shoulder w/L hand w/R fist next to your R ear, un-pivot *(L ball/R heel)* to 10:30 R side horse w/R In raking hammerfist or hook punch thru R or L kidney *(best available)*, weight to L leg *(10:30 R rev close kneel)*.
6. Right side thrust kick to the back or outside of his left knee.
<u>Extension Begins Here</u>
7. With R kick still in air step R towards 1:30 w/L side thrust kick thru back of his R knee *(regulate these 2 kicks so he is buckled but not kneeling)*.
8. Continue turning L toe to R *(spinning CW)* to R rear scoop kick thru his groin at 9.
9. Bounce ball of R foot off ground w/R rear thrust kick into his tailbone then R front crossover step out towards 3 to exit.

## TWIRLING FIST *(Twirling Hammers)*
### Left Crossing Punch Stepping Thru from 12
1. LNB/natural position, L front crossover to 1:30 w/L Ext Block outside his L wrist.
2. R step behind his L heel hooking his foot *(R knee checks his L knee in R side horse)* w/In whipping BKS thru his R mastoid *(GB20)* while your L hand checks his L elbow.
3. Adjust R to 12 *(R close kneel w/L knee checking his L knee)* w/L in elbow his L ribs or temple *(if his L arm drops)* w/R check to L shoulder.
4. Adjust L *(offensive front turn)* to w/L out hooking check top of his L wrist w/R In handsword his R kidney *(possible neck tweak in transition)* as R knee checks his L knee.
5. R push sweep L foot to 7:30 *(widen his base w/L hand at L shoulder pushes weight off that foot)*, R at back of his head as L punches his face *(sandwich)* in front twist to 7:30.
6. Step L toe to R pushing *(Off switch)* L checks his L knee *(possible neck tweak in transition)* step back R to 1:30 LNB w/L horiz 2-finger eye poke, R position check L elbow.

## PARRYING GRAB *(Snaking Talon)*
### Left Jab / Right Cross Boxers Combo from 12
1. L step back *(12 RNB)* w/R In parry catching and guiding outside of his L punch.
2. R cat w/R Out parry outside his follow up R punch attaching and grabbing his right wrist pulling him forward and off balance with a left-hand position check.
3. R front snap kick groin, R front crossover to 7:30 *(rear twist to 1:30)* pulling him forward and down by his R wrist.
4. L Up hook kick face *(if head low)*, step out, R Side Thrust Kick to R knee at 1:30.
<u>Extension Begins Here</u>
5. From kick R toe to L *(spinning maneuver)*, L Out leg sweep inside his R shin *(circular sweep spreads his legs and break his balance)* until you are in a 12 L reverse bow.
6. Cover to 12 LFB w/dbl In ear box, grab around his head w/both hands *(Thai clinch)*.
7. R front knee kick his solar plexus, extend R Up stiff leg lifting shin kick into groin.
8. Loosen clinch, R Up knee kick his face, extend R front push kick into his chest or solar plexus to clear him away, then step back right to a LNB.

**Ground Option:** While mounted or in Half-Guard L In parry, R In parry combo punch attack *(or dbl lapel grab or 2 hand choke weaving R arm over collapsing his L arm, then under and back of his R arm)*, L knee tailbone *(pushes body weight forward)*, apply R side arm triangle or rear naked choke. Either post L foot outside R heel then bridge to roll over your L shoulder to top position *(them possibly on side)* or Hip Escape out L from underneath driving them face first into floor, use tenderizing or ground & pound to escape *(Hip Escape: Take back; Closed Guard: elbow-punch-palm strike/press inner knees & groin, pinch tender skin areas, heel palm bladder, knee tailbone, Open Guard: elbow-punch-palm legs, knee on groin or side, kick inner legs, crossover knee drop on legs, etc)*.

## ENTWINED FISTS *(Entwined Maces)*
### Left Jab / Right Cross Boxers Combo from 12
1. L step back to 12 RNB w/R In parry catching and guiding outside his L punch.
2. R Out parry R cross punch grabbing his R wrist to pull adjusting to RFB w/L vert thrust punch to his R jaw hinge.
3. RNB with a right inward handsword strike to the left side of his neck.
4. L rear crossover outside his L foot w/R In Raking Finger Slice eyes, R In elbow L jaw.
5. Transition thru R rev cat, R rear sliding leg sweep thru inside L knee w/R right back hammerfist groin as L hand checks *(possible palm or finger poke)*.

6. Modified RNB w/R Out raking hammerfist thru his nose pivoting to R front twist *(R heel pivot)* w/L arm cross-body check across his chest line *(possible pec pinch)*.

7. L then R chicken knee kick to his groin with R arm cocked to your R.

8. Settle weight forward to 12 RNB w/R down hammerfist onto his L collarbone.

9. R front crossover step out exit to 6 then *(go back for seconds)* L rear crossover towards him w/R side thrust kick best available body target, R front crossover out to 6.

## CIRCLING PARRIES *(Circling Fans)*
### Left Jab - Right Cross Boxers Combo from 12
1. Step back L *(12 RNB)* w/R In parry catching guiding his L punch down to your left.
2. R cat w/L In parry catching and guiding R punch down to your R as R chambers.
3. Right front snap kick to his groin.
4. Step forward *(RNB)* w/R inv horiz snap punch *(uppercut)* between his eyes or under his chin or half-fist his throat *(as he bends)* as L hand checks across the top of his arms.
5. L front crossover to front twist w/R cross body check down across his arms and left vertical thrust punch to his sternum driving him backwards.
6. R front knee kick his groin w/L cross body check *(possible pec pinch)*, R chambers.
7. Step forward to rev RNB *(or side horse)* w/R Uprolling forearm strike under his chin *(continues driving him backwards)*.
8. L rear crossover step to 12 w/R side thrust kick to best available body target then R front crossover step out towards 6 to exit.

**Ground Option:** While mounted R In parry catches L punch, L In parry catches R punch grabbing & holding wrist across centerline *(both his arms could be crossed)*, L knee kick tailbone *(pushes him forward)* applying R side arm triangle or CAC. Bridge to roll over L shoulder or Hip Escape L, tenderizing or ground & pound to escape *(Hip Escape: Take back; Closed Guard: elbow-punch-palm strike/press inner knees & groin, pinch tender skin areas, heel palm bladder, knee tailbone, Open Guard: elbow-punch-palm legs, knee on groin or side, kick inner legs, crossover knee drop on legs, etc)*.

## PROTECTIVE PARRIES *(Protective Fans)*
### Left Jab / Right Cross Combo from 12
1. From LNB R In parry catching the outside his left jab.
2. L In parry catches outside R punch w/L slip and step to 10:30 *(LFB)* w/R Out parry above R elbow *(possible elbow tweak)*, sliding down to counter grab his R wrist.
3. Transition thru R cat to 1:30 pulling him forward and down by his R wrist w/R front snap kick to his groin and left horizontal two-finger thrust into his right eye.
4. Step forward to a 1:30 RNB as your L hand checks his R arm down w/R inward elbow strike into his solar plexus *(bring his head down)*.
5. Rebound off his chest w/R Out finger flick thru his R eye turning your shoulders to modified RNB then shift your weight back to a R rear bow stance.
6. R In eye rake thru L eye w/R front scoop kick thru his groin stepping back to exit.

**Ground Option:** While mounted R catches L punch, L catches R punch followed by R Out parry, L eye poke w/L knee kick to tailbone *(breaks balance)* w/R side arm triangle or rear naked choke. Bridge to roll over your L shoulder or Hip Escape L to crawl out from underneath, tenderizing/ground & pound to escape *(Hip Escape: Take back; Closed Guard: elbow-punch-palm strike/press inner knees & groin, pinch tender skin areas, heel palm bladder, knee tailbone, Open Guard: elbow-punch-palm legs, knee on groin or side, kick inner legs, crossover knee drop on legs, etc)*.

# UNDERNEATH ARM DEFENSES
## PROTECTIVE CIRCLES *(Circles of Protection)*
### Right Overhead Strike Stepping from 12
1. R Up parry ducking under punch stepping forward to LNB w/forward horiz elbow strike into attacker's R armpit nerve *(training partners check this point for safety)*.
2. L Out claw face, grab inside his R wrist posting back of his R wrist to your L hip circling R to underhand heel palm *(possible groin grab or glancing strike)* on way to wrap under his R arm locking elbow joint adjusting to 10:30 LFB.

3. Step R to 6 RFB *(offensive cover)* pushing his wrist w/L hand pulling his elbow joint w/R arm *(pressure moves him to your R)*.

4. L front crossover push sweep inside L ankle widens base *(best before weight settles)*.

5. Step L to your L then R front step thru sweep (looks like a roundhouse kick) inside his R ankle at 10:30 *(further widening his base)*.

6. Continue moving L bringing R toe spinning w/L rear thrust, rear stiff leg lift, or rear scoop kick his groin *(depends on range)* then R front crossover step out exit towards 7:30.

## TURNING WINDMILLS *(Circling Windmills)*
### Two-Hand Push then High Right Punch from 12

1. Wall behind you: Rebound from wall or just step forward to 12 LNB w/R Up parry ducking under punch w/R forward horiz elbow R armpit nerve *(partners check for safety)*.

2. L out claw his face on path to grab inside his R wrist circling R hand Out, LFB as L hand posts his R palm to your L hip w/R In hammerfist his solar plexus.

3. Reach under his R elbow *(possible tweak)*, lift his R arm over head R grabs back of his R wrist posting his inner wrist to your R hip w/L In hammerfist R kidney or elbow.

4. L step back L grabs his L elbow, step forward R *(def switch)* w/R In hammerfist thru his nose, R Out 2-finger slice *(palm down)* thru R eye, In 2-finger slice *(palm up)* thru L, then 4-finger Out splay using each finger thru both eyes on way to grab his R wrist.

5. Front rotating twist with L vertical thrust punch to his face.

6. Un-pivot to a RNB with a L outward two-finger slice thru his R eye.

7. R to R front crossover sweep to 7:30, R pulls R wrist w/L In horiz 2-finger poke R eye.

8. Grab his R wrist w/L hand, step out L *(along wall)* w/R straight palm to R side of his face *(St5-6)*, Out / In windshield wiper finger slice eyes, Out crane hook over R side neck.

9. Adjust to R rev close kneel pushing his head down, R Up heel kick face, R front crossover step *(still moving along wall)* circling R arm to back hammerfist R collarbone or jaw.

10. Un-pivot L placing both hands on the wall for support then L side thrust kick inside his L knee *(or best available)*, L front crossover out along the wall to exit.

## DESTRUCTIVE PARRIES *(Destructive Fans)*
### Right High Cross Punch Stepping Thru from 9

1. L Inward parry outside his high R punch, L cat to 9 w/R Out parry back of his R elbow *(tweaks elbow)*. Note: Original EPAK technique and Form 5 starts w/R Up parry.

2. L circles up, grabs back of R elbow *(above joint)*, step 9 LNB behind his R foot *(L knee checks back of his R knee)* w/R In hammerfist R ribs *(Liver side)* holding R elbow w/L.

3. L front crossover pushing sweep inside R ankle to 3 pulling his R arm w/L hand *(widens his base)* ending in a front twist stance.

4. Un-pivot R *(L heel / R ball)* to 1:30 R rev cat *(him over R shoulder at 1:30)*, possible elbow tweak w/your L, R Out whip BKS R kidney, L hand checks outside his R shoulder.

5. R rear sliding leg sweep back of R knee w/R vert thrust punch nose driving him back onto the ground *(7:30 LFB)*.

6. Jump R front stomp kick onto his face at 6, R front crossover towards 4:30 to exit.

## 12. KICK INTO DARKNESS *(Thrust into Darkness)*
### Right High Reverse Punch from 6

1. Step forward R to 12 *(6 L rev close kneel)* looking over left shoulder with a left rear thrust kick into attacker's groin then replant that left foot.

2. Pivot L to 6 L front twist *(facing opponent)* then R front snap kick his solar plexus *(or groin)*, step forward to a RNB with a right straight palm strike to his nose.

3. Hook R hand over back of his R elbow hopping onto your L foot to 3 *(L one-legged stance outside his R leg with universal check)*.

4. Right side snap kick to back of his R knee *(buckle him to his knees)*.

5. Step down to 9 RNB w/L on top piggyback punch low spine *(make him arch backwards)* then R front crossover out away to 3.

6. L rear crossover towards him at 9 w/R side thrust kick to the back of his neck *(or side stomp onto the back of his left knee if he is face down)* then front cross out to exit.

276

# CLUB / KNIFE / GUN WEAPON ATTACKS

Attacker threatening or aggressively attacking with a *Club, Knife*, or holding a *Gun* within reach.

Note: These formulations evaluate the positioning for defending against weapon attacks if no other option is available. Running away would be the recommended first choice, zigzag if running from a pointed gun. If unable to avoid a club or knife attack, find an equalizer weapon like a knife, gun, baseball bat, tree branch, trash can lid, shoe, jacket, rock, dirt, etc. An empty-handed defense against a weapon wielding attacker should be the last choice.

The *Club* technique formula here defends against the overhead downward swing by moving inside, outside, or under the weapon arm; against the horizontal swing by moving inside the forehand arc or outside the backhand arc; and moving the weapon (and possibly us) offline against the club poke.

Note: The original EPAK technique club attack design was against the shorter one handheld club, like an escrima stick, or more likely a hammer in our time, but these should also be practiced against the longer baseball bat used with two hands, as this is common in our culture. The techniques still work under these circumstances but with slight modifications that should be practiced.

The *Knife* is considered the most dangerous close-range weapon and is often not seen, being perceived as a punch in the heat of battle, but if seen then environmental props should be used to help defend against this deadly weapon.

Contained here are: 1 *Threatening Knife Defense*, 4 *Linear Thrust Defenses* at different quadrants, and 3 *Circular Motion Defenses* that evaluate the overhead, forehand, and backhand swipes. See "Knife Defense Formula" video at BarryBBarker.com for the full explanation.

The *Gun* technique formula has only 4 techniques in the Kenpo system. They are *inside* and *outside* gun defenses with one each against front and rear close attackers holding the gun in one hand. Practicing these against a two-hand held gun would also be recommended.

Note: *Defying the Gun* is a rear gun attack here, as done in Form 6, to create this balance. See "Gun Defense Formula" video at BarryBBarker.com for these and other useful gun takeaways not covered in the Kenpo techniques.

Caution: These or any empty-handed technique against a trained expert intent on using any of these weapons against us is almost impossible. Trained people are less likely to allow themselves to be in a position for these defenses to even start (sorry if that is breaking news). Luckily, trained people are not who we are generally concerned with attacking us in the civilian self-defense environment.

# CLUB

CHECKING THE CLUB *(Checking the Storm)* Pg 278
EVADING THE CLUB *(Evading the Storm)* Pg 278
BRUSHING THE CLUB *(Brushing the Storm)* Pg 279
OBSTRUCTING THE CLUB *(Obstructing the Storm)* Pg 279
CAPTURING THE CLUB *(Capturing the Storm)* Pg 280
CALMING THE CLUB *(Calming the Storm)* Pg 280
DEFYING THE CLUB *(Defying the Storm)* Pg 280
SECURING THE CLUB *(Securing the Storm)* – plus Ground Option Pg 281
RETURNING CLUB *(Returning Storm)* Pg 281
CIRCLING THE CLUB *(Circling the Storm)* Pg 282

# KNIFE

LEAP OF DEATH *(Leap of Death)* Pg 282
GLANCING BLADE *(Glancing Lance)* Pg 283
CLIPPING THE BLADE 1-2 *(Clipping Lance/Clipping the Storm)* Pg 283
UNEXPECTED BLADE *(Unfurling Lance)* Pg 283
THRUSTING BLADE *(Thrusting Lance)* Pg 284
ENTWINED BLADE *(Entwined Lance)* Pg 284
PIERCING BLADE *(Piercing Lance)* Pg 284
RAINING BLADE *(Raining Lance)* Pg 285

# GUN

CAPTURING THE GUN *(Capturing the Rod)* Pg 285
TWISTED GUN *(Twisted Rod)* Pg 285
DEFYING THE GUN *(Defying the Rod)* Pg 286
BROKEN GUN *(Broken Rod)* Pg 286

# CLUB

**CHECKING THE CLUB** *(Checking the Storm)*
***Right Overhead Club Step Thru from 12***
1. R step to 3 w/R inward parry to the inside of attacker's right wrist.
2. L foot to L cat *(facing 10:30)* w/L Out parry sliding to grab the stick w/R hand position check. The Ext grabs inner R wrist w/slight Out twist to disrupt posture.
3. L front snap kick groin, R front snap kick sternum/solar plexus *(chicken kick)* stepping R forward to 10:30w/R palm to his R bicep or wrist taking weapon w/L hand.
Extension Begins Here:
3. R step to 10:30 RNB *(holding his R wrist in L hand),* R stiff-armed lifting punch up thru his nose *(lifts his head),* if not bent from kick strike solar plexus then R hand up.
4. R rear bow w/R front scoop kick thru his groin w/R down heel palm claw his face.
5. Step forward to RNB, L rear crossover *(rear twist)* w/R Up elbow under chin *(still holding R wrist),* R down heel palm nose, grab hair *(collar or hook neck if no hair)* w/R.
6. Step out L to 4:30 *(R rev close kneel to 10:30)* w/R side thrust kick to R ribs *(L hand strips weapon if still holding)* driving him away, R front crossover step out exit to 6.

**EVADING THE CLUB** *(Evading the Storm)*
***Right Overhead Club Step Thru from 12***
1. Step L to 9 w/L In parry outside R wrist, grab that wrist w/R *(possible R Up block dbl factor slows arm with possible elbow tweak),* L check leaning onto L foot *(R rev bow).*
2. Pull his R arm to break his balance w/R ball wheel kick to his groin.
3. R to 3 *(RFB)* w/L horiz thrust punch R kidney then pushing R hip *(hold R wrist).*
4. L front knee kick back of R knee *(or side of thigh depending on angle)* to buckle his R knee, place your L foot on ground to the inside of his R foot towards 12.

5. R down knee to 12 drops on his R calf or Achilles *(depends on his foot position)*.

6. Stand up, step back R extending his R arm w/L inv palm *(fingers down)* to his R elbow then into a left bicep strike *(compound break)*.

<u>Extension Begins Here:</u>

5. R down knee *(12)* on R calf or Achilles feeding his R wrist to your L hand, R arm under elbow crease *(hook & bend his R elbow up)* R hand on upper back *(hammerlock)*.

6. Cover step R driving him face down onto the ground to 1:30, L knee drop on R kidney jamming his arm as R hand releases lock, grab his bent R elbow *(fingers to you)*.

7. Cover step L dropping R knee to brace his medial R scapula and neck to ground as L hand switches grip to back of his wrist *(your two arms crossed at his wrist and elbow)* pulling his R wrist and elbow *(damaging his shoulder)*.

9. Jump up crossing your feet in the air *(front twist)* landing a R inv stomp kick onto his upper spine then step back R to exit.

**BRUSHING THE CLUB** *(Brushing the Storm)*
***Right Overhead Club Step Thru from 3***

1. L In parry outside R wrist, step R to 3 outside his rear foot, or place your foot inside w/your knee outside to jam his knee with a R straight palm heel thrust under his chin.

2. L front crossover to 3 L close kneel *(if inside foot R knee buckle)*, L hand checks his R arm w/R In flapping elbow his solar plexus, R underhand heel palm his groin.

3. Step/swing R leg back around to 7:30 L cat as R arm slides down his R leg picking it up *(inner knee then slide down to ankle)* as L hand pushes his R hip down from behind to make him bend forward putting his hands on the ground.

4. L upward front kick his groin then down to a L front twist stance.

5. R side snap kick back of his L knee *(buckling him to ground)*, R step back over his R leg *(Out hook kick motion possibly passing his R leg to your L hand behind your back)*.

6. R knee drops on back of R calf *(possible R elbow his tailbone to make him lay flat)* as L picks up his L foot *(L hand to top of foot w/R over outside holding back of heel)*.

7. Stand up, cover step R turning him over onto his back *(ankle twist turnover)*, L knee drop above his R knee *(holds him down)* sliding R hand outside his L ankle, inverted palm strike *(fingers down)* his inner knee to tweak and clear his leg away opening his groin.

8. Stand up moving L w/R glancing front heel kick thru his groin then step R outside his R hip *(toes in)* turning left *(spinning motion)*.

9. Spin L w/out stomp kick his sternum *(or Out hook kick his chin)*, step outside his R shoulder *(toes out)*.

10. R roundhouse ball kick under his chin and thru his face then picking up club *(or scissoring with your feet)* while exiting towards 4:30.

**OBSTRUCTING THE CLUB** *(Obstructing the Storm)*
***Right Overhead Club from 12***

1. Step forward *(12 modified LNB)* w/Up cross block *(L hand below R)* under wrist(s), intending to counter grab and move offline using weapons downward momentum.

2. Grab his R wrist in R hand pivoting L forearm on R forearm until your L hand is up w/L ulna bone against his R elbow joint *(tricep tendon at TW10/11)*, welding inside *(medial)* R wrist against your R hip, adjusting your R foot back to 7:30 *(LNB facing 1:30)*.

3. L forearm vigorously rubs his elbow joint (MSC) while moving your feet as necessary *(cancel height, width, and depth)* until his left hand reaches for the ground.

4. R front knee kick his R ribs, step back down to take the club w/R hand to exit.

<u>Extension Begins Here:</u>

4. R front knee kick his R ribs as R hand strips the club from his grip ending w/R hand behind you *(club inverted in your right hand cocked behind your right hip)*

5. Step back R *(or step forward to RNB depending on distance)* to 1:30 LFB w/R Up lifting club strike to face, L hand helps rotate club *(from inverted club position)* to hold the handle *(club tip up now and still in your right hand)*.

6. Step L to 10:30 w/Out club strike to back of his R elbow.

7. R front crossover *(twist stance)* outside R foot w/R In club strike thru R front knee.

8. Step out L to 12 behind him at 6 w/R Out club strike inside his right knee.

9. Push drag forward w/Up club strike between his legs into his groin.

10. Continue moving around him gauging L foot to 3 w/R In club strike thru inside L knee, R front crossover to 4:30 *(front twist)* w/R down club on head, step L to 4:30 exit.

**CAPTURING THE CLUB** *(Capturing the Storm)*
***Right Overhead Club Step Thru-12***

1. Step forward *(12 modified LNB)* w/Up cross block *(L hand below R)* under wrist(s), intending to counter grab and move offline using weapons downward momentum.

2. Guide weapons down momentum turning L palm up to grab his R wrist as R hand pivots under *(your hands palm-up holding his R wrist w/L feeling for wrist lock grip)*.

3. Pivot L foot open *(heel pivot)* guiding club down and thru front of his R knee with both hands then duck under his right arm with a right front step thru towards 9.

4. L rear crossover to 9, R taking club up and out as L applies inward wristlock.

5. Un-pivot to 3 RNB w/R down club strike to back of his head/neck *(can start w/glancing strike thru his R elbow)* into low R In club strike thru front of his right knee.

7. Using reverse motion w/R Out whipping club strike thru the back of his R knee.

8. R Up In club strike face *(lifts his head)* twisting R arm behind his back *(hammerlock)*.

9. Continue circling your R hand to repeat previous club strike but w/L front crossover pushing sweep thru the back of his right foot *(opens his stance)*.

10. Cover R to 4:30 rev cat *(10:30 L cat)* R arm over head as L checks R elbow, R rear sliding leg sweep R knee w/R club end strike to sternum *(drives him back to ground)*.

11. Leap forward winding up the club landing w/R down club strike onto the best available target the step back left foot towards 4:30 to exit.

**CALMING THE CLUB** *(Calming the Storm)*
***Right Roundhouse Club from 12***

1. Step forward to 12 RNB *(R leg jams &/or checks his R leg)* w/R vert thrust punch *(or palm strike)* into his face w/L waiters' tray *(two-bone)* block to his right wrist.

2. Slide R hand to push his R bicep muscle *(squares his shoulders)* adjusting to RFB w/L vert thrust punch sternum *(L punching arm above your R arm checking his R bicep)*.

3. RNB sliding L hand down his arm, grab medial side R wrist *(need for Ext to work)*, pull him into R back of wrist strike to R ribs *(Axillary nerve or 5th intercostal space)*.

4. R toe to L *(spin L)* grabbing club w/L *(keep wrist in Ext)* bumping his R arm w/your R arm turning to L spinning rear thrust kick to groin, L front crossover exit towards 6.
Extension Begins Here

4. Holding medial R wrist wrap R arm under his R elbow *(R knee can buckle inside his R knee to help break balance)*, R step back *(10:30 LFB)* levering his elbow *(arm bar)* to pull him forward slightly.

5. As or before his weight settles from the pull R Out whipping BKS thru R side *(Liver or Kidney area)*, R inward vertical forearm strike the left side of his neck.

6. R forearm hooks over neck & under R armpit to fulcrum his neck, step L to 6 *(shuffle as needed)* pressing down on his neck w/R forearm, pulling R wrist w/L to drag him face to floor, drop R knee on his L scapula *(wide kneel)*, grabbing his neck w/R *(push & hold his head on floor)*.

7. Bounce up w/L rear crossover to 12 low rear twist w/R down BKS on R Kidney.

8. Hop up out of twist stance to 6 L wide kneel dropping R knee on his L kidney w/R down palm thrust to back of his mastoid, L hand checks back of his L shoulder.

9. Lift R foot forward over his head *(possible glancing heel kick)* R straight downward ax kick neck, jaw, temple area.

10. Pivot R foot open, L down knee drop on back of his neck *(low twist)* w/possible R down vert punch onto his middle spine, L step out over his head towards 9 to exit.

**DEFYING THE CLUB** *(Defying the Storm)*
***Right Roundhouse Club Step Thru-12***

1. R forward *(12 RNB, possible knee jam w/yours)* w/L ext out block inside R wrist, grab his wrist *(C grip thumb down)* w/R In handsword block his R bicep, hook over back of his R elbow or shoulder crease.

2. R cat pulling his R shoulder forward and down lifting his R wrist up *(breaks his center levering his body down)* w/R Up knee kick his chest *(R arm circles overhead)*.

3. Settle weight *(RNB)* w/R down elbow to middle spine or neck *(his R hand up w/club)* as your L hand twists his R wrist inward so your L hand can reach the weapon.

4. Grab club w/R hand then right rear step thru striking his head with it.
Extension Begins here

2. L step forward to 10:30, R front knee kick inside R knee *(sweeps his leg out)* while pulling R shoulder forward and down lifting his R wrist up *(break his center levering his body to bend down)* w/R Up knee kick his chest *(R arm begins circling overhead).*

3. RNB w/R down elbow onto his middle spine or back of his neck while your L hand twists his R wrist inward so your R hand can grab the end of the opposite club end.

4. Rotate R *(1:30 front twist w/or w/out club in hand)* w/L inside down club strike &/or L inside down elbow thru R mastoid moving your elbow just below his head.

5. Un-pivot standing up *(reverse motion)* w/L obscure elbow under his chin, &/or L upward club tip strike *(or left upward hammerfist strike)* lifting under his chin.

6. RNB w/R Up lifting club tip *(or R uppercut punch)* then R Up elbow under the chin.

7. Turn L to 12 R rev close kneel *(opponent behind over R shoulder)* w/R rear scoop kick thru groin, step R toe to L looking over L shoulder *(defensive reverse switch).*

8. Jump off R foot turning 180° landing on L w/R In crescent kick thru his left jaw hinge continuing thru to a R front crossover step out towards 6 to exit.

## SECURING THE CLUB *(Securing the Storm)*
### Right Roundhouse Club Step Thru from 12

1. Step L forward to 10:30 *(outside his R foot, if in front)* jamming attacking arm w/L ext block inside R wrist w/R straight palm between his eyes *(or best face target)* either simultaneously or staggered as a quick 1-2.

2. R step thru forward to 10:30 R cat stance outside and behind his R leg *(rev cat)* as L arm wraps around his R arm above the elbow *(grab your own shirt or figure 4 lock)* w/R forward elbow flap into his solar plexus *(brings his head down).*

3. Hold R arm, R rear sliding leg sweep back of R leg *(or both legs but not in training)* w/R In crab pinch throat driving him onto his back *(possible elbow dislocation on fall).*

4. Step over to mount (Standard) or standing at his side w/L knee on his face and R on ribs: Apply arm bar, Kimura (R knee on ground), or Americana (from mount).

<u>Extension Begins Here</u>

3. R rear sliding leg sweep thru back of R leg *(possibly both legs but not in training)* w/R In crab pinch striking grabbing and pushing his throat driving him onto his back.

4. Pin his body to the ground w/R knee against his R side *(possible elbow lock)* then slide L hand to his R wrist reaching across w/R hand to grab far end of the club *(either end can work)* taking the club from his hand *(possible whip thru his face).*

5. Straight club poke into his throat while locking his R elbow around your left shin.

6. L shin pressure turns him on L side, gauge forward w/club behind his R arm *(arm across his chest)* w/far club tip on ground above L shoulder *(club shaft under his chin).*

7. R front crossover step forward past his head grabbing end of the stick w/both hands together *(pull-up hand position)* locking shaft tight against his chin and levered against the top of his left shoulder.

8. L toe to R then back R to LNB above his head pulling the club thru his chin.

9. L heel pivot to open foot, R front crossover sweep *(TSK)* thru L side of his head circling club CCW in front settling your weight into a front twist stance with a right downward outward snapping club strike into his face then left foot then steps out to exit.

**Ground Option:** While Mounted L Ext Block R round punch w/R palm strike face, wrap L arm around his R elbow, w/R crab pinch choke his throat, post L foot outside his R heel, lift hips to Bridge over L shoulder to top guard, use tenderizing or ground & pound to escape *(Closed Guard: elbow-punch-palm strike/press inner knees & groin, pinch tender skin areas, heel palm bladder, knee tailbone, Open Guard: elbow-punch-palm legs, knee on groin or side, kick inner legs, crossover knee drop on legs, etc).*

## RETURNING CLUB *(Returning Storm)*
### Two-Hand Roundhouse then Backhand Club from 12

1. Step back L to 7:30 *(corner #1)* to a R rear bow *(zone of sanctuary)* with both hands up letting the forehand club swing go past you.

2. As outward club swing returns step forward to 1:30 *(corner #2)* w/dbl *(2-bone blocks)* forearm block to back of R arm and shoulder then grab his R wrist in your R hand applying left forearm pressure against his right elbow.

3. Step back R to 4:30 *(corner #3)* levering arm driving him around and down in front.

4. Grab just above his R elbow w/L followed by R front snap kick into his groin or left knee his ribs *(depending on range)* while your right-hand cocks behind you.

5. Weight forward w/R stiff armed lifting punch face, L holds R elbow against R hip.

6. Reach back R grab his R wrist, pin to your R hip then R rear step thru cover step to 10:30 *(corner #4)* pressing R elbow w/L hand levering him face down to the ground.

7. Step over R shoulder toe in *(possible glancing heel kick head)* continuing to hold R wrist in R hand as your L feels for his elbow crease, bend his R elbow to a hammerlock position by twisting his wrist and collapsing his elbow as you step back R over his head, drop L knee across his R scapula pulling up on his arm to dislocate his shoulder.

8. Bounce up jumping off knee switching in the air landing on L foot above his head w/R side stomp across the back of his neck, R front crossover step exit to 10:30.

## CIRCLING THE CLUB *(Calming the Storm)*
### Right High Club Poke Step Thru from 12

1. Step back R *(12 LNB)* w/R Out parry outside club or wrist, L In parry R elbow, circle R arm over and around the club to strip it out of his grip *(could hold & use)*.

2. R step thru behind his R leg w/R In elbow and/or club strike glancing thru his R rib cage checking his R shoulder with your L hand.

3. Keep turning L until to L Out elbow face w/R check at R elbow gauging to a L cat.

4. Step *(hop)* back L behind his R leg *(L one-legged stance)* to 6 w/R In heel palm claw thru his face checking his R shoulder with your L hand *(possible neck tweak)*.

5. R side snap kick the back of his L knee *(break balance)*.

6. Land w/R inv Up 5-finger strike testicles w/L cross body shoulder line check.

7. Gauge R foot to the R as needed, R hand circles up w/R In heel palm claw thru face then becomes a R cross body check across his shoulder line *(replacing your left)*.

8. L TSK back inside of his R leg *(spreading him)* settling weight to 6 front twist w/L Up 5-finger strike his testicles *(still behind)* as R hand checks his shoulder line.

9. Un-pivot R ending w/weight on L *(R rev close kneel to 6)* then a right rear scoop kick thru his groin while crossing out towards 10:30 to exit.

# KNIFE

## LEAP OF DEATH *(Leap of Death)*
### Right Threatening Knife from 12

1. Scissor slap disarm *(L hand hits back of knuckles, R hand hits medial wrist flexors)* threatening knife *(or L In parry if against R punch as in original technique)*, R countergrab back of R wrist stepping back R to 6 pulling him off balance w/L inv palm thru R elbow glancing to L bicep strike *(compounded move)* turning to a 6 RFB.

2. Maintain R wrist grab, adjust to 12 LNB w/R Out BKS his right rib cage or groin.

3. L palm strike his R elbow, C clamp grab *(thumb down)* at joint welding medial side of his wrist to your R hip gauging R foot *(off cover step)* turning your hips to a 6 RFB applying armbar pressure forcing him face down to the ground.

4. Jumping L heel stomp L kidney, R foot lands outside his R hip *(dbl stomps in air)*, squat *(diamond stance)* w/dbl palm strikes down to back of head driving face into ground.

5. As his head bounces up catch and cradle his chin *(R hand on chin, L supports that hand)*, concave stance locking his middle spine against your closed knees and shins as you pull up against his chin *(caution: this could break his back and neck)*.

6. Pull R hand out and up next to your R ear *(cocked)* while turning and cradling his head in your L hand so he looks to the right *(possible left thumb gouge to his left eye)*.

7. Right downward handsword strike the right-side bridge of his nose.

8. Circle L elbow out so L hand can pivot from L to R side of head, L Out claw face *(neck tweaked w/R during transition)* slamming his head onto ground w/L palm *(possible R ear compression)* w/L knee drop on upper thoracic spine *(your L foot outside his L hip)*.

9. Bounce your L knee off his back switching in the air over his body landing on L foot outside his R hip w/R round ball kick to his R temple, front crossover exiting to 10:30.

**GLANCING BLADE** *(Glancing Lance)*
### Right High Cross Knife Thrust from 12
1. R step back to 12 LNB *(possibly further back to 1:30 LNB)* w/L In parry outside his R arm *(close to his elbow)*, R Out parry outside R wrist w/both hands grasping *(L grabs his elbow joint with R grabbing back of his R wrist)*.
2. Weld medial side of his R wrist to your R hip applying elbow pressure pulling him forward and down then R front snap kick his groin *(or TSK if his right knee)*.
3. Step forward to RNB *(possibly hooking R foot behind his R heel, R knee attack)* w/R vert 2-finger poke R eye while L hand continues to hold his R arm against your hip.
4. Hop to 9 behind his R leg land L, tweaking R elbow w/both hands at elbow & wrist.
5. R side snap kick the back of his R knee while your L hand helps pull down at the arm/shoulder driving him onto one or both knees facing 3.
6. *(Moves 6-7-8-9 connect quickly)* Step down from kick inside his bent R lower leg hooking R eye from behind w/R inward two-finger hook anchoring your right elbow at the back of his right shoulder as your left-hand transitions thru the chamber.
7. Modified RNB with a L middle knuckle punch to his L temple
8. RNB w/R In elbow R mastoid and L In heel palm L mastoid sandwiching neck.
9. Optional L claw pulls his face up as R hand presses back of his lower neck *(tweaks/breaks his neck)* ending w/R universal check pushing him onto his face to 3.

**CLIPPING THE BLADE 1-2** *(Clipping the Storm)*
### Right Low Cross Knife Thrust from 12
Version 1: Your right leg slightly forward
1. R foot crosses back towards 6 *(12 front twist)* w/R down out hooking parry over his R wrist, un-pivot w/L down handsword R radial arm nerve *(scissors wrist glancing thru and down as your R hand maintains contact while pivoting to grab his right wrist from the top)*.
2. LFB w/L Up lifting palm heel thru R elbow as R pushes R wrist down *(tweaks elbow)*.
3. RNB pulling his R wrist w/L Out handsword R side of his neck/throat.
4. L hand slides down to grab and hold back of R elbow *(weld R wrist to your R hip)* adjusting to LFB w/R straight horizontal 2- finger thrust into his right eye.
5. R hand slides down to grab R arm, still against your R hip, step thru forward to R cat w/L inverted vertical middle or index knuckle fist strike behind his right ear *(TW17)*.
6. L hand slides down to grab R arm stepping thru forward to 12 RNB w/R straight palm strike to his R jaw hinge.
7. Slide R hand down his R arm to inside of his thenar eminence *(carpal tunnel groove)*, peel knife out of his hand stepping R back thru *(possible invert pull sweep as you exit)*.
Version 2: Your left leg slightly forward
1. Step L towards 10:30 *(left 45o horse)* w/L inside downward parry (fingers down) to the outside of his right wrist while positioning your right fist near your right ear.
2. LFB dropping R hip behind R down vert thrust punch back of his R hand *(causing release of weapon)*, grab his R wrist w/R hand. Moves 3-7 from version #1 to finish.

**UNEXPECTED BLADE**
### Right High Straight Knife Thrust from 12
1. Step L foot back behind R towards 4:30 to R rev 45o horse w/R In parry inside his R wrist followed by L Out parry, grab medial side of R wrist *(wrist held thru move #6 - twist outward here to affect his posture and open elbow nerve target)*.
2. Transition back to 10:30 R cat stance; R inward knocking punch glancing thru his inside R elbow *(SI11)* then R front snap kick his groin.
3. Step forward from kick to 10:30 RNB w/R Out elbow stabbing his R rib cage.
4. R vert BKS bridge of nose, L foot forward w/R back hammerfist groin. *(Note: EPAK version & Form 6 insert L heel palm claw before BKS. I prefer not to let go of weapon hand)*
5. Straighten w/R obscure elbow under chin shifting weight back *(rear bow)* w/simult R outward heel of palm claw thru and right front scoop kick thru his groin.
6. With R knee in air R side thrust kick inside L knee simult w/R inv palm heel strike to his left jaw hinge *(optional rear sliding leg sweep to his left knee)*.
7. R front crossover *(front twist)* to 9 *(optional R knee to medial R knee to break posture)*, readjust grip for In wrist twist takedown locking his elbow tight under your R armpit.

8. L toe to R, step back R, cover to 6 w/elbow & wrist pressure driving him face down on ground *(ends w/back of his R hand locked tight against your lower abdomen w/your L knee locking his R shoulder to ground, knife in your hand pointed at back of his head).*

## THRUSTING BLADE *(Thrusting Lance)*
### Right Low Straight Knife Thrust from 12
1. Step L back behind R to 4:30 R reverse 45o horse w/R palm strike to R forearm *(Lu6)* grabbing that wrist w/ L 2 or 4-finger eye poke *(finger pads to forehead in training).*
2. Grab back of his R thumb joint w/L as R grabs back of his R hand *(wristlock prep),* R rear step thru w/R wrist out turning him inward *(cancels balance & possible weapon release or take)* ending in 12 L cat stance *(opponent should be bent over forward).*
3. L then R Up front kick groin &/or chest positioning R straight arm behind you.
4. Step forward 12 RNB w/R stiff arm lifting punch R temple *(or up thru nose)* bringing that hand up above his head *(left hand holds his right wrist at your left hip).*
5. Right downward BKS *(or right forearm)* onto the back of his neck.
6. Bounce off his neck, R down forearm his R elbow *(optional 2nd R down BKS his neck).*
7. R crane hook over his arm grabs his elbow crease, pull up to bend stepping forward to 1:30 L cat rolling his fingers under his armpit to secure braced wristlock w/both hands *(know where the weapon is at this point).*
8. L rear sliding leg sweep inside R knee to 10:30 w/sudden pressure to break R wrist.
9. Shoulders turn L to 12 LNB w/L back hammerfist groin w/R inward hammerfist nose *(universal block position)* or possible R knife stab his chest if you have the knife.

## ENTWINED BLADE *(Entwined Lance)*
### Right High Roundhouse Knife from 12
1. Step L across your bodyline to1:30 *(front twist stance)* w/L ext block *(hand open)* to R wrist, grab medial side of that wrist *(squeeze to affect nerve & blood flow to the hand)*
2. Step R to 12 w/L inv horiz palm strike to his left chin *(fingers in)* causing him to look over his right shoulder while slightly twisting and pulling his right wrist with your left.
3. R hand replaces L to R wrist w/R pulling sweep to R leg w/L horiz 2-finger eye poke.
4. L hand re-grabs his R wrist with a R side snap kick inside his L knee.
5. Step down forward inside and behind his R foot if possible, w/R Out BKS R ribs, R Up flapping elbow under his chin allowing your R arm to reach over his R arm.
6. If he still has the knife: Grab over his hand w/R to inv grip at hilt side of the handle, R rear step thru slicing his neck with the knife in your right hand as you exit.
If he dropped the knife: Step back R w/R Out, then L Inward whipping hammerfist strikes thru R jaw hinge or mastoid as you exit towards 4:30 *(picking up knife as you go).*

## PIERCING BLADE *(Piercing Lance)*
### Right High Roundhouse then Backhand Knife from 12
1. Step back L to 7:30 *(back L corner)* to R rear bow to 1:30 *(zone of sanctuary)* with both hands up as inward knife swing goes past you.
2. As outward knife swing follow up returns step forward to 1:30 *(front right corner)* to LNB w/R universal block *(R hand down / L hand up)* surrounding to grab his R hand and wrist pressing R elbow against your L lat muscle or side of your bent L elbow.
3. Swing R foot back to 10:30 *(front L corner)* into 4:30 L rev bow applying R elbow pressure w/L side of your body, his R wrist levers him to step with his left foot forward and around to your 4:30.
4. Adjust to grab his wrist for an Out wristlock *(pushing TW2 & pulling Lu9)* adjusting towards him turning his hand inward and up *(possible knife slice his throat)* w/R front crossover step-thru running towards 4:30 driving his R hand over his R shoulder and him onto his back, locking R elbow *(TW10/11)* around your L shin driving R knee down onto his R rib cage *(Liver)* twisting and holding his right hand tightly outward.
5. R down palm strike back of his R hand *(at TW2)* causing weapon release, R hand grips back of his hand w/fingers in thumb webbing as L hand slides down to the back of his bent right elbow *(TW10).*
6. Drag R foot to L twisting his hand behind his back w/R while L pushes elbow *(begins to turn him onto his L side)* until turned over onto his stomach stepping L over his R shoulder to 4:30 *(completes drag step)* dropping L knee on his R scapula *(holds him down)* pulling up against his R arm w/both hands dislocating his R shoulder.

7. Jump up and back landing L foot above and outside his L shoulder w/R front downward stomp across the back of his neck, then crossover to exit towards 1:30.

## RAINING BLADE *(Raining Lance)*
### *Right Overhead Downward Knife from 12*

1. L inward parry outside his r wrist guiding it downward.
2. Guide down past your sternum insert R hand inside of your L connecting your wrists forming a cross, stepping L to 12 modified LNB driving knife into his R leg *(or groin)*.
3. LFB w/R In elbow solar plexus as L hand holds knife against and in his right leg.
4. R hand slides down to hold his R wrist adjusting to 12 LNB reaching up to grab his throat with a left outward crab pinch *(palm up)*.
5. L hand slides down holding his R wrist adjusting to a 12 modified LNB with R inward thumb/index grab *(eagles' claw)* his eyes throat grab.
6. R hand and arm slide down checking his arm at his low back stepping L to 10:30 *(LFB)* w/L Out rev handsword *(palm up)* his throat *(combo begins to arch him backwards)*.
7. Outward crane hook his throat or grab across his shoulder line holding his clothing w/R front step thru to 10:30 dropping your L knee to ground leaving R knee up as both hands force him back and down *(R hand stays under training partners low back to ease them down)* breaking his back over R knee *(if too big bring him all the way to the ground)*.
8. Grab knife and pull it out of his leg w/R as L claws thru his face, use your forearms to push him off your knee to the ground then stand up and step back right to exit.

# GUN

## CAPTURING THE GUN *(Capturing the Rod)*
### *Right Pistol Close from 12*

1. L Out parry gun barrel *(inside their arm)* turning your shoulders L *(narrows target line)* grabbing barrel w/L hand *(fingers over top)* as R hand grabs gun handle *(trapping his hand)* all as your R foot steps forward *(two hands holding gun tight against your chest; do not hook R elbow over his)*. Optional L 2-finger eye poke *(EPAK version and Form 6)*.
2. While hugging weapon and opponent's hand turn your shoulders R using hands and torso to point the gun at opponent while transitioning back thru a R cat to a LFB.
3. R front snap kick groin pulling gun away w/R *(cocking it behind R hip)* as L checks.
4. Step forward RNB with R up-out pistol-whip thru his chin *(1:30)*.
5. R down-in pistol whip thru his L temple *(7:30)* then up to *(10:30)*.
6. R out-down pistol whip thru R temple *(4:30)* stepping back R then rear crossover stepout to exit ending with gun pointed at attacker.

## TWISTED GUN *(Twisted Rod)*
### *Right Pistol Close from 12*

1. R Out parry gun barrel (outside his R arm) turning your shoulders R (narrows target line), grab it w/R hand (fingers over top) as L grabs handle (trapping his hand) all as your L foot steps forward (hands holding gun tight against your chest pulling him forward off balance; L elbow can temporarily hook over his arm).
2. Rotate shoulders L as hands (R palm pushing against back of little finger knuckle) and torso to twist his hand (and gun) over his R shoulder (possible gun strike his face and/or R In elbow), R In down elbow R collarbone w/R front step thru behind his R leg covering to 7:30 LFB twisting his hand out tripping w/R elbow tip driving his back onto the floor.
3. Still holding gun and hand (your R palm pressing back of his little finger knuckle) wrap R elbow around L shin dropping R knee onto his right floating rib (Liver).
4. With pressure against elbow joint lift R knee up (possible R glancing heel kick ribs), R down heel stomp solar plexus bouncing off turning to R down round ball kick his L bicep.
5. R TSK face stepping over and above his R shoulder ending in L front twist pulling up to break his R elbow at leg junction stripping gun, step out L to 4:30, exit ending with gun pointed at opponent.

## DEFYING THE GUN *(Defying the Rod)*
### *Right Pistol Close from 6*

1. Turn shoulders to your L *(narrows target line)*, cross step back L to 4:30 w/L arm down, cover to LNB facing opponent at 6 as L arm wraps up and around his R arm trapping back of his wrist tight against your L shoulder *(gun pointing outward left)*. Note: This is a different gun disarm then done in the EPAK version and in Form 6.

2. LFB w/R palm strike into his chin followed by a 4-finger poke into his eyes and with no loss of motion execute a right front knee into or front kick up into his groin.

3. R foot down inside of his R foot *(6 RNB)* w/R down crane hook striking crook of his R elbow *(collapses his arm, cancels height)*, up flapping elbow under chin reaching R hand over his R arm to grab his elbow joint.

4. Step back thru R cat w/L down shoulder pressure against his hand/wrist as your R hand pulls his elbow joint until R back to 7:30 LFB w/pressure causing him to drop down in front *(his L hand on the ground)*

5. L hand on his R elbow to check and hold as R hand grabs gun barrel peeling it out of his grip and whipping the handle down thru the back of his head.

6. Circle R arm overhead w/R Up front knee kick lifting his face and body up then settle your weight forward w/R downward gun handle strike onto his head.

7. Turn L *(R rev close kneel)*, R rear scoop kick L jaw stepping R toe to L spinning L w/L rear thrust kick best available body target to clear him away. L front crossover step out and cover towards 3 to exit ending with gun pointing at opponent.

## BROKEN GUN *(Broken Rod)*
### *Right Pistol Close from 6*

1. Turn shoulders R *(narrows target line)* pivoting R heel / L ball *(rear rotating twist)* lifting R hand next to your R shoulder so forearm bumps outside gun at your back.

2. Grab medial wrist w/R pinning back of his hand to chest stepping L *(6 L side horse)* wrapping L arm under to trap and dislocate his elbow w/L elbow crook, *(still holding his R elbow)*, slide R hand down to grab guns hammer or slide mechanism. *(Variation: Grab back of wrist crease rolling elbow point up reaching over R arm w/L (optional palm strike) to trap joint under L armpit w/down pressure. This would change the ending however.)*

3. L Out BKS groin circling thru and up outside R arm *(possible fingers in palm strike or eye poke)*, push down check his R arm w/R TSK front knee stripping the gun w/R hand settling weight in front twist stance towards 6.

4. Un-pivot to 6 RNB w/upward inward pistol whip that circles overhead, shuffling forward with inward downward pistol barrel tip strike stabbing into his left collarbone.

5. Step L to 4:30 LFB pushing gun thru his face, lift and cock R knee behind him w/R Out pistol handle whip thru back of R elbow as L hand grabs back of his R shoulder.

6. R side snap kick back of his R knee *(buckles him to knees)*, step down between his feet w/R In pistol whip across R side of his face into R sleeper choke.

7. R Out gun scrape across face, return w/R In gun strike thru face rotating L to rear twist stance *(rear rotating twist)* looking over L shoulder at opponent while re-gripping gun. Step out R then back thru L to 4:30 ending to 10:30 w/gun pointed at opponent.

Attacker is trying to strike with their legs and feet, then possibly follow with a punch. When kicking, the hips could be square to the front or rear or turned sideways. The kick attack techniques covered here are sorted by these different hip alignments, whether to low or high targets.

As with all impact defenses there are the 3 possibilities of blocking, avoiding, or jamming the kicking attack, then the best follow-up timing happens before or as their kicking foot touches the ground, and in Kenpo this is often a kick or strike to the groin. This timing after defending the initial effort is critical for a successful kick defense because if their weight reaches the ground before this occurs, they then regain leverage and can move and/or attack with something else.

## INSIDE STRAIGHT KICK DEFENSES

THRUSTING PALM *(Thrusting Salute)* Pg 287
DEFENDING CROSS *(Defensive Cross)* Pg 288
CIRCLING THE KICK A *(Circle of Doom)* Pg 288
CIRCLING THE KICK B *Pg 288*

## INSIDE ROUND KICK DEFENSES

ROLLING FISTS *(Long Form 2)* Pg 289
BOUNCING PENDULUM *(Swinging Pendulum)* Pg 289
DETOURING THE KICK *(Detour from Doom)* Pg 289
THE NUTCRACKER *(Bowing to Buddha)* – Starts Kneeling Pg 290
UNROLLING CRANE *(Unfurling Crane)* Pg 290
REVERSING CIRCLES *(Reversing Circles)* Pg 291

## OUTSIDE STRAIGHT KICK DEFENSES

BUCKLING THE LEG *(Buckling Branch)* Pg 291
DEFLECTING PENDULUM *(Deflecting Hammers)* Pg 291
HUGGING PENDULUM *(Hugging Pendulum)* Pg 292
RETREATING PENDULUM *(Retreating Pendulum)* Pg 292
SLEEPER *(Sleeper)* Pg 292
DANCING IN THE DARK *(Dance of Darkness)* Pg 293
UNTWIRLING PENDULUM *(Unwinding Pendulum)* Pg 293

## INSIDE STRAIGHT KICKS

**THRUSTING PALM** *(Thrusting Salute)*
***Right Front Kick Stepping Thru from 12***
1. Step back R to LNB slightly off angle facing 10:30 w/L down out block *(dbl factor)* to the inside of attacker's R kicking leg ending w/R hand in the chamber.
2. Left hand position check with a right front snap kick to his groin
3. Step forward to RNB between his legs *(10:30)* w/R straight palm to his chin.
<u>Extension Begins Here</u>
4. L front crossover to 10:30 *(L front twist)* w/L vertical thrust punch to his sternum.
5. Un-pivot to LNB w/L In elbow his R jaw sandwiching w/R In heel palm his L jaw.
6. L out heel palm claw L face & jaw, causes him to look R as your R hand circles out.
7. LFB w/R down In hammerfist to L floating rib *(Spleen area)* or L Kidney *(depends on body & L arm position)*.
8. Rebound off previous strike w/def rev switch *(L toe to R)* into R spinning side thrust kick his chest *(or out hook head kick)*, R front crossover step out towards 6 to exit.

## DEFENDING CROSS *(Defensive Cross)*
### *Right Front Kick Stepping Thru from 12*

1. L down out hooking parry traps inside his R ankle, L hand on top stepping back R to 10:30 or 9 LFB pulling his R leg past your left hip towards 6 with your two hands.
2. In the same flow adjust to a modified LNB w/R Out BKS to his R temple.
3. L In heel palm R jaw adjusting to LNB hooking back of his head inward w/L hand.
4. LFB w/R front stiff leg lifting shin kick into groin positioning R fist behind you.
5. R foot back to LFB w/R stiff-armed lifting punch up between his eyes.
6. Gauge R forward near L, L front snap kick into his solar plexus *(bends him over)*.
7. Gauge L to 7:30 *(to his R)*, R Out crescent kick thru R jaw hinge stepping back.
8. Bounce R foot off ground w/R round shin kick to face, step back or thru to exit.

## CIRCLING THE KICK A *(Circle of Doom)*
### *Right Front Kick Stepping Thru from 12*

1. From 12 RNB, R hand down *(bating him)* turn shoulders L to R rev bow w/R In down parry inside his R ankle bending your elbow to grab and trap his leg.
2. RNB to 12 throwing his leg to your R w/R extended block motion.
3. Drag L to R then R stiff leg lifting rear kick up between his legs into his groin then R toe to L *(defensive reverse switch)* looking over left shoulder.
4. Complete spin w/L side thrust kick to back of his R knee *(driving his knee to the ground)* then L toe to R w/R spinning outward hook kick to his face.
<u>Extension Begins Here</u>
4. Spinning L thrust kick to back of R knee *(knee to ground)*, L step to 6 looking R, push drag to 12 R close kneel w/L on top piggyback punch to L kidney *(he arches back)*.
5. Reach L hand over his R shoulder hooking back of his neck as R hand hooks inside his R arm, begin turning his head to his L as R hand hooks inside his R arm, pull his head to his L pulling his R arm back, two moves together begin to turn him L.
6. As he turns step L forward to 10:30 *(just past his L foot)* to L close kneel w/R vert hook punch thru L jaw hinge *(your L hand can slide over to support R side of his face to sandwich)*, R In elbow thru same target *(resembles similar manipulation in Leopard Set)*.
7. Swing R foot back behind L thru 1:30 LNB *(un-pivot on L heel)* w/R outward whipping BKS thru his right temple followed by a left palm strike to his face.
8. Keep turning/spinning L bringing L toe to R into R spinning rear thrust kick (moves 7-8 are done in one 270º pivot on the left heel) to the best available target (chest, groin, knee) then right front crossover towards 9 to exit.

## CIRCLING THE KICK B
### *Right Front Kick Stepping Thru from 12*

1. From 12 RNB R hand down *(bating opponent to kick)* turn shoulders L to R rev bow w/R In down parry inside R ankle *(missing Version A leg trap or prefer this technique)* shifting weight to L foot w/R rear thrust kick to his groin *(his kicking leg still in the air)*.
2. Gauge L to 9 *(outside his R foot)*, circle R Out down ax kick onto back of his R knee buckling it to the ground *(your R calf hits then your R foot on ground behind his R leg)* with a possible right downward heel-of-palm strike onto his right collar bone.
3. Step R toe to L into L spinning out hook kick to back of his head.
<u>Extension Begins Here</u> *(Same as Version A but at a different angle)*
3. Step thru forward L to 10:30 covering to 4:30 RNB, push drag forward to R close kneel w/L on top piggyback punch into his left kidney *(causing him to arch backwards)*.
4. Reach L hand over his R shoulder hooking back of his neck as R hand hooks inside his R arm, turn his head L as your R hand hooks inside his R arm, pull his head to his L pulling his R arm back as these moves together begin to turn him to his left.
5. As he turns step L forward to 1:30 *(just past his L foot)* to L close kneel w/R vert hook punch thru L jaw hinge *(your L hand can slide over to support R side of his face to sandwich)*, R In elbow thru same target *(resembles similar manipulation in Leopard Set)*.
6. Swing your R foot back behind your L thru a 7:30 LNB *(un-pivot on L heel)* w/R Out whipping BKS thru his right temple followed by a left palm strike to his face.
7. Keep turning/spinning L toe to R into R spin rear thrust kick (moves 7-8 one 270º pivot on L heel) to best available target (chest, groin, knee), R front crossover exit to 3.

# INSIDE ROUNDHOUSE KICKS

**ROLLING FISTS**
*Right Roundhouse Kick Stepping Thru from 12*

1. Step forward L *(12 LNB)* w/L universal block inside kicking leg *(above knee better)*. Note: If kick correctly done w/knee lifted in front, zig zag R-L inside leg above knee.
2. L close kneel stance w/R forward reverse hammerfist groin as L hand lifts to apply a cross body check along his shoulder/chest line *(possible outward face claw)*.
3. Stand up to LFB maintaining L cross body check w/R Out BKS R side of his nose.
4. LNB w/L Out BKS L temple/eye, modified LNB w/R Out BKS R temple/eye *(rolling)*.

<u>Extension Begins Here</u>

5. R front step thru between his feet w/R down out BKS groin as L hand hooks and anchors over L side of his neck.
6. Facing 6, R knee to ground pulling his neck down *(his head between his legs)* lifting R arm between his legs *(make him roll over onto back, feet at 6)* driving R elbow then R down heel palm onto his chest/sternum *(prevents rolling thru)*.
7. Sit back onto your R calf w/R back elbow strike under his chin.
8. Stand up w/R Out down ax kick between his legs into his groin.
9. As his head reflexes up from kick lift R foot, R side thrust kick his face towards 12.
10. Step R above his head towards 12 then L front crossover sweep kick *(TSK)* thru his chin as you cross out towards 12 to exit.

**BOUNCING PENDULUM** *(Swinging Pendulum)*
*Right Roundhouse Kick Step Thru from 12*

1. From 12 RNB step L back offline to 12 rev 45o horse *(moving away but inside his kick)* w/L universal block as insurance against the kick and to potentially block it *(optional R side thrust his standing leg)*.
2. As or before his foot touches the ground push drag forward to RNB between his feet w/R forward/back hammerfist groin w/L position check *(or palm strike face in Ext)*.
3. Adjust L foot back offline *(9 R Side Horse)* w/R obscure elbow strike under his chin.

<u>Extension Begins Here</u>

3. Adjust L foot back offline and forwards towards opponent to R rev cat *(him at your 9 w/wall behind you both)* w/R obscure elbow under his chin, R BKS his groin.
4. R rear sliding leg sweep *(R rev bow along wall)* thru inside L knee w/R Up lifting forearm under his chin *(same as "Sweeping the Leg")*.
5. R rear scoop kick groin then R toe to L *(def rev switch)* looking over L shoulder then L rear sliding leg sweep *(L rev bow along wall)* thru inside of his R knee w/L heel palm to his groin w/R palm strike to his chin *(Universal Check)*.
6. Adjust to LNB between his feet moving into him w/L Out horiz elbow to solar plexus followed by L outward heel of palm to his sternum pinning him against the wall.
7. LFB w/R palm between his eyes *(drives back of his head into wall)* glancing thru to hook around the right side of his neck as his head bounces off pulling him forward into R front knee kick into his urinary bladder or groin while chambering your left hand.
8. LNB as R pulls neck down driving L Up lifting forearm under his chin *(your R hand lets go of his head, so your L strike whiplashes his head back up and into the wall again)*.
9. R In 2-finger slice thru his L eye as his head bounces forward, L front crossover step towards 3 w/L outward snapping handsword into his throat as you exit.

**DETOURING THE KICK** *(Detour from Doom)*
*Right Roundhouse Kick Stepping Thru from 12*

1. From 12 RNB step L back offline and forward behind your R to 10:30 R cat *(offline & forward)* w/L down block *(higher block if higher kick)* w/R vert thrust nose punch.
2. R front snap kick groin w/R cross body check as L hand chambers.
3. Step forward *(10:30 RFB)* w/L vert thrust sternum punch w/R arm check.
4. L foot back offline *(9 R close kneel)* w/R Out whipping BKS thru groin as L hand hooks and pulls down on back of neck *(possible L glancing out handsword strike then hook as in Six Hands)* anchoring L elbow to keep him bent as R hand circles overhead.
5. R reverse wide kneel to 9 w/R overhead downward ulna side wrist strike on back of neck *(wrist contours neck so possible regular wide-kneel to align weapon)*.

<u>Extension Begins Here</u>

6. With your right hand still on his neck adjust to a RFB hooking and pulling the top of his neck with your right ulna side wrist strike (pulling him slightly towards you) with a left inverted palm strike thru his left jaw hinge (tweaks his neck).

7. Hold R side of his head w/L hand, step L to 6 (12 R rev bow) w/R inward elbow strike (possible hook punch first) sandwiching his head.

8. Swing your right foot back around to a 10:30 LNB facing him with a R outward whipping BKS thru his R temple then L inward heel of palm his R jaw hinge or R mastoid (could also be a left inward handsword strike) then wrap your left hand around to grab the back of his neck.

9. Adjust to a RFB with a R inward handsword to the L side of his neck (or inward heel of palm his L jaw hinge) sandwiching his neck then wrap your R hand around to grab the back of his neck (Thai clinch).

10. Pull him into a R knee kick into his solar plexus then extend a R upward lifting shin kick into his groin maintaining L hand clinch with space between your R arm and his collarbone (your R knee still up).

11. Step forward from the groin kick to 10:30 RNB w/R forward vert elbow strike into his left collarbone then pull him forward & down with a R rear step thru towards 4:30.

12. Push the back of his head and neck driving his face onto the ground ending w/L knee across the back of his neck then optional L or R stomp kick his head as you exit.

**THE NUTCRACKER** (Bowing to Buddha)
**Right Roundhouse Kick Step Thru from 12**
1. <u>From Knees</u>: Lift your R knee up to stand on your R foot (left knee still on ground) with a double forearm block above his right knee (gauge forward as needed).

2. As his weight settles check his R arm w/L hand w/R forward vert elbow strike to his solar plexus (gauge forward as neeeded).

3. Your L clears his R arm, then L underhand groin grab followed by R downward BKS sandwiching his testicles between your L and R hands.

4. R uppercut punch under chin to lift his head and shift weight back.

5. L step thru forward between legs grabbing back of his L leg w/R hand (ankle pick) as L forearm pushes across his hip back and down onto ground (face up).

6. L back over R leg, L knee drop on R knee (L foot outside his R leg) as R hand grabs top of his L foot (top of toes), L reaches over under to L heel (possible ankle/calf lock).

7. Cover step L applying pressure against his foot (ankle twist turnover, R pushes down as L pulls up) flips him over to his stomach (he is face down), drop R knee onto the back of his R thigh (your L foot now between his legs).

8. Hold his L ankle high in your two hands, R front knee kick inside his L inner thigh (clears his leg opening his groin), step R toe to L between his feet looking over L shoulder (spinning L), L sliding heel stomp pinching testicles to ground, front crossover exits to 6.

**UNROLLING CRANE** (Unfurling Crane)
**Left Punch w/Right Front Kick, then Right Round Punch (or L-R Round Punch) from 12**
1. Step back L to 12 RNB w/L down block inside R front kick (or check if not kicking) w/R Out block inside L punch, R In block/parry (possible hammerfist thru nose) his follow up R punch (gauge forward as needed), L Out block/parry (double factor) w/R forward hammerfist strike to groin.

2. L palm strike catches his face as he bends from groin strike, claws down to become a left cross body check with a right vertical BKS onto his nose.

3. Drag L foot next to R (drop weight slightly) w/R back hammerfist to his groin while your left hand checks his right arm (you are sideways towards opponent).

4. Straighten up under him w/R obscure elbow lifting under his chin, R Out claw his face, R cat w/L (fingers in) palm strike to sternum (creates space) w/R front scoop kick thru his groin (end with your R hand palm up to the outside standing on your left foot).

5. Turn your hips over w/R side thrust kick thru inside of his R knee w/R inv horiz (fingers in) palm strike his L jaw (rotates him to his R) or kick then strike if needed, R front crossover exit to 4:30.

**REVERSING CIRCLES** *(Reversing Circles)*
**Left Roundhouse Kick with Left Step Thru Punch from 12**

1. R step 12 RNB w/R universal block jams L round kick *(above knee, Rolling Fists).*
2. R up parry under L punch to RFB w/L out handsword *(reversing circles)* L ribs.
3. L hand up counter grab his L wrist pulling his arm down to your L hip w/R Out handsword to his L rib cage *(hands circling in rev).*
4. R front crossover to 7:30 front twist pulling his wrist placed on your R hip w/R downward forearm strike to the back of his left elbow *(keeps him canceled down).*
5. R side snap kick inside R knee w/R out BKS L temple, return to twist stance *(optional move and traditional end to this technique).*
6. Both hand grab back of his L hand, step L toe to R then R foot back to 7:30 w/Out wristlock throw taking him down onto his back, step over his body w/L w/L down knee drop across chest or throat pinning him to ground w/his R elbow around your R shin.
7. Step R back over his body to 4:30 pulling him up by wristlock *(he starts to come up),* step thru back L to 4:30 whipping his L wrist down turning it In *(opposite direction)* slamming him face down onto the ground w/his L wrist on your L hip crease putting your R knee against his L elbow to break or lockdown that joint.

# OUTSIDE STRAIGHT KICKS

**BUCKLING THE LEG** *(Buckling Branch)*
**Right Front Kick Stepping Thru from 12**

1. Step L back to 1:30 RNB w/L down in / R down out dbl factor block outside R kicking leg *(turns him so his back is facing you).*
2. As or before his R foot touches the ground L Up lifting front kick groin *(punting),* L front twist w/R cross body check to back shoulders, L position check behind L elbow.
3. Lift R knee, R side thrust kick *(extend leg, turn hips, drop weight)* thru back of his L knee to buckle his leg, cross out exit to 9.
Extension Begins Here
3. R side snap kick back of his L knee then your R foot behind his R leg *(RNB to 3).*
4. Grab his R shoulder w/R hand circling L hand overhead, down hammerfist his R collarbone w/L front knee kick his middle spine, L crosses back towards 7:30 as L hand checks his R shoulder w/R right fist cocked above your R shoulder.
5. Un-pivot to 1:30 RNB w/L Out whip BKS his face, R In heel palm his left temple.
6. 3 optional endings from here:
A) Follow to ground w/R down Round kick torso *(Broken Kneel),* front cross out exits to 6.
B) Weight to R foot w/L down rhouse kick solar plexus, L front cross out exit to 6.
C) Weight to R foot w/L stiff arm lifting punch thru nose *(your R hand turns his head into this strike)* into L down round kick solar plexus *(same kick ends version #2),* exit.

**DEFLECTING PENDULUM** *(Deflecting Hammers)*
**Rt Front Kick Stepping Thru from 12**

1. Step back L *(12 RNB)* w/R down out *(closed hand)* parry hammering thru outside his R kicking leg w/L hand position check *(R arm circles back thru like a pendulum).*
2. As or before his R foot touches the ground push drag forward w/R inward elbow strike to his face as your left-hand pins and grabs right elbow *(your left thumb down).*
3. Drag L foot forward to R rev cat behind his R leg w/R down whipping BKS thru back of his neck *(right mastoid).*
4. R rear sliding leg sweep *(10:30 LFB)* back of his R leg with a R palm strike to the front of his R shoulder driving him onto his back.
5. Right TSK into his face then step back right then left to exit.
Extension Begins Here
3. Slide L hand down his R arm inverting to thumb up R wrist grab *(L middle finger on pisiform bone, L thumb on back of thumb joint),* R hand grabs back of neck *(C clamp grip).*
4. L hand twists his R wrist behind his back *(hammerlock,)* R hand pushing down on neck w/L step forward to 12 L toe to R, R foot back to 6 LFB bringing him w/you *(both spin 180°). He is bent over towards 12 w/you above him at 6 holding his neck down w/R his R arm behind his back, rev arm lock).* Optional Guillotine Choke finish.

5. R front knee kick either up into R collarbone or straight into top of his head *(this can cause a cervical compression that could be fatal so not done in training)* while your L continues to hold his right arm behind his back as your right holds his head down.

6. Step back from knee kick to LFB *(still to 6)* w/R straight down palm on top of his R scapula pulling his R wrist w/your L hand *(possible shoulder dislocation)*.

7. R front knee or push kick clears him away then back right to exit.

## HUGGING PENDULUM *(Hugging Pendulum)*
### Right Step Thru Side Thrust Kick from 12

1. Step back L *(12 RNB)* w/R down out *(closed hand)* parry hammering thru outside his R kicking leg w/L hand position check *(R arm circles back thru like a pendulum)*.

2. L grabs R shoulder w/L front crossover behind his R leg *(possible TSK back R knee)* w/R In middle finger fist *(or hook punch)* thru R eye *(your arms "hugging" w/R on top)*.

3. Still holding his R shoulder R side snap kick the back of his L knee pulling down on that shoulder *(buckles him down onto his L knee)*.

4. R foot behind his R hip *(1:30 R close kneel)* pressing R knee against R hip w/R Out whipping BKS thru R mastoid *(L hand holds & controls his R arm outside his shoulder)*.

5. Adjust to a *(1:30)* RNB with R inward heel of palm lifting his face.

6. Rear rotating twist *(L heel/R ball)* w/R In face claw *(L rear twist)*, toe to toe switch.

<u>Extension Begins Here</u>

5. Swing L foot back *(off cover step)* w/R In heel palm claw thru face moving into L rear rotating twist looking over L shoulder w/L outward BKS to his left temple.

6. Continue rotating around to your L with R roundhouse punch into his sternum *(360° of rotation with the three strikes from moves #5-6)*.

7. R roundhouse kick or R front push kick his sternum *(depending on angle, range, and preference)* then R step back to exit.

## RETREATING PENDULUM *(Retreating Pendulum)*
### Left Front / Right Spin Rear Kick Combo-12

1. L back L *(12 RNB)* w/L down out hooking parry outside L kick *(spins to R rear kick)*.

2. R rear crossover *(front twist)* w/R down out parry hammering inside R rear kick w/L hand position check *(your R arm continues circling back and thru like a pendulum)*.

3. R side snap or front snap kick back of his L knee as R hand circles up overhead, step down to 12 RNB w/R down hammerfist strike onto back of his neck *(C7)*.

4. Shift L *(1:30 R rev close kneel back to back w/him)* w/R Up hook kick groin *(timed as he goes down from hammerfist)*, return to rev close kneel *(kick bounces up/down)*.

5. Extend and lock your R leg out *(R rev bow)* w/push drag driving back of your R hip pushing him away then R front crossover to exit.

<u>Extension Begins Here</u>

4. R rear sliding leg sweep to 4:30 thru inside angle at back of his R knee *(splits his legs apart to open targets and keep his balance checked)*.

5. R close kneel to 1:30 w/L Up 5-finger strike to testicles *(could be groin grab)* w/R hand cross body check across his shoulders.

6. RNB *(groin rip, L hand chambers)* w/R Out BKS his L kidney.

7. RFB w/L In handsword L side of neck *(L SCM muscles)*, grabbing his chin hooking L forearm over his L shoulder to pull his chin up and take the slack out of his neck.

8. RNB w/R In handsword R side of neck, grab his chin w/R hand *(Thai clinch)* as R forearm hooks over his R shoulder *(anchors his head & neck, chin up)*.

9. L front knee kick lower/middle spine arching him back w/neck pressure *(caution)*.

10. Step forward to LFB releasing chin then aggressively push him forward face down on the ground with your two palms *(end standing between his two feet)*.

11. R front snap kick between his legs then step back to exit.

## SLEEPER *(Sleeper)*
### Right Front Kick followed by Right Punch from 12

1. <u>From a RNB</u>: Adjust back to 12 R cat w/R down out hooking parry outside kicking leg, then or w/L in parry catch outside R punch switching w/hop to drive a L knee into his R thigh *(Iliotibial band)* with left check against his right arm.

2. Step down to 12 LFB w/R In rev handsword into L side of his neck *(under his R arm)*.

3. Slide L forearm against R side of his neck as L grabs his L trapezius muscle *(your L hand keylocks w/your R arm)* using your head and R shoulder to eliminate space by pushing his arm up *(standing arm triangle)* to choke him.

4. R step thru behind his R leg sweeping back taking him down on top of your left knee; or to the floor as you fall on top of him with submission choke, L back to exit.

### DANCING IN THE DARK *(Dance of Darkness)*
#### Right Front Kick - Right Punch Step Thru from 12

1. <u>From RNB</u>: R rear crossover *(front twist to 12)* w/R down out parry hammering then glancing thru outside his R kick w/L hand checking.

2. L In parry his follow up punch, opponent still far away, R Out parry R elbow stepping forward R to a 12 RNB outside his R leg.

3. L step thru forward to 10:30 close kneel, push R arm into groin R knee jams R knee.

4. Hands thru L chamber to 3 R close kneel w/L on top piggyback punch low spine as L knee jams and checks the back of his R knee.

5. L hand checks and holds R elbow down rolling R hand up, Out BKS thru back R mastoid, down tracking R arm before circling up and in w/R 2-finger poke to R eye.

6. Slide R hand down to grab his R wrist w/L front crossover pushing sweep thru his R leg *(front twist to 4:30)* to widen his stance, w/L Out forearm across his throat *(originally another eye poke)* while extending his R arm to tweak his R elbow across your chest.

7. Un-pivot R *(L heel / R toe)* to R rev cat *(behind his R leg)* w/possible R Out whipping BKS thru R kidney *(or Out glancing elbow thru back of head, or circle hand over his head)*.

8. R rear sliding leg sweep thru back of his R leg w/inward heel of palm strike to his sternum driving him to the ground.

9. R inv roundhouse ball kick his R jaw hinge then jump switch landing w/L side thrust kick under his chin then cross out along his body line towards 4:30 to exit.

### UNTWIRLING PENDULUM *(Unwinding Pendulum)*
#### Right Front Kick / Right Punch Step Thru 12

1. <u>From RNB</u>: R rear crossover *(12 front twist)* w/R down out parry hammering then glancing thru outside of R kick w/L hand checking, opponent is close so un-pivot to LNB with a left inward block outside his right cross punch.

2. R front crossover push sweep inside L ankle opens legs *(front twist)* w/R Up 5-finger strike under his groin.

3. Shift weight L, *(R heel/L toe)* to R rev cat w/R rear scoop kick thru groin, reset foot behind his R leg into R rear sliding leg sweep back of his R leg to widen his base. Your arms in R side universal check or insert any strikes that do not cause him to fall forward.

4. R toe to L rev switch looking over your L shoulder to a L rear sliding leg sweep thru the back of his left leg to further widen his base.

5. Adjust L foot outside and past his L foot towards 1:30, R front crossover pulling sweep inside his L ankle to spread his legs further apart cocking R foot above his exposed L knee, R side thrust kick down onto that knee. R front crossover step out exit to 1:30.

# TACKLE & TAKEDOWN ATTACKS

Attacker is trying to hit with their entire body. This is an extremely dangerous range due to the weight and force applied, especially in an environment with obstacles.

The two main defensive methods each cover three major depth ranges. The two methods are moving *Off-the-Line* of attack, like a matador avoiding a Bull, and the other is getting caught *On-the-Line* of attack where we are forced to stop or ride the mass. The three depth zones (dz= Depth Zone, see Mind) in either case is contact with the hands (dz1), the elbows (dz2), and lead side of the body (dz3).

*Skipping Tackle* is added from Form 5 to complete the off-line tackle formula. I created *Jamming the Tackle* as a first contact goal against the on-line tackle attempt and modified *Dangerous Tackle* to address to real possibility of getting taken down.

The scenario where we are laying, or falling, to the ground with an opponent standing over us (original EPAK "Dangerous Tackle" scenario) is defended with ground maneuvers, covered in the basics chapter, and is designed to get us back onto our feet.

## OFF-LINE TACKLE DEFENSES
CHARGING TACKLE *(Charging Ram)* Pg 294
BROKEN TACKLE *(Broken Ram)* Pg 295
SKIPPING TACKLE *(Long Form 5)* Pg 295

## ON-LINE TACKLE DEFENSES
JAMMING THE TACKLE Pg 296
MEETING THE TACKLE *(Intercepting the Ram)* Pg 296
DANGEROUS TACKLE *(Encounter with Danger)* Pg 296

## OFF-LINE TACKLE DEFENSES
**CHARGING TACKLE** *(Charging Ram)*
***Two Arm Tackle from 12***
 1. Step back R to 4:30 *(forward 45o horse)* w/L straight palm jams L collarbone/neck.
 2. Absorb momentum w/L rear step thru to 4:30 *(R rev 45o horse)* w/R overhead down handsword to back his neck *(drives him to his knees)*.
 3. Right upward front shin kick into his left rib cage.
 4. L front ball kick his face *(chicken kick style)* then step back L to exit.
<u>Extension Begins Here</u>
 5. As he rolls onto his back away from the L front kick L step forward to front twist, R down roundhouse ball kick inside his R knee/thigh *(opens his legs)*.
 6. R foot between his legs followed by L front snap ball kick inside his L knee *(widens his legs)*, rebound back w/L rear sliding heel kick inside his R knee *(opens legs more)*.
 7. L step to 6 LFB *(towards his torso standing between his legs)* then R front snap ball kick into his testicles then step back right then left back thru to exit.

**BROKEN TACKLE** *(Broken Ram)*
*(Two-Arm Tackle from 12)*

1. Step back R to 4:30 *(forward 45o horse)* trying to do Charging Tackle w/L straight palm to L collarbone/neck, but he gets past your L hand making your L elbow (depth zone 2) using the humerus bone alignment as the next line of defense to stop his momentum jamming his L collarbone/neck.

2. Continue absorbing his momentum w/L rear step thru to 4:30 *(R rev 45o horse w/him too close for downward handsword)* w/R overhead down elbow to his upper back.

3. LFB to 4:30 *(10:30 rev bow)* w/R down in heel palm to R jaw hinge or temple as L grabs above to hair/head, hooking R hand under to grab his chin.

4. Drag L foot to R cranking his neck by lifting R hand up *(forearm anchored against his back to keep his body down)* pushing head down w/L *(practice with caution),* R Up hook kick under groin as R hand releases chin circling overhead.

5. R push-drag to 10:30 R rev bow towards opponent w/R back elbow L collarbone.
Extension Begins Here

6. After elbow adjust to 10:30 RNB w/R back heel of palm lifting under his chin or R obscure handsword strike up into his throat.

7. Adjust to a RFB w/L upward lifting palm strike under his chin.

8. L then R front knee kicks *(chicken kick)* groin w/L cross body check across front shoulder line w/R hand by R ear.

9 Option 1: With your R leg still in the air from the second knee kick R side thrust kick inside his L knee w/R In inv horiz palm *(fingers in)* to his L temple.

    Option 2: If you lose your balance after the second knee kick, put R foot on ground inside his R leg hooking your foot behind his R foot then R knee buckle.

10. In either case R foot to L *(def reverse switch)* looking over L shoulder, L rear scoop kick groin &/or L rear thrust kick best available target clears him, cross out exit to 6.


**SKIPPING TACKLE**
*Tackle - 12, Right Arm Pinned / Left Arm Free*

1. Step back R to 4:30 *(12 L forward 45o horse)* w/L straight palm to L collarbone / neck. His L shoulder & weight against you his L arm trapping your R arm.

2. Absorb momentum L foot back to 4:30 *(R rev 45o horse)* R hand on L both push down his head w/off cover turning hips forcefully to 6.

3. Push his head down between his legs as R arm lifts levering his R arm up rolling / flipping him over onto his back, ending w/his head close to you and feet away w/your R knee on the ground and your right hand on his chest to keep him from rolling up.

4. Stand up w/R down stomp his chest jumping off to L foot outside his L hip, R rear stomp between his legs into his groin as you exit towards 4:30.
Extension Begins here

4. As his back hits the ground *(optional dbl down heel palm his collarbones)* grab his chest *(pec muscle pinch)* or shoulders to lift him to seated position, R front knee kick middle spine, let go of his shoulders circling back thru your chamber.

5. Step back R *(6 LFB)* w/dbl In ear box, reach around his face *(possible dbl In claws)* grabbing his chin *(overlapped hands)* w/forearms against sides of his neck w/elbows down on back of his shoulders *(tweaks neck back),* R front knee kick upper spine.

6. R step back *(LNB)* pulling him back down, slam back of head on ground w/hands pinning body down, L down knee drop L collarbone/throat *(10:30 R close kneel).*

7. Bounce off previous knee turning to 6 L close kneel w/R down knee drop onto his nose w/R down vert thrust punch into his solar plexus, L hand position check his legs.

8. Stand up w/R glancing front heel kick thru his face, lift R knee up followed by R front stomp kick onto his solar plexus or sternum.

9. Jump off his chest onto L foot outside his L hip then R rear stomp kick between his legs into his groin, 4:30 R front crossover to exit.

# ON-LINE TACKLE DEFENSES

**JAMMING THE TACKLE**
*(Attempted Tackle from 12)*

1. Jump both legs back *(jams before sprawling necessary)* w/dbl palm heel strikes to his two collarbones *(if he gets past your hands then forearms into the humerus bones are the next line of defense)*, grab their shoulders *(clothing, trapezius muscles or neck clinch)*.

2. Step back R pulling him forward then pushing him <u>face down</u> onto the ground *(shuffle backwards with tenderizing knee strikes as needed)*.

3. Drop L knee across back of his neck holding shoulders down *(compliance hold)*.

<u>Extension Begins Here</u>

4. Bounce up shifting L *(cover)* to R down knee drop across neck *(cervical spine)*.

5. Bounce up *(above his head facing 6)* w/R front stomp kick onto his middle spine *(thoracic, as technique moves down his body line)* standing on L above his R shoulder.

6. Jump to R foot outside his L hip w/L down heel stomp to his lower spine *(lumbar)*.

7. Jump up turning L in the air landing on your L foot outside his L hip *(where R foot was)* facing 6 w/R downward roundhouse kick between his legs into his groin.

8. Drop R shin onto his tailbone *(coccyx)* w/R palm down onto the base of his occipital lobe *(drives his face into the ground)*.

9. Bounce up w/R front crossover to 6 *(now moving up his body line)* w/R inv side stomp *(or TSK)* thru the back of his head as you exit towards 6.

**MEETING THE TACKLE** *(Intercepting the Ram)*
*(Two-Arm Tackle from 12)*

1. Jump both legs back w/dbl palms to collarbones *(dz1, trying to do "Jamming the Tackle" before sprawling is necessary)* but he gets past hands where front of elbows *(dz2)* slow his tackle, but he gets past the elbows with his shoulder against body *(dz3)*, step back R w/L down elbow tip hits and presses his upper spine down, changing his height zone.

2. Keep riding the tackle w/L rear step thru *(avoiding his single leg)*, L hand can hook & moves his head if needed, w/R inside down elbow *(could lead hook into this move)* thru L jaw hinge &/or temple, changing his width zone.

3. R back elbow *(or hammerfist)* L collarbone, jamming his depth zone *(1-3 requires timing)*.

4. R hand holds head down, R rear scoop kick thru face or groin w/exit to 6.

<u>Extension Begins Here</u>

4. Absorb any residual momentum w/R rear crossover or step thru w/R down BKS to neck into LNB w/L down palm strike middle spine *(possible horsebite kidney area)*.

5. Keep moving back gripping, pressing down, while pulling w/both hands driving him face down to the ground *(moves 5-6 look like mauling his back)*.

6. L knee drop across back of his neck holds him down or bounce up crossing feet in the air ending w/R inv side stomp kick on his neck, R step back exit to 6.

**DANGEROUS TACKLE** *(Encounter with Danger)*
*High or Low Right Shoulder Tackle from 12*
Version 1 - Opponent successful in applying a high body tackle *(his right shoulder against you and above your hands)*:

1. Hook R hand around back of his neck, L grabbing his L arm *(above elbow)*, sit on your L hip controlling his arm & pulling his neck down to your R shoulder; R up front shin kick groin *(or spider guard foot/knee position or heels on hips)* w/R back shoulder roll w/opponent ending mounted on top *(if he falls to side, scramble to same position)*.

2. Mounted on top, L-R In palm thru R-L sides of face, R grabs his L wrist as L arm reaches under his R upper arm w/over shoulder lock *(Americana Lock)*. Submit or dislocate, R forward shoulder roll over his head exit to 12.

Version 2 - Opponent successful in applying a low body tackle *(his right shoulder against you and below your hands)*:

1. Hook R arm over back of his neck, reach under to apply R radius bone against his trachea as L arm hooks around and traps his R arm *(Guillotine Choke)*, sit wrapping both of your legs around his waist *(Guard Position)* then lean back and choke him out.

2. If his head lifts out of hold, sit up w/L foot on ground outside his L knee reaching over L shoulder w/L arm using L hip to push him over to top mount facing 6.

3. Same ending as move #2 in Version #1 except to 6.

# HUGS/HOLDS & LOCKS

Attackers uses their hands and/or arms to apply a body controlling technique intended to lift, throw, and/or submit.

A *Hug* is a type of *Hold* used here as a *Bear-Hug* to describe moves where the arms are wrapped around the torso. This type of attack can be applied from various directions around the body with arms free in space, both pinned against the body, or one free and the other pinned. Only front and rear *Bear-Hug* attacks are covered here to simplify the analysis.

A *Lock* for this section describes ways the arms and hands are interlocked around the throat or neck.

Whether "in process" or if "fully applied" defending this type of attack requires time to work free, where the attacker loosens or gives up on the position. This is accomplished by fighting the grip while maintaining balance and the relative hip position to find and maintain a *Zone of Sanctuary* while *"riding the storm."*

Controlling hip position, or perhaps attaching with leg and arm hooks, help to avoid being lifted or thrown. Maintaining air and blood passageways is crucial to remaining conscious, so fighting grips are mandatory. All are done while trying to continually obtain a better position.

*Tenderizing Techniques* are especially useful at this range of fighting to soften an attacker's grip, distract their mind, cause them to loosen or give up on a position, or make them want to let go entirely. These are used individually, sequentially, or in combination as needed to affect a release.

Depending on positioning, *Tenderizing Techniques* include groin attacks with hands, knees, and feet, plus foot stomps, body punches, pinches, biting, fingers to eyes, head butts, etc. Any or all of these can minimize an attacker's effectiveness until an escape can be made.

## HUGS
### FRONT BEAR HUGS
THRUSTING THUMBS *(Thrusting Prongs)* Pg 298
TRIPPING LEG *(Tripping Arrow)* Pg 298

### REAR BEAR HUGS
CRUSHING PALM *(Crushing Hammer)* Pg 298
CAPTURED ARMS *(Captured Twigs)* Pg 299
CRASHING ELBOWS *(Crashing Wings)* Pg 299
STRADDLING THE LEG *(Squatting Sacrifice)* Pg 300
SPIRALING WRIST *(Spiraling Twig)* Pg 300
SWEEPING THE LEG Pg 301

## LOCKS
ARMS OF SILK *(Wings of Silk)* Pg 301
SCRAPING STOMP A *(Scraping Hoof)* Pg 302
SCRAPING STOMP B *(Twirling Sacrifice)* Pg 302

LOCKED HORNS *(Locking Horns) Pg 302*
LOCK OF DEATH *(Grip of Death) Pg 303*
PINCH FROM DEATH *(The Grasp of Death) Pg 303*
ESCAPING DEATH *(Escape from Death) Pg 304*
ELUDING DEATH A-B-C *Pg 304*

## HUGS
## FRONT BEAR HUG ATTACKS

**THRUSTING THUMBS** *(Thrusting Prongs)*
***Bear-Hug Arms Pinned from 12***
1. Step back R to 12 LFB w/dbl forward thumb strike into urinary bladder *(groin area)* with a possible front head butt.
2. R front knee kick his groin *(hips forward, head back)* chambering your two hands.
3. Step forward r from knee w/r cross body check to push and clear him away.
<u>Extension Begins Here</u>
2. L hand under R armpit & over R shoulder w/R front knee kick groin, R chambered.
3. Forward to RNB *(checking/buckling R knee)* w/R In elbow to L side of his face *(pressing your elbows together crimps his neck).*
4. R Out crane hook back of his neck *(over his R shoulder)* pulling down as L hand circles overhead as R steps back to 1:30 LNB into L down handsword back of his neck.
5. L palm holds head down, R Up knee kick face as R arm circles overhead into 1:30 RNB w/R overhead down palm *(fingers point away)* onto the base of his head/neck.
6. Hold head down w/R shifting weight L *(1:30 R rev close kneel)* w/R rear scoop kick L jaw *(or best available),* R side thrust kick inside L knee, R front crossover out to 7:30.

**TRIPPING LEG** *(Tripping Arrow)*
***(Bear-Hug Arms Free from 12)***
1. Dbl In ear box *(possible thumbs in eyes)* &/or dbl In hooking BKS mastoid(s), L hand over grabbing L side of his head stepping L outside his R foot *(modified horse)* pulling his R ear to his R shoulder *(L slides off his head to grab his R elbow)* w/R inv horiz palm strike *(fingers in)* L temple/jaw *(his weight should be shifted to his R heel).*
2. R Out claw face w/R step behind R to cat *(4:30 R rev cat)* holding R arm in L hand.
3. R In thumb/index throat *(Tigers mouth)* w/R rear sliding leg sweep back of R leg drives him back onto ground at 10:30 *(possible arm bar break or tweak wrapped elbow).*
4. His R arm slides until your L hand holds back of his R wrist as your R hand reaches under and back to grab the inside of his right wrist *(wrist flex lock).*
5. Holding his R wrist in both hands pivot L foot open, R knee up then R front stomp onto his R shoulder joint/jaw/throat pulling up w/both hands *(shoulder dislocation).*
6. R TSK clears his arm down to floor, R inv stomp R forearm crossing out to 7:30.
<u>Extension Begins Here</u>
6. R foot above his L shoulder to 1:30 clearing his R arm to side w/L down knee drop onto R collarbone *(moves #6-9 use opponent's body to bounce up from w/each move).*
7. Bounce up w/cover step L landing to 4:30 w/L foot still next to his R hip landing w/R downward knee drop onto his left collarbone.
8. Bounce up w/jump switch over his body turning slightly R *(or stagger R then L foot over his R shoulder & L hip)* to 10:30 w/L down knee drop onto his solar plexus or ribs.
9. Bounce up covering in the air to 4:30 w/R down knee drop sternum as your arms check his legs, R front crossover sweep kick thru L knee/foot as you exit towards 1:30.

## REAR BEAR HUG ATTACKS

**CRUSHING PALM** *(Crushing Hammer)*
***(Bear-Hug Arms Pinned from 6)***
1. Close rear attack tenderizing technique Index: *(Used collectively here for reference)* Trap his hands w/R hand reaching back w/L thumb/index finger pinch to upper inner L thigh, L rear stomp kick top of L foot, R Up hook kick groin, rear head butt nose.
2. L hand pinning check traps his dropping your weight and stepping L *(12 horse stance)* w/R back elbow to solar plexus followed by R back hammerfist strike to groin.

3. R foot to L then step outside & behind his L foot *(4:30 R rev bow w/your R hip against his L hip)* w/R back underhand heel palm strike to his groin *(crushing palm)*.

4. RNB towards 4:30 opponent *(heel pivots used to penetrate)* as R knee checks *(slightly buckles)* back of his L knee w/R obscure elbow strike up under his chin *(lifting his head & straightening his body)* while chambering your left.

5. RFB to 4:30 w/R Out claw face w/L horiz palm thrust *(fingers out)* L ribs *(Spleen)*.

Extension Begins Here

5. L foot to R *(slight squat to 3)* as both arms wrap R over front & L under behind his legs hugging his knees, lift him up causing him to fall backwards onto back of his head & shoulders to 6 *(let legs slide thru your arms until shins/tops of feet against your chest)*.

6. R rear step back to 1:30 *(to 7:30 LNB)* flipping him over by his feet onto his face dropping his legs *(he should be face down with head away at 6 w/you outside his L leg)*.

7. *(Moves #7-10 move up his body line)* R inv side stomp back of his L knee, step R over his body next to his R hip w/L downward knee drop onto his lower spine *(lumbar)*.

8. Step L to 4:30 on his L side w/R down knee drop on his middle spine *(thoracic)*.

9. Step R to 7:30 outside his R shoulder w/L down knee on his upper spine *(cervical)*.

10. Hop forward to 7:30 onto your R foot w/L rear thrust kick back and down onto his head and/or neck, L front crossover exit to 7:30.

**CAPTURED ARMS** *(Captured Twigs)*
**(Bear-Hug Arms Pinned from 6)**
Use tenderizing techniques as needed.

1. L hand pinning check traps his hands dropping weight stepping L *(12 horse stance)* w/R back hammerfist into his groin *(you cannot see his left foot between yours)*.

2. Break out of hold explosively turning shoulders R *(flaring elbows out to make space)* to 3 R cat ending w/R universal check position *(possible left poke/claw to his eyes)*.

3. R front stomp top L foot, R obscure elbow under chin *(like a ball bouncing)*.

Extension Begins Here

4. From obscure elbow extend hand to R obscure handsword throat, L inverted horizontal snap punch stomach *(bends him forward)* as the right-hand checks.

5. L rear crossover to 6 as L hand reaches up and hooks over the L side of his neck w/R outward whipping BKS glancing thru his groin.

6. Transition thru R rev cat R arm lifts behind and into back of L armpit pocket grabbing your L w/R hand over his shoulder, R rear sliding leg sweep thru inside L knee leveraging his head down w/both hands *(same as Skipping Tackle except he bends instead of flip over)*. Optional ending: Step R between his legs *(possibly striking R inner knee w/R knee)* to 4:30 pushing his held arm to send him to the ground on his back with any follow up.

7. R Up knee kick lifts his face *(same as Gripping Wrist)*, release R grip 10:30 front crossover step-out, drag step L to R *(or leap)* w/R side thrust kick to chest, R front crossover exit to 10:30.

**CRASHING ELBOWS** *(Crashing Wings)*
**(Bear Hug Arms Free from 6)**

1. Establish balance & hip position w/tenderizing moves, attack back of his hands w/In knocking punches &/or fight his hands, push down at his thumb joints to loosen his grip. When grip softened step R to 3 *(12 horse stance)* w/dbl down elbow strikes to his hands/arms to separate his hands *(his R foot seen between your feet)*

2. Move L foot to R, step behind his R leg to 7:30 *(your L hip against his R hip)* transitioning thru 7:30 L rev bow *(L knee checks his R knee)* to 7:30 LNB *(pivot on heels, toes move towards him)* w/L obscure elbow under chin, R hammerfist cocked at R ear.

3. Continue transitioning to 7:30 LFB w/R In down hammerfist urinary bladder *(groin area)* w/cross body check to shoulder line &/or L Out claw face, L step thru back exit.

Extension Begins Here

4. From hammerfist slide L hand down to grab back of his R elbow *(thumb down pushing his R arm in front of his R hip)* gauging L foot L to 7:30 LFB w/R up lifting palm under chin.

5. Still connected to chin w/R palm, hook R elbow over back of his R shoulder *(taking slack out of his neck w/forearm)*, arch him back at neck placing L hand at front of his forehead *(him looking up)*, pull his head back down into R Up knee kick to back of neck *(cervical)*. Note: This is a potentially lethal or disabling move so practice very cautiously.

6. W/knee in the air R front crossover step out and thru to 4:30 slamming his head on ground *(end in LNB above opponent's head facing him on the ground at 10:30).*

7. R step thru low roundhouse ball kick thru R temple, R toe to L spinning L w/L low out heel kick thru same R side head target *(looks like spinning leg sweep in the air)* ending in RNB facing opponent on the ground.

## STRADDLING THE LEG *(Squatting Sacrifice)*
### (Bear-Hug Arms Free from 6)

1. Establish balance and hip position w/any tenderizing techniques, attack back of hands w/In knocking punches &/or fight hands by pushing down at his thumb joints to loosen grip. When grip softened step R to 3 *(12 horse)* w/dbl down elbow strikes onto his hands and arms to separate his hands *(his R foot seen between your feet).*

2. Squat, tailbone back against top of his R knee *(his R heel plants, his toes lifting slightly),* reach back between your legs w/both hands to grab back of his R foot.

<u>Version 1: (successful squatting knee bar)</u>

3. As his knee locks, and his weight shifts to his R heel, keep applying pressure w/tailbone against his knee lifting his R foot up causing him to fall backwards, immediately turn your body R to 3 dropping L knee on the ground hugging his R knee (his R knee tight against back of your R thigh, possible knee bar).

4. Grab top of his R foot w/L hand & back of his R heel w/R hand, stand up, R step back over his L knee (possible out hook kick face), drop R knee onto his L thigh (to 3).

5. Cover step R (to 9) w/ankle twist turnover (push down L, pull up R) turning him to his stomach, L knee drop back of L thigh (possible ankle lock), re-grab top R foot w/R.

6. Stand up still holding top of R foot in R hand, step drag forward to 6 (him face down w/head towards 6) sliding a R front kick between his legs into his groin.

7. Reach down w/L hand to pick up his L wrist (use collar or hair if he rolled over his arm), R front scoop kick thru groin lifting knee up above his back, R front stomp kick down onto his middle spine while pulling up on his leg and arm (could break his back).

8. R TSK his L elbow, inv stomp his arm as you exit towards 4:30.

*Options:* (unsuccessful squatting knee bar and/or he pushes you)

<u>Version 2: (unsuccessful squatting knee bar with rollover counter where they roll to back)</u>

3. L shoulder two-man front rollover w/him rolling over face up, scramble up until your R leg can either drop R knee on his L thigh (#4 of base technique) or step over his R knee (#3 of base technique) w/R thigh, finish base technique from either point.

<u>Version 3: (unsuccessful squatting knee bar with rollover counter where they roll to stomach)</u>

3. L shoulder two-man front rollover w/R ax kick back of his R knee pushing him face down ending w/top of his R knee in your hip, apply knee bar to finish (rolling knee bar).

## SPIRALING WRIST *(Spiraling Twig)*
### (High Bear-Hug Arms Free from 6)

1. Establish balance and hip position w/any tenderizing techniques, attack back of his hands w/In knocking punches &/or fight his hands at thumb joints to loosen grip, step R to 3 *(12 horse stance)* w/dbl down elbow strikes to separate hands & arms *(you cannot see his R foot between your feet),* grab his R wrist w/both hands *(L thumb down / R thumb up)* securing his R elbow joint under your R armpit *(his little finger pointed up).*

2. Pivot open R foot *(heel pivot)* to 1:30 *(press down against his elbow, begins breaking his balance),* step L to 1:30 pressing down against his elbow pulling him towards 1:30 *(him moving forward & down, when L hand reaches for the floor his balance is broken).*

3. Transition back thru 7:30 R cat as R hand slides to back of his locked R elbow or armpit crease still pulling his arm, continue R step back thru to 7:30 LFB *(his L hand to the ground to balance with you holding his right hand in the air).*

4. R front snap kick groin or up into solar plexus *(knee if close)* cocking R arm behind R hip, step forward w/R stiff arm lifting punch to R temple. R rear step thru exit or reapply elbow pressure w/R rear step thru cover locking him face down *(In armpit trap).*

<u>Extension Begins Here</u>

4. R round ball kick inside his R knee *(turns him slightly)* holding R wrist w/L hand as R straight arm cocks behind your R hip, step between his feet to 6 RNB w/R In whipping punch to L temple glancing thru to in front of your L shoulder *(keeps turning him to his right),* still holding his right wrist in your left hand.

5. L rear crossover to 9 w/R Out whipping BKS thru R temple, chamber R hand still holding his R wrist in your L while transitioning to a 7:30 right reverse cat stance.

6. R rear sliding leg sweep *(R rev bow)* thru inside L knee w/R vert thrust punch *(possible R In elbow strike)* thru his L jaw *(your hand goes down in front of his chest)*, L hand becomes position check *(possible In heel palm to R temple tweaks his neck)*.

7. R Out elbow sternum straightens him up *(stay in R reverse bow between his legs)*, R rear scoop kick groin, R leg still in the air *(ok to bounce off ground to regain balance if needed)* R side thrust kick inside his R knee, R front crossover step out exit to 12.

## SWEEPING THE LEG
### (Bear-Hug arms free from 6)

1. Establish balance w/tenderizing moves, fight hands at thumb joints to loosen grip, L to 9 *(12 horse)* moves hips away, push down separating hands *(spot his L foot)*.

2. Turn R to 3 R cat w/R obscure elbow under his chin then R down out BKS groin.

3. R rear sliding leg sweep thru inside L knee driving his leg towards 7:30 *(separates his legs canceling 3 zones and bending him forward)* catching his chin w/R Up lifting forearm under chin under and around his throat. L hand reaches to Gable or 'S' grip w/R hand to choke him *(reverse headlock)*.

4. Pull his head, turning face to you, w/R Up knee kick *(to 3)* R temple w/L down palm strike sandwiching head as R arm circles outside R thigh and overhead.

5. Settles weight to 3 RNB w/R downward elbow onto spine, neck, or scapula *(use strongest alignment)* while maintaining a L hand position check at his L shoulder.

6. Shift weight L *(R rev bow)* w/R down palm strike his head holding it down, R rear scoop kick his face *(possibly groin)* as you exit towards 10:30.

<u>Extension Begins Here</u>

6. From downward elbow strike drop R down in heel palm to his R mastoid *(or jaw hinge)*, reaching under to grab his chin as R forearm anchors across back of his neck and L hand braces back of his left shoulder.

7. Step forward L toe to R *(off switch)* levering his chin up w/grip *(him looking over his R shoulder turning)* while L hand pushes his L shoulder forward until his back to you, R back to 4:30 LFB as L hand becomes a cross body check across his rear shoulder line.

8. R holds chin posting back of his R shoulder, R inv side thrust kick *(TSK)* back of R knee, R back to LNB pushing R shoulder with chin pull back over R shoulder *(neck tweak)*.

9. L toe to R *(def rev or jump reverse switch)*, spin R rear thrust kick spine, R front crossover step towards 12 to exit.

# <u>LOCKS</u>

## ARMS OF SILK *(Wings of Silk)*
### (Two-Arm Double Wing Lock from 6)

1. Tenderize by reaching back w/L hand thumb/index pinch to L inner thigh, L rear stomp L foot leaning forward w/R Up hook kick groin pulling R elbow up & out from grip *(possible R obscure elbow under chin)*.

2. R step forward to 10:30 *(toe in)* holding his L arm w/your L hand/arm, step L foot back thru to 10:30 *(1:30 horse stance)* sliding L hand down to grab his L wrist as R arm wraps under to break/hyperextend his left elbow joint.

3. L rear crossover behind his L foot w/R Out whipping BKS thru ribs/groin bringing R hand up to an In blocking position behind his L shoulder.

4. R rev cat, R rear sliding leg sweep thru inside L knee *(above his knee)* w/R forward vert forearm *(In Block)* continuing to hold his left wrist in your left hand *(If he falls face down then lock him down to finish; if he keeps his balance move on to extension)*.

<u>Extension Begins Here</u>

5. Adjust hands to hold his L hand for Out wristlock *(thumbs on back of his hand)*, cover R *(4:30 RFB)* w/Out wristlock & possible L In elbow face *(stands him, shifts his weight L)*, L knee kick groin wrapping R arm over around his L, grabs his elbow *(wraparound technique)*.

6. Step back L *(wraparound in place)*, cover step to 10:30 LFB while applying forward pressure against his locked left elbow *(moves him forward)*.

7. Cover R *(4:30 RFB)* letting him run into L straight palm under chin *(possible eye poke)*, L front knee to groin/solar plexus *(could hook neck to pull into knee)*, extend foot from knee *(if in range)* w/L front push kick to torso driving him away, L back to exit.

301

**SCRAPING STOMP A** *(Scraping Hoof)*
**(Attempted Full Nelson Hold from 6)**
   1. Before hold is locked *(reach back peel fingers off &/or dbl inv punch temples)* &/or just drop weight to 12 horse crashing elbows down onto his forearms, straighten legs extending both arms down to break grip *(punching down motion)*, grab your L wrist w/R hand *(allows Lat muscles to engage holding his arms)* w/rear head butt to his face.
   2. Shift weight L turning slightly looking over R shoulder, R Out hook kick inside his L knee followed by R side snap kick inside his R knee *(rolls his R foot out onto its side)*, scrape down R shin w/R front stomp to inside arch of his R foot *(Scraping Stomp)*.
   3. Grab R wrist w/L hand stepping L towards 1:30 *(LFB)* pulling opponent then immediately shift to a RNB towards him with a right outward elbow strike to his face.
   4. Transition thru modified RNB w/R Out handsword R side of neck hooking over grabbing back of his neck or clothing collar as you shift back to R rear bow stance.
   5. R front scoop kick his groin *(possible upward knee his face)*, R step thru back to 1:30 pressing down on his neck and still holding his right arm in your left hand.
   6. L rear crossover step out to 1:30 pulling his arm and pushing his neck down until face down on ground w/R wrist on your L hip pocket as R hand presses his neck down driving R knee onto back of his R shoulder *(position locks him down onto the ground)*.
<u>Extension Begins Here</u>
   3. From foot stomp R rear sliding leg sweep inside L knee w/R lifting BKS to nose.
   4. R forward behind R foot hooking back of ankle as R knee presses and buckles his inside R knee pulling down on his R wrist w/L as R arm pushes him down to ground.
   5. L rear crossover heel stomp his groin *(his head should come up)*, R side thrust kick his face *(or side stomp his torso)* then right front crossover to towards 12 to exit.

**SCRAPING STOMP B** *(Twirling Sacrifice)*
**(Locked Full Nelson Hold from 6)**
   1. Against locked hold grab back of your own L wrist w/R hand placing back of your right hand against your own forehead and press back to support your neck.
   2. With both hands supporting your neck use any tenderizing techniques to soften his grip. Standard sequence: L rear heel stomp L foot, R Up heel kick groin.
   3. When possible step R wide outside his R foot to 9 *(12 horse stance)* then slide L foot next to your R and behind his R leg to 7:30 *(L rev close kneel checks his R leg w/your L)* w/L back underhand heel palm strike into his groin *(bend forward as needed to reach)*.
   4. Stand up adjusting to 7:30 LNB towards opponent w/L obscure elbow under his chin, LFB w/R horiz palm strike to his Liver *(R ribs)* or solar plexus *(depends on his position)* drives him away *(looks like Crushing Palm ending)*, L rear step thru to exit.
<u>Extension Begins Here</u>
   5. Bounce R hand off previous strike, LFB w/R inv palm groin, L hand checks R arm.
   6. L pushes his R arm in front as R right arm grabs back of his neck, R front step thru knee sweep inside his R knee pulling him to your R and down *(he bends forward w/his hands on the ground to brace his front fall)*.
   6. R rear sliding leg sweep inside his R arm making him fall flat face down.
   7. R Out down ax kick between his legs into his groin, L front step thru to 4:30, R front crossover *(TSK thru his right Achilles tendon)* towards 4:30 to exit.

**LOCKED HORNS** *(Locking Horns)*
**(Right Reverse Forearm / Guillotine Choke from 12)**
Note: If feeling this hold being applied put your head under his armpit vs letting a skilled person put the back of your head against his torso before applying pressure.
   1. L hand grabs his R choking wrist *(shaped like doing a chin up)*. If R arm free defend w/R arm over his L shoulder or post at hip or around his waist w/tenderizing moves to ride the storm and soften his grip *(knees & punches to groin, body, & legs, pinches, foot stomps, biting, fingers to eyes, etc.)*.
   Option: If R arm held *(after tenderizing)* R step thru outside R foot to 10:30 driving R arm & head up and out under his R armpit escaping hold *(like Eluding Death B)*.
   2. Step forward R *(12 close kneel)* w/R vert snap punch to his groin/lower abdomen.
   3. Shift weight L *(R rev wide kneel)* w/R vert hook punch above inside R knee taking R arm off back of your neck w/L hand and pulling his weight down at that wrist.

4. Stand up *(12 RNB)* w/R obscure elbow under his chin, pulling down on his R arm, followed by possible R outward claw thru his face.

5. Push drag forward w/R In elbow his L jaw (St6) sandwiching w/L In heel palm his R temple *(staggered high/low snaps head, disrupts CNV & VII causes probable knockout)*.

Extension Begins Here

6. Glancing thru previous strikes, L front crossover towards opponent at 12 w/L inv horiz *(fingers-in)* palm strike sternum w/R forward BKS into his solar plexus.

7. R front knee kick his groin w/L hand check as R hand chambers.

**Option 1:** *(if able to hook his right foot)*

8. From knee kick step R inside behind his R foot R knee, press & buckle R knee pushing his body with your two arms causing him to fall backwards onto the ground.

9. W/R foot in place L rear crossover heel stomp groin *(his head comes up)*, R side thrust kick face *(or rear stomp torso if too far)*, exit to 6 with R inv side thrust kick *(TSK)* thru R knee *(same ending as Scraping Stomp A)*.

**Option 2:** *(Option 1 not set up or you prefer this option)*

8. Grab R wrist w/L hand then do any hip throw *(under arm, over shoulder or around waist)* with your own follow up before exiting.


**LOCK OF DEATH** *(Grip of Death)*
**(Right Arm Headlock Pulling You Down from 9)**

1. Ride headlock stepping R to 10.30 *(dbl hammerfists load around him)* settling in R close kneel *(L knee checks outside his R knee)* w/L In hammerfist R kidney/spine sandwiching w/R In hammerfist to his groin.

2. Grab his R wrist w/R hand as L reaches over his R shoulder to grab his hair, nose *(index finger bar)*, or chin, step drag forward buckling back of R knee w/L knee pulling his head back & down *(pull down height check w/L elbow fulcrum at upper spine)* ducking out from R arm driving your chest into back of his straight R elbow.

3. Adjust L w/R In elbow to face sandwiching w/L hand holding L side of his head, drop R knee onto his R calf or Achilles tendon. Stand up then step back left to exit.

Extension Begins Here

3. Maintain R hand grip of R wrist, step L outside his R leg as L arm hooks & collapses his R elbow crease folding his arm to over shoulder lock *(Americana)*, cover step L towards opponent at 4:30 w/R In elbow thru his face driving his R hand over his R shoulder w/R front knee kick to solar plexus, all driving him back & down.

4. Follow him *(adjusting feet as needed)* to L close kneel on his R side w/R knee drop pinning his R ribs *(Liver side)* to ground as you dislocate his shoulder outward.

5. Continue holding his R wrist w/R but L lets lock go to grab above the back of his R elbow joint *(base of tricep w/C clamp grip)*, drag R foot next to L pushing his elbow & twisting his wrist to force him to roll over *(same maneuver in Piercing Blade)* moving L foot over as he rolls, step back R dropping L knee bracing back of his R scapula pulling up on his arm to dislocate his R shoulder.

6. Jump up from L knee brace switching feet in the air landing R front stomp kick onto his R scapula, gauge R w/optional L roundhouse or front shin kick to his neck/collar bone area then step back L to exit.


**PINCH FROM DEATH 1-2-3** *(The Grasp of Death)*
**(Right Arm Headlock from 9)**

1. Tuck chin to L shoulder grabbing R wrist w/R hand, step R foot forward to 12 R close kneel *(L knee checks outside R knee)* w/L horse bite pinch R upper inner thigh.

2. Option 1: *(he releases & lunges forward)*. R takes arm off neck w/L vert forearm against back of R elbow or armpit w/L front step thru driving him forward & down.

3. R inv vert punch R mastoid or temple or press behind his R earlobe (SJ17).

2. Option 2: *(he releases & steps back L)*. L grabs his waist posting your L foot behind his L foot, sit pulling him back & down *(rear heel trip takedown)*, end mounted on top.

3. If he holds headlock apply a neck lock arm bar, or if he lets go step over armbar.

2. Option 3: *(successful headlock takedown)*. L grabs around his waist as R posts against inside L or outside R leg, barrel roll R ending mounted on top.

3. If he holds headlock apply a neck lock arm bar, or if he lets go step over armbar.

**ESCAPING DEATH** *(Escape from Death)*
**(Attempted Sleeper Choke from 6)**
   1. Defend choke placing two hands up next to your temples so forearms protect your throat from attempted choke *(tucking your chin toward your left shoulder)*
   2. Step R to 3 *(12 horse)* looking L at opponent w/L back elbow his solar plexus followed by L back hammer fist strike to his groin.
   3. Bring L foot to R as L hand goes under his L armpit cocked behind his back *(or circle L arm over his R shoulder as in Short Form 3)*, L step behind his R at 7:30 *(L knee checks his R knee)* w/dbl In hammerfists sandwiching R kidney and groin.
   4. L reaches over his R shoulder hooking under nose w/L braced index finger bar *(or grab hair, collar, chin)*, LNB to 7:30 anchoring L elbow as fulcrum into upper spine pulling his nose up *(or hair, collar, chin)* to force him face up.
   5. L releases to track his upper R arm out adjusting to 7:30 LFB w/R straight palm strike under his chin *(possible finger poke)*.
<u>Extension Begins Here</u>
   6. R hooks behind R side of neck, pull to R front knee kick groin.
   7. Step R to 9, L pushes R arm in front of him w/L knee kick to R knee *(buckles)*.
   8. Step back L, cover step to 4:30 L close kneel w/R In heel palm L jaw (turns his head), attach palm to chin hooking R forearm over his R shoulder anchoring at back of shoulder (same as Crashing Elbows taking slack out of his neck).
   9. L hand across his forehead, R Up knee kick back of his neck *(also like Crashing Elbows)*, R side stomp kick back of his R Achilles *(or calf, back of knee, or sweep one or both legs)*, R front crossover to 4:30 pulling him back and down as you exit.

**ELUDING DEATH A-B-C**
**(Applied Right Arm Sleeper Choke from 6)**
   1. Grab wrist and elbow crease w/two hands *(fingers towards you chin up position)* dropping your weight *(keeps air/blood pathways open and makes him carry you)*.
   2. Based upon his body dynamics and/or personal preference use one of 3 counters to get out of the hold and get him to the ground.
   <u>Option A:</u> If his weight high or forward hip throw over R shoulder.
   <u>Option B:</u> If his weight in place step R w/L back elbow solar plexus creating space, L cross step back in front of his R foot to 3 *(between your R & his L)*, duck out under his arm, unpivot facing 6 w/R front shoulder pressed against his R elbow joint.
   <u>Option C:</u> If he is pulling you backwards spot his R foot, place back of your R ankle against back of his R ankle *(heel to heel)*, step L around 180° *(6 Horse)*, drop R shoulder turning hips L to LFB pulling down on his arm putting him on the ground.
<u>Extension Begins Here</u>
Same ending regardless of Option with stepping direction the only question:
   3. Grab back of his R wrist w/R hand *(fingers holding thumb webbing side)* as L hand slides down to grab back of his R elbow joint *(thumb inside elbow crease)* w/R front crossover step outside his R hip *(to 10:30 in A or 4:30 in B-C)*.
   4. Push him over L side on his stomach by twisting his R hand CW, push his elbow joint as you step L toe to R, back R to LNB facing him on the ground just outside his R shoulder.
   5. L hand re-grabs back of his R wrist *(his palm/fingers up, held in L palm up hand)* as R chambers, RFB w/R straight palm across back of knuckles *(breaks wrist)*.
   6. Grab R wrist w/R hand *(both hands holding his wrist)* dragging R foot to L *(drag step)*, L In ax kick his R elbow *(L foot above his R shoulder on ground near his head)*.
   7. R step back over his head as L hand slides down his arm to grab back of R elbow bending it as R hand twists his R wrist bending his arm behind his back *(Hammerlock)*, drop L knee on scapula pulling up on his arm *(shoulder dislocation)*.
   8. Step *(or jump)* up and back L w/R front stomp kick onto his R scapula or head/neck *(#7-8 same ending as Piercing Blade)* then R back to exit.

# MULTIPLE ATTACKERS

Addressing the multiple opponents or "mass attack" scenario is unique to street arts, like Kenpo. It is physically the most exhausting and the essence of awareness practice. Keys are to keep moving from one attacker to the other while keeping them busy and/or putting them in each others way until they can't continue, or we can get away safely. This is done while not exposing our blind angles to attack and searching for or creating a safe exit angle.

Attacks can come from any of the previously described ranges or angles but are done by more than one person. The techniques described here are empty-handed two-man samples of these angles, ranges, and types of attacks. However, the possibilities are endless and could include more than two opponents, with or without external weapons.

I have added the concept of using attackers against each other to a few techniques in this formula by adding "stacking" and "crowding" options. Separating opponents is covered extensively in the original EPAK multiple opponent techniques and is still covered here. There are 10 techniques total, 4 with attackers on the left and right sides, then 6 with them to the front and rear.

COURTING THE TIGER *(Courting the Tiger)* Pg 305
FINGERS OF WISDOM *(Snakes of Wisdom)* Pg 306
MATING THE RAMS *(Marriage of the Rams)* Pg 306
FLOWING HANDS *(Falcons of Force)* Pg 306
OPPOSING PALMS *(Grasping Eagles)* Pg 300
RAM AND THE EAGLE *(The Ram and the Eagle)* Pg 307
DIVIDING THE ENEMY *(Parting of the Snakes)* Pg 307
BEAR AND THE RAM *(The Bear and the Ram)* Pg 307
TRAINING THE BEARS *(Reprimanding the Bears)* Pg 308
GROUPING THE ENEMY *(Gathering of the Snakes)* Pg 308

**COURTING THE TIGER** *(Courting the Tiger)*
**(Right & Left Double Wrist Grabs at 3 & 9)**
Note: Attacker #1 starts on your right *(3)* with #2 on your left *(9)*.
　1. Shift weight L while bending L elbow *(palm up)* to stab #1 abdomen *(put his hips back, weight on heels)* counter grabbing #2 R *(twist to lift R elbow up)* w/R rear crossover to 9.
　2. Counter grab #2 L wrist *(use hand bones as handles, twist & lift his L elbow)*, backs move towards each other, R side snap kick #1 R knee then R front crossover towards 9.
　3. L knee lifts #2 L leg under front L thigh *(foot if needed)*, L side snap kick supporting R leg still holding #2 L wrist.
　4. L rear crossover to 3 *(rear twist)* w/R Out snapping BKS #1 temple.
　5. L/R front kicks *(chicken kick)* #2 groin and/or stomach *(or R knee)* settling weight to 9 RNB w/R forearm strike back of his L elbow *(or stiff-arm punch face or body if wrist lost)*.
　6. R rev cat, R rear thrust kick #1 torso w/R palm strike #2 face *(or L elbow)*, 9 R front crossover *(front twist)* clears #2, L foot back to 6, R rear step thru exit between #1 and #2.

**FINGERS OF WISDOM** *(Snakes of Wisdom)*
**(Right & Left Shoulder Grabs at 3 & 9)**
Note: Attacker #1 starts on your R *(3)* with #2 on your L *(9)*.

1. Step back *(12 mod LNB)* w/dbl out heel palm claws *(lead w/ elbows if in range)* thru attackers faces/eyes wrapping down around both arms at elbows, your elbows forward in front of your hips for leverage *(wrists against back of your shoulders from initial grab).*

2. R front step thru *(your hands together for structural support)* bringing them forward w/you using their arms stretch reflex to accelerate dbl out BKS thru their groins *(or solar plexus)* circling hands out and up then smashing their heads together.

3. Push their two heads down onto a L up knee kick, step back L as your arms flow down to dbl out BKS inside of their knees (Ki10 area).

4. Rebound off to scoop L leg of #1 w/R and #2 R leg w/L hand.

5. Standard: They fall, R down round ball kick #2 groin on your L, openR foot *(front twist)* w/L down round ball kick #1 groin on R then cross out to 6.

Note: If either or both standing on one leg up shin kick their groin(s) then exit back to 6.

### MATING THE RAMS *(Marriage of the Rams)*
### (Close Right & Left Shoulder Grabs at 3 & 9)
Note: Attacker #1 starts on your right *(3)* with #2 on your left *(9)*.

1. Step back R *(12 modified LNB)* w/dbl down back finger whips thru both groins.

2. Arms track up behind their backs hooking armpit creases *(SI9)* hands trapped to back of your shoulders *(based upon attack)*, R front step thru clapping hands above your head *(Gable grip)* slam their faces together, then interlocked arms hold them down together.

3. L Up knee kick their faces, step back L to R close kneel collapsing forearms down on their upper arms further *(keeps them bent over, possibly damages their shoulders).*

4. Relax both, slide down and out from shoulder lock *(gauge back as needed)* into dbl Out BKS thru inside front inner knees *(above bone)*, turn your two hands In to scoop Out picking up and pulling their front legs at the ankles *(same ending as "Fingers of Wisdom" where they either fall on their sides or remain standing on one leg).*

5. Standard technique they fall: R down round ball kick #2 groin *(on L)*, open R foot *(front twist)* w/L down round ball kick #1 groin *(on R)*, L front crossover exit to 6.

Note: If either or both on one leg change kick to up front shin kicks groin(s), exit back.

### FLOWING HANDS *(Falcons of Force)*
### (Right & Left Shoulder Grabs at 3 & 9)
Note: Attacker #1 on R *(3)* w/#2 on L *(9)*. Grabbing hands on sides or back of shoulders.

1. Step R *(3 side horse)* w/R obscure handsword #1 throat *(trachea)*, L checks hand.

2. Rebound weight to 9 L close kneel w/R In 2-finger slice #2 eyes *(L hand under R).*

3. R step thru forward *(10:30 R close kneel)* w/L Out handsword L side of #2s neck.

4. L rear crossover to 10:30 grabbing back of his neck *(or collar)* as a handle *(moves 2-4 connect as one flowing motion with the right step).*

5. Base technique: #1 R follow up punch. Unpivot to 4:30 R Cat pulling #2 head down in front of #1 w/R In block against punch *(or hammerfist #1 and/or forearm strike #2).*

6. R Up knee kick #2 face *(his neck in L hand)*, R front snap kick #1 groin *(or knee)*, R side snap kick to L knee of #2 before stepping down R next to L *(defensive switch).*

7. L step forward to 4:30 w/R Out handsword #1 R neck slicing thru, hook over to grab his neck or collar *(holding both opponent's necks or collars w/arms crossed, L under R).*

8. L rear crossover step out to 6 pulling #2 w/L in front of #1 w/R *(they trip over each other)* stacking #1 on top of #2 *(carefully practiced or just visualized alternate version, place L foot inside #1s R foot, inv pull sweep exposea now straight R knee to #2s body falling forward and down to break it.*

### OPPOSING PALMS *(Grasping Eagles)*
### (Right Lapel Grab-12 / Left Collar Grab-6)
Note: Attacker #1 in front *(12)* w/#2 behind *(6)*. Moves 1-2-3 are rapid-fire on L foot.

1. Shift weight L w/L In block *(clear #1s lapel grab)* w/R front snap kick groin w/R back hammerfist #2 groin *(possible rear or R side head butt).*

2. On L foot lean forward slightly w/R straight palm under #1 chin w/R rear thrust kick into #2 lower abdomen *(groin area).*

3. On L foot straighten up /R inv side thrust kick *(TSK)* to #1 closest knee w/L fingers-in palm strike face w/R rear lifting heel palm claw up into #2 face.

4. R step forward *(12 front twist)* between opponents using both hands to check and separate them, L back towards 9 followed by R rear step thru towards 9 to exit.

**RAM AND THE EAGLE** *(The Ram and the Eagle)*
**(Left Rear Collar Grab-6 / Right Punch-12)**
Note: Attacker #1 starts in front *(12)* with #2 behind *(6)*.

1. Step back R *(12 LNB)* w/R Out raking hammerfist *(Out block raking to ext position)* thru #2s nose clearing L collar grab simult w/L inward block outside #1s right punch.

2. *(Flashing Fist)* Pivot L foot open *(heel pivot)*, R step thru outside R foot to 10:30 w/R vert hook punch *(or middle finger fist)* thru #1 R eye, cover L to 430 LNB *(both attackers in front)* w/L Out BKS under R arm into #1 R ribs *(Liver)* as R checks back R shoulder.

3. *(Six Hands)* Front rotating twist w/two arm block inside #2s follow up R punch *(base technique presumes this)*, R front snap kick groin, step forward *(4:30 RNB)* w/R Out handsword R neck side, RFB w/L straight palm thrust under chin *(possible 4-finger poke)* as R chambers, R inv horiz snap punch up into solar plexus, rebound L hand off R shoulder to L Out handsword L neck side as L foot adjusts back slightly *(3 RFB)*, hook over neck to pull his head down w/R handsword next to R ear *(possible R Out whipping BKS thru groin)*, 3 RNB w/R downward handsword strike to the back of his neck.

4. Step L open *(front rotating twist)* w/R In elbow thru #2 L jaw hinge.

5. R roundhouse ball kick #1 sternum of at 12, R rear crossover back to 6 *(gauge)* L rear thrust kick #2 torso at 6, L front crossover to 12 between 12 & 6 opponents using your hands to separate and check, step back R towards 3 then L rear step thru to exit.

**DIVIDING THE ENEMY** *(Parting of the Snakes)*
**(Right Punch-12 / Approach-6)**
Note: Attacker #1 starts in front *(12)* with Attacker #2 starting behind *(6)*.

1. Step forward L to 12 close-kneel dropping under #1 punch w/L Up parry punch & R Up rev handsword between his legs into groin *(or inv horiz snap punch into his bladder)*.

2. Reach L to grab over back of neck *(his R side)* pulling his head down into a R Up knee kick to his face as your R hand chambers.

3. Still holding back of #1s head pull to R horiz thrust punch his nose w/R rear thrust kick to lower abdomen *(groin)* of #2 approaching behind.

4. R foot down, L rear crossover to 6 w/R Out snapping BKS to #2 R temple.

5. L then R front chicken kick to #1 groin-stomach, R forward 12 RNB w/R straight palm under chin *(or best available)*.

6. R leg back to 6 *(potential R Up hook kick #2 face if bent enough)*, L rear thrust kick #2 torso *(rear chicken kick)*, L front crossover step to 12 *(front twist)* using hands to separate and check opponent's, R back exit to 9.

**BEAR AND THE RAM** *(The Bear and the Ram)*
**(Bear Hug Arms Free-6 / Right Punch-12)**
Note: Attacker #1 starts in front *(12)* with Attacker #2 starting behind *(6)*.

1. *(Taming the Fist)* Step L to 9 *(12 horse, more weight on L)* w/L In parry #1 punch R In raking hammerfist nose en route to collapsing R elbow *(shifts weight to outside R heel)*.

2. Optional: R Out handsword R side #1 neck w/R Up hook *(or scoop)* kick #2 groin.

3. *(Crashing Elbows)* R front snap kick #1 groin w/dbl forward 2-finger poke eyes, step R to 3 *(12 horse w/more weight on R)* w/dbl down elbows on #2 forearms *(breaks grip & shifts his weight to his R, you should be able to see his R foot between your two feet)*.

4. L foot to R, step behind #2 R leg *(7:30 L rev bow L hip checks R hip)* w/L obscure elbow under chin *(R hand by R ear)*, LFB w/R In down hammerfist groin w/L cross body check, grab across chest line *(possible out claw face &/or grasp pinch pec muscles)*.

5. Hold clothing or chest muscles w/L, L rear crossover to #1 at 12 *(rear twist)* w/R heel palm to chest *(or Out handsword R neck side)*, R cross body check grabs across chest line.

6. Hold attackers across chest lines, R rear thrust kick #1 groin/knee rebound R front snap kick #2 groin/knee *(kicks can turn them back to back, not face to face)*, R steps to L.

7. L back *(completes Off Switch)* to 7:30 RFB *(holding attackers in hands)*, L front snap kick #2 groin or knee, L foot to R *(clacker ball footwork)*, R rear thrust kick #1 groin/knee.

8. Front crossover to 6 *(front twist)* pulling attackers heads together face to face or back to back *(kicks & body manipulation sets up)* L back, R rear step thru exit to 3 *(9 LNB)*.

**TRAINING THE BEARS** *(Reprimanding the Bears)*
**(Bear Hug Left Arm Free-6/Right Punch-12)**
Note: Attacker #1 starts in front *(12)* with Attacker #2 starting behind *(6)*.

1. Step L to 9 *(12 horse, more weight on L)* w/L Inward parry catching outside #1 R punch *(attempting to guide that punch into the face of Attacker #2 behind you)*.

2. R front snap kick #1 groin w/R back hammerfist #2 groin rebounding back to R rear sliding leg sweep thru inside angle of #2 L knee *(sweeps back to 7:30)* w/R vert stiff-arm punch *(or BKS)* up into #2 nose, hooking both hands over the L side of his neck/head.

3. Pull #2s head down into R Up knee kick, R front crossover to 12 *(front twist)*.

4. Step out w/L side snap kick #1 front knee, R rear crossover towards 12 *(rear twist)* w/L Out snapping BKS to his nose or temple.

5. Separate attacker's w/R front snap kick to #2 groin *(at 6)* then feet together *(gauge as needed)* followed by L rear thrust kick #1 torso *(at 12)*, L front crossover to 6 *(front twist)* between attackers using arms to maintain space, R back to 9 then L rear step thru exit.

**GROUPING THE ENEMY** *(Gathering of the Snakes)*
**(Left Punch - 12 / Approach - 6)**
Note: Attacker #1 starts in front *(12)* with Attacker #2 starting behind *(6)*.

1. *(From Destructive Circles)* R In parry outside #1 L punch, L Out parry at back of his L elbow *(possible elbow tweak)* stepping R forward to 12 RNB *(outside his L foot)* w/R Out whipping BKS thru left ribs *(back of your L hand still attached outside his L elbow)*.

2. L rear crossover to 12 *(R front twist, further around than base 1 attacker technique)* moving behind #1 w/L In heel palm L temple, grab his chin anchoring L forearm behind his upper L scapula *(take slack from his neck)* cocking R hand near your R ear.

3. Un-pivot *(6 RNB)* w/L hand neck control guides #1 as shield against approaching #2 w/R straight palm to L mastoid *(tweaks neck)*, release shoulder grip into R rear bow.

4. R front scoop kick groin, R side snap kick back of L knee pulling his R shoulder and pushing his L shoulder *(rotates him down onto his left knee)*.

5. R front crossover around #1 L leg *(still holding shoulders from behind)* towards approaching #2, L roundhouse shin kick #2 R stepping leg *(buckles him to ground)*, step behind his R leg to a LNB w/L Out BKS to #2 face w/R hand check to #1 L shoulder.

6. Air version: L rear crossover to 12 *(6 front twist)*; Body version: If no room to step back L then jump in place crossing feet *(6 front twist)*; In either case weight settles w/R Out BKS to #1 face w/L hand check to #2 R shoulder.

7. Un-pivot to 7:30 RNB w/R stiff arm lifting punch thru #2 face bringing that hand up to assist spinning around to your left to grab #1 shoulders from behind.

8. L rear thrust kick *(spinning kick)* #2 back rebounding into L front knee kick *(front snap kick in Mass Attacks Form)* into the back of Attacker #1.

9. L inv side stomp #1 calf/Achilles *(holding shoulders from behind)*, L front crossover, R step out, L rear step thru all to 3 pulling him back & down to ground, then R front crossover step *(possible TSK face)* and step out and thru to exit towards 3.

# BIBLIOGRAPHY

Deadman, Peter. <u>A Manual of Acupuncture</u>. 1998 Journal of Medcine Publications, 22 Cromwell Rd Hove East Sussex BN3 3EB England

Parker, Edmund K. <u>Infinite Insights into Kenpo Series 1-5</u>. 1982 Delsby Publications, Pasadena California

Parker, Edmund K. <u>Encyclopedia of Kenpo</u>. 1992 Delsby Publications, Pasadena California

Liu, Sing-Han. Ba Gua: Hidden Knowledge in the Taoist Internal Martial Art. 1998 Liu Sing-Han and Bracy, John Publishing

Adams, Brian. The Medical Implications of Karate Blows. Published 1969

<u>Websites</u>
Howstuffworks.com
Nutritiondata.com
Webmd.com
Mathisfun.com
Molossia.org
Wingchunonline.com
Scientificpsychic.com
Nlh.nih.gov/medlineplus
Pitt.edu
Mediral.com
Your-doctor.com
Scribd.com

# ABOUT THE AUTHOR

Barry B Barker (aka Mr. B) is a father of 5 kids, with 6 grandkids, and 87 Black Belts as of this 2021 4th Edition (See Black Belt Family Tree in 'Spirit'). Mr. B is a 9th Degree Kenpo Black Belt in his American Kenpo Alliance (AKA) Kenpo system having been a full-time school owner and teacher for over 35 years while running Poway Kenpo Karate/Poway Martial Arts, which he founded in 1984. He is also a Licensed Acupuncturist, Author, BarryBBarker.com owner, and a competitive Salsa Dancer.

Mr. B became interested in martial arts after watching Bruce Lee as a child. He first enrolled in martial arts at Brian Adams Kenpo Karate School in San Diego, California in 1973 for a brief time, Parker Linekin was his instructor.

He dabbled in various martial arts styles until 1980 when he found an Ed Parker Kenpo Karate School located in El Cajon, California. That school was run by a very technical instructor, and private student of Mr. Parker, Jim Mitchell (does the stance work photos in Mr. Parker's Book #2). Mr. Barker earned his 1st Degree Black Belt at this school in 1983, with Mr. Parker as a member of his testing board.

In 1984, Jim Mitchell promoted Mr. Barker to 2nd Degree Black Belt and in the same year Mr. B opened Aaction Kenpo Karate, as a Jim Mitchell affiliate school, then later changed that to Poway Kenpo Karate.

He was promoted to 3rd Degree in 1987 then 4th Degree in 1990. Mr. Mitchell moved out of state shortly thereafter, so Mr. B formed his own American Kenpo Alliance (AKA) martial art association in 1992 to administer to his own Kenpo students.

Additional certification came in 1994 by Orned "Chicken" Gabriel and Steve "Nasty" Anderson, recognizing Mr. Barker as a 4th Degree in their United Karate Federation (UKF). IKKA Master Instructor Ernest George Jr. promoted Mr. Barker to 5th Degree in 1995 then 6th Degree in 2000.

Mr. Barker expanded his training facility in 1998 when he opened a Muay Thai gym called World Class Kickboxing, later becoming The Boxing Club. He added Brazilian Jiu Jitsu in 2005 and MMA in 2008. All of that became part of what is now known as Poway Martial Arts.

He was promoted to 7th Degree in 2005 by Rick Hughes and Willy Steele, both Ed Parker Black Belts and IKKA Master Instructors'. In 2010 he was promoted to 8th Degree by GM Parker Linekin, with additional authorization provided from SGM Brian Adams and in 2015 to 9th Degree as authorized by SGM Brian Adams, GM Parker Linekin, GM Orned "Chicken" Gabriel, and GM Reynaldo Leal.

In addition to running Poway Kenpo Karate and Poway Martial Arts, Mr. Barker pursued his education and graduated from Pacific College of Oriental Medicine with a Master's in Traditional Oriental Medicine (MSTOM) in 2007. He is a Nationally Certified (Dipl. O.M.) and a California Acupuncturist (L.Ac.).

This Mind-Body-Spirit book series is a project he gave himself to further his personal growth and contribute to his family, students, and the martial art community.

Mr. Barker has turned daily operations of Poway Kenpo Karate and Poway Martial Arts over to his children for them to continue the family legacy. He still teaches seminars/workshops and treats his Acupuncture patients and manages his Kenpo video site BarryBBarker.com where his entire Kenpo System is available to see and learn. In 2014, his school celebrated 30 years in business, then 36 years in 2020, and the school he founded is highly regarded in the local community.

As an avid learner and student of martial arts, Mr. Barker has also sought additional training over the years to continue and enhance his own skills.

Additional training:
Ed Parker, Advanced Kenpo Theory • Jeff Speakman, Kenpo Seminar • Joe Lewis, several Fight Training Seminars • Steve Nasty Anderson, several Fight Training Seminars • Orned Chicken Gabriel, 2 Years Personal Training & many Fight Training Seminars • Brian Adams, Knife & Stick Fighting Seminar • Dave Hebler, Power & Speed Seminar • Richard Post, Knife Fighting Seminar • Rick Hughes, many Classes & Seminars • Willy Steele, many Classes & Seminars • Toke Hill, Olympic Style Sparring Seminar • Mike Stone, Martial Arts Seminars • Eric Lee, Martial Arts Training Seminar • Parker Linekin, many years of Seminars & Training • John Denora, Daito Ryu Seminar • George Dillman, Pressure Point Seminar • Prof. Wally Jay, several Small Circle Jiu Jitsu Seminars • Royce Gracie, Brazilian Jiu Jitsu Seminars • Nelson Monteiro, Brazilian Jiu Jitsu 2 Years Training & Seminars • Carlos Valente, Brazilian Jiu Jitsu 1 Year Training and Seminars • Vic Zamora, Boxing Personal Training • Vincent Soberano, Muay Thai Personal Training • Melchor Menor, Muay Thai Seminars & Classes • Nelson Siyavong, several Muay Thai Seminars • Kaewsamrit Muay Thai Training Camp, 2 Weeks Bangkok Thailand • Cepeda Brothers, Arnis de Mano Classes • Krav Maga, Certification Seminar • CDT, Certification Seminar • Cung Lee, San Shou Seminar • Jim Tian, Tai Chi Chuan several years • Frank Primicias, Lo Han Chi Gung Seminars • Chen Sitan, Taiji Seminar • Rey Leal, Tai Chi Personal Training • International Training Program, Chengdu University of Chinese Medicine in Chengdu, China

Mr. Barker has also been recognized more formally in other ways. Some of those recognitions are listed below:

• Inducted Golden Global Martial Arts Hall of Fame 1998
• Inducted Masters Hall of Fame 2000
• Inducted World Amateur Martial Arts International Federation 2006
• Listed Heritage Registry of Who's Who 2007
• City of Poway Mayors Commendation for Civic Work 2010 & 2014
• CA State Senate Community Service Commendation 2012, 2014, 2017
• Inducted USA Martial Arts Hall of Fame 2014
• Presidential Fitness Award 2017

Made in the USA
Las Vegas, NV
15 February 2024

85830113R10175